Approaches to Teaching
the Works of Ovid
and the Ovidian Tradition

Approaches to Teaching
World Literature

For a complete listing of titles,
see the last pages of this book.

Approaches to Teaching the Works of Ovid and the Ovidian Tradition

Edited by
Barbara Weiden Boyd
and
Cora Fox

The Modern Language Association of America
New York   2010

© 2010 by The Modern Language Association of America
All rights reserved. Printed in the United States of America

MLA and the MODERN LANGUAGE ASSOCIATION are trademarks
owned by the Modern Language Association of America. For
information about obtaining permission to reprint material from
MLA book publications, send your request by mail (see address below),
e-mail (permissions@mla.org), or fax (646 458-0030).

Library of Congress Cataloging-in-Publication Data

Approaches to teaching the works of Ovid and the Ovidian tradition /
edited by Barbara Weiden Boyd and Cora Fox.
   p. cm. — (Approaches to teaching world literature ; 113)
   Includes bibliographical references and index.
   ISBN 978-1-60329-062-3 (hardcover : alk. paper)
   ISBN 978-1-60329-063-0 (pbk. : alk. paper)
   1. Ovid, 43 B.C.–17 or 18 A.D.—Study and teaching.
 2. Ovid, 43 B.C.–17 or 18 A.D.—Criticism and interpretation.
         3. Latin poetry—Study and teaching.
   I. Boyd, Barbara Weiden, 1952–. II. Fox, Cora, 1968–.
               PA6537.A77 2010
        871'.01—dc22   2010011992

Approaches to Teaching World Literature 113
ISSN 1059-1133

Cover illustration of the paperback edition:
Diana and Actaeon, by Titian (Tiziano Vecellio). Purchased jointly by the National Galleries
of Scotland and the National Gallery, London, by private treaty from the Duke of Sutherland,
with the aid of the Scottish government, the National Heritage Memorial Fund, The Monument
Trust, The Art Fund, and through public appeal, 2009

Published by The Modern Language Association of America
26 Broadway, New York, New York 10004-1789
www.mla.org

CONTENTS

Acknowledgments ix

Preface 1

Editions Used in This Volume 3

PART ONE: MATERIALS

Ovid's Life and Legacy

Introduction 7
Ralph Hexter

Roman Religion and Ovid 13
Christopher M. McDonough

Ovide moralisé 18
Raymond Cormier

Speaking Pictures: Ovid and the Visual Arts 23
Bruce Redford

Ovid's Texts in the Classroom

Commentaries on Ovid 27
Peter E. Knox

Ovid in Premodern English Translation 31
Cora Fox

Ovid in Modern Translation 34
Barbara Weiden Boyd

Surveying Pedagogy and Practice: A Report on the MLA Survey 39
Barbara Weiden Boyd and Cora Fox

PART TWO: APPROACHES

Introduction 49
Barbara Weiden Boyd and Cora Fox

Ovid's Classrooms

Caveat Lector: Learning to Read through Ovid 57
Wendy Chapman Peek

Genre Transformed: The "Heroes" of Ovid's Epic 64
Lorina N. Quartarone

Approaches to Teaching Ovid's *Tristia*   73
  Samuel Huskey
From Ovid to Elvis: Teaching Mythology in the Classical Tradition   80
  Nikolai Endres
Reading and Teaching Ovid's *Amores* and *Ars amatoria* in a
  Conservative Christian Context   88
  M. L. Stapleton
Ovid and His Human Animals   95
  Frank Palmeri
Teaching Medea to Freshmen: Ovid, Thematic Criticism, and
  General Education   102
  Ronald W. Harris

Political Ovid

Always Hopeless, Never Serious: Wit and Wordplay in Ovid's *Amores*   109
  R. W. Hanning
Transforming Exile: Teaching Ovid in Tomis   117
  Matthew McGowan
Teaching the *Really* Minor Epic: Literature, Sexuality, and
  National Belonging in Thomas Edwards's "Narcissus"   126
  Jim Ellis
Teaching the Ovidian Shakespeare and the Politics of Emotion   133
  Cora Fox
Reforming *Metamorphoses*: The Epic in Translation as a
  "Major Work" of the English Renaissance   142
  Scott Maisano
Ovid's Genial and Ingenious Story of King Midas   151
  William S. Anderson

Gendered and Embodied Ovid

Sex and Violence in *Amores*   161
  Paul Allen Miller
Ovid's Thisbe and a Roman Woman Love Poet   170
  Judith P. Hallett
The Lay of the Land: The Rhetoric of Gender in Ovid's "Perseid"   178
  Alison Keith
Teaching Ovidian Sexualities in English Renaissance Literature   189
  Goran V. Stanivukovic

Teaching Marlowe's Translation of *Amores*   197
   Patrick Cheney

Teaching Tiresias: Issues of Gender and Sexuality in Ovid and Beyond   204
   Phyllis Katz

Metatextual Ovid

Metamorphoses Metamorphosed: Teaching the Ovidian Tradition   212
   Jamie C. Fumo

Metamorphoses, Its Tradition, and the Work of Art   219
   Sean Keilen

Island Hopping: Ovid's Ariadne and Her Texts   225
   Barbara Weiden Boyd

The Case of Ovid in Dante   234
   Madison U. Sowell

Captured in Ekphrasis: Cervantes and Ovid   241
   Frederick A. De Armas

Ovid and Ransmayr: Translating across Cultures and Times   250
   Susan C. Anderson and Mary Jaeger

Notes on Contributors   257

Contributors and Survey Participants   261

Works Cited   263

Index   289

ACKNOWLEDGMENTS

For their assistance and guidance in bringing this collection to completion we want to thank first and foremost Joseph Gibaldi and James Hatch: both have been exemplary correspondents, responding to e-mails and phone calls on all sorts of topics, patiently waiting for the various stages of the proposal and manuscript, judiciously sharing with us the comments of anonymous referees, and communicating to us the suggestions of the MLA Publications Committee. We are grateful, too, to all the contributors to this volume, who in some cases endured lengthy delays in hearing back from us regarding their submissions and who in others cheerfully responded to our nudging. It has been a pleasure to work with each one of them; we have made some wonderful new friendships and have renewed some old ones in the process. We also appreciate the time and dedication of all those scholars and teachers who responded to the questionnaire about teaching Ovid and the Ovidian tradition that we circulated at an early stage in the development process; their thoughts, suggestions, and desiderata helped define the shape that this collection has taken, and their names are included in the list that appears at the end of this volume. Not mentioned there are several other scholars and students who, while not directly involved with the development process, gave sound advice, made good suggestions about possible contributors, or just listened. Most important among these is undoubtedly Leo Landry (BA in classics, Bowdoin College, 2005; PhD candidate in classics, Brown University), who somehow managed during summer 2005 to impose order on the chaotic mass of fact generated by the questionnaire and to assemble a very helpful synopsis of results. Last but not least, we thank Angela Gibson, associate editor at the MLA, for her eagle eye and painstaking and patient copyediting. She has helped us immeasurably to impose order on this collection, and any errors that remain are entirely of our making.

Of less practical help but all important as emotional mainstays are those family members and friends who saw us through this, especially Michael Boyd, Rachel Boyd, and Lily Fox. Without them—well, without them we probably wouldn't have worked so long and hard on this. We are eternally grateful for their patience and for their presence as living reminders that teaching well really does matter.

PREFACE

When we were invited by Joseph Gibaldi, who was then the series editor, to develop and edit a volume of essays on teaching Ovid and the Ovidian tradition for the Approaches to Teaching World Literature series, we signed on enthusiastically. Ovid plays a central role in our scholarly and teaching lives, and we both have many professional friends and acquaintances who share our interest. We were also aware, if on an entirely anecdotal basis, that Ovid's poetry and the works it has inspired are taught in a wide variety of college and university classrooms in the United States and elsewhere. Only as we got further into the project, however, did its daunting character become fully evident: the variety of Ovid's audiences—like the variety of his subject matter—made the establishment of reasonable parameters for the collection a challenge. As the development of the collection proceeded, therefore, we found ourselves overseeing an artful (we hope) combination of careful planning and nature's course, with Ovid, as always, as our best guide to the negotiation of (seeming) inconsistency, multidirectionality, and polymorphous variety: "ars . . . latet arte sua" 'art lies hidden thanks to its own artfulness' (*Met.* 10.252; our trans.). The result is an array of approaches to our subject, of which we like to think Ovid himself would have approved: though some roads remain untraveled here, many other paths have been forged, or at least cleared, to welcome future visitors embarking on the scholarly and teaching journeys we have made.

Part 1 of this volume, "Materials," is a team effort that brings together a range of useful introductory material for any instructor contemplating the inclusion of the works of Ovid the Ovidian tradition in a course. A concise introduction to Ovid's life and legacy (by Ralph Hexter) is complemented by three essays, on Ovid and religion (by Christopher McDonough), and on the *Ovide moralisé* (by Raymond Cormier), on Ovid and the visual arts (by Bruce Redford). Each of these essays offers a brief but authoritative introduction to a topic that is particularly challenging for nonspecialists. A survey of Ovid's afterlife in the Latin classroom (by Peter Knox) paves the way for a survey of translations of Ovid (by the editors). We focus here on premodern and contemporary English translations of *Metamorphoses*, since translations of this poem are perhaps the single most important vehicle for Ovid's continuing vitality both in and outside the classroom. The "Materials" section concludes with a report on the survey we conducted of a broad spectrum of instructors engaged in teaching the works of Ovid and the Ovidian tradition and draws some general conclusions about educational trends.

In part 2, "Approaches," we have organized essays under four broad headings, each intended to suggest a different lens through which to consider the works of Ovid and the Ovidian tradition. The sections are thematic and interdisciplinary. These include "Ovid's Classrooms," featuring essays that exemplify the range of contemporary contexts for the teaching of the works of Ovid and the Ovidian tradition and explore some of the challenges posed by these different contexts; "Political Ovid," composed of essays focusing on the political and moral discourses shaping the works of Ovid and the Ovidian tradition and the politics of adapting Ovid's poetic voice over two millennia; "Gendered and Embodied Ovid," with essays about the centrality of constructions of gender and the body in the works of Ovid and the Ovidian tradition, which either locate these constructions in broader discourses in classical antiquity or examine the consequences of this centrality for the history of postclassical depictions of gender and the body; and "Metatextual Ovid," which includes essays that treat various aspects of the self-conscious appropriation and transformation of Ovid's works or that focus on their role as metatextual figures for the classical tradition. Within each subcategory, we have organized the essays in a loosely chronological sequence to highlight developments and changes in both contexts and critical approaches from antiquity to the present; at the same time, each essay stands on its own and can be used independent of other contributions in this volume. All the essays are either explicitly pedagogical in focus or easily applicable to a classroom context. Our introduction to the "Approaches" section discusses trends in scholarship on Ovid and the Ovidian tradition.

BWB and *CF*

EDITIONS USED IN THIS VOLUME

Except when noted otherwise, the editions of Ovid's poetry cited throughout this collection are as follows:

Amatory Works, including *Amores*, *Ars amatoria*, *Medicamina faciei femineae* and *Remedia amoris*

P. *Ovidi Nasonis Amores, Medicamina faciei femineae, Ars amatoria, Remedia amoris*. 1961. Ed. E. J. Kenney. Corrected 2nd ed. Oxford: Clarendon, 1995. Print.

Epistulae ex Ponto

Ovidii Nasonis Tristium libri quinque, Ibis, Ex Ponto libri quattuor, Halieutica, fragmenta. Ed. S. G. Owen. Oxford: Clarendon, 1915. Print.

Fasti

Ovidii Nasonis Fastorum libri sex. Ed. E. H. Alton, E. W. Wormell, and E. Courtney. Leipzig: Teubner, 1978. Print.

Heroides

Heroides *and* Amores. Trans. Grant Showerman. 1914. Ed. and trans. G. P. Goold. 2nd rev. ed. Cambridge: Harvard UP, 1977. Print. Loeb Classical Lib.

Metamorphoses

Ovidi Nasonis Metamorphoses. Ed. R. J. Tarrant. Oxford: Clarendon, 2004. Print.

Tristia

Ovidii Nasonis Tristium libri quinque, Ibis, Ex Ponto libri quattuor, Halieutica, fragmenta. Ed. S. G. Owen. Oxford: Clarendon, 1915. Print.

Because of the variety of texts and perspectives on the texts in this collection of essays, we have not imposed consistency in the translations authors cite. Because of the popularity of *Metamorphoses* in the classroom, however, we have encouraged contributors to use either their own or Mandelbaum's translation when discussing this poem, except when issues of translation itself are a topic of discussion. Where only a page number occurs for translations of *Metamorphoses*, the reader can assume Mandelbaum is the source.

Many nonclassicist readers and teachers of Ovid and the Ovidian tradition are most familiar with his poetry from the bilingual edition of his works in six volumes in the Loeb Classical Library series. Users of this collection should be aware that these volumes, originally translated and published in the early twentieth century, were thoroughly revised by the series editor George P. Goold in the 1970s–80s; whenever these volumes are cited, therefore, the reference is to the Goold revision. While Goold was unable to produce entirely new editions of these volumes, the text he presents in each is a significant improvement on what had appeared in the first edition, and his editions are now considered by scholars to be, at least where no other modern edition has appeared, the best working edition of Ovid's poetry.

Part One

MATERIALS

OVID'S LIFE AND LEGACY

Introduction
Ralph Hexter

The Roman poet Ovid (Publius Ovidius Naso) was born in 43 BCE, the year following the assassination of Julius Caesar. The tumult of the years that followed and that led to the consolidation of power by Julius Caesar's grandnephew and adopted heir Octavius (the later version of whose name, Octavian[us], indicates his adoptive status) seems to have had little impact on Ovid, the younger son of a wealthy landowner in Sulmo, now Sulmona, in the Abruzzi. The radical change of Rome's government, however, from republic to dynastic empire was to have fateful consequences for the poet.

As a member of the equestrian (knightly) order, Ovid was groomed for a life of public service and received intense training in rhetoric and letters, Greek as well as Latin. His prodigious verbal talent was apparent early on, and he began writing poetry, especially elegiac love poetry, that caught people's attention. Unusually, he made an explicit decision to abandon his public career and devote his life to writing poetry—he had no reason to worry about money. The first set of letters that compose the *Heroides*, which presents famous women of myth and legend, each writing a letter to the lover who has abandoned her, is the earliest of his productions to have survived, although a five-book collection of elegiac poems celebrating his amours with (a fictitious) Corinna was apparently circulated earlier. A second, three-book edition of that work (dated c. 1 BCE) has come down to us as *Amores*. Ovid was not content in that collection to cap a tradition that included, to name only Roman examples, Catullus, Gallus, Tibullus, Sulpicia, and Propertius. With characteristic ingenuity, he revisited the same world of lovers sighing outside their mistress's doors and bribing maids to get past jealous guardians in a mock didactic poem. Books 1 and 2 of *Ars amatoria*

(*Art of Love*) purport to instruct young men in the arts of seduction—of single women only, the earnest Ovid assures us, since Octavianus, now titled Augustus, had established severe sanctions for adultery, for which he would eventually have to exile both a daughter and a granddaughter, executing their lovers.

But such scandals and their public penalties lay in the future when Ovid published the first two books of *Ars amatoria* (also c. 1 BCE) and, shortly thereafter, a third, which he directs to (unmarried) ladies so that they, too, could become learned in the game of love. Ever eager to show his creative wit with a sequel, when readers might have imagined there was no more to be said, Ovid promptly released, in one book, *Remedia amoris* ("The Cure for Love"), which, in defiance of its title, would not be likely to cure anyone of his or her desires. *Heroides* offers another example of Ovid's revisiting an earlier poetic work only to recast it. A friend, Sabinus, had been inspired by Ovid's foray in the epistolary genre to pen the responses of several of the heroes to whom Ovid's heroines had addressed their pleas. Sabinus's responses are lost, but they inspired Ovid to publish his own set of paired letters (in modern printed editions of *Heroides*, letters 16–21). In these pairs Ovid, never one to imitate without stamping his individual genius on the work, has the man lead off, the woman follow.

Early on, Ovid also attempted tragedy; his *Medea* impressed some readers in the first century CE but is lost. Whether he attempted an epic poem about the gigantomachy remains uncertain; his references to his inability to achieve so serious a work may be sincere but are more likely mock modesty that also slyly digs at Augustus's pretensions and at those poets who would celebrate his rise to power, for the princeps would be the Jupiter who prevailed over such giants as Antony and Cleopatra. In *Metamorphoses* Ovid did of course succeed in writing one grand work in epic verse (i.e., hexameters; all his other extant poems are in elegiac couplets). This is not, however, an epic with a hero. Instead, after the fashion of some of the Alexandrian works of Callimachus and other Hellenistic Greek poets, it is a grand amalgam of many hundreds of stories linked, on the one hand, by dazzlingly contingent transitions (and layered by means of dizzying framed narratives) and, on the other hand, by a common theme of transformation—metamorphosis, or change of shape. The poem proceeds chronologically, ostensibly at least, from the creation of the world through myths of Greek gods and heroes to Roman historic times, all in fifteen books and 11,995 verses. Though Ovid became a byword for the lover and the teacher of love—"magister amoris"—his greatest achievement is *Metamorphoses*, the work on which he staked his claim to fame and his single most influential work over the centuries.

Ovid delighted in the world of myth and religion and, in characteristic Ovidian fashion, found another form with Alexandrian overtones in which to display his learning, wit, and poetic skills, this time with an even more directly Roman slant. *Fasti* was to be an account of the Roman festivals in calendar form, featuring one book for each of twelve months and ample opportunity for narrative in the αἴτια (*aitia*, Greek for "causes," the "how so" or "backstories") for each festival or holiday. Only six books (January–June) are extant; it is likely that the other six were never finished, given the break that occurred in Ovid's life in 8 CE. (See the essay on Ovid and Roman religion by McDonough, in this volume.)

In that year, Augustus exiled Ovid—"relegated" was the technical term for the particular form of banishment, which did not strip him of his estate—to Tomis, on the Black Sea. No state document or testimony by a contemporary or near contemporary details the reason for his punishment. Ovid himself tells us that the causes were two: a poem ("carmen") and a mistake ("error") (*Tristia* 2.207). The former is believed by many scholars to be *Ars amatoria*, which as an affront to Augustus's attempt to correct Roman morals must have annoyed the princeps not a little. But the proximate cause and no doubt the decisive impulse was a private scandal in which Ovid had some peripheral role. Whatever the incident was, it must have been a matter that touched and angered the emperor—involving either the emperor's private, familial life or his public one, in which case Ovid's role must have been very indirect and minor. The offense occasioned the well-nigh sadistic mandate that Ovid, the consummate poet of Roman urbanity and luxury, should live in a distant colonial outpost far from the capital city.

Ovid documented the travails of banishment, of a long and difficult journey, of life in a new and in his view not merely frigid but "barbarous" setting through five books of *Tristia*. Books 1 and 3–5 of *Tristia* are composed of laments directed to unnamed but often identifiable persons, unnamed because the disgraced Ovid did not wish to put any of his friends at risk by publicizing their names. *Tristia*, book 2, is a long and passionate defense of Ovid's career to that point, almost an autobiography, and is addressed directly to the emperor. Also unnamed is the addressee of *Ibis*, a highly allusive and coded attack on the person Ovid felt betrayed him.

At a certain point, Ovid realized that he would likely never be recalled to Rome. His pleas then were for transfer to a less inhospitable place of exile, but they fell on deaf ears, both Augustus's and, after his death in 14 CE, his successor Tiberius's. Ovid's final collection, *Epistulae ex Ponto* ("Letters from the Black Sea"), in four books—the fourth clearly an amalgam of all that remained when Ovid died, most likely in 17—does make explicit the identities of the addressees and leaves us with the image of an Ovid who is in some way, and to some degree, resigned to his fate. He had given up all hope.

Ovid's facility with Latin verse lent his elegiac couplets and hexameters extraordinary suppleness and speed, making them models of elegant ease for generations of Roman poets. But Ovid was not a required author in the curricula of the schools of the empire, unlike the more "serious" and "substantial" Vergil, most famous as the author of the great epic of Rome, the *Aeneid*. The two near contemporaries—Vergil was twenty-seven years old when Ovid was born and died when the younger poet was twenty-four; Ovid reports that he "only saw Vergil" 'Vergilium vidi tantum' (*Tr.* 4.10.51; my trans.)—have often been set as diametrically opposed poles, a scheme that does not do full justice to the complexities of Vergil's own stance toward Rome's new government. Still, in his pre-exilic poetry Ovid constructed a persona—recall that the word is Latin for "stage mask"—"Ovid," who was the poet of carefree elegance and delicious love affairs, the lightweight temperamentally unsuited to the demands of military epic, and the humorous deflater of imperial pretension and hypocrisy. In the poetry he wrote after his banishment, one can see Ovid at times struggling against the self-constructed image that brought him such fame (and, in part, to this pass), even as he cannot conceal the pride he takes in his independent, even oppositional stance.

If, like Horace, Ovid could only imagine his reputation surviving so long as Rome did, in fact both pre- and postexilic Ovids spoke to readers and poets long after Rome was no real center of power, even as the place-name *Rome* was still a talisman of authority and Rome's tongue, Latin, remained the language of literacy across most of western Europe. As monks from Ireland and Anglo-Saxon England fanned out across the Continent and founded monasteries and schools, Ovid was read, book 1 of *Ars amatoria* even receiving glosses in Latin and Welsh. The Latin poets of the court of Charlemagne and his immediate successors—"Carolingian," we call them, after the Germanic emperor who unified not only realms but also a liberal arts curriculum that would be influential for centuries—took a particular interest in exile and put Ovid, rusticated from Rome and transferred to the North, at the head of long lists of exiled writers.

In the high Middle Ages, which saw the rise of cities and cathedral schools, the urban and urbane Ovid was increasingly attractive. The twelfth and thirteenth centuries are often referred to as the "aetas Ovidiana," the "age of Ovid," a name so apt that it has been applied more broadly than its creator, Ludwig Traube, intended (2: 113). (One of the founders of the discipline of medieval Latin studies, Traube was actually describing a succession of poetic models for medieval Latin poets.) All Ovid's works were studied in the schools, receiving lengthy commentaries, many of which have come down to us, and the secular poetry of many clerics, including the most unbuttoned of them known as goliards, are full of Ovidian echoes and even Ovidian attitudes. As medieval courtliness advanced, Ovid made his way into the vernacular, with multiple adaptations and translations of his erotodidactic poetry in Italian and French.

The longer *Metamorphoses* was also read and studied. Alfonso the Wise is famous for having termed it "the pagans' bible," and while there were some who were quite nervous about handling all this pagan lore, it was more valuable as a source of mythological lore and learning. Many in the schools were capable of studying it as historical pagan material. Others created elaborate allegories, natural as well as explicitly Christian, and moralizations to render *Ovidius major*, as it was called, usable in a Christian world that was making increasing demands on piety, both clerical and lay. In the fourteenth century, almost simultaneously, the French *Ovide moralisé* provided a "safe" *Metamorphoses* for vernacular readers in France, and the Franciscan Pierre Bersuire turned the poem into a collection of tales ready to serve as sermon material for his preaching brethren. (See the essay on *Ovide moralisé* by Cormier, in this volume.) The accretive biographies of Ovid that circulated, beyond repeating old speculations on the "error" that incensed Augustus and that led to Ovid's exile and inventing a few new ones, occasionally imagine him a Christian convert: from his place of exile he visited Saint John during the saint's sojourn on the island of Patmos. The longest of the pseudo-Ovidian poems that circulated, "De vetula" ("On the Old Woman"), casts Ovid first as an erotic dupe and then as an unwitting prophet of Christ.

Petrarch, whose Italian poetry especially is replete with allusions to Ovid, rejected the attribution of "De vetula" to Ovid, and humanist scholars stripped away the unhistorical accretions. As the humanists became ever more scholarly, they were relatively less interested in explicated Ovid, since they could show their mettle with more "difficult" poets. *Fasti*, however, rich with religious lore and needing commentary, finally came into its own, especially in the Roman academies of the sixteenth century, and scholars relished the difficulties of *Ibis* and the novelty of the "Letter of Sappho" (*Heroides*, letter 15, in modern collections), which came to light at this time. Indeed, particularly from the Renaissance through the eighteenth century, *Heroides* was extraordinarily popular not only in the original and in translations but also as a genre in which hundreds of authors worked, creating new collections of fictitious letters, especially from women. The great eighteenth-century epistolary novels of Samuel Richardson and Choderlos de Laclos build on the base of this fashion.

Ovid's narrative poems, which recount hundreds of mythological stories, often with memorable moments of pathos and striking visual details, served as veritable sourcebooks for visual artists as well. Texts, especially translations of *Metamorphoses*, were supplied with illustrations, and entirely pictorial *Metamorphoses* were popular, especially in the sixteenth century. Thousands of independent works present an Ovidian scene or scenes, from Italian wedding *cassoni* and bronze panels on Saint Peter's Basilica to notable canvases by Pieter Brueghel the Elder (*Fall of Icarus*), Peter Paul Rubens (*Rape of Ganymede*), Rembrandt (*Abduction of Europa*), and Titian (*Actaeon, Venus and Adonis*), to name but a few of the significant painters who worked from Ovid, to sculpture (e.g., Bernini's *Apollo and Daphne*). (See the essay on Ovid and the visual arts by Redford, below.)

Moreover, Ovid was the source for music as well. Although it was generally the idea of Greek tragedy that late-sixteenth-century theoreticians and the artists they influenced proposed to revive, Latin versions of mythology were the actual sources of the plots of most operas. The very first opera, Jacopo Peri's *Dafne* (1597), was based on an Ovidian story, and Ovid lies behind many hundreds, including George Frideric Handel's *Acis and Galatea* and Wolfgang Mozart's youthful *Apollo and Hyacinth*. In the twentieth century and near the end of his own career, Richard Strauss returned to opera's ultimate antecedents in Greek tragedy and myth with his own *Daphne* (1938). As the European world he had known crashed around him, he turned to the underlying principle of Ovid's greatest work, change itself, and wrote the meditative orchestral piece *Metamorphosen* (1945, first performance January, 1946, in Zurich).

In the aftermath of World War II and in a century that had seen massive displacements of entire peoples, the exiling (and self-exiling) of intellectuals and artists, state-sponsored ethnic cleansing, and the creation of seemingly permanent refugee populations, it is the fact of Ovid's own exile and, if to a lesser extent, Ovid's exile poetry that once again caught hold of writers' imaginations. Two late-twentieth-century novels that best exemplify this are *An Imaginary Life: A Novel*, by the Australian David Malouf (1978), and *Die letzte Welt* (1988 [*The Last World*]), by the Austrian Christoph Ransmayr. In the latter, postmodern magic realism meets Ovidian magic realism, and an imagined Pontic landscape is populated not just by an imaginary Ovid but by figures from Ovid's mythological poetry. A third, David Wishart's *Ovid* (1995), represents the genre of historical detective novel: the mystery Wishart's fictitious Marcus Corvinus must solve to get to the bottom of the case the private detective has been asked to work on is none other than the nearly two-thousand-year-old puzzle Ovid himself set when he did not tell his readers what the "mistake" ("error") was that angered Augustus to the point that the emperor exiled the poet to the Black Sea in the first place.

Roman Religion and Ovid

Christopher M. McDonough

The work of Ovid, particularly the six books of *Fasti (The Book of Days),* is suffused with a thoroughly religious sensibility. The Romans, however, judged what was religious differently than we do in the West today. Personal belief and behavior are central to contemporary religious thought, in contrast to the ancients' thinking about the divine. The general lines along which the educated classes in Ovid's day understood the nature of their relation to the gods had been established a half century earlier by the erudite Marcus Terentius Varro, in whose *Divine Antiquities* three genres of theology were distinguished: the "mythicum" 'the mythical,' which was poetic in nature; the "physicum" 'the natural,' which was philosophical in nature; and the "civile" 'the civic,' which was political in nature (qtd. in Augustine, 112–13; bk. 6, sec. 5).[1] Let us use this Varronian threefold classification in considering Ovid's engagement with ancient Roman religion.[2]

Unsurprisingly, much of Ovid's overtly religious work falls into the category of *genus mythicum.* By and large, the Roman elite of the first century BCE considered poetry about the gods to be little more than fatuous if not actually scandalous anthropomorphic entertainments. In Cicero's *On the Nature of the Gods (De natura deorum),* for instance, such poetry was compared by one interlocutor (the Epicurean Velleius) with the ravings of lunatics, while another (the Stoic Balbus) spoke regretfully of the "crazy beliefs, hysterical mistakes, and old wives' tales" to which poetic depictions of the gods gave rise.[3] Still, the tradition in Roman epic poetry of portraying the gods as sponsors of the Roman state, which finds its (ambiguous) culmination in Vergil's characterization of Jupiter in the *Aeneid,* was strong.[4] Ovid was certainly the heir to this tradition, but it would be hard to claim of *Metamorphoses* that it seeks, like *Paradise Lost,* to "justify the ways of God to men."[5] The divinities of Ovid's magnum opus, in fact, seem to exist in ironic counterpoint to their more dignified Vergilian prototypes. While *Metamorphoses* would become a primary source of Greek mythology for the subsequent European literary and artistic traditions, traditionalists like Varro or Cicero would not have recognized it as a genuine exposition of Roman religious belief or practice.

Ovid's philosophical engagement with religion—Varro's *genus physicum*—must be considered in the broader intellectual context of the late Republic. The tumultuous political conditions of the period gave rise to sustained philosophical examination of traditional religion. Turning again to Cicero's *On the Nature of the Gods,* we find the interlocutor Gaius Cotta saying:

> In an inquiry as to the nature of the gods, the first question that we ask is, do the gods exist or do they not? "It is difficult to deny their existence." No

doubt it would be if the question were to be asked in a public assembly, but in a private conversation and in a company like the present it is perfectly easy. This being so, I, who am a high priest, and who hold it to be a duty most solemnly to maintain the rights and doctrines of the established religion, should be glad to be convinced of this fundamental tenet of the divine existence, not as an article of faith merely but as an ascertained fact. (59, 61 [trans. Rackham]; bk. 1, sec. 61)[6]

Such skepticism, even from a man in high religious office, was apparently common among first-century elites. Despite the conflict between the validity he senses in his priestly role and the doubts arising from his philosophical inquiry, Cotta should not be taken for a hypocrite. This attitude, called "brainbalkanization" by scholars in recent years, can be found in Ovid as well.[7] In a famous passage of the *Art of Love*, for instance, the Casanova-like narrator instructs lovers in the making of oaths:

> Don't make timid promises, since it's promises that lure the ladies.
> Add whichever gods you like to your promises
> . . . .
> It's convenient that there are gods, and as it is convenient, let's pretend they exist.
> Let incense and wine be given to their ancient hearths.
> (*Ars* 1.631–32, 637–38)

Whether Ovid speaks for himself here or not, we cannot say. While we should not expect any more consistency from a poet during the principate than we might have from a pontiff in Cicero's time, it seems certain that Ovid's remark, less a product of genuine doubt than Cotta's, struck a jarring note in the political atmosphere under Augustus.[8] The enumeration elsewhere in the *Art of Love* of temples and other holy sites as apt places for romantic assignations certainly put the irreligious insight to cynical practice.[9]

Nonetheless, religion was for most citizens a matter of *pietas*, the proper performance of the ceremonies that, countless in number, kept relations between the state and the gods in good repair. "Roman religion was the ritual, to be followed and observed by everybody, but to be understood and studied only by the priests (and scholars)," as Jerzy Linderski has succinctly put it (613). Of all Ovid's works, it is *Fasti* that most meaningfully engages this central concept of Roman religion. In the poet's attention to individual details of cult, we could hardly ask for a more picturesque snapshot of Varro's *genus civile*. For many years, *Fasti* was studied from a strictly anthropological perspective as little more than a conglomeration of weird tales and observances. Only recently has the work begun to receive serious scholarly appreciation as a bona fide work of literature documenting the religious mentality of the Augustan era.[10]

As the proem states, *Fasti* presents "tempora cum causis," 'the festivals and their aetiologies,' so offering a mélange of myth and ritual held together by the structure of the calendar (1.1).[11] As a religious work, *Fasti*'s significance reflects the central place the calendar held in Roman religious life, as well as the "restoration" of Roman religion that formed the centerpiece of the Augustan revolution. The Republican calendar was a ten-month schedule of cultic festivals and political activities under the management of the *pontifices*, the chief priestly college that (as we can see from Cotta's remarks above) was not necessarily motivated by deep piety. So badly mishandled had the calendar been during the political turbulence of the first century BCE that it required a complete overhaul by the Pontifex Maximus, Julius Caesar, in 46 BCE.[12] To Caesar's scientific improvements of the calendar Augustus added ideological elements, thus turning what had been an unorganized series of religious events into a tool of harmonious Augustan propaganda.[13] That Ovid fell afoul of Augustus and was exiled by him, perhaps for political reasons, has greatly influenced recent study of the poem. If *Fasti* is an Augustan panegyric, its abrupt conclusion at the end of the sixth book, just before the exposition of the months named for Julius and Augustus Caesar, nonetheless seems egregious.[14]

It is against this centralized control of time with the princeps at its very heart that *Fasti* evidently makes demonstration. In the manner of an antiquarian rather than a propagandist, Ovid often attributes the details of his depiction of the Roman holidays to informal interlocutors instead of authoritative accounts. A good example of this tendency is to be found in the treatment of the ides of March, a date on which some commemoration of Caesar's assassination might well have been expected.[15] Instead, Ovid interviews a drunken old couple about Anna Perenna's "festum geniale," 'jolly feast,' which also takes place on this day (2.523). With this disregard for (or rejection of?) official order, the *Fasti* narrator is reminiscent of George Orwell's Winston Smith, who, when interrogating older proles in *1984*, wants to know "what it was like in the old days, before the Revolution" (89).[16]

Pursuing an intentionally irregular exegesis of rituals and myths with a deliberate inconsistency of tone, Ovid seems to undermine the carefully constructed seamlessness of Augustan ideology. But if the poem fails to toe the party line of the princeps, it offers in its haphazard way a colorful vista of religious life at the beginning of the first century CE. In *Fasti*, we find compelling descriptions of unusual ceremonies (such as the paterfamilias's strewing of beans around the house to drive away ghosts on the Lemuria, or "All Souls' Day" [5.427–44]), longer set pieces from Roman legend (such as the story of Claudia Quinta's ferrying of the Great Mother's statue at her holiday, the Megalensia [4.179–328]), and a host of other memorable vignettes. It may well be that, in a society as multicultural and polytheistic as imperial Rome was, Ovid's presentation of a pantheon more like pandemonium accurately captures the religious sensibility of his time, one immune to the political systematics of as masterly a propagandist as even Augustus, as well as to the theological classification of so learned a scholar as Varro (with whom this essay began).

NOTES

[1] All translations, unless otherwise noted, are mine. For background, see discussions by Momigliano, especially 202, and Rawson 299–301.

[2] The tripartite perspective of Ovid's work was noted in passing by Schilling 152, although the idea has now been more thoroughly treated by C. M. C. Green; compare the apt caution of Boyd, who "can easily imagine Ovid wilfully resisting at every turn G[reen]'s attempts to fit him and the *Fasti* into an ill-fitting Varronian straightjacket" (Rev. of *Ovid's* Fasti).

[3] Cicero, *De Natura deorum* bk. 1, sec. 42 (Velleius 43) and bk. 2, sec. 70 (Balbus 191). The disparaging of poetic representations of the gods, as old as the critique of Xenophanes of Colophon in the sixth century BCE, was powerfully argued by Plato in book 10 of the *Republic*. On the topic, see the collected citations of Pease in his magisterial commentary, 1: 280–83. See also Momigliano: "In Rome the poets could be dismissed more easily than in Greece because after all it was known that the best stories about the gods were written in Greek and did not really belong to the original Roman tradition" (202).

[4] This tradition begins with national epics of Naevius and Ennius in the third and second centuries BCE. See Feeney, *Gods* 98–187, for further discussion.

[5] Note, however, the allegorical usage to which *Metamorphoses* was put in the fourteenth-century *Ovide moralisé*: see Cormier's essay, in this volume.

[6] The extensive commentary of Pease (1: 351–53) on this passage is worth consulting.

[7] The term, coined by Veyne 41–59, is applied specifically to the religious mentality of Rome by Feeney, *Literature* 14–15, as the ability to "entertain different kinds of assent and criteria of judgement in different contexts."

[8] On Augustus's moral legislation, see the good summation of Galinsky, *Augustan Culture* 128–30.

[9] In particular, the designation of the Temple of Venus, built to honor the Julian family, as a good spot for illicit lovemaking must have grated on the princeps's nerves (*Ars* 1.81–87).

[10] The literary prototypes for *Fasti* were Callimachus's *Aitia* and, more immediately, the fourth book of Propertius's elegies. Until recently, the standard English-language reference on the poem was the six-volume commentary by James G. Frazer of *Golden Bough* fame. Cultic information from *Fasti*, with a distinctly Frazerian cast, had already been incorporated into Fowler's study of Roman festivals. As a literary work, *Fasti* was dismissed as "trite" by Wilkinson (*Ovid Recalled* 269) and condemned by the great historian Syme as "[n]ot a good idea" (105). The radical realignment of critical opinion on the poem since the 1980s is well documented by Fantham, "Recent Readings." See too the essays in Boyd, *Brill's Companion*, by both John F. Miller ("The *Fasti*") and Fantham ("Ovid's *Fasti*").

[11] Ovid offers many depictions of rites and the pious folks who carry them out, chiefly but not solely in *Fasti*. In *Amores* 3.13, for instance, we find a relatively sincere recreation of a festival honoring Juno in the rural town of Falerii, on which see the illuminating discussion by Miller, *Ovid's Elegiac Festivals* 50–57.

[12] See Suetonius 40 and Plutarch, "Julius Caesar" 58.5–6, and the scholarly discussions in Michels 16–18 and Bickerman 43–46. In his reform of the calendar, Caesar apparently relied on the calculations of the Greek astronomer Sosigenes.

[13] On this topic, see Wallace-Hadrill.

[14] Ovid himself attributed his exile to "carmen et error," 'a poem and a mistake' (*Tr.* 2.207). While the fateful poem is thought by many scholars to have been the *Art of Love,* the "mistake" is anybody's guess. Although Ovid claims to have written twelve books of *Fasti* (*Tr.* 2.549–50), no trace of books 7 through 12 has been identified. On the silence of *Fasti* at the end of June, see the remarks of Newlands, *Playing with Time* 3–5, and Barchiesi, *Poet and the Prince* 259–62.

[15] The assassination, impossible to ignore altogether, is treated as a footnote later in the book (3.697–711). See Newlands, who notes that, with this arrangement of events, Ovid "seems to prefer the populist strain in Roman religion to the new moral and political decorum promulgated by the Julio-Claudian family, which was inserting itself obtrusively into Roman time and religious cult" (*Playing with Time* 61).

[16] See also John F. Miller: "Significantly, most of the [*Fasti*] interlocutors are old, as if to suggest that these are the *antiqui* whom Ovid elsewhere cites generally as a source" ("Callimachus" 404).

Ovide moralisé
Raymond Cormier

Ovid's boundless *Metamorphoses* begins with the genesis of humankind and concludes with the promised apotheosis of the Roman emperor Caesar Augustus. Soon perceived as a kind of pagan bible, the text qua medieval artifact—along with its myriad subsequent marginal annotations and commentaries—at once poetizes allegory, anthropologizes hermeneutics, and treats archaeology and historiography in literary terms. Known in fact as the "poets' bible" in the Middle Ages, it was endlessly studied, taught, copied, imitated, glossed, and interpreted—thus providing a prime example of the process of reconciling Graeco-Roman antiquity with medieval Christian perspectives. As Robert Levine phrases it, dogma was thus conveyed by means of highly imaginative allegorical exegesis, a "popular activity . . . because it gave men license to read and write about [often horrible] sex and violence . . ." (197). A titillating narrative thus escaped the scrutiny of conservative biblical commentators.

In the early fourteenth century (c. 1300–30), an anonymous French cleric, doubtless a Franciscan from the Burgundian area, set about to embroider the work with a massive philosophical paraphrase of about 72,000 lines—a sixfold exploitation of Ovid—in Middle French octosyllabic couplets.[1] Working for his patroness Jeanne of Navarre, queen of Philip the Fair, the medieval poet of the "moralized Ovid" saturated Ovid with exegetical moralization and allegorical interpretation, as well as with pseudo-historical narrative. Ovid's gallery of heathendom now had its Christian curator. Drawing methodologically on earlier medieval allegorical traditions, such as the gestalt, aura, and style of the thirteenth-century *Roman de la Rose*, the medieval poet adapted each Latin fable and then amplified the episode—and more—with a vernacular exposition, attempting to synchronize sacred traditions and moralize secular ones. Despite the poet's occasional misogynistic, anti-Semitic, and anticlerical arrows, the result is an encyclopedic summa, at once breathtaking, copious, and influential. The didactic work synthesizes sources as diverse as ancient biblical commentary and late antique and early and late medieval allegorical glosses on all Ovid's works. It also includes "a library-full of well-known medieval texts on mythological themes" (Morse 129), encompassing ancient mythographic and Homeric lore as well as story matter from twelfth-century vernacular accounts. For just a single gloss, the approach uses a pluralistic system, drawing on imagery from geographic, euhemeristic, moralistic, theological, exegetical, and apocalyptic modes. Apparently chaotic and irreconcilable elements are deftly orchestrated: pagan fable becomes redemptive myth in the hands of this inventive French "compiler-expositor" (Copeland 116). Like what one might call anthropological "bricolage," the "cherry-picking" of Ovid seemingly starts with such expansive medieval harmonizing.[2]

Excruciating in its unflagging commentary on Ovidian story, polyvalent to a fault (and thus ironically postmodern in its quest for diversity), *Ovide mora-*

lisé enjoyed an immense subsequent popularity, since it made antique legends more accessible. In diverse vernacular dress, it was widely imitated by writers like Guillaume de Machaut, Eustache Deschamps, Geoffrey Chaucer (in the *Legend of Good Women*), John Gower, and Christine de Pisan. The Benedictine scholar-translator Pierre Bersuire (fl. 1340) used it for his learned Latin prose *Ovidius moralizatus*, part of an erudite and legitimizing sixteen-book compilation that became a standard reference work for Renaissance artists. Moreover, the text was subjected to further treatments (Caxton's 1480 English prose translation; a French prosification by Colard Mansion; and a fifteenth-century French prose summary [*Ovide* (1954)]) and was used as well in the *Bible des poètes* (printed by Vérard in the early sixteenth century; full details in Amielle 13–30). Like a kaleidoscope, this mosaic of semantic metanarrative connected, to the delight of intellectuals and sermonizers, the classical world with that of Christian *pietas*. Thus did Ovid's urbane and witty antique verse find new life in typical medieval exempla of vice and virtue. Such was the case, for example, with three Ovidian heroines—Thisbe, Echo, and Procne (in Old French, Tisbé, Dané [sic], and Procné)—vividly reborn in Old French as rebellious females who subvert or repudiate "the frustrating or demeaning conditions imposed" by "dominant patriarchal society" (Cormier 102).

In her study of the poetics of *mutacion*, Ana Pairet has shown how distinct generic contexts were analogized (through Ovidian poetry, courtly literature, mythography, and historiography) so that the Middle Ages turned this polysemic figure—Ovid's "endless song"—into a literary artifact. Renate Blumenfeld-Kosinski explores the appropriation and transformation of classical mythology in French culture from the mid–twelfth century to about 1430. Her third chapter focuses on interpretive techniques and key terms, such as *allegory, fable, exposicion*, and *istoire*, and she argues that the Christianization of *Metamorphoses* created a "new Ovid" (91) in the person of a fourteenth-century Franciscan friar. Blumenfeld-Kosinski points out that *Ovide moralisé* represents the first French translation of Ovid's epic poem and the first systematic allegorization of "Ovid's pagan fables"—the value of which in turn increases through the application by intellectuals and clerics of biblical-style exegesis (135). She views the gigantic undertaking as a hermeneutical "rescue mission" to preserve classical mythology (101), an endeavor so successful it displaced Ovid's text in the process (136). While the translation segments alone account for about half of the text, it is the balance—copious allegorical and historical interpretations, "exposicions" and deeper meanings adduced—that make up the other half (102). Often, too, the interpretations or allegorizations are subjected to further construals, so that the whirling process becomes mind-numbing, something like counting angels on the head of a pin.

With the pagan and Christian worlds seen in parallel, taking Orpheus or Theseus or Jupiter as a typological *figura* for Christ, for instance, allows the medieval poet to emphasize soteriology—Christ's Incarnation representing "the ultimate metamorphosis" (101). Again, in book 14, the ship of Aeneas stands for Saint Yglise in its avoidance of two dangers, Scylla and Charybdis, viewed as Jews and heathens (118). Blumenfeld-Kosinski's analysis of this "interpretive plenitude" (132) follows progressively coherent developments of several Ovidian episodes, from G. Julius Hyginus, librarian of Augustus and contemporary of Ovid (64 BCE–17 CE), up to John of Garland's antecedent and influential *Integumenta Ovidii* (thirteenth century). The medievalist Sarah Kay has similarly focused on what she calls anamorphosis in the text, positing violent sexual transgression in the Ovidian stories, for which the moralizations function just as brutally (and often more obscenely) because they extract pagan contexts and resituate them within a Christian paradigm.

The monumental length of the rhyming text, the difficulty most readers will have in acquiring a copy of the long out-of-print five-volume compilation, and the frustration of following the poet's extraordinarily paradoxical and hermeneutical vagaries allow me here only to feature one part of *Ovide moralisé* for brief discussion. As well, Paule Demats notes that book 7 of the *Metamorphoses* represents a crucial "axis," a turning point from "pure fable" to a new era of heroism (89). We turn then to one of Ovid's most striking female characters, Medea, in book 7, who illustrates the "moralized" version's Christianization of an extraordinarily charismatic "barbarian" witch.

In the twelfth century, urbane Benoît de Sainte-Maure's *Roman de Troie*, innovative in vernacular fiction, synthesizes antecedent accounts of the Trojan War and incorporates Jason's betrayal of Medea as one love interest among several moralized entertainments—the tales of Troilus and Briseida, Achilles and Polyxena and, of course, Paris and Helen (Morse 89). But it is the dangerous and cunning Medea—foreigner and victim, but also a brilliant (yet sadly gullible and foolish) trickster—whose "erotic passion" personifies a feminine threat to social order and the patriarchy (Morse 107, 113). Elsewhere anticipating a kind of Don Juan, in the Christian paradigm Jason becomes allegorized as the virtuous and powerful soul (i.e., *male*), tempted and delayed by feminine wiles. The betrayed princess Medea, however, unchanged, becomes "inscribed within the anagogical trajectory . . . a trope of misogyny" (Morse 126).

Ovid's five-part arrangement of this story in book 7 includes Medea's love soliloquy; Aeson's rejuvenation; Medea's vengeance on Pelias; Medea's escape and eventual marriage to Aegeus, king of Athens; and Medea's exit just after attempting to murder Theseus, son of Aegeus. By following the extended narrative of the Troy romance, one can grasp more precisely how Benoît very freely condensed Ovid while drawing as well on *Heroides* (esp. 12) for the episode of Medea's abandonment by Jason in order to amplify the Jason-Medea episode into some eight hundred lines of compelling and dramatic storytelling (out of his 33,016 octosyllabic lines of Old French).

The Argonauts, led by Jason, are welcomed with opulence to the court of Aeëtes in Colchis, and there meet Medea, whose many secret talents and "immense and diverse" knowledge will help the adventurers capture the magical and marvelous Golden Fleece (Benoît, line 1228). But Medea's imprudent and passionate intentions miscue her excessive and erotic attentions: "Mout li tressaut li cuers el ventre, / Mout l'a espris de granz amors . . ." 'Her heart throbs and pounds as Love's flames have engulfed her' (lines 1464–65; my trans.). She falls for Jason, who as it turns out is a perfidious and cupidinous cheat and philandering scoundrel. In the secrecy of her bedchamber, Medea, just before being deflowered, makes Jason swear on a statue of Jupiter to marry her and be faithful forever (this intimate scene is omitted from *Ovide moralisé*; see Feimer 44). Benoît observes immediately that Jason pledged but later broke his promise, to his own sorrow and shame. Once he has secured the precious Fleece, they depart for Greece, actions that Benoît condemns because Medea must abandon her family and homeland, as Jason will then abandon her. Like Helen, Medea is abducted from home. Nevertheless, for medieval writers, the fault lies with Medea: "she was doubly in error," observes Morse, "first in not foreseeing that Jason would betray her, then in counting on his word, though he swore upon the image of a deity" (152). Guido delle Colonne adapts Benoît's romance in a Latin prose work, completed around 1287, which is yet another important iteration and precursor for *Ovide moralisé*. In it, Jason carries out Medea's plan: offering "himself with devout expression and touching the image physically with his hand, [he] swore to observe and carry out . . ." (3.64–66).

The *Ovide moralisé*, demonstrating encyclopedic exertion, following Benoît and Guido, and amplifying yet again, restores all five of Ovid's segments, expanded here into some 2,000 lines of Middle French, including fable and allegory (see Jung, "*L'Ovide moralisé*" 110, for a brief account of additions to book 7). In the allegorical segment (using typology), the Franciscan author of the *Ovide moralisé* interprets the Golden Fleece as representing the Lamb of God; the task of plowing of the furrows by Jason figures the Harrowing of Christ; and Christ's Incarnation is anticipated by several marvelous metamorphoses. The whole story in fact, much like the massive text itself, takes on a retelling of the Incarnation and Passion of Christ (Possamaï-Pérez 559–65). When Medea (viewed as Christ), escaping with Jason, carves up and hurls the parts of her brother's body across a field to distract her father's pursuit, the *Ovide moralisé* poet takes the action as comparable to Jesus's surrendering his body, suffering "ill treatment and death" 'mort et laidure' to "save humankind" 'pour sauver humaine nature' (7.811–12). The chariot Medea uses to gather magical herbs is assimilated to the womb of the Virgin Mary that bore the Redeemer (Possamaï-Pérez 690–91), and the poison that she later prepares in Athens for her presumed rival Theseus prefigures the mortal beverage of anguished and bitter death that God had his dear son Christ drink ("Son chier fi, que tant dut amer, / A boivre le bevrage amer / De mort angoisseuse et amere . . ." 'his dear son whom he loved so had to drink the sour brew of painful and bitter death' [7.2117–20; my trans]).

A classroom activity that communicates some of the flavor of *Ovide moralisé* to contemporary students would be to have them read *Metamorphoses*, book 7, and then discuss Medea's behavior and character. By introducing the brief assessment of Benoît's and of the Middle French versions included here, the instructor can suggest to his or her students how the transformation of a figure of classical myth into a lesson or paradigm for the Christian Middle Ages could result.

NOTES

[1] All references to the *Ovide moralisé* in this section are to the 1966 edition.

[2] According to Levine (198n), Smalley dates the poem 1316–28 (247–48). Boer proposes 1305 (4).

Speaking Pictures: Ovid and the Visual Arts
Bruce Redford

> Poesy therefore is an art of imitation, for so Aristotle termeth it in his word *mimesis*, that is to say, a representing, counterfeiting, or figuring forth—to speak metaphorically, a speaking picture.
> — Philip Sidney, *An Apology for Poetry* (1595)

In his preface to *Ovid's Epistles, Translated by Several Hands* (1680), John Dryden distinguishes three kinds of translation: "metaphrase," "paraphrase," and "imitation." "Metaphrase" consists of "turning an author word by word, and line by line, from one language into another." Dryden defines "paraphrase" as "translation with latitude, where the author is kept in view by the translator . . . but his words are not so strictly followed as his sense." The third approach, "imitation," gives the translator "liberty not only to vary from the words and sense, but to forsake them both as he sees occasion" (268). To illustrate these contrasting approaches, Dryden adduces contemporary examples of translation from classical literature: Ben Jonson's metaphrastic version of Horace's *Ars poetica*, Edmund Waller's paraphrastic rendering of Vergil's *Eclogues*, and Abraham Cowley's imitations of Pindar. Dryden then clarifies his terminology by means of visual metaphors: Jonson is a "verbal copier," Waller aims "to vary but the dress, not to alter or destroy the substance," while Cowley seeks "not to translate [Pindar's] words, or to be confined to his sense, but only to set him as a pattern" (268–72). Dryden's pictorial language prompts us to apply his "heads," as he calls them, to the translation of words into images; it also invites analysis of artistic responses to Ovid in terms of the spectrum that runs from faithful metaphrase through flexible paraphrase to libertine imitation. This spectrum includes hundreds of examples in many periods, mediums, and styles: as Nigel Llewellyn emphasizes, *Metamorphoses* rivals the Bible and the epics of Homer and Vergil as "the source for most of the visual art produced until the later eighteenth century" (151). Any brief account, therefore, must narrow the field to those examples that are both historically representative and pedagogically rewarding.

Every student of Ovidian visual culture should keep three facts firmly in mind. First, we have no evidence from the ancient world for an illustrated *Metamorphoses* or for painting or sculpture that derives unambiguously from Ovid's versions of mythic narrative. Second, most artists who responded to Ovid during the late Middle Ages and the early modern period were unable to read Latin and therefore worked from translations, retellings, and iconographic manuals. Third, the doctrine of decorum, with its emphasis on the integrity and dignity of the human body, directed most artists to moments preceding the metamorphic climax; the effect of this doctrine was reinforced by the technical difficulty of translating time into space, textual process into visual product.

Imitation

Allegorical interpretation begins to transform the reading and reception of Ovid during the twelfth century. This didactic rescue mission accelerates thanks to illuminated manuscripts of *Ovide moralisé*, an anonymous French poem of the early fourteenth century. The images in these manuscripts consolidate and even amplify the text: they interpret the judgment of Paris, for example, as a contest among the contemplative life (Minerva), the active life (Juno), and the voluptuous life (Venus). All the figures wear contemporary costume and the gods golden crowns; the illuminators base their renditions of metamorphosis on the grotesques that appear in cathedral sculpture and the marginalia of manuscripts. As Carla Lord emphasizes, "it is just these French illustrations that during the course of the fourteenth century kept the Ovidian tradition visually alive" (170). They create the conventions that influence the decorated panels of early Renaissance wedding chests and the first illustrated editions of *Metamorphoses*, which appeared in Venice at the end of the fifteenth century.

A generation later Correggio painted for Federigo Gonzaga, Duke of Mantua, four pictures that have long been known as the *Loves of Jupiter* (1530–33). These four, which may have decorated the "sala di Ovidio" in the duke's pleasure dome, the Palazzo del Te, divide unmistakably into two pairs: Io and the rape of Ganymede and Danaë and Leda. In both pairs Correggio takes great liberties with his source material, but the picture of Io exemplifies a paradox of verbal to visual translation: masterful imitation sometimes involves daring inversion.

Ovid's account in *Metamorphoses*, book 1, makes it clear that Io flees the lustful Jupiter in terror and that the dark cloud manufactured by the god is designed to stop her flight and conceal the rape from Juno. Correggio completely reimagines the tale, using all his resources of design and color to turn violence into voluptuousness. Io reclines on a grassy knoll, her head tilted backward in ecstasy as she welcomes the embraces of a god who has changed himself into a blue-gray cloud, the more completely to envelop and arouse her. The picture is built out of interlocking curves—the loosening limbs of Io welcome the divine cumulus that functions, as Paul Barolsky observes, not as the means of concealment but as "the agent of love-making" (469). Through his melting artistry Correggio does not simply illustrate metamorphosis, he performs it.

Paraphrase

The most profound visual responses to Ovid are those by Titian, who late in his career painted for Philip II of Spain six mythologies called *poesie*: *Venus and Adonis*, *Perseus and Andromeda*, *Diana and Actaeon* and *Diana and Callisto*, *The Rape of Europa*, and *The Death of Actaeon*. In the words of Giorgio Vasari, "these last works are executed with bold strokes and dashed off with a broad and even coarse sweep of the brush, insomuch that from near little can be seen, but from a distance they appear perfect" (2: 794). This daring yet scrupulous brushwork is both the vehicle for and analogue to Titian's "translation with latitude": each one of the *poesie* combines close attention to Ovid's narrative with inspired departures from it.

The three *poesie* that engage most fully and most inventively with their textual sources are *The Rape of Europa, Diana and Actaeon,* and *The Death of Actaeon*. In *Europa* Titian responds fully to Ovid's description:

> Europa now is terrified; she clasps
> one horn with her right hand; meanwhile the left
> rests on the bull's great croup. She turns to glance
> back at the shore, so distant now. Her robes
> are fluttering—they swell in the sea breeze.
> (73; *Met.* 2.873–75)

As we compare poem with picture, we grasp that the painter has registered but reworked every detail. Europa's scarf, not her robes, flutters, its iridescent curves helping unite setting and action. It is not Europa's right but left hand that clasps the bull's horns, a decision that extends the dramatic diagonal line of her splayed torso. Europa turns to glance not backward but upward, as her thighs slacken in a pose mingling terror with excitement.

Ovid is likewise "kept in view" when Titian translates the story of Actaeon. *Diana and Actaeon* creates a generic hybrid by grafting landscape onto mythological painting, just as Ovid takes unusual pains to describe the woodland setting in which the hunter stumbles upon the naked goddess:

> And within the deepest shade,
> the innermost recess, there lay a cave
> most perfect. Though no mortal art had shaped
> that grotto, Nature's craft can imitate
> the ways of art. (82; *Met.* 3.157–59)

While faithfully conjuring up the *locus amoenus* atmosphere, Titian devises rusticated architecture that inverts Ovid's description: nature imitating art becomes art imitating nature. The pool in the foreground likewise reflects the scene in reverse. As Erwin Panofsky observes, "what looks like a triumph of poetic license is in reality the triumph of an imagination fertilized by attentive reading and intelligent thought" (157). The same kind of imagination forecasts the tragic outcome of the story and links this picture to its companion by placing the skull of a stag on a pier in the background.

The Death of Actaeon defies the doctrine of decorum and celebrates the power of the brush by capturing the very moment of transformation. As in *Metamorphoses,* book 3, the change has begun with the head: Actaeon's body, assaulted by his hounds, remains that of the young hunter. The decision to create at this preliminary stage the painterly equivalent of a cinematic freeze-frame accentuates the horror of Actaeon's plight. Titian has found perhaps the only spatial means of communicating what Ovid narrates: "He wants to shout, / 'I am Actaeon! Don't you recognize / your master?' But his heart has been denied / all speech" (85; *Met.* 3.230–31). Through "bold strokes" both literal and figurative, Titian devises the ultimate in speaking pictures.

Metaphrase

Gian Lorenzo Bernini's *Apollo and Daphne* is the third of three life-size sculptures illustrating classical subjects that were commissioned by Cardinal Scipione Borghese; all three are still to be seen at the Borghese Gallery in Rome. Before sculpting *Apollo and Daphne*, for his *Aeneas and Anchises* Bernini had turned to Vergil and for his *Rape of Proserpina* to Ovid. Though he closely follows his classical sources in the first two groups, *Apollo and Daphne* best illustrates his breathtaking virtuosity in the service of visual metaphrase. This sculptural group is unusual in two respects. First, Bernini, who read Latin, closely follows not only the details but the exact sequence of Ovid's narrative, brilliantly translating time into space, flesh into marble. Second, he chooses to capture the decisive moment of metamorphosis, seconds after Peneus has answered Daphne's prayer to "transform, dissolve / my gracious shape" (24; *Met.* 1.547). Bernini guides the viewer through a sequence that recapitulates the sprouting, encasing, and rooting of Daphne: the eye moves diagonally from agitated hair and splayed hand, both of them halfway to vegetation, past the "thin bark [that] begins to gird her tender frame" (24; *Met.* 1.549) to the agitated drapery swirling around the thighs of the incredulous Apollo. Through carving of extraordinary delicacy and precision, Daphne's toes mutate into "sluggish roots" (24; *Met.* 1.551). Such naturalistic details serve the human drama and enhance the sculpture's pictorial qualities, which Bernini designed to be seen from a single vantage point. Its original installation completed the homage to Ovid and the challenge to the resources of painting.

In both matter and manner, Ovid's *Metamorphoses* is a picture-making poem— an influential example of a tradition that reaches back to Homer. In *The Sister Arts*, our most incisive guide to this tradition, Jean H. Hagstrum argues that "in order to be called 'pictorial' a description or an image must be, in its essentials, capable of translation into painting or some other visual art" (xii–xiii). The translations we have just been examining illustrate some of the ways in which Ovid has stimulated the imagination of artists as well as readers, both of whom take their cue from the poet's artful commitment to "representing, counterfeiting, or figuring forth" (101).

OVID'S TEXTS IN THE CLASSROOM

Commentaries on Ovid
Peter E. Knox

In its most basic aspects the approach to teaching classical texts in the original language has not changed much since antiquity: a teacher with a small group of students parses individual words and phrases, with the aid of commentaries compiled from notes accumulated by predecessors (Reynolds and Wilson 9–15). We can see the process at work best in the case of Vergil, for whom much ancient scholarship survives, most notably the extensive commentary on the *Eclogues*, *Georgics*, and *Aeneid* that was largely the work of the fourth-century grammarian Servius. For his students Vergil's Latin was already a remote literary language, perhaps as remote as Elizabethan English is from students of today, and the text contained many obscurities—mythological allusions, historical references, intertextual references, lexical and grammatical oddities—in need of a teacher's explication. The production of commentaries on Vergil began shortly after his death in 19 BCE, and yet many problems remained in the text for Servius and his students to address, and many answers recorded by ancient commentators are clearly misguided. The centuries separating Vergil from Servius's students also opened up an interpretative gap into which Servius and other commentators rushed, to explicate potentially problematic issues of ideology or morality (Knox, "Savagery"). And so commentaries on his works have continued to be produced through the centuries to address the shifting needs and interests of readers and, chiefly, of students and scholars.

The case of Ovid is somewhat different. His works, unlike those of Vergil, Horace, Cicero, or Juvenal, never entered the ancient curriculum, and so there was no tradition of grammatical, rhetorical, or critical exegesis passed on from antiquity through the Middle Ages. Students did not study Ovid in school, but it is abundantly clear from references to his works and imitations by other authors that Ovid remained a popular author until the end of classical antiquity and beyond (Dewar). For a number of reasons, Ovid was only slowly absorbed into the medieval curriculum, partly because conservative tendencies resisted the introduction of new texts into the canon and partly of course because the subject matter of his amatory works was difficult to reconcile with the Christian context in which schooling took place (Glauche). By the twelfth century, however, a number of Ovid's works were being read in schools, most commonly *Epistulae ex Ponto*, *Heroides*, and *Metamorphoses*. Reasons for his inclusion in the curriculum are not accessible to us, but an easy guess would be popular demand, for Ovid has always been a hit with readers. Surviving medieval commentaries show teachers proceeding down one of two exegetical paths. At one level teachers had to explain the difficulties in understanding Ovid's Latin, by glossing unusual words, parsing grammatical obscurities, and identifying historical and mythological references (Hexter, *Ovid and Medieval Schooling*). Much of this form of commentary remains to be explored in the marginalia of Ovid's medieval manuscripts, which still offer a largely unexploited trove for students of Ovidianism. A second form of commentary provided guidance in ethically acceptable and edifying interpretations. One important product of this latter effort to "decode" Ovid's pagan myths to reveal their hidden Christian meanings was a series of allegorizing paraphrases and commentaries on *Metamorphoses*, culminating in the early years of the fourteenth century in the anonymous French verse *Ovid moralisé* (see Cormier, in this volume). The modern commentary, which combines these two aspects of grammatical explication and critical exegesis, is largely the invention, or reinvention, of the Renaissance humanists, who took the ancient commentators as their models, chiefly Servius's commentary on Vergil, in registering their observations "line by line and often word by word" (Grafton 48). The greatest humanist commentator on Ovid, Raffaele Regio, describes his task in terms that have a contemporary ring: "the first task is to read a corrected text and to explain what seems too difficult in a way that can be easily understood."

The importance of Regio's and other contemporary commentaries in the reception of Ovid's works in the Renaissance and after can hardly be overstated, but it has scarcely begun to be assessed (Guthmüller). Moralizing interpretation, though stripped of its allegorical overlay, remains an important element in Regio's readings. So the story of Daphne, for example, continues to teach a lesson, but it is not an overtly Christian message, as Regio frames it in his introductory note: "What else should we think is signified by the transformation of Daphne into an evergreen laurel than that undying fame awaits maidens who take considered care for their modesty?" Ovid's translators, through whom most writers came to know his works (Lyne, "Ovid"), were clearly influenced by the prevailing interpretations to be found in the notes of the commentaries used in teaching the Latin text, but this aspect of the Ovidian reception remains largely unexplored territory.

The problem faced by the contemporary commentator still remains how to negotiate the twin requirements of grammatical explication and critical exegesis; and with the multitude of approaches used by scholars or advocated by university presses, the problem for the classroom instructor is to match the needs of the student with the available options. In recent years the role of the commentary as a work of criticism and a pedagogical tool in the classroom is increasingly the focus of academic discussion (Most; Gibson and Kraus), but it can hardly be said that a consensus has been reached, and arguably it never should. For the teacher of Ovid, there is a vast array of options to consider, and yet inevitably compromises have to be made to account for students' reasonable needs and demands, including budgetary demands. For instance, any attempt to teach Ovid's masterpiece, *Metamorphoses*, at an advanced level by way of the commentary approach confronts certain stark realities. The only complete modern commentary intended for scholars is a magpie's nest of disassociated notes, as the author himself acknowledges in his preface (Bömer 1: 5). At a slightly lower level of scholarly aspiration, there is a complete one-volume edition of the poem, handsomely produced with facing translation and copious notes by Luigi Galasso, Guido Paduano, and Alessandro Perutelli that will serve students well for many years—in Italy. The most notable commentaries in English will all require that the teacher adopt a selective focus on a book or a small number of books, a circumstance that has probably contributed to the generally compartmentalized approach to the critical interpretation of the poem over the years. Precisely because commentators offer so much information, they more than other interpreters expose themselves to criticism for errors and omissions. The commentaries by the well-regarded literary critic W. S. Anderson are less sure guides in matters lexical, metrical, and grammatical (Kenney, Rev. of *Ovid's* Metamorphoses); the more rigorously philological work of A. S. Hollis may fall short in attuning students to Ovid's literary accomplishments. The same observations may generally be made, *mutatis mutandis*, about Ovid's lesser-known narrative masterpiece, *Fasti*. The student of Ovid's amatory poetry is generally better served, with more options ranging across all the works. They may run the gamut from J. C. McKeown's monumental work on *Amores*, intended for advanced scholars, to selections from *Heroides* in the now ubiquitous and flourishing series of Cambridge "green and yellows" intended for advanced students (Knox, *Ovid*; Kenney, *Ovid:* Heroides) to notes on a text of the second book of *Amores* with facing translation by J. Booth in a series intended to address some of the needs of the Latinless reader as well. Something of the same sort was attempted for *Metamorphoses* (Hill), but the scale of Ovid's long narrative poem seems to overwhelm this genre of commentary. Accordingly, minimalism as an approach to the classroom commentary also finds its advocates, as represented in the Bryn Mawr series, which is characterized by a bare text accompanied by basic notes aimed at assisting comprehension rather than interpretation (e.g., J. Miller, *Ovid*).

At every period, technology has had a profound influence on the form, and hence the classroom use, of the commentary. The earliest commentaries produced in Alexandria circulated separately from the texts they were intended to explicate, on papyrus roles with citations (lemmas) from the originals to key the comments to the text. Many of these notes, disengaged from their original contexts, ended up in the margins of texts for ease of reference, a format that became increasingly common as the papyrus roll was supplanted by the parchment codex as the standard format for books. With the advent of printing, this format for commentary, text surrounded by notes, became standard, as it remains today, with some variations, chief among which is that embraced by more advanced commentaries, with notes bundled after the text. With the slow, gradual migration to electronic forms of publication, it is likely that the format of the commentary too and, with it, the way it is used in classrooms will change. Some developments may actually assist teaching Ovid and the Ovidian tradition. For example, a consistent problem in teaching Ovid in the original involves the wide variation in language skills among students in any particular classroom. While N. Hopkinson's commentary on book 13 of *Metamorphoses* might strike some students as too basic, others will need more help with fundamental questions of grammar and vocabulary not addressed in it. Publication of commentaries in digitized form may allow for more customization by teachers, as in the layered commentaries now offered online by Cambridge University Press.

In such cases the impact of technology may be classed primarily as changing the delivery method of the commentary without essentially altering the nature of the learning experience for students reading Ovid. Potential developments for the study of the Ovidian tradition are likely to be more dramatic. That Ovid's influence on the literature and learning of the Middle Ages and Renaissance was vast has long been acknowledged, but the full extent and nature of this influence remains to be assessed. Medieval commentaries, ranging from full-scale notes for classroom use to intermittent marginalia in copies of Ovid, have only begun to be investigated for what they can tell us about the intellectual life of the period and Ovid's place in it. Difficulty of access to the material in hundreds of manuscripts in libraries across Europe and North America hampers any but the most dedicated investigator. Likewise early printed editions, with their marginal notes, as well as the commentaries of the Renaissance, such as Regio's, remain largely inaccessible. But as more and more libraries make their unpublished materials available online, students will have access to primary materials documenting Ovid's place in world literature. Regio's commentary, for example, can now easily be accessed from the digitized images of the collection of Wolfenbüttel Digital Library. What is evident from a survey of the range of approaches in contemporary commentaries is that the role of the classroom teacher, to act as gatekeeper and guide through the exhibits on display, remains as important as it was in Servius's time.

Ovid in Premodern English Translation
Cora Fox

The two most important early English translations of Ovid appear in the Renaissance and are both of *Metamorphoses*—by Arthur Golding (1567) and George Sandys (1621). Written only about fifty years apart, these two translations announce in different ways their contemporary cultural authority, especially among the educated elite who would have encountered *Metamorphoses* first in Latin. Although there are also important early translations of *Heroides*, *Ars*, *Amores* (see Cheney, in this volume, on Marlowe's), and *Tristia*, these two translations of Ovid's most influential work stand out as central to the literary culture of the time. They are important, not just because they are the first full translations of the poem into English, but because they profoundly influenced the development of the canonical literary tradition in English. Written in a prolific period, they provide a version of Ovid—his language, style, and themes, as well as the ideologies and assumptions that are encoded in his works—in an age that defines Ovidianism in English literature.

As Raphael Lyne has pointed out, the history of translations of Ovid into English is really the history of print, beginning with the first printer in England, William Caxton, and his *Ovyde his booke of Methamorphose* in 1480–83 ("Ovid" 249). Caxton's text, however, is not a translation in the modern and narrow sense but a collection of prose summaries framed as moral exempla, most likely derived from a variant of the *Ovide moralisé*. There is critical debate about whether it was printed at all, since it survives in only one manuscript, although Caxton refers to it in his *Golden Legend* as a work he has "accomplished," along with a number of works that survive in print.[1] So while it is significant that Ovid's work holds a prominent place at the origins of English print culture, this first rendering of the poem is significantly removed from the Latin original.

Golding, however, in his translation, makes loud claims to some kind of textual accuracy and wholeness: "This worthie worke . . . I present / To your good Lordship once ageine, not as a member rent / Or parted from the resdew of the body any more: / But fully now accomplished" ("Epistle of 1567," lines 581, 585–88).[2] Playing on the trope of dismemberment that is particularly appropriate to the poem's matter, Golding is seeking further patronage from the Earl of Leicester, who had already supported his translations of books 1–4 in 1564. This focus on the fullness of the work probably reflects and certainly would have inspired a renewed attention to the poem as a whole, and it must have marked a change in the reception of the work from the piecemeal, highly moralized, and usually prose forms of the Middle Ages. This first full English translation, therefore, must be counted as responsible for ushering in the new Ovidian age of the late sixteenth century.

Golding's poem is characterized by readers today as energetic or hearty, although some in previous generations have not been so kind. Although Ezra

Pound repeatedly called it "the most beautiful book in the language," C. S. Lewis commented that it "ought to be unendurable, and it almost is" (qtd. in Nims xxxi). Golding's landscape and his loyalties are profoundly English and Protestant, although he does remain faithful to many of the details of the stories that might be most troubling to the taste and morality of an English Protestant reader. Philomela, for instance, is led by Tereus to a "pelting graunge that peakishly did stand / In woods forgrowen" (*Met.* 6.663–64), where Tereus

> Did catch hir by the tung,
> And with his sword did cut it off. The stumpe whereon it hung
> Did patter still. The tip fell downe and quivering on the ground
> As though that it had murmured it made a certaine sound.
> And as an Adders tayle cut off doth skip a while: even so
> The tip of Philomelaas tongue did wriggle to and fro,
> And nearer to hir mistressward in dying still did go.
> (6.709–15)

In fact, the most striking aspect of the translation is the tension between Golding's seemingly loving attention to the details and style of Ovid's narrative and his anxious insistence in the prefatory material that the immorality of the poem must be avoided by a cautious reader, always reading metaphorically and typologically. He provides short traditional commentaries on many of the tales in his preface to the reader, all drawn from the moralized tradition, but then reproduces the hard, frightening ambiguities and nuances of Ovid's fictional world. This disparity must ultimately be ironic, and Golding practically acknowledges this in his final lines of the preface, where he protests:

> If any stomacke be so weake as that it cannot brooke,
> The lively setting forth of things described in this booke,
> I give him counsell to absteine until he bee more strong,
> And for to use Ulysses feat ageinst the Meremayds song.
> Or if he needes will heere and see and wilfully agree
> (Through cause misconstrued) unto vice allured for to bee,
> Then let him also marke the peine that dooth therof ensue,
> And hold himself content with that that to his fault is due.
> (428–29, lines 215–22)

Painstakingly attempting to turn the responsibility for the moral content of the poem to the readers rather than himself in the preface, Golding produces a stunningly varied *Metamorphoses* and sets the stage for new interpretations and rewritings that respond to Ovid's siren song in at least some of its original stylistic complexity and moral ambiguity.

Sandys's translation is similarly remarkable in standing as a monument of the literary culture of the time. Produced in an elaborately illustrated folio edition, the poem introduces not only a new style of translating the Latin poem but also a new kind of embedded commentary, drawing from widely varied contemporary sources and personal experience as well as medieval mythographic readings and exegetical moralization. The remarkable historical fact that Sandys completed his translation in the Virginia colony where he was treasurer, and the ways his experiences as a traveler and travel writer inflect (and sometimes seem to have no bearing on) his commentary, have been acutely examined by Lyne. Sandys's translation attempts to be more refined than Golding's, and it repeatedly advertises its serious literary value: in the prefatory materials (with a dedication to the king), the illustrations, and in the Latinity of the translation itself. He and his circumstances produce a very different Ovid from Golding's, but one similarly designed to be central to contemporary literary undertakings.

To modern readers at least, Sandys's translation is also less "English" in obvious ways than Golding's. He keeps the landscape and atmosphere of the poem mainly mythical (instead of reproducing Golding's English countryside) and the violent descriptions concise and therefore less dramatic. For example, the description of Philomela's severed tongue, so gruesome in Golding, is presented more matter-of-factly in Sandys. Tereus ". . . her tongue in pincers caught, / His sword divideth from the panting root: / And as a serpent's tail, dissevered, Leaps: / Even so her tongue: and dying sought her steps." Sandys's description of this action is much shorter than Golding's and is in fact shorter than Ovid's Latin. It is less visual: there is no wiggling and writhing as in Golding. And instead of describing the murmuring of the severed tongue, he only implies the sound of the crime in the "panting" root. He also chooses not to translate the Latin "dominae," which removes some of the macabre humor of not just personifying the tongue, but specifying its relation to Philomela. His commentary on the tale is mainly a protonaturalist discussion of the natures and behaviors of swallows and nightingales, proving that they are apt figures for Philomela and Procne and that the detail of their metamorphoses is the only "feigned" part of the story, representing their escape to Athens to avoid Tereus's revenge. Overall, Sandys's translation and commentary betray a desire to justify and naturalize the extremities of the poem, whereas Golding only worries about these desires in the prefatory material. Sandys's Ovid is still Ovid but slanted toward a seriousness and dignity that most likely reflects the attitude toward this classical author at the end, rather than the beginning, of an Ovidian age.

NOTES

[1] Lyne assumes the work was printed ("Ovid" 250–52), but Kuskin refers to the *Methamorphose* as "apparently unprinted" (241).

[2] All citations of Golding's *Metamorphoses* are from Nims's edition. Forey has also edited a recent paperback edition.

Ovid in Modern Translation
Barbara Weiden Boyd

Many of the more modern commentaries mentioned by Peter E. Knox (in this volume) can be of great value to the instructor who knows at least some Latin; but by and large, most of the nonclassicist instructors Cora Fox and I surveyed rely primarily if not exclusively on translations when they teach Ovid's poetry. In our report on the survey results, which follows this essay, we provide a list of those translations most frequently used in the non-Latin classroom; here, I briefly compare nine contemporary English translations of *Metamorphoses* currently available in paperback. I also do not include the premodern translations of Arthur Golding, George Sandys, and others; for them, see Cora Fox, "Ovid in Premodern Translation," in this volume. Nor do I include the translations available in the (bilingual) Loeb Classical Library edition of Ovid's works, since neither their original translators nor George Goold, the series editor who revised them all, was particularly concerned with crafting a work of literary merit on its own terms; rather, as with the Loeb series generally, the goal was to offer serviceable translations for use by those eager for help with Ovid's Latin. (Goold also took the opportunity, while modernizing the Loeb translations, to improve the Latin texts printed alongside, capturing improvements in our knowledge of the manuscript transmission since the translations were first done and relying on his own impressive scholarly acumen.) Finally, I do not include prose translations other than that by Michael Simpson, which because of its recent publication has been adopted by some for classroom use.

The translations included in this discussion are by Rolfe Humphries (1955), Horace Gregory (1958), A. D. Melville (1986), Allen Mandelbaum (1993), David Slavitt (1994), Michael Simpson (2001), David Raeburn (2004), Z. Philip Ambrose (2004), and Charles Martin (2004). To provide a basis for comparison, I have chosen a brief excerpt from an episode that virtually all survey respondents include in their teaching: the opening and closing lines of the Daphne and Apollo episode. With each example, I note a few important features that illustrate *in parvo* the translator's treatment of the poem as a whole. First, Ovid's Latin:

> Primus amor Phoebi Daphne Peneia, quem non
> fors ignara dedit, sed saeva Cupidinis ira.
> . . . .
> finierat Paean; factis modo laurea ramis
> adnuit utque caput visa est agitasse cacumen.
> (452–53, 566–67)

Humphries's version:

> Now the first girl Apollo loved was Daphne,
> Whose father was the river-god Peneus,

And this was no blind chance, but Cupid's malice.
. . . .
    . . . He said no more. The laurel,
Stirring, seemed to consent, to be saying *Yes*.
                              (16, 20)

The choice of "malice" as a translation for Ovid's "saeva . . . ira" points up the relation between this beginning ("primus amor") and that of the *Aeneid*, where Vergil foregrounds Juno's long-lasting wrath as a driving force behind the travails of Aeneas (*Aen.* 1.4, "saevae memorem Iunonis ab iram" 'on account of the mindful wrath of cruel Juno' [my trans.]).[1] Humphries interprets the final action of Daphne, now turned tree, as one of consent and underlines it with a concluding "*Yes*" that is a closural gesture not found in Ovid.

Gregory's version:

Apollo's first love was elusive Daphne,
The child of Peneus, kindly tyrant of the river,
Nor did the god pursue the girl by chance—
The cause was Cupid's anger at Apollo: . . .
. . . .
    . . . As Phoebus spoke,
The laurel shook her branches and seemed to bow
A timid blessing to her lover's pleasure.   (43, 47)

Like Humphries, Gregory concludes with a positive interpretation of Daphne's nod; the combination of "timid blessing" with "lover's pleasure"—neither phrase precisely paralleling anything in Ovid—brings out Apollo's dominance, as does the alliterative juxtaposition of "god" and "girl." At the same time, the description of Apollo as "lover" neutralizes the unsettling features of Ovid's story, while "anger" is a comparatively bland translation for "saeva . . . ira." Gregory's addition of the epithet "elusive" to describe Daphne and of the phrase "kindly tyrant" to denote her father supplements Ovid for readers who may be unfamiliar with the dramatis personae.

Melville's version:

Daphne, Peneus' child, was the first love
Of great Apollo, a love not lit by chance
Unwitting, but by Cupid's spiteful wrath.
. . . .
Thus spoke the god; the laurel in assent
Inclined her new-made branches and bent down,
Or seemed to bend, her head, her leafy crown.
                              (20, 25)

With "spiteful wrath" for "saeva . . . ira," Melville hints at the *Aeneid*'s opening as Ovid's model; his decision to translate *Phoebus* as "great Apollo" nods to the god's lofty epithet while helping the reader. Similarly, Melville replaces "Paean" with "god," preferring a straightforward emphasis on Apollo's divinity to the specificity in each epithet. His emphasis on Daphne's "new-made branches" and "leafy crown" contributes to the vividness of her metamorphosis, and the emphatic placement of the verb "seemed" in "[o]r seemed to bend" counterbalances the earlier phrase "in assent" and so leaves the character of Daphne's final gesture open to interpretation. Melville's concluding "leafy crown" recalls Ovid's last word, "cacumen."

Mandelbaum's version:

> Now Daphne—daughter of the river-god,
> Peneus—was the first of Phoebus' loves.
> This love was not the fruit of random chance:
> what fostered it was Cupid's cruel wrath.
> . . . .
> Apollo's words were done. With new-made boughs
> the laurel nodded; and she shook her crown,
> as if her head had meant to show consent.
>
> (20, 25)

Mandelbaum, like Humphries and Gregory, helpfully identifies Peneus but assumes familiarity with the epithet "Phoebus." The subtle shift from "primus amor" to "the first of Phoebus' loves" reminds us that Phoebus will have many such encounters in his career post-Daphne—she is first but hardly last. Mandelbaum offers a neutral translation of "adnuit" and relegates the question of Daphne's consent, or lack thereof, to a conditional clause. His placement of "consent" as the last word in this condition heightens the problematic nature of her (perceived) behavior.

Slavitt's version:

> Apollo, you will remember, was smitten with love for Daphne,
> the beautiful daughter of Peneus (he was a river god).
> It was not merely a chance infatuation, but rather
> the mischief—and some say more, the positive malice—of Cupid . . .
> . . . .
> The Paean god fell silent. The laurel rustled her branches
> and nodded her leafy crown in assent to the world's winds.
>
> (1.449–52, 563–64)

Slavitt omits Ovid's detail regarding the temporal precendence of Apollo's love for Daphne and instead, with "you will remember" (a parenthesis entirely absent from Ovid) locates the story in a timeless past. His "double" translation of "saeva . . . ira" as "mischief" / "positive malice" brings out the duplicity of

Cupid; and a second parenthesis, "and some say more," underscores the story's infamy. Slavitt translates "Paean" as "the Paean god," and so invites his reader to query the epithet's meaning without giving any clues to its association with medicine—ironic here, of course. Slavitt opts for a consenting Daphne; her audience—"the world's winds"—is absent from this episode in Ovid but may be meant to recall the earlier scenes in book 1 regarding the creation of the cosmos.

Simpson's version:

> Apollo's first love was Daphne, Peneus' daughter, a love
> blind chance was not the cause of, but Cupid's savage anger.
> . . . .
> Before the Healer had finished, the laurel moved her new
> branches to reply, nodding the ones at the top as though
> nodding her head.   (18, 20)

Simpson's rendering of the opening lines is literal enough but lacks the elegance possible only with the flexibility of Latin word order. His translation of "Paean" is helpful, and his repetition of "nodding" echoes Ovid's "adnuit" and "agitasse" without imposing an extraneous suggestion of consent onto either verb.

Raeburn's version:

> Apollo's first love was Daphne, the child of the river Penéüs.
> Blind chance was not to be blamed but Cupid's spiteful resentment.
> . . . .
> Apollo the Healer had done. With a wave of her new-formed branches
> the laurel agreed, and seemed to be nodding her head in the treetop.
>   (1.451–52, 566–67)

Raeburn approximates the structure of Ovid's lines, and the juxtaposition of "[b]lind chance" and "spiteful resentment," phrases emphasized by Ovid through chiasmus, here frames the verse. The elevated patronymic "Peneia" is here echoed by the (exotically) accented "Penéüs," and "Apollo the Healer" is an effective handling of "Paean." Raeburn does not attempt an open-ended treatment of Daphne's nodding but offers the unequivocal "agreed" for "adnuit." His final word, "treetop," nicely parallels Ovid's last word, "cacumen."

Ambrose's version:

> The first of Phoebus' loves was Daphne, Peneus' child,
> which no unwitting chance supplied, but rather Cupid's cruel wrath.
> . . . .
> The words of Paean were done. Now the laurel with her leaves
> gave nod and seemed to have moved her top like a head.
>   (1.452–53, 566–67)

Like Mandelbaum, Ambrose suggests with "[t]he first of Phoebus' loves" that we are to remember Apollo's other love affairs too. His translation of Ovid's "dedit" as "supplied" is probably the best as well as the least intrusive of any of the versions listed here, in that it avoids introducing non-Ovidian metaphors to the scene. Ambrose refrains from equating her nodding with consent; the precision of "to have moved" (for the perfect infinitive "agitasse") enhances the indeterminate character of Daphne's movement.

Martin's version:

> Daphne, the daughter of the river god
> Peneus, was the first love of Apollo;
> this happened not by chance, but by the cruel
> outrage of Cupid; . . .
> . . . .
> Phoebus concluded. Laurel shook her branches
> and seemed to nod her summit in assent.
> (1.628–31, 782–83)

Martin's version of "saeva . . . ira," "cruel outrage," moves away from the echo of Vergil evident in other translations; it also deemphasizes the playful vindictiveness motivating Cupid in this scene. Martin nicely captures the linguistic play between the Greek name "Daphne" and the Latin "laurea" by using "Laurel" not as a generic name for a type of tree but as a proper name. Like most of the translators sampled here, Martin offers a closed reading of the episode by ending with the word "assent."

NOTE

[1] I cite Mynors's edition.

Surveying Pedagogy and Practice: A Report on the MLA Survey

Barbara Weiden Boyd and Cora Fox

Contexts of Ovid and the Ovidian Tradition

The forms taken by the study of Ovid and his influence in contemporary classrooms vary almost as much as does the poetry of Ovid itself. The unusual range of this collection of essays demonstrates that the study of Ovid's poetry takes two very different routes through American higher education, which are by and large parallel and therefore rarely intersect. Classicists regularly incorporate Ovid into Latin courses offered in the context of a program in ancient Roman studies or teach reading courses in which Ovid's poetry is the primary focus. They also include his works in translation in courses on classical civilization that serve students with little or no background in Latin. Instructors in other disciplines, however, often use Ovid—primarily, *Metamorphoses*—as one of many texts read in a given course, in which Ovid's poetry per se is not likely to be the primary focus. In such courses, selections from Ovid may be used for anything from a single week to an entire semester, but the key point here is that these selections tend to serve as a reference point for other studies rather than as the end goal. In analyzing the survey results, therefore, we found few dominant patterns, and even fewer that seem to us to have real significance when account is taken of the very different contexts in which Ovid is taught. The one powerful conclusion to be drawn is that Ovid's very versatility—not to mention the sheer size of his poetic corpus and its popularity over the centuries—means that almost as many Ovids (and Ovidian traditions) are being taught as there were participants in this survey. We list below the titles of courses in which Ovid is taught by survey respondents and contributors to this volume, whenever these titles can offer some insight into the topics and themes of the course. We therefore omit from this list what are usually introductory or survey courses with generic titles such as World Masterpieces, World Literature, and Comparative Literature.

Myth and religion

    Folklore
    Mythology / Classical Mythology
    Myth, Ritual, and Society in the Ancient World
    Roman Religion: Jupiter to Jesus
    Religions of Rome

Postclassical literature and culture

> The Classical Tradition in Western Literature
> Troubadours
> Introduction to British Literature
> Chaucer and Medieval Schooling
> *Canterbury Tales*
> *Troilus and Criseyde*
> Ovid's *Metamorphoses* and Dante's *Divine Comedy*
> Italian Poetry Survey
> Early Seventeenth-Century Literature
> The Epyllion
> English Drama before Shakespeare
> English Drama to 1642
> Shakespeare
> Spenser's *Faerie Queene*
> Milton and the Literature of His Time
> English Renaissance Literature
> Tudor Renaissance Literature
> European Renaissance Literature
> The Literature of Metamorphosis
> The Transformations of Ovid
> Ovid's Afterlife

Ovid read in Latin

> Ovid's *Metamorphoses*
> Ovid's Roman Calendar
> Ovid
> Latin Didactic Poetry
> Catullus and Roman Elegy
> Elegiac Poetry
> Age of Augustus
> Advanced Latin Literature
> History and Development of the Latin Language

Gender and sexuality

> Literature and Sexuality
> Women in Classical Literature
> Women in Epic
> The Birth of Romance
> The Love Lyric
> Love Poetry from Sappho to Shakespeare
> Queer Renaissance

        Gay and Lesbian Literature
        Women in Antiquity

Other special topics in literature and classical studies
        Considering the Canon
        Survey of Latin Literature
        Heroes and Hustlers in Latin Literature
        Diversity in the Classics
        Human-Animal Hybridity
        Exile Literature from Antiquity to the Present
        The Classical Tradition in Contemporary Fiction and Film
        Creative Writing: Poetry Workshop

Trends in the Teaching of Ovid's Poetry

In the remainder of this summary, we highlight those survey results that are, while not destined to predict the shape of future studies in this area, at least suggestive of some of the reasons for Ovid's endurance and durability. They also offer valuable insight into the diverse character of our pool of respondents.

Among the instructors surveyed, *Metamorphoses*, in whole or in part, is far and away the most commonly taught work of Ovid (used in 78% of the courses described); *Amores* is a distant second (used in 20% of the courses described), but every work of Ovid (with the exception of *Ibis*) was championed by at least one respondent. The time devoted in a single course to either *Metamorphoses* or *Amores* (or the other works) can range from a week to a month to a semester, depending on the course topic and themes; particularly in the case of *Metamorphoses*, the amount of time devoted on the syllabus to the work determines whether it is read in its entirety (33% of those who gave specifics) or selectively. Again, selective reading has a wide range of meanings also, from those instructors who may read several books to those who assign a half-dozen, or fewer, discrete episodes.

Among those who read substantial portions of *Metamorphoses* in their classes, the relative popularity of the individual books (including both readings of entire books and readings of a single episode within a book) are indicated below:

Book Number	Percentage Who Assign It	Book Number	Percentage Who Assign It	Book Number	Percentage Who Assign It
1	100	6	61	11	50
2	67	7	61	12	33
3	72	8	67	13	56
4	72	9	39	14	39
5	50	10	72	15	56

A number of factors probably contribute to this distribution, including the preponderance of stories concerning divine-human interaction early in the poem, a general preference for the Greek over the Roman sections of the poem, and the support given to readers of the first ten books by the availability of W. S. Anderson's two separately published volumes of commentary on these books (*Books 1–5*, *Books 6–10*). These two volumes, available in inexpensive paperback format, are a popular choice for Latin instructors planning all or part of a semester on *Metamorphoses*, and thus they encourage a focus on the first ten books. Nonclassicist instructors with some background in Latin may well have used Anderson's editions themselves when studying Latin and are thus likely to feel on solid ground with these books when questions relating to the Latin text and translation arise.

The "preferred" books—in other words, those read in whole or in part by at least two-thirds of respondents (books 1–4, 8, 10) show significant overlap with the most popular individual episodes, among which the following six stand out: Apollo and Daphne (book 1), read by 39%; Baucis and Philemon (book 8), read by 33%; Narcissus and Echo (book 3), read by 28%; Daedalus and Icarus (book 8), read by 28%; Pygmalion (book 10), read by 28%; and Pyramus and Thisbe (book 4), read by 25%. Many other episodes have their enthusiasts, and these preferences are usually strongly held, but, again, because the courses in which Ovid is taught vary so widely, few meaningful patterns are to be discerned. It should be noted that, of the six most popular episodes, all but one (Narcissus and Echo) have been required components in the syllabus for the advanced placement examination Latin Literature: Catullus and Ovid, offered at the time the survey was conducted (but terminated in 2009) by the College Board for college-bound high school students studying Latin; they are therefore the most easily available, in a number of recent intermediate-level textbooks (LaFleur; Jestin and Katz), to teachers and students reading these selections in Latin, and at least some part of their popularity is doubtless a correlate of textbook selection (and vice versa).

Similarly, it is likely that the standing of *Amores* as the second-most-read work of Ovid has in part resulted from its inclusion in the current advanced placement Latin Literature syllabus and in the textbooks that have been designed to provide access to the poems on this syllabus. Of the nine instructors who incorporate selections from *Amores* into their courses, seven gave specific details of the poems they assign; of these seven, 100% assign *Amores* 1.1, and 86% assign 1.3, 1.4, 1.5, 1.11, 1.12, and 3.15; of these, all but 1.4 and 1.5 appear on the Ovid syllabus for the current advanced placement Latin Literature examination and so are readily available in Latin textbooks.

Finally, we note that, while *Metamorphoses* and *Amores* top the list of texts most frequently taught, they may play a relatively minor role in some of the courses described by survey respondents and contributors; the variety of Ovid's poetry invites his other works into courses as diverse as those on the literature of exile (*Tristia*, *Epistulae ex Ponto*, *Heroides*), on gender and sexuality in the ancient world (*Heroides*, *Ars amatoria*, *Remedia amoris*), or on Roman religion and politics (*Fasti*). Ovid's versatility makes him a poet for every pedagogical occasion, it seems.

Trends in the Teaching of the Ovidian Tradition

The Ovidian tradition is as extensive and varied as are the works of Ovid himself. Scores of authors and texts, from Andreas Capellanus's *De amore* and the anonymous *Pamphilus* to Josef Brodsky and Seamus Heaney, were mentioned by survey respondents and contributors among the works of the Ovidian tradition they teach. We list here those works and authors most frequently identified, but, as with the works of Ovid described above, the amount of any given work read in a particular course, as well as the level of sophistication with which, and by whom, it is read, varies widely. The information provided here is therefore descriptive and makes no pretensions to being comprehensive or finely graded. Many of the essays in this volume supplement this list with rich catalogs of works taught.

Authors and works most frequently mentioned include (in rough chronological order):

> Apuleius, *The Golden Ass*
> Dante, *Divine Comedy*
> Petrarch, *Canzoniere*
> Edmund Spenser, *The Faerie Queene*; *Muiopotomos*
> Christopher Marlowe, *Hero and Leander*
> William Shakespeare, *Sonnets, Venus and Adonis, The Rape of Lucrece, Two Gentlemen of Verona, A Midsummer Night's Dream, Titus Andronicus, Romeo and Juliet, The Tempest, Cymbeline, The Winter's Tale*
> Franz Kafka, *The Metamorphosis*
> Ezra Pound, *Cantos*
> T. S. Eliot, "The Waste Land"
> Christoph Ransmayr, *The Last World* (*Die letzte Welt*)
> Mary Zimmerman, *Metamorphoses: A Play*

Several other works deserve mention because of the special contributions they make to a variety of different classrooms: Arthur Golding's translation of *Metamorphoses* (1567) marks an important turning point in the study of Ovidianism, not only because Golding made Ovid newly available to a wide audience (which indeed he did) but also because of the status of this work in the history of English literature and culture writ large (see Fox, above). As a result, his translation is taught frequently not simply as a historical artifact allowing us to see through the lens through which earlier writers gained access to Ovid, but as a work of literature on its own terms. Marlowe's *Amores* likewise has a special status in this category and is frequently taught for its insights into a variety of late-sixteenth-century cultural discourses. And three recent collections of poems or short stories, all inspired in one way or another by *Metamorphoses*, have achieved something like textbook status in a wide variety of Ovidian courses: Michael Hofmann and James Lasdun's *After Ovid: New Metamorphoses*, Ted Hughes's *Tales from Ovid*, and Philip Terry's *Ovid Metamorphosed*. Christopher Martin's *Ovid in English* provides a valuable survey of Ovid's career in translation across the millennia.

Books on the Instructor's Shelf

The history and merits of various translations and editions are described in the preceding essays by Knox, Fox, and Boyd. Here, based on the responses to our survey, we provide a snapshot of the translations most commonly in use in today's classrooms. We also note several translations too new to have acquired a readership at the time the survey was done.

Among translations of *Metamorphoses*, those by Allen Mandelbaum, A. D. Melville, and Rolfe Humphries are most commonly used, and each has its strong proponents. Though further distinctions are difficult to discern, many classicists surveyed give Melville's translation a slight lead, and they are also less likely than nonclassicists to use Humphries. Several other modern translations were mentioned as well: those by Mary M. Innes, Charles Martin (newly published at the time of the survey), Michael Simpson, and Goold. The last of these, the Loeb edition, is of course useful in more advanced courses on the Ovidian tradition, in which at least some participants are likely to have some Latin and so use the translation primarily as an aid for making sense of the facing Latin text.

In addition to Martin's translation, two others appeared as this volume was in production and so were not widely known among our respondents. David Raeburn's is likely to win converts because of its availability and reasonable price and, along with Melville's and Mandelbaum's, is likely to dominate Ovidian classrooms for the foreseeable future. Z. Philip Ambrose's, on the other hand, will be most useful to those with some Latin, since it offers a translation that, while not the easiest to read, gives a strong sense of what the reading experience in Latin is like.

Cost and availability are important factors for some survey respondents, and the wide availability of Mandelbaum, Melville, and Humphries on the used-textbook market helps perpetuate the popularity of this triumvirate.

For Ovid's other works, most nonclassicists rely on Penguin or Oxford World's Classics translations (amatory elegy: P. Green, *Ovid: The Erotic Poems* or A. D. Melville, *Ovid: The Love Poems*; *Heroides*: Isbell; *Fasti*: Boyle and Woodard; *Tristia*: A. D. Melville, *Ovid: Sorrows of an Exile*; *Tristia* and *Epistulae ex Ponto*, P. Green, *Ovid: The Poems of Exile*) or the relevant translation in the Loeb series. Classicists also turn to some less-widely-known resources, such as John

Barsby's edition with translation of *Amores*, book 1; Guy Lee's translation of *Amores*; and Betty Rose Nagle's translation of *Fasti*.

Again, cost and availability are important factors, and the editors note that, while the clothbound Loeb volumes revised by Goold have a limited student appeal, many instructors, classicists and nonclassicists alike, find them a valuable resource.

We conclude this snapshot of today's classrooms with a list of those secondary or reference works most frequently cited by survey respondents as essential components in the library of teachers of Ovid and the Ovidian tradition and supplement their suggestions with a few recent publications.

By far the most frequently cited volume is Philip Hardie's *Cambridge Companion to Ovid*, because of its up-to-date and readable assessment of Ovidian studies, along with its extremely reasonable price and the reliability of a well-respected series and imprint. Two other titles have achieved similar status, if not classroom use: Barbara Weiden Boyd's (unfortunately overpriced) *Brill's Companion to Ovid* and Sara Mack's *Ovid*. Karl Galinsky's *Ovid's* Metamorphoses*: An Introduction to the Basic Aspects* was also cited by numerous instructors as a reliable starting point. Since the survey was completed, Elaine Fantham's *Ovid's* Metamorphoses has provided yet another strong introduction, while Sarah Annes Brown's *Ovid: Myth and Metamorphosis* is an engaging if brief essay offering readings of several famous episodes together with some of their modern retellings. Knox's recent *Oxford Readings in Ovid* is a convenient one-volume collection of papers that were originally published elsewhere and that have in many cases become standard in the field of Ovid studies. For Ovid's elegiac poetry, two new introductions are available: Rebecca Armstrong's *Ovid and His Love Poetry* and Genevieve Liveley's *Ovid: Love Songs*. The essays in this volume offer an abundance of further suggestions for studies appropriate to specific topics or themes.

Many instructors teaching *Metamorphoses* complement it with selections from *Iliad*, *Odyssey*, and *Aeneid*; and nonclassicists generally find any of a number of up-to-date (and frequently updated) mythology textbooks to be an important resource (e.g., Morford and Lenardon's *Classical Mythology*, Powell's *Classical Myth*, and Harris and Platzner's *Classical Mythology: Images and Insights*). Classicists are likely to turn to the rich resource on variants in Greek myth assembled by T. Gantz (*Early Greek Myth*). Other works occasionally mentioned as important resources include a number of monographs on individual works or themes (Bate, *Shakespeare and Ovid*; Boyd, *Ovid's Literary Loves: Influence and Innovation in the* Amores; Enterline, *The Rhetoric of the Body from Ovid to Shakespeare*; and Tissol, *The Face of Nature: Wit, Narrative, and Cosmic Origins in Ovid's* Metamorphoses); as well as the collection of essays edited by Stanivukovic, *Ovid and the Renaissance Body*. Theodore Ziolkowski's survey of the modern Ovidian tradition (*Ovid and the Moderns*) and Leonard Barkan's study of its prominence in the poetry, art, and thought of the medieval era through the Renaissance (*The Gods Made Flesh: Metamorphosis and the*

Pursuit of Paganism), together with the contemporary responses to Ovid offered by Terry, Hofmann and Lasdun, and Hughes, round out the instructor's library as recorded in the survey.

Two Web resources were also mentioned, the first for its bibliography, which is primarily (but not exclusively) classical: Ulrich Schmitzer's *Tenerorum lusor amorum: Ovid im WWW—die Homepage*; the second for its assemblage of electronic texts (including Golding's and Sandys's translations), images, and many other resources for Ovid's reception: the University of Virginia's *The Ovid Collection*.

Part Two

APPROACHES

Introduction

Barbara Weiden Boyd and Cora Fox

Ovid and Classical Studies

In the study of Latin poetry, the hegemony of Vergil has gone all but unchallenged for over two thousand years. His impact on the Roman classroom was immediate and his work held sway in the classroom so long as there were little Roman boys to fill it; long after the disappearance of the classical world as we know it—in those so-called dark ages of medieval Europe—Vergil continued to be read, indeed revered, as a font of pagan wisdom and, thanks in part to the "messianic" fourth eclogue (predicting the birth of a child who would herald the coming of a new Golden Age [see Clausen's introduction to *Eclogue* 4]), as a proto-Christian of sorts, worthy to conduct the likes of Dante through hell and purgatory. Of course, Dante, like others before and after him, recognized other great Latin poets too—Statius, Lucan, and Ovid—but only Vergil achieved the status of guide, only Vergil was universally recognized as the somber, sober soul of the pre-Christian world. His apparent transcendence of history and its vagaries culminated in T. S. Eliot's coronation of Vergil as "the classic of all Europe," in an essay that is itself a product of a complex matrix of historical and political circumstance ("What Is a Classic?" 70).[1]

In other words, Vergil has long been a hard act to follow, and yet the assumption has long been made that the pursuit of Vergil is exactly the impossible task that his successors carved out for themselves. Indeed, Statius would seem to have codified this approach to Vergil when, at the close of his *Thebaid*, he in one breath wishes long life for his poem ("vive, precor" 'Live, I pray') and cautions his poem not to try to attain the heights reached by Vergil's *Aeneid* but to follow worshipfully in the earlier poem's footsteps ("nec tu divinam Aeneida tempta, / sed longe sequere et vestigia semper adora" 'And do not try for divine *Aeneid*, but follow at a distance and worship always its footsteps' [12.816–17; Boyd's trans.]). Yet behind Statius's worshipful mention of Vergil—or perhaps we should say alongside it—lurks Ovid, whose language richly infects Statius's poem (note, for example, how Statius's closing address to his poem, "vive," reworks Ovid's final word, "vivam" [*Met.* 15.879]), whose very sensibility, in all its centrifugal rupturing of epic convention, is as much the ancestor of Statius's dystopic poem as is the centripetal force of Vergilian epic. Statius's pursuit of Vergil—at an awed distance—is evident, but only recently have scholars begun to realize that the pull exerted by Ovid on Statius is just as powerful, if less conventionally "epic," standing as an exemplar of the Ovidian tradition writ large. It is the nature of Ovidian influence and reception—the tendency to lurk and to infect rather than to announce its presence—that has shaped most Ovidian scholarship, at least among classicists, in the modern era as the study of secondariness and inferiority, a scholarship that looks for and finds in Ovid the excess that Vergil avoids, the fragmentation and subversiveness that Vergil (at least in the dominant reading) transcends.[2] The Ovid of pre–World War II criticism was essentially the "anti-Vergil," a poet whose desire to model himself on his predecessor was as obvious and inescapable as was his failure to meet the self-imposed challenge.

A new era in Ovid studies began around the middle of the twentieth century, with the appearance in quick succession of a triad of books that, despite a certain datedness, continue to merit a reading by scholars looking for the beginnings of a particular question or approach.[3] Hermann Fraenkel's *Ovid: A Poet between Two Worlds* (1945), L. P. Wilkinson's *Ovid Recalled* (1955; abridged as *Ovid Surveyed* in 1962), and Brooks Otis's *Ovid as an Epic Poet* (1966) all brought new attention and a sense of urgency to the questions that have long been a staple of Ovid studies: How serious is Ovid, if at all? Is there any trace in his poetry of the reasons for Augustus's decision to send him into exile? What literary sources and influences shaped his poetry? The attention these scholars gave to *Metamorphoses* first and foremost centered on what we would now consider primarily formalist issues: Is Ovid's diction truly epic, or does he innovate—or contaminate—epic with elegiac diction? Are Ovid's refinements to the dactylic hexameter the result of a desire for perfection or of trivialization? Can *Metamorphoses* be considered an epic, and, if so, what are its generic characteristics? What is the structure of *Metamorphoses*? What is the theme of *Metamorphoses*? How do structure and theme unify a poem that, superficially at least, would seem to be characterized by lack of structure and a dizzying variety of themes?

These three books helped both create and respond to scholars' growing desire to move Ovid out of Vergil's shadow. Several essay collections soon followed that contributed to a widening conversation about Ovid, not only about *Metamorphoses* but also about the rest of the Ovidian corpus, particularly the erotic and erotodidactic elegies. These collections continue to offer much of value and are standard reference works in most scholarly studies of Ovid: *Ovidiana* (1958), edited by the Romanian classicist N. I. Herescu (himself living in exile in Paris), and *Ovid* (1973), edited by J. W. Binns. A year after the publication of Binns's collection, Howard Jacobson published *Ovid's Heroides* (1974)—the first major study in English of the collection as a whole (although Jacobson did not include the double letters, or those featuring an exchange between women and their male lovers, 16–21, in his survey) and, like much other scholarly work in Latin poetry at the time, a serious reassessment of the importance of elegy at Rome. Karl Galinsky's overview of *Metamorphoses* (1975), meanwhile, built on the work of Fraenkel and Otis while striving to make Ovid's poem ever more accessible to a wide audience. In this same period (1969–86) Franz Bömer was working on his encyclopedic multivolume commentary on *Metamorphoses*, geared toward serving the needs of scholars; simultaneously, Ovid entered the classroom—at least the college and university classroom—in newly accessible form, thanks to William S. Anderson's commentary on *Metamorphoses*, books 6–10 (1972), John Barsby's commentary on book 1 of *Amores* (1973), and A. S. Hollis's commentaries on *Metamorphoses Book VIII* (1970) and *Ars amatoria Book I* (1977). (A. G. Lee's 1953 commentary on *Metamorphoses*, book 1, was something of an outlier and passed under most readers' radar until the 1970s, when the new interest in things Ovidian provided cause for a reprint.) With his first critical edition of the amatory works (1961), E. J. Kenney began a remarkable career of scholarly dedication to Ovid, among several other Latin authors. Last but not least, the 1970s saw the first complete critical edition of *Metamorphoses* in the twentieth century, by Anderson (1977); its publication made the complete text of the poem easily accessible at last.

The new era of Ovid studies that had emerged in the middle of the twentieth century reached critical maturity in the 1980s. Within a single year, two transformative studies of *Metamorphoses* appeared: Peter Knox's *Ovid's* Metamorphoses *and the Traditions of Augustan Poetry* (1986) and Stephen Hinds's *The Metamorphosis of Persephone: Ovid and the Self-Conscious Muse* (1987). In addition to the sheer delight each exhibits for Ovid's sharply defined wit, both books bring welcome focus to the engagement of Ovid with Greek Hellenistic poetry, in particular that of Callimachus, who may well be Western literature's first postmodern poet. With their attention to Ovid's sophisticated adaptation and exploitation of Callimachean poetics, both Knox and Hinds successfully moved Ovid studies generally toward a new awareness of the importance of what was then beginning to be called intertextuality for the study of Ovid and of Latin poetry generally. Their books were soon followed by Joseph Solodow's *The World of Ovid's* Metamorphoses (1988), which in its astute attention to Ovid's style and narrative techniques remains two decades later an extremely valuable resource.

The renovation—indeed, the (re)discovery—of Ovid continued apace in the 1990s, so much so that this overview can itself offer only a superficial sketch of the richly textured expanse of research in the period. *Ars amatoria*, book 2, was the topic of an important application of reader-response theory to Ovid's erotodidaxis, by Alison Sharrock, and *Amores* received its first book-length treatment from Barbara Weiden Boyd (*Ovid's Literary Loves*), combining analysis of Ovid's style with the suggestion that the three books of elegies are structured as a narrative. *Heroides* provided material for not one but two Cambridge commentaries, by Knox (*Ovid*) and Kenney (*Ovid:* Heroides *XVI–XXI*).

This decade also saw the first real efflorescence of interest in Ovid's calendar poem, *Fasti*, and the elegies he wrote in exile. Alessandro Barchiesi's *Il poeta e il principe* (published in English as *The Poet and the Prince*) and Carole Newlands's *Playing with Time*, soon followed by Elaine Fantham's commentary on *Fasti*, book 4, opened up this previously misunderstood poem to new audiences eager for an introduction to Ovid's most explicit and extended response to the Augustan regime after Actium. Hinds and especially Gareth Williams, meanwhile, shed new light on the poetics of Ovid's *Tristia, Epistulae ex Ponto*, and *Ibis*, the three works he wrote during the last nine years of his life in Tomis (Hinds, "Booking"; Williams, *Banished Voices*, *Curse*, "Ovid's Exile Poetry," and "Ovid's Exilic Poetry"). And more commentaries appeared, including Anderson's edition with notes of *Metamorphoses*, books 1–5; one of Anderson's former doctoral students, Garth Tissol, has been entrusted with the task of completing the series with a commentary on books 11–15. Over the decade, aspects of Ovid's work provided the subject matter for dozens of scholarly articles and dissertations.

In the first decade of the twenty-first century, work on Ovid continues apace. Two volumes featuring the title *Companion to Ovid* appeared in 2002—one from Cambridge, edited by Philip Hardie, and the other from Brill, edited by Boyd; a third, edited by Knox, was published by Blackwell in 2009. Numerous commentaries on individual books have either recently appeared or are in progress, and Richard Tarrant's long-awaited Oxford edition of *Metamorphoses* finally appeared in 2004, quickly to become the new standard. Bimillennia continue to be celebrated: the two thousandth anniversary of *Fasti* saw the publication of a collection of essays edited by Geraldine Herbert-Brown, and the (roughly) two thousandth birthday of *Ars amatoria* and *Remedia amoris* was fêted with a collection of essays edited by Roy Gibson, Steven Green, and Alison Sharrock. Increasingly, these collections find room for discussion of Ovid's reception as well as of Ovid's poetry; indeed, if the response we received to our invitation for submission to the current volume is any indication, the reception of Ovid is likely to remain a rich vein to be mined for years to come.

As we noted at the opening of this introduction, Vergil continues to loom large in Ovid studies; yet it is no longer a matter of displacement or of mere comparison, a simplistic game of "who is better?" Rather, a newly heightened awareness of the differences between the two—including not least of all the difference in the social and political contexts in which they worked—has enriched both fields of study, allowing for a kind of cross-fertilization that is just beginning to show results (Hinds's *Allusion and Intertext* is a first step in this new direction). Scholarly interest in this area promises to continue for at least the coming decade and to make Ovid's assertion of eternal survival (*vivam*) secure despite all he himself did to ensure its contingency.

Ovid's Renaissance

Ovid's words have certainly had life, although in some periods and modern languages his influence has been more fully captured by scholars than in others. Even before Ludwig Traube referred to the twelfth and thirteenth centuries as the "aetas Ovidiana" 'age of Ovid,' some scholarship had traced how Ovid's works survived and influenced European literature during the Middle Ages. As a central part of the school curriculum, Ovid's works were important sources for countless writers, both major and minor, in every age of this period, and it is telling that both Dante and Chaucer have earned entire scholarly works devoted to tracing their Ovidianisms: on Dante, Madison U. Sowell's *Dante and Ovid: Essays in Intertextuality* and Rachel Jacoff and Jeffrey Schnapp's edited collection *The Poetry of Allusion: Virgil and Ovid in Dante's* Commedia (1991); and on Chaucer, Richard Hoffman's *Ovid and the* Canterbury Tales (1966), John Fyler's *Chaucer and Ovid* (1979), Michael Calabrese's *Chaucer's Ovidian Arts of Love* (1994), and Marilynn Desmond's *Ovid's Art and the Wife of Bath: The Ethics of Erotic Violence*. While a full discussion of this critical period is beyond the scope of this section (and the disciplinary boundaries of these authors), excellent overviews of the scholarship on the medieval Ovidian tradition are provided by Jeremy Dimmick in the *Cambridge Companion to Ovid* and by Ralph Hexter in *Brill's Companion to Ovid*. It is unquestionably the Renaissance, and one might argue the English Renaissance, however, that has dominated studies of Ovidian influence in the past twenty years, partly because of the renewed attention to Ovid in classical literary studies and partly because of developments in theoretical and methodological approaches within literary studies more broadly and Renaissance studies specifically.

There has never really been controversy over whether the Renaissance was another great Ovidian age, but the energetic critical exploration of Ovid's influence on the culture of this period really began around the same time that scholars of the English Renaissance embraced new historicism, with its focus on dominant and subordinate texts and textual processes, and it came of age with the turn toward the marginal in historical and cultural studies. Although W. R. Johnson identified Ovid as the origin of the counterclassical tradition in English literature in 1970, the theoretical focus on how important any marginal or counterdiscourse is to defining the dominant one began to explain more fully Ovid's pervasive influence on Renaissance literature and culture. While both Vergil and Ovid are overtly acknowledged through allusion as major sources for Renaissance texts, critics had focused primarily on Vergil's works as central to the ideological negotiations of the period. In fact, we have still not fully accounted for how seriously Ovidian works and translations construct their own often subversive, anti-authoritarian, metamorphic Renaissance discourses. Studies of this kind of influence began to emerge with Leonard Barkan's seminal *The Gods Made Flesh* (1986). Two years later Charles Martindale edited *Ovid Renewed*, which added a chorus of voices insisting on Ovid's central influence on Renaissance literature and art. There had previously been scholars who painstakingly recorded Ovidian allusions in their notes to Renaissance texts, and even some extended discussions of Ovid's influence, for example Douglas Bush's *Mythology and the Renaissance Tradition in English Poetry* (1963), especially chapter 4, "Ovid Old and New." In addition, there were already important works on the influence of paganism on Renaissance culture, such as Jean Seznec's *The Survival of the Pagan Gods: The Mythological Tradition and Its Place in Renaissance Humanism and Art* (1953) and Edgar Wind's *Pagan Mysteries in the Renaissance* (1968). Not until Barkan's book appeared, however, did a study of the influence of "Ovidianism"—a discourse with a defined set of values and themes—emerge to replace the sometimes limiting model of textual influence that was behind Ovidian source study and that defined its subject as the Ovidian tradition. We originally described our subject matter for this volume as "Ovid and Ovidianism," responding to this distinct poststructuralist trend in Renaissance criticism, but we have agreed to use "Ovidian tradition" as a substitute, because the works taught in the classroom are indeed part of a multiplicitous and fluid but definable tradition emerging from this single author's works.

As such a shift in terminology reveals, the larger critical interest in reception studies, at least in the English Renaissance, has turned toward uncovering cultural and discursive shifts that register the wider cultural impact of Ovid's works in the Renaissance and in subsequent centuries for which Renaissance texts became canonical. Recent studies reveal that a major shift occurred in the sixteenth century in the kind of influence Ovid had as well as its extent. While the Ovid that emerged from the period of the late Middle Ages was a bifurcated Ovid—half pagan preceptor of love and half moralized Christian mythographer—studies of the Renaissance reveal the ways Ovid retained these characterizations while at the same time being reborn in many other guises, his works translated (sometimes anxiously) in whole or in part into all major European languages and his career emerging as a counter-Vergilian authorial model (see, e.g., Cheney, *Marlowe's Counterfeit Profession* and Introduction; Lyne, *Changing Worlds* and "Ovid in English Translation"; and Oakley-Brown). Even when scholarship focuses on a single Renaissance author, recent criticism tends to read the author's works in relation to larger cultural questions and paradigms, and all the canonical heavyweights of the English Renaissance have recently gained monographs or edited volumes that focus on their dialogues with Ovid. Ovid's works have been revealed to be central intertexts in the writings of Christopher Marlowe (Cheney, *Marlowe's Counterfeit Profession*), John Milton (DuRocher), and William Shakespeare (Bate, *Shakespeare*; James, *Shakespeare's Troy*; Taylor, *Shakespeare's Ovid*), and Shakespeare is often the terminus for studies of Ovid's literary influence from antiquity through the Renaissance (Christopher Martin, *Policy*; Stapleton; Enterline). Edmund Spenser, long acknowledged as perhaps the prime Ovidian author of the period, finally received a book attending to his Ovidianism when Syrithe Pugh published *Spenser and Ovid* (2005). Most of these works start from the assumption—a correct one—that Renaissance writers are particularly self-conscious in their imitations of Ovid and that therefore the privileging of this authorial relationship makes sense as a way to uncover complexities in the Renaissance works that would otherwise remain hidden to modern readers and students. In addition, however, some of these works also participate in the analysis of Ovid's wider cultural influence, working to point out thematic and ideological relations between a canonical English author and this transgressive classical intertext. Heather James, for instance, while focusing on Shakespeare, uncovers the politics of the larger English translation of empire, and in recent work she has continued to point to how the politics of Ovidianism shape English national and gender politics ("Ovid"). Lynn Enterline similarly uses Shakespeare as the critical crux for a much wider-ranging and theoretical analysis of how Ovid shaped Western constructions of the relation between subjectivity and voice.

Another even more recent current in scholarship on Renaissance English Ovidianism does not focus primarily on single authors, but frames study of Ovid in wider cultural terms. Such studies include both essay collections, notably Goran Stanivukovic's *Ovid and the Renaissance Body*, and monographs like those by Jim Ellis on the sexual and national politics of the English epyllion or by Georgia Brown (*Redefining*) on the multifaceted and pervasive use of Ovid to authorize countercultural and marginal literatures and values in Renaissance England. Classicists have also contributed greatly to this kind of wider analysis, often including chapters on reception in their studies of Ovid or devoting entire books to the subject, such as *Ovidian Transformations: Essays on Ovid's* Metamorphoses *and Its Reception* (Hardie, Barchiesi, and Hinds). Because scholarship that bridges classical and modern literary studies approaches the question of influence from an already broad perspective, these studies also tend to see the ways Ovid's works have been foundational not only as literary sources but also as lenses and mirrors through which later cultures negotiated some of their most essential cultural questions. There is an obvious need for more interdisciplinary work on Ovidianism in both art and literature, and the recent collection *Metamorphosis: The Changing Face of Ovid in Medieval and Early Modern Europe* (Keith and Rupp) promotes some of these crucial discussions by bringing together scholars from classical and modern literary studies and art history.

A great deal more could be said about how Ovid's works and Ovidianism are a continuous presence and exert particular kinds of cultural pressure in literary periods following the Renaissance, and Sarah Annes Brown's *The Metamorphosis of Ovid: From Chaucer to Ted Hughes* begins to trace such a history, at least in English. There has also recently been important work, notably Theodore Ziolkowski's *Ovid and the Moderns*, on how the Ovidian tradition influences later literatures. This overview has attempted, however, to do justice to the burgeoning critical subfield in studies of Ovidianism in the English Renaissance, privileging this area of scholarship primarily because it was so clearly important when we surveyed teachers for this volume; its dominance is also evident in the volume's list of works cited. Some of the trends described have been paralleled in studies of other European Renaissance languages and nations, and scholarship in later periods has also seen rising interest in studies of Ovidianism. We expect and welcome similar "new Ovidianisms" (to borrow Valerie Traub's description of recent Renaissance studies [261]) in the study of later Ovidian ages, including our own.

Ovid in This Volume

The essays in the first section, "Ovid's Classrooms," offer a sampling of the classroom contexts in which the works of Ovid and the Ovidian tradition are taught.

The variety of classrooms in which these works are found—from introductory writing-intensive courses and courses intended to develop students' critical reading and thinking skills to courses focusing on a specific literary genre, topic, or theme—illustrates Ovid's versatility and adaptability. Each essay in this section addresses some of the challenges—cultural, social, religious—confronted by students meeting the works of Ovid or the Ovidian tradition for the first time; each essay also emphasizes commonalities and offers practical ideas for classroom exercises and assignments.

"Political Ovid," the second section, features essays that consider the political and moral discourses shaping the works of Ovid and the Ovidian tradition; they either scrutinize Ovid's political or moral attitudes or focus on the adaptations of such attitudes to new circumstances. Contributors describe the investments of readers and writers in using Ovid's representations of different kinds of power, and they offer strategies for confronting the politics of Ovid's works and the Ovidian tradition in a variety of classroom contexts.

The third section, "Gendered and Embodied Ovid," focuses on the centrality of constructions of gender and the body in the works of Ovid and the Ovidian tradition; essays either locate these constructions in broader discourses in classical antiquity or examine the consequences of this centrality for the history of postclassical depictions. The range of approaches includes both historically oriented treatments of sexual relations and gender roles in antiquity as reflected in Ovid's poetry and essays examining how the complex constructions of gender and sexuality articulated in later literatures find their roots in Ovid's poetry.

In "Metatextual Ovid," the fourth section, contributors treat various aspects of the self-conscious appropriation and transformation of Ovid's works (including a case study of such appropriation and transformation by Ovid himself) or focus on the role of Ovid's works as metatextual figures for the classical tradition. Each essay is grounded in classroom experience and offers guidance on issues of translation, rhetoric, and poetic language, as well as techniques for introducing students to complex models for understanding literary and cultural transmission.

NOTES

[1] See the essays collected in the first section of the *Cambridge Companion to Virgil* for a good introduction to the influence and reception of Vergil (Martindale). For Vergil's reception in Europe in the decades leading up to World War II, R. F. Thomas is thought provoking (*Virgil*).

[2] See Hardie, *Epic Successors*, for an introduction to Vergil's reception in later Latin epic; and see Keith, "Ovidian Personae" and "Ovid's Theban Narrative," for the Ovidianism of Statius.

[3] Our focus here is on scholarship in English. In terms of general critical trends, however, the patterns of study we limn follow a similar trajectory in the other critical traditions dominant in the twentieth century, i.e., the German, French, and Italian.

OVID'S CLASSROOMS

Caveat Lector:
Learning to Read through Ovid

Wendy Chapman Peek

I teach Ovid's *Metamorphoses* in a required 100-level general education course entitled Critical Encounters: Literature, which introduces first-year students to both literary study and college writing. Several years of teaching this course have instructed me in the value of beginning the syllabus with *Metamorphoses,* which serves as a primer in the art of reading well. Although students enter the course confident in their ability to read in a literal sense—they can usually follow plots, and the stronger students may notice elements of setting and characterization—they often miss the essential details that make Ovid distinct, important, and wickedly fun. While the content of these myths is an important feature, both to refresh the students' familiarity with the stories and to help them appreciate the influence of Ovid on medieval and early modern literature, Ovid's narrative strategies, namely his skillful and subtle manipulation of narration, voice, and point of view, are the focus of our study. I find that *Metamorphoses* in particular makes a convincing case for the value of reading closely because Ovid's humor, complexity, and vivid imagery richly reward the student who attends to the details of his world.

The lesson begins with book 1, where the gap between what we are told by characters and what we "see" in the third-person narration reveals that Ovid's readers will not be mollycoddled. Of differing accounts, Ovid will not tell us which is accurate; we must learn to rely on our own interpretive skills, which become increasingly sharpened as we read further.

It is first important to distinguish among the various storytellers of book 1. Initially, the first narrator seems to be omniscient. The historical sweep of his story, "from the world's beginnings to our day" (3; 1.3–4), suggests a broad knowledge. At the same time, a deep familiarity with the stuff of nature is suggested by the penetration of his purview, which descends through the stratosphere filled with winds that "forever clash" to focus on strife at the atomic level (5; 1.60)—the "heap of seeds that clashed" (3; 1.8–9). Yet even this narrator has his limits. Who made this first universe? He confesses only that it is "a god" (3; 1.21). A few lines later the narrator's uncertainty will be manifest, when he refers to the maker as "whichever god it was" (4; 1.32). Fifty lines later he offers competing accounts: "Either the Architect / of All, the author of the universe . . . created man from seed divine—or else / Prometheus . . . made man" (5–6; 1.78–86).

Clearly, traditional ways of describing narrative modes will not suffice to capture Ovid's method. Our narrator is less than omniscient, although neither is he an objective third-person observer. He knows too much—the thoughts of Jove, the piety of Deucalion and Pyrrha, the suspicions of Juno—to be merely an onlooker. Yet he is neither strictly impersonal nor noticeably intrusive. If anything, he behaves like a discreet gossip. He signals through indirection and sleight of hand. If Apollo is the revealer (as he boasts to Daphne), Ovid is the judicious concealer. Like the dance of the seven veils, Ovid's prose offers glimpses of a more tantalizing revelation—glimpses meant to catch the notice of the careful reader.

Lycaon further develops the lesson, as we switch to another narrator. At stake in this story is responsibility for the origin of evil. Jove insists that evil resides in the nature of humankind. He informs the other gods that he must destroy "the mortals' race" because of their impiety and wickedness (10; 1.188), their "vast cabal of crime," the "fierce Fury [that] reigns" wherever men hold sway (12; 1.241). Yet two additional accounts, one underdeveloped, the other deliberately concealed by Ovid, challenge Jove's version of events. The first describes the destruction of the landscape. While Jove paints a picture of sin run riot under the rule of humankind, our narrator tells us, instead, that the flood swept away "orchards and groves, and herds, and men and homes, / and shrines and all the sacred things they hold" (14; 1.285–87). In place of a landscape ruled by ferocity and undisciplined fury, we see products of human industry and signs of civilization—farming, herding, pious worship—all of which question the veracity of Jove's account. These scenes testify to the piety of human beings just as they are in the process of being destroyed. Of further irony is Jove's claim that he must destroy humanity for the protection of the nymphs and demigods who inhabit the lowlands with them: "half-gods / and rustic deities—Nymphs, Satyrs, Fauns, / and woodland gods . . . let's ensure their safety on the lands we have assigned them" (10; 1.193). Yet the only stories in book 1 of nymphs violated tell of their mistreatment at the hands of the Olympian gods: Apollo and Daphne, Jove and Io, Pan and Syrinx.

A second version of the origin of evil occurs earlier in book 1, tucked away in a side note when Ovid relates the fall from the golden age to the silver. What precipitated this decline? "[A]fter Saturn had been banished, sent / down to dark Tartarus, Jove's rule began" (7; 1.113–14). Primal patricide initiates the fall, yet this cause rests occulted in a subordinate clause (an ablative absolute in Latin). If we listen only to Jove's account, we are convinced of the innate brutality of humankind; if, however, we attend carefully to Ovid's artful allusions, his demisilences, then we see the outlines of a contrary and more disturbing narrative, one about violent, disordered, and capricious gods.

Instead of "all knowing," one might call the narrator of *Metamorphoses* "many knowing," in the sense that his voice moves among the limited points of view of his characters, sharing the perspective of each before moving on. In the story of Europa and Jove, for example, the reader first sees the transformed god through the eyes of the curious Europa. This bull is "a handsome presence," opines perhaps not the narrator but the girl who is in the process of being seduced by the god (72; 2.850–51). "His horns, it's true, are small," speaks her silent, assessing voice, "but so well wrought, one would have thought a craftsman had made them.... He seems so calm" (72; 2.855–58). This last sentence means different things according to whom one imagines as the speaker. If Ovid himself, the reference to how the god "seems" signals the deception of that seeming, for in the next lines Ovid notes that it is "no easy test to check his eagerness" (72; 2.863). The reader savors the dramatic irony of the situation while also seeing the bull from Europa's limited point of view: "He seems so calm"—so harmless, so docile, a bull that a even a slip of a girl could manage by herself. "[H]e is so shapely, so unthreatening" (72; 2.858–59), she continues—unthreatening, however, only to someone who has not yet read book 1 of *Metamorphoses*. Four lines later the perspective shifts again from the increasingly trusting girl to the ever-anxious god: "Delighted, as he waits—a lover—for still other, greater joys, / he kisses her fair hands—no easy test to check his eagerness, delay the rest" (72; 2.862–63). Ovid's coy periphrasis—"greater joys" ("sperata voluptas" [2.862]) and "the rest" ("cetera" [2.863])—would no doubt be lost on the innocent girl, although the knowing reader, trained by Ovid to read the salacious in the obscure, understands fully the stuttering drive of Jove's desire, an effect heightened by the Latin original of the line translated above, "vix iam, vix cetera differt!" (2.863). All these opposed forces come together in the final scene of book 2, when Europa, mounted on the bull's back, realizes that her control is an illusion, that nothing will be again as it was, that, in Ted Hughes's words, she has "stumble[d] out into the mythic arena" (x). The clash of perspectives—the depth of her terror, the anxious force of Jove's desire, and the reader's knowing comprehension of both—raises the final image to a level of intensity that we might call the Ovidian sublime. This aesthetic typically combines narratives of human fragility undone by divine power with flashes of outrageous and inappropriate humor, as when Io spells out her name with her hoof or Eurydice, fresh from her snakebite, limps toward Orpheus in the underworld or Philomela's severed tongue comes to rest at her feet. Here, however, Ovid offers us something different but equally characteristic: a devastating portrait of endangered "delicacy" (to use Burke's term [116]), which sublimates the impending violence of Jove's ardor with the seemingly irrelevant and yet madly distracting beauty of the final image: "Her robes are fluttering—they swell in the sea breeze" (73; 2.875).

The story of Daphne, too, not only repeats the lesson of the gods' excesses but also demonstrates how easily Ovid moves in and out of subject positions, shifting among his characters to offer multiple perspectives on a single event, heaping irony on irony in an effort to complicate the ostensibly straightforward message of this cosmogonic account. Initially, this tale appears in book 1 as yet another story of a first: "Daphne . . . was the first of Phoebus' loves" (20; 1.452). Yet the events of the tale ironize even this first sentence, for the story memorializes not Apollo's achievement of his desire but his failure to get the woman he loves, at least in the form in which he hopes to enjoy her. Offered as an explanatory account of the laurel as symbol of athletic prowess, the tale features only compromised successes: Apollo fails to "love" the nymph as he would wish, and Daphne's achievement in thwarting his desires comes at the price not only of being rooted in place, a terrible cost for one who desires "to roam uncurbed" (21; 1.479), but also of having her very self defined by him. At the end of the story, Apollo assumes the position of narrator, as he dictates what the newly transformed Daphne signifies, addressing her with the perorative "O" that Ovid himself had used earlier to address Daphne (22):[1]

> ". . . since
> you cannot be my wife, you'll be my tree.
> O laurel, I shall wear your leaves
> To wreathe my hair, my lyre, and my quiver.
> . . . .
> And you will also be
> The faithful guardian who stands beside
> The portals of Augustus' house and keeps
> A close watch on the Roman crown of oak leaves."
> (24–25; 1.557–59, 562–63)

Apollo at this moment assumes what had previously been the narrator's role in pointing out the significance of events. Yet Ovid has already tutored the reader in shifts between perspectives when, earlier in the same tale, the narrative voice assumes the subjective position of Apollo, as it assesses the hapless Daphne through her pursuer's eyes:

> . . . He looks at Daphne's hair
> as, unadorned, it hangs down her fair neck,
> and says: "Just think, if she should comb her locks!"
> He sees her lips and never tires of them;
> her fingers, hands, and wrists are unsurpassed;
> . . . .

> whatever he can't see he can imagine;
> he conjures it as even more inviting.
>> (22; 1.497–502)

And later:

> ... the sight of her was striking.
> The wind laid bare her limbs; against the nymph
> it blew; her dress was fluttering; her hair
> streamed in the breeze; in flight she was more fair.
>> (23; 1.527–30)

The first passage repeats the word "he" in its reverie on Daphne's beauty to remind the readers that we see Daphne's flight through the eyes of another; thus, we are not necessarily responsible for the kind of look that is being conveyed.[2] In the second passage, however, no such comforting pronoun shields the reader from responsibility for gazing in delight in the same manner as her would-be seducer, with a rapacious scopophilic gaze. While we may sympathize with Daphne's plight, we too have made her subject to what Claudette Colbert in another context called "the Look, you know. 'How's about this evening, babe?'" (*Palm Beach Story*). Ever so subtly, Ovid has made his reader complicit in the crime committed against Daphne. Perhaps we even enjoy inhabiting the perspective of a god, so easily does it slip upon us.

But from whose perspective do we read the final alarming lines of the story? After Apollo tells Daphne of her new meaning, that she must serve as a symbol of his divinity, "With new-made boughs / the laurel nodded; and she shook her crown, / as if her head had meant to show consent" (25; 1.566–67). This moment recalls the Greek practice of sprinkling the heads of sacrificial animals with water so that the beasts would appear to nod and assent to their sacrifice (Burkert 56). Students often glide over these lines without a second thought and quickly move to blame Daphne for her own condition. If she accepts what Apollo has done to her, the logic suggests, then she deserves no pity. This response shows the triumph of Apollo's perspective: Ovid has my students reading Daphne through Apollo's eyes, so that she becomes an image of perversity, a woman consenting to serve a god from whom she fled in terror just a few lines earlier. If, however, we recall Ovid's characteristic mode of narration, we understand how much is packed into that "as if," and we see that there is a world of difference in how we read Daphne's gesture—if it is in fact a gesture at all.[3]

The details of Daphne's story prepare the reader for Actaeon's equally unexpected encounter with a god in book 3. According to some other accounts of Actaeon's deeds, his crime is not wholly accidental; rather, he stopped to enjoy the vision he stumbled on. Ovid, however, repeatedly insists on Actaeon's innocence: "there is no crime in making a mistake" (82; 3.142). To further this point, Ovid makes no mention of what Actaeon does or does not see. The reader, however, sees everything, and lest we be inattentive observers, Ovid insists that we look. The scene of Diana being undressed by her attendant nymphs is told in such scandalous detail that it resembles, in the phrase of one of my freshmen, "a movie kept in the section of the video store where they don't let me go." If, however, the reader has failed to take proper note of these details, Ovid arouses him with an "Ecce" 'behold!' (3.174; my trans.) when Actaeon enters the scene. Here too the reader may see more than Actaeon does, since Ovid directs the reader to notice the problem of being a lanky goddess: "[the nymphs] crowded around Diana, / trying to hide her body with their own. / But taller than her nymphs, above the rest, / the goddess could be seen—up from the neck" (83; 3.180–82). Perhaps, though, we have glimpsed enough. After all, we have already seen her stripped naked and bathing, all before Actaeon enters the grotto. Once again, we have been seduced by the ability of Ovid to shift quickly among the perspectives of his characters. Though the story begins by attending specifically to Actaeon's activities, the narrative voice moves on to enter the scene in the grove before him and thus to see more than Actaeon ever does. The reader has in effect become the more successful Peeping Tom. Yet he will escape his just retribution and can only read on helplessly as the catalog of Actaeon's executioners is enumerated: "swift Pterelas, / keen Agre, and Hylaeus, battling dog" (84; 3.212–13). Thus, when Ovid invites us to "behold!" in a tale about the dangers of looking, what we see is that the innocent Actaeon will be the martyr for our own voyeurism, since he bears the punishment for our guilty desire to see Diana unrobed.

I teach these stories in a class organized around the theme of speech and silence, particularly the silencing of the powerless, usually women. The syllabus mixes ancient, medieval, early modern, and modern texts, ignoring chronology (though not history) by teaching the works out of historical sequence so that they correspond to five subsections of the class's theme. In every section, tales from *Metamorphoses* begin the discussion. "Women Who Say 'No'" combines the stories of Apollo and Daphne and Jove and Io from book 1 with Chaucer's *Parliament of Fowls* and The Clerk's Tale and Melville's *Bartleby the Scrivener*. Section 2, "Learning to Talk," pairs Ovid's Pygmalion with Chaucer's The Merchant's Tale. "Silence Will Speak," the next topic, begins with the Ovidian stories of Tereus, Procne, Philomela, and Arachne and joins them with Isak Dinesen's short story "The Blank Page" and Jane Campion's film *The Piano*. A unit on gender impersonation, "I Am Not What I Am," links Ovid's tale of Iphis and Ianthe with Shakespeare's *Twelfth Night* and the Afghani film *Osama*. Lastly, "The Girl with No Door on Her Mouth" pairs Echo with Chaucer's Wife of Bath.

Once students are schooled in the art of reading for detail, all these texts become less mystifying. The repeated danger of hidden groves in book 3 (Cadmus and Actaeon) teaches them to notice setting, so that they will later understand the importance of Bartleby's cramped work space that looks out on a "dead brick wall" (H. Melville 17). Having learned that Arachne is punished as much for the events her weavings narrate as for the excellence of their execution, they will scrutinize the relation of "Bluebeard's Castle," the play within the play in *The Piano*, to the text that frames it. Their newly minted attention to the narrator and his investment in a story, which they learned by looking at the tales told by Jove of Lycaon and by Orpheus in book 10, leads them to question why an unmarried cleric is so interested in a story of marital obedience, as in Chaucer's Clerk's Tale. The quick shifts between humor and pathos in Ovid's stories prepare them for the surprising darkness lurking amidst the levity of *Twelfth Night*.

In an essay originally published in *Life* magazine on the director John Huston, James Agee wrote:

> Huston is one of the few movie artists who, without thinking twice about it, honors his audience. His pictures are not acts of seduction or of benign enslavement but of liberation, and they require, of anyone who enjoys them, the responsibilities of liberty. They continually open the eye and require it to work vigorously; and through the eye they awaken curiosity and intelligence. (380)

Ovid honors and challenges his readers in much the same way, although he is never above seduction. Sometimes I worry that my students will appreciate only Ovid's characteristic dark humor, that creepy, campy element that lurks under his narratives like a severed tongue lapping at Philomela's feet. What I hope they remember, though, is how Ovid encouraged them as readers to match his game—his wit, his wordplay, his ability to shift perspective in an instant—and that the skill of reading attentively may some day save them from a bad fate, even if it is too late for poor, misreading Europa.

NOTES

[1] The repetition of "O" in Mandelbaum's translation serves in place of Ovid's "te . . . / tuo tua" in the first passage (1.488–89) and "te . . . te . . . te" (1.559) in the second, both texts using verbal repetition to draw these two moments into comparison.

[2] In Latin, this effect is created through the repetition of verbs of seeing: "spectat, videt, videt, vidisse."

[3] See Boyd, "Ovid in Modern Translation," in this volume, for the challenge of translating this line.

Genre Transformed: The "Heroes" of Ovid's Epic

Lorina N. Quartarone

"The stories are fun, but I keep getting lost." "I'm reading about Io, and the next thing I know, I'm reading about Syrinx." "I can't keep track. There are so many stories and characters, I just don't know how they fit together." Whenever I teach *Metamorphoses*, whether in a mythology, survey of classical literature, or epic course, I hear comments like these. Students generally enjoy reading Ovid, but encouraging them to regard the poem as a work of unity rather than a collection of unrelated episodes—an encyclopedia of myth, as it were—and helping them appreciate how artistically Ovid segues from one tale to another can be challenging. The framework below is designed to help first-time readers of the poem focus on its most salient and meaningful features. Whether students read the entire poem or selections (which should include at least books 1–2, 5–6, 8, 10, and 15), they can, with proper guidance, come to appreciate the elegance in Ovid's sleight of hand—or, rather, word.

The first matter for consideration is the poem's genre. If students are reading *Metamorphoses* in a classical epic or survey course, they are familiar with epic, but even students who haven't read Homer or Vergil have impressions of the genre. Asking a question such as, When you approach a work labeled "epic," what do you expect to find? will help them generate a list of principal elements or features. At some point, "the hero" is sure to emerge as a, if not the, central feature of an epic poem.

The predictable objection, But there isn't a hero in *Metamorphoses*, will trigger the next line of questioning. If some students resist considering *Metamorphoses* an epic because it lacks a central character, it may help to quote E. J. Kenney, who calls it "a special kind of epic, an epos *sui generis*" ("Ovid" 140). Next, point out its other epic features, for example, its length, meter, scope, presentation of legendary material, concern with the human-divine relationship, focus on "heroic" exploits, confrontations with mortality, and so on. Then have them reconsider the notion of a central figure by asking them to assume that Ovid, adhering to the epic tradition, presents some kind of hero in this poem and to answer the question, Who or what could we consider the hero of *Metamorphoses*? Titles of other epics offer convenient comparisons. *Odyssey* and *Aeneid* reflect the identity of the central figure. Noting that Achilles is *Iliad*'s protagonist and *Argonautica* features Jason can help elicit the observation that sometimes the title reflects something broader, such as the scene of the epic. What, then, does the title *Metamorphoses* signify? Presenting the title's Greek roots should encourage the suggestion that "change" or "change of shape" is the hero of the poem. Help students notice how this is a combination of the two varieties of title discussed above: it incorporates both the specific "name" of the central "figure" and the broader scope of the "journey." Examine this notion by walking students through a few episodes, focusing not only on actual metamorphoses but also on the transitions between tales and emphasizing how subtly the poem pivots from one story to the next. Helping students shift their focus from the episodes themselves to how Ovid "morphs" from one to another can also allay their concerns about feeling overwhelmed or getting lost in the poem. As they cover at least one book or reading assignment, suggest that they write an outline in which they carefully note the transitions between stories. This exercise will assist them in following the flow of the narrative.

After discussing the implications of the poem's title, proceed from the introduction. It is profitable to walk students through the poem's first four lines, in Latin, even if they don't know any. Call attention to Ovid's initial clause "In nova fert animus mutatas dicere formas / corpora" and help them notice that "mutatas . . . formas" is the Latin equivalent of *meta-morphoses*. Make a special point of the intervening word "dicere" 'to say or speak': "My spirit moves me *to tell* of shapes changed into new bodies."[1] Good initial questions will help students get their bearings: Specifically, what does this introduction tell us? What is its central focus? How does it set the parameters of the epic? What, if anything, does it emphasize? Are there words that seem particularly important? Help students notice that while Ovid adheres to tradition in certain ways (e.g., the invocation to the gods, establishing the scope of the poem and, arguably, its central focus—change), he also breaks from it. Unlike other epic authors, he emphasizes the poet's role through the pride of place of his "animus" ("mind," "spirit," or "imagination") and the adjective "meus" ("my" [lines 3, 4]); he also presents a scope much broader than that of any preceding epic.

Comparing Ovid's first four lines (in English) with the introductions of other epic poems (*Iliad, Odyssey, Argonautica,* and *Aeneid*) can generate a profitable discussion and bring the importance of Ovid's narrator and his "animus" into special focus:

> In nova fert animus mutatas dicere formas
> corpora: di, coeptis (nam vos mutastis et illa)
> adspirate meis primaque ab origine mundi
> ad mea perpetuum deducite tempora carmen.
> (*Met.* 1.1–4)

> My spirit moves me to tell of forms changed into new bodies: gods (for you have changed yourselves and them), inspire my undertakings and spin out a seamless poem from the earliest origin of the world down to my own times. (*Met.* 1.1–4)

> Wrath, goddess, sing the wrath of Achilles, son of Peleus, the destructive wrath, which put countless pains on the Achaeans and sent many heroes' brave souls to Hades, and made them food for all the dogs and birds, and

the will of Zeus was accomplished, from that time when the son of Atreus, lord of men, and godlike Achilles first stood apart in conflict. Which of the gods was it who first made them fight in their strife?   (*Il.* 1.1–8)

The man, Muse, sing for me the man of many ways, who suffered many terrible things, when he sacked the sacred city of Troy.

Goddess, daughter of Zeus, speak also to us of these matters from someplace or other.   (*Od.* 1.1–2, 10)

Beginning with you, Phoebus, I shall recount the glories of men of old, who, at King Pelias's command, sailed the well-benched Argo down through the mouth of the Pontus and between the Cyanean rocks in pursuit of the golden fleece.   (*Argonautica* 1.1–4)

Arms and the man I sing, the man who first, exiled by fate, came from the shores of Troy to the Lavinian shores; was tossed about much both on land and at sea by the might of the gods, because of cruel Juno's remembering anger, and he suffered many things also in war, until he could establish the city and bring the gods to Latium, whence came the Latin nation and the Alban fathers and the walls of high Rome. Muse, recount for me the reasons. . . .   (*Aen.* 1.1–8)

Ask students to compare how each poet invokes the Muse and establishes the central character and boundaries of the poem. Help them notice the similarities and contrasts. In both Homeric epics the Muse is invoked in the first line and again a few lines later; the central characters and significant events then receive immediate focus. Apollonius emphasizes the poet's role through a first-person verb ("I shall recount," as well as the participle, "beginning," modifying the subject and placed prominently as the first word), then invokes Phoebus and quickly establishes the domain of the epic. Vergil likewise uses a first-person verb ("I sing") but gives his role as poet no special emphasis; he then describes Aeneas, his plight, and Juno as the instigator of the poem's action. His invocation to the Muse appears at line 7. It is useful to observe that both Apollonius and Vergil employ verbs that have poetic overtones: "I shall recount" ("μνήσομαι") is etymologically related to memory and the Muses, the patrons of poetry.[2] "I sing" ("cano") elicits the musical, metrical elements of epic; is the usual verb used by poets and prophets; and is related to the Latin (and English) word *canon*. In contrast, Ovid's "animus" bids him "to speak" 'dicere'—a much more general term than either "to sing" or "to remember." As W. S. Anderson notes in his commentary on *Metamorphoses*, books 1–5, "[*dicere* is] carefully inserted between the two words that define Ovid's subject. In epic convention, the poet and his Muse(s) *sing*, although some poets do indeed use the verb *dicere*" (150).

Anderson doesn't name those other poets, but two nonepic poets—Tibullus and Horace—use *dicere* (e.g., at 1.3.31 and 1.12.25, respectively).

Thus, the use of "dicere" is arguably a subtle suggestion of other poetic genres and serves as Ovid's first indication that *Metamorphoses* comprises many nonepic episodes and features. While Brooks Otis's charge that "the epic style is only a facade and the chronological progression only a trick" so that "[t]here is no real substance to either" may sound extreme (77), many scholars have examined the poem's various nonepic features. As Joseph Solodow, following Georges Lafaye (89–90), observes, *Metamorphoses* clearly "handles the themes and employs the tone of virtually every species of literature" (18). Some scholars, like Gregson Davis, focus on a single genre's influence (in this case, elegy); fruitful as that is, appreciating the poem's intricate complexity demands a simultaneous awareness of features from the tragic, comic, elegiac, philosophical, rhetorical, and pastoral genres, and this list is not exhaustive (Solodow 17–25). The presence of features from other genres is so legion that it pushes the boundaries of epic itself. In fact, Stephen Hinds's observation on Ovid's elegy could also apply to his epic:

> Within elegy he achieved an unparalleled variety of output by exploiting and extending the range of the genre as no poet had before—not by ignoring the traditional norms, but by carrying to new extremes the ... tendency to explore a genre's potentiality by testing its boundaries.   ("Ovid" 1086)

Reading even the first few lines of each poem above will help students notice *how* Ovid approaches epic differently from these four predecessors, all of whom immediately establish the central character(s) and invoke a specific deity. Ovid's introduction does neither. Rather, he places immediate focus on the poet's imagination as the creative source and declares a much less specific, much broader domain than any of the previous epics. This broader scope offers the reader nothing but a starting place, the "earliest origin of the world"; no specific characters or events, not even particular gods, are mentioned. This lack of specificity makes even the idea of a central character seem impossible, for no single figure could span the poem's scope unless she or he were immortal—and heroes are always, of necessity, mortal. This suggests that the protagonist must be understood differently.

Since in earlier epics the hero is the unifying element, is it fair, then, to expect *Metamorphoses* to be unified? Yes, indeed, for the narrator himself tells us that the poem will be "seamless" (1.4). How will it be so if there is no central character? What will produce that continuity? Can the "change of form" suggested by the title qualify as the bona fide hero of the epic?

Some students will likely find "change" a plausible central figure, particularly if they have actively traced the pivots between episodes, but some will find it slippery or elusive, despite the significance of the title, and reject this nonpersona as the poem's protagonist. Indeed, change of shape is a central theme, not a character. Thus, it may prove helpful to approach the issue of unity from a different perspective. After they have read a generous portion of their assignment (at least three books), ask students to compare Ovid's different descriptions of the process of metamorphosis: On what does Ovid focus as he describes transformations? Is there any particular aspect of change that seems to capture his attention? Reading aloud the principal transformations from just book 1 (Lycaon, Daphne, Io, even Syrinx) should highlight the figure's ability (or inability, during and after the transformation) to speak. It helps to list other characters or episodes where students notice Ovid's tendency to focus on speech during the metamorphosis (e.g., Callisto, Actaeon, Philomela, Baucis and Philemon). Also helpful is to make a list featuring the different kinds of speech Ovid represents as catalysts of change, such as a promise that cannot be broken (as with Semele and Phaethon), boasting or hubristic speech (Arachne, Niobe, and Erysichthon), an ignored command or warning (Adonis and Battus), a desperate plea (Daphne and Ianthe), or a wish fulfilled (Pygmalion and Myrrha); however the words are delivered, they ultimately lead to transformation. Furthermore, this focus on speech can be expanded to help students interpret many episodes (e.g., Echo and Narcissus, the Raven, Philomela, Teiresias, Caenis) as variations on a theme. Through this discussion, the professor can suggest that Ovid presents speech as the primary vehicle of the poem's action, parallel, in a way, to Achilles's wrath or Aeneas's *pietas*. As the principal catalyst of change, speech underlies the entirety of the epic. In fact, as Ovid pushes the boundaries of the genre, it is tempting to imagine that he also plays with what the word *epic* means. He was certainly fully aware of the range of the Greek word *epos*, whence the genre is named, and he likely alludes to its several meanings through his various representations of the impact of speech. While its primary meaning is "word," *epos* governs territory that is general (meaning "any utterance," "story," "speech"), specific ("promise," "oracle," "proverb"), and technical ("lines," "verses," and "poetry").

Some critics have certainly noted that speech holds a special interest for Ovid (e.g., Zyroff; Forbis; De Luce), and even those who don't pursue it at length remark on its significance:

> It is another important feature of Ovidian narrative that he puts so much stress on speech as the mark of humanity. Whenever a person is transformed into a lower form of life, the poet will emphasize this loss of speech and of power to communicate with other humans.
> (Fantham, *Ovid's* Metamorphoses 18)

No matter what critics say, though, the most convincing proof for the students emerges from their own close examination of the text. Either ask them to reflect on what they have read or instruct them to read with an eye to tracing speech, not only as a theme or catalyst of change but also, most concretely, as the voice of the narrator—the one whose *animus* bids him *to speak*. He interrupts the text in various ways, some obvious, others more subtle: direct addresses to the reader and to characters, rhetorical questions, parenthetical asides, expressions of disbelief, laments, references to the future—whatever the form, his comments pepper the narrative and serve as continual reminders of his presence and manipulation of the material. (For a good synopsis of such devices, see Solodow, esp. 37–73.) Through these various kinds of comments he pulls his audience back and forth in time, in and out of the narrative, at times drawing the reader into the story, at others inviting the reader's reflection.

The several apostrophes in books 1 and 2 demonstrate not only the frequency but also the variety of such remarks. In book 2, Ovid's narrator delivers over fifty such comments, some more blatant than others. Direct addresses to the reader and characters are the easiest types of apostrophe (literally, a "turning away" from the narrative) for readers to notice and are also the most likely to be accurately represented in translations. In Books 1 and 2, Ovid addresses characters twelve times (the gods, Augustus, Python, Daphne, and others) and the reader only once; this apostrophe, which uses the second-person verb form *scires* ("you would know" [1.162]) is rendered by Mandelbaum as "it's clear to see" and thus is less easy to notice in translation (9). Many other types of apostrophe take some form of conveying the narrator's thoughts or opinions, such as parenthetical remarks (usually indicated by editors as such in the Latin text) or alternative statements. Such comments frequently inspire reflection or thought on the reader's part, and sometimes supply an exegesis of the circumstances. For example, the remark at book 1, line 318, "nam cetera texerat aequor" 'for the water had covered all the other places' functions as a note to the reader explaining why Deucalion and Pyrrha came to Parnassus. Likewise, the statement "namque reperta / fistula nuper erat" 'for the shepherd's pipe had recently been invented' explains why Argus asks Mercury about the instrument (1.687–88). The narrator also uses rhetorical questions to spur thought; such questions are clearly directed at the reader and often evoke sympathy for a character. At 2.436–37, "sed quem superare puella / quisve Iovem poterat?" 'but whom could a girl overcome, and who could overcome Jupiter?' invites us to empathize with Callisto's plight, and the simple "quid faciat?" 'what could he do?' (2.187) conveys the sense of helplessness poor Phaethon felt once he realized he had taken on a task beyond his power. The narrator more obviously invites the reader to share his perspective through the use of first-person-plural verb forms, as he does at 1.414–15, "inde genus durum sumus experiensque laborum / et documenta damus qua simus origine nati" 'whence we are a race tough and accustomed to toil, and we offer evidence of the source from which we came.' The first-person verb forms create a sense of unity, since "we" not only refers to all human beings but, more specifically, to the narrator and reader, the "we" in the present context. On a more detached level, anachronistic remarks interrupt the narrative by shifting the reader's thoughts to a time outside the story at hand, whether before or after it, and sometimes evoking another story or contemporary reference. Such interruption occurs in the simile describing the gods in the tale of Lycaon: "sic, cum manus impia saevit / sanguine Caesareo Romanum exstinguere nomen" 'just as when an impious mob rages to extinguish the name of Rome through the blood of Caesar' (1.200–01). The modern reference evokes historical time outside the narrative and engenders a link to earlier events. Anachronistic references can be as simple as a single word, such as a future participle, for example "dicturus" (1.713)—Mercury was "about to say" such things (which compose a dozen or so preceding lines, a quasi-ekphrasis, if you will, of the things he was about to say but didn't, and so they stand outside the actual tale). Anachronistic references can also function more integrally to the narrative, such as "nondum laurus erat" 'the laurel tree did not yet exist,' a comment that both explains why Phoebus crowned his brow with other types of leaves and prompts the story of Daphne (1.448). This apostrophe functions as the pivot, or "narrative metamorphosis," to the next tale. To alert readers, then, apostrophes of various sorts demonstrate the narrator's manipulation of the material.

It is striking that Ovid uses apostrophes far more frequently than do earlier epic poets. According to the study by Ellen S. Zyroff, Ovid's text displays a dramatic increase in the use of the apostrophe. In addition, unlike his epic predecessors, Ovid clearly prefers the direct address to the reader. Per 3,000 lines of poetry, Homer uses this type of apostrophe only once in *Iliad* and never in *Odyssey*; Apollonius three and a half times; Vergil once; and Ovid seven and a half times, or thirty-one times in toto, an average of twice per book (Zyroff 498, 506). Ovid also addresses characters more frequently. Per 2,000 lines, *Iliad* averages two such apostrophes, *Odyssey* three, *Argonautica* one, *Aeneid* six, and *Metamorphoses* ten (Zyroff 503). Ovid addresses characters a total of fifty-nine times in the poem—averaging nearly four times per book—far more frequently than any earlier epic poet. Overall, Ovid's text contains 148 apostrophes, or one every eighty-one lines (Zyroff 490).

This increased use of the apostrophe suggests, at the very least, a less omniscient and removed, more directly involved narrator. Whereas in the earliest epics the narrators asked to be used by the Muse as a vehicle, as it were, through which to tell the story and seemed to fade into oblivion behind the verses, Ovid's narrator plays a much more direct, visible role, frequently addressing both the poem's characters and readers, interrupting the continuity of the narrative and repeatedly calling attention to himself. The effect is the reader's continual awareness of the narrator's manipulation: of the stories, characters, readers' responses, even the very words on the page. Through the technique of apostrophe, the reader's own role shifts and changes from that of detached onlooker to invited addressee to involved figure of empathy. The epic genre, once the lofty domain of divinely inspired storytellers, has become the property of a clever wordsmith and his reader, whoever that may be, and thus the text changes with every new audience. The oral tradition of epic, which kept the story and its characters, the poet, and the audience all quite distinct, has evolved into a literary labyrinth that collapses its narrator, poet, and reader into the text. (See Boyd, "Two Rivers," for a step-by-step account of this process in book 8.)

The narrator's frequent comments, then, should nudge even an inattentive reader into asking, Why *does* this narrator keep interrupting? Why indeed! Once Ovid has manipulated the audience into asking, he has pushed us halfway toward the answer. While different characters appear to speak, Ovid wants us to notice that the words of every character are, in fact, the narrator's. To follow his voice and its many permutations is to witness yet another form of metamorphosis in the poem. The narrator's voice morphs into that of every character; and where one story is embedded into another (and still another), that voice changes again and again. Book 5 offers perhaps the best illustration of this technique, where the voices of characters are layered one on the other in as many as five levels. To help students recognize this morphing of voice, have them focus on pages 156 to 174 of Allen Mandelbaum's translation and follow the quotation marks, which gradually become embedded. The narrator's voice first becomes that of an unnamed Muse, whose voice becomes that of Pyreneus, then that of a Pierid, then Minerva's, when it becomes Calliope's voice, which then speaks severally as Venus, Cyane, Arethusa, Jupiter, and Triptolemus. The final layering of multiple voices occurs when Arethusa (already in the mouths of Calliope and the unnamed Muse) speaks as Alpheus. Through such stacked overdubbing, as it were, we must remember that all these voices emerge, ultimately, from the narrator.

It is significant not only that but also how Ovid frames the poem by giving speech particular prominence in both the introduction and the epilogue. As noted above, it is hardly accidental that in the poem's first line "to speak" ("dicere") lies noticeably between "changed" ("mutatas") and "forms" ("formas"). In the epilogue, the references are less blatant but perhaps more powerful. The narrator claims that the common instruments of change will be, paradoxically, ineffective on his work: "iamque opus exegi, quod nec Iovis ira nec ignis / nec poterit ferrum nec edax abolere vetustas" 'and now I have completed my work, which not the anger of Jupiter, nor fire, nor the sword, nor voracious time will be able to destroy' (15.871–72). If this work—his "opus" —is indestructible, it must not be a physical entity. What part of a written work is not physical? The author's name and the stories the author tells—the words, which may be recited or memorized. Thus, he proclaims his immortality as immortality *in speech*: "I shall be read by the lips of the people." Even his claim, "I shall be borne, eternally, beyond the stars" ("super alta perennis / astra ferar" [15.876]) is a double entendre, since "ferar" can also mean, "I shall be spoken (of)." Furthermore, all the first-person verbs, "I shall be borne" (876), "I shall be read" (878), and 'I shall live" (879), obviously do not mean "I" but rather "my words." If we read this in the light of the quintessential Homeric definition of a hero as a "doer of deeds and a speaker of words" (describing Achilles [*Il.* 9.443] and Odysseus [*Od.* 2.272]), we understand that the narrator is thus identifying himself as the poem's hero and hearkening back to the oral beginnings of epic. Moreover, if his prediction "I shall" really means, "my words shall," the true hero is not really the narrator himself but his composition of *words*; hence he states that his body will die while "I shall live." Of course, Ovid—who appears never to take anything too seriously—must cast doubt on this lofty prediction: "In fame, through all the centuries—if the predictions of poets have any truth in them—I shall live." Thus the poem's final metamorphosis slips elusively beyond our grasp.

The poet's final statement may not be satisfying, but it is quite Ovidian—he can't be pinned down. This reader, at least, often imagines Ovid putting pen to papyrus while plying his tongue into his cheek, as if saying to himself, "Let's see who catches this!" His sense of humor pervades his poetry, no matter how lofty, erudite, socially conscious, or moving it may be. If we allow his deliberate mélanges of elements and personae associated with various genres to speak for themselves, we will catch on.

NOTES

[1] All translations are my own. I have used prose rather than poetry, since the meaning is the focus, and I have maintained the initial words of each epic in these translations.

[2] Apollonius employs the verb μνήσομαι (mnesomai), which shares its stem with the word for *memory* and is the name of the mother of the Muses Μνημοσύνη (Mnemosyne). Since early epic poets performed orally, they invoked the Muses, whose domains are the arts and memory, to assist them.

Approaches to Teaching Ovid's *Tristia*
Samuel Huskey

By placing *Tristia* last on the reading list for my undergraduate survey course on Latin literature in translation up to the Augustan Age, I do not mean to suggest that it is the zenith of Roman literary achievement, although recent scholars (e.g., Gareth Williams; Claassen) have shown that the poems evince the same artistry as that found in Ovid's earlier works. Rather, I choose to end the semester with *Tristia* because this collection of poems clearly represents the end of an era. After I have introduced my students to the auspicious beginning of Augustus's reign, it seems appropriate that they also consider what happened at its end, when Augustus, great patron of the arts that he was, banished the greatest poet of his day to Tomis, a backwater town on the edge of the empire.

The exact reason for Ovid's relegation remains a mystery, but Ovid blames it on "a song and a mistake" ("carmen et error" [*Tr.* 2.207]). Of the latter, he says only that it was something that he saw (*Tr.* 2.103–04); he says nothing more about it, for fear of making his situation even worse. Regarding the former, however, he frequently reminds us that his *Art of Love* destroyed him (e.g., *Tr.* 1.1.111–16, 2.1–12), presumably because it offended Augustus's moral standards. The banishment of a citizen for something that he wrote marks the beginning of a new era in Roman literature, and Ovid's *Tristia* is its inaugural work. But just as Ovid looks back to Rome from Tomis, *Tristia* also looks back to previous eras of Roman literature. Indeed, because its poems allude to the works of so many of Ovid's predecessors, a judicious selection of readings from the collection doubles as a review of the material covered previously in the semester. If my students read Ovid's poems from exile attentively and carefully, they will recognize Aeneas behind Ovid's exilic self-portrait; they will hear Cicero in Ovid's defense of his poetry; and they will see Ovid's own pre-exilic works anew in the light of his exile.

Of course, it can be depressing to end the semester with exile poetry, especially when the collection is entitled *Tristia* (*Sadnesses*), but these poems also provide a chance to test students' appreciation of literary style and artistry. It is easy to dismiss Ovid's exile poetry as monotonous, depressing, and inferior to his other work, as did many earlier scholars (e.g., Wilkinson, *Ovid Recalled* 347, 359–61). Who can blame them? Even Ovid bemoans his flagging talent and the poor quality of his work in exile, worrying about the deterioration of his Latin as he grows accustomed to the barbaric sounds emitted by the inhabitants of Tomis (e.g., *Tr.* 3.1.17–18, 3.14.43–52, 5.7.57–58). But how seriously ought we to take Ovid's self-disparaging remarks, especially when he couches them in perfect elegiac couplets? What of the unmistakable style that identifies the work as Ovidian, even should it lack a proper title page (*Tr.* 1.1.61–62)? When I introduce *Tristia*, I challenge my students to appreciate the poems, even if they do not particularly enjoy them—a valuable distinction, and one worth learning. Reading *Tristia* also provides a good opportunity for practicing some of the critical approaches that students have learned earlier in the semester. The many ways of identifying the first-person narrator challenge assumptions about authorial intent. For example, are Ovid the poet and Ovid the person identical, or different personas? The difference between the realities of the Black Sea region and the fantastic features of Ovid's "poetic Pontus" illustrate the problems with reading the exile poetry literally and as biography. In general, the poems repay close reading, as Ovid himself suggests when he invites us to "read more" in *Tristia* 1.1.

"Reading More" in Tristia

Ovid's high expectations for readers of *Tristia* are made clear through the allusive artistry of the first twenty-two lines in the collection. On the surface, the message of these opening lines is that the shabby appearance of Ovid's personified book of exile poetry reflects not only its author's reduced circumstances but also the quality of the poems that it contains. Disheveled and unpolished though the book may be, the witty contrast between it and Catullus's charming and polished book (Catullus, poem 1) exemplifies a wryness familiar from Ovid's previous works. Indeed, if students have paid enough attention in their reading of Catullus's first poem earlier in the semester, they will recognize the game that Ovid is playing. They may also recall Ovid's pun on metrical "feet" in *Amores* 1.1.3–4 when he says in *Tristia* 1.1.15–16, "Go, book, and bring to the places I loved my greeting— / let me reach them with what 'feet' I may!" (P. Green, *Ovid: The Poems*). The book's shabby appearance might also evoke a contrast with the grooming instructions that Ovid gives to young lovers in *Art of Love*. This last point becomes more and more important in *Tristia* 1.1, as in the entire collection, since Ovid will continue to allude to his erotic work.

Most important for my purpose, however, is the command that Ovid gives his book in lines 21–22: "atque ita tu tacitus (quaerenti plura legendum) / ne, quae non opus est, forte loquare, cave." There are as many opinions about the meaning of this difficult couplet as there are editors and translators (for a survey, see Huskey, "*Quaerenti*"). This gives me an opportunity to introduce other facets of classical scholarship into my lecture, such as textual criticism and the art of translation, both of which, I emphasize, are important kinds of reading. For example, in his translation Peter Green reluctantly accepts Georg Luck's emendation "quaerent si plura legentes" for the reading of most of the manuscripts, "quaerenti plura legendum," which can be construed as meaning, "the one who seeks more must read" (*Ovid: The Poems* 204). Arguing that "such perusal will provide no more information" (204), Green translates the couplet, "For the rest, keep silent. If people demand more details / take care not to blab out / any state secrets." In his revision of A. L. Wheeler's Loeb translation, however, G. P. Goold sticks to the text of the manuscripts and translates the couplet, "Except for this be silent—for he who requires must read more—and take care that you chance not to say what you should not." Neither Wheeler nor Goold comments on the text or translation, but Sergio Casali discusses the problem at length, ultimately taking the couplet as an invitation to read beneath the surface, to plumb Ovid's text for extra meaning. This is a fruitful way of looking at Ovid's *Tristia*, since it encourages readers to move away from the gloominess of the surface message about the life of an exiled poet and toward appreciation of Ovid's poetic skill and sparkling wit. Of course, the couplet has also been read as encouragement to readers looking for "secret messages" about the reason for Ovid's exile, but I take this opportunity to discuss with my students how this quixotic pursuit for a long time distracted scholars from reading and appreciating the exile poetry as poetry. Given the number of theories that have been proposed over the centuries regarding Ovid's exile (for which see Thibault), I maintain that it is best to take Ovid at his word when he says on many occasions that he will not reveal the nature of the mistake that led to his banishment. Instead, it is more useful to explore other ways of "reading more" in Ovid's poems.

Reading the Metamorphoses *in* Tristia *1.1*

Heeding the instruction to "read more," we continue our exploration of *Tristia* 1.1, paying particular attention to the theme of transformation. At lines 58–59, for example, Ovid wishes that he could become his book, an idea that he returns to at the end of the poem when he wishes to add to *Metamorphoses* the transformation of his fortune from good to bad. He also alludes to *Metamorphoses* when he compares himself to Phaëthon (79–80) and Icarus (89–90). These details should be relatively easy for students to recognize, but there are also some that reveal themselves only in the Latin text. I focus on one in particular, since it demonstrates on many levels why we should not take Ovid seriously when he complains that his talent is flagging.

At *Tristia* 1.1.39–44, each couplet begins with a form of the word "carmen" 'song':

> carmina proveniunt animo deducta sereno;
>   nubila sunt subitis pectora nostra malis.
> carmina secessum scribentis et otia quaerunt;
>   me mare, me venti, me fera iactat hiems.
> carminibus metus omnis obest; ego perditus ensem
>   haesurum iugulo iam puto iamque meo.

> Poetry comes fine spun from a mind at peace; my mind is clouded with unexpected woes. Poetry requires the writer to be in privacy and ease; I

am harassed by the sea, by gales, by wintry storms. Poetry is injured by any fear; I in my ruin am ever and ever expecting a sword to pierce my throat. (Ovid, Tristia [trans. Goold])

Although I use Green's translation in my class, I use Goold's revision of Wheeler's translation of these couplets because it highlights their rhetorical features. Anaphora at the beginning of the three hexameter lines draws attention to Ovid's subject, but *variatio* (i.e., changing from "carmina" to "carminibus") mitigates the monotony of the repetition. The alternating hexameter and pentameter of each couplet give structure to the syncrisis. (My students have already encountered these terms earlier in the semester, so this is a helpful review.) Ovid's literary artistry is not simply a matter of rhetorical technique, however. Using Ovid's allusive technique as a "touchstone for the refutation of the pose of decline" (Gareth Williams, *Banished Voices* 58), I lead my students in an investigation of Ovid's image of "finely spun poetry" (line 39; my trans.) to demonstrate just how complex an allusion can become.

Since Vergil had coined the term "deductum carmen" in the sixth eclogue (line 5) as a shorthand allusion to Callimachean poetics (Ross 26–27), it is reasonable to conclude that Ovid's phrase "carmina . . . deducta" would recall Vergil's poem. The pastoral setting of *Eclogues* certainly provides a stark contrast to the gloomy circumstances of Ovid's exile, effectively buttressing the comparison; but Ovid did not write pastoral poetry before, so why should he introduce it now as a contrast to his current effort? More lurks behind Ovid's use of the image of a finely spun poem. If we review the content of Vergil's sixth eclogue (which my students have read previously in the semester), we find that Tityrus's "deductum carmen" covers a wide range of topics: the origin of the universe, the creation of human beings, and the transformations that various heroes and heroines underwent. In other words, Tityrus gives us a preview of Ovid's *Metamorphoses* (Knox, *Ovid's* Metamorphoses, esp. 10–14). When we turn to the proem to *Metamorphoses* (1.1–4), we find that Ovid plays with the image of a finely spun song, and with Callimachean poetics as a whole, when he asks the gods to spin out his perpetual song: "perpetuum deducite . . . carmen" (Van Tress 68–69). Thus, we have in *Tristia* a double allusion to Vergil's *Eclogues* and to Ovid's own *Metamorphoses*—all held together by the thread, as it were, of the finely spun song (Huskey, "Ovid's Metamorphoses"). It is difficult to take seriously Ovid's comments about the poor quality of his poetry when his allusive artistry is as alive as ever and flourishing, as examples below demonstrate.

Reading Vergil in Tristia

Students who have read Vergil's *Aeneid* can appreciate seeing how Ovid's departure from Rome and journey into exile recall Aeneas's struggles in the first six books of Vergil's epic poem. While exploring the effect of Ovid's allusions to *Aeneid*, we focus on the problematic comparison of Ovid to Aeneas. After all, Aeneas was not only a national hero for the Romans but also the ancestor of Augustus. What, then, is the effect of Ovid's placing himself on a par with Aeneas? Is there an anti-Augustan undertone to this comparison, or does the comparison transcend politics? Does the comparison engender more or less sympathy for Ovid in his readers?

These and other questions guide our discussion of 1.3, in which Ovid describes his departure from Rome (Huskey, "Ovid"), and 1.2, 1.4, and 1.11, in which he describes the gales and wintry storms that toss his ship during the journey to Tomis. When we "read more," we discover again that we cannot take Ovid's descriptions literally. Vivid though the picture may be that Ovid paints of scribbling poetry while his ship takes on water and the winds threaten to rend the sails (1.11.13–18), it is unlikely that Ovid could maintain his composure well enough to craft elegiac couplets that describe the storms as they toss him about the sea. "Mountains of heaving water" whose peaks nearly touch the stars and whose valleys seem to reach Tartarus itself may inspire poetry (1.2.19–24), but they do not provide a suitable environment for writing it, so we need to consider instead the symbolism of the storm at sea in the context of Ovid's experience of exile (Dickinson 162–63, 167–68; Nagle, *Poetics* 147–50).

It is useful to consider here a character who appears in all three of the storm poems, the helpless helmsman who has lost control of his "art." He is named variously in the three poems as "rector" (1.2.31–32), "navita" (1.4.11–12), and "gubernator" (1.11.21–22), but the image is always the same: his ship is at the mercy of the storm, since his skill ("ars") is not sufficient to master the winds and the waves. As shorthand for *Ars amatoria*, the word "ars" is always a charged word in the exile poetry; it is therefore easy to see in the helpless helmsman a metaphor for the poet whose skill is useless, even harmful, to him as he faces the upheaval of relegation (P. Green, *Ovid: The Poems* 220). Moreover, we may recall Ovid's boast, in reference to the celebrated helmsman of the Argo, that he had become the Tiphys of love (*Ars* 1.8). Now on his way into exile because of his *Ars amatoria*, Ovid revisits the image.

The storms themselves also deserve attention. Close reading reveals that they bear a striking resemblance to the storm in the first book of Vergil's *Aeneid* (Videau-Delibes 73–82). The mountains of water in *Tristia* 1.2.19 recall the mountain of water that crashes down on Aeneas's fleet (*Aen.* 1.105). The soaring heights and plunging depths of the waves in *Tristia* 1.2.20–22 evoke memories of the monstrous waves in *Aeneid* 1.106–07. In *Tristia* 1.11.21–22, our helpless helmsman stretches out his hands to the stars, exactly the same posture that Aeneas adopts at *Aeneid* 1.93 before he begins to speak; and both Vergil and Ovid end their hexameters with the phrase "ad sidera palmas." Even the detail of ropes whistling in the wind (*Tr.* 1.4.9–10, 1.11.19–20) has a Vergilian antecedent (*Aen.* 1.87). Is Ovid writing "mock-epic," as Evans argues (35–36)? Is this merely an elaborate form of hyperbole? Or is Ovid writing his own "epic of exile," seriously comparing his experience with that of Aeneas and other epic heroes, as Jo-Marie Claassen argues (*Displaced Persons* 68–72)?

Reading Cicero et al. in Ovid's Defense of His Poetry

If I had to select only one poem from *Tristia* to include in my survey course, it would be the single poem of book 2, since it brings together so much of the material from the rest of the semester. Ovid's goal in this poem is to defend his character and his poetry to Augustus, so naturally he adopts the structure of a formal oration for his poem: lines 1–26 constitute the *exordium*, or introduction, followed briefly by the *propositio* (27–28), or Ovid's declaration of his intent; the body of the argument, or *tractatio* (29–578), is composed of the *probatio* (29–154), or the presentation of evidence; an *epilogus* (155–206), or conclusion to the first part of the argument; the *refutatio* (207–572), or rebuttal; and another *epilogus* (573–78), in which Ovid rests his case and pleads for mercy (Dickinson 172). After the unit on Cicero earlier in the semester, my students are familiar enough with this kind of structure to appreciate Ovid's innovative use of it in poetry.

Of course, book 2 allows us to review much more than rhetorical form. It also presents a survey of literary history from the beginnings up to Ovid's day, the goal of which is to show that Ovid is not the only one who composed erotic verses. Although his list features the usual suspects (e.g., Catullus, Calvus, and Propertius), he argues that poets such as Ennius and Lucretius have also written salacious poetry; at the climax of the argument, he even claims that people read *Aeneid* mostly for the "union of illicit love" between Aeneas and Dido (533–36). Students who have read works by some of these poets earlier in the semester can evaluate Ovid's arguments and recognize that some are reasonable, but many are specious.

The poem is also worth studying for its own literary merits. As ever, Ovid's allusive artistry is on display as Ovid makes his case. He frequently alludes to his own works, as when he compares himself to Actaeon (*Tr.* 2.105–06), who also suffered for seeing something that he should not have seen (cf. *Met.* 3.143–252), or when he quotes directly from his *Ars amatoria* (*Tr.* 2.247–50; cf. *Ars* 1.31–34). But he also alludes to other poets. When he protests, "My morals, believe me, are quite distinct from my verses" (2.354), he echoes Catullus's assertion in poem 16: "Squeaky-clean, that's what every proper poet's / *person* should be, but not his bloody squiblets" (P. Green, *Poems of Catullus*, lines 5–6). He quotes Vergil directly, and subversively, when he says, at *Tristia* 2.533–34, "Yet even the fortunate author of your own *Aeneid* brought his / Arms-and-the-Man into a Tyrian bed" (P. Green, *Ovid: The Poems*). Indeed, as he proceeds through his survey of literary history, he alludes to or quotes directly from many of the works that he mentions.

Most of all, however, the poem betokens the difficulties of being a writer in the Roman Empire. For this reason, book 2 is a superb choice for the final reading in a survey of Latin literature to the age of Augustus. Foreshadowing future regimes, it depicts an anonymous informant bringing Ovid to the attention of a capricious emperor (77–80), who summons the poet to his chambers and unilaterally decides to banish him (121–38). There was no recourse of any kind for Ovid, or anyone else for that matter—not when the emperor might as well have been a god, as becomes clear through Ovid's many comparisons of Augustus to Jupiter (e.g., 2.33–40). Thus, in Ovid's nervous yet spirited defense of his poetry, and in his obsequious yet disingenuous praise of Augustus (Claassen, *Displaced Persons* 147–53), we witness the birth of the dissimulation that characterizes the work of Ovid's literary successors (Rudich).

More to Read in Tristia

Constraints on space prevent me from discussing in detail the poems in books 3–5, but I do not mean to suggest by omission that the poems of the latter books are not worthy of inclusion in a reading list for a course on Latin literature. Ovid's guided tour of Rome in 3.1, for example, offers a unique perspective on the Augustan transformation of the city. His descriptions of the conditions in Tomis in 3.10 and 5.10 often foster a discussion of poetic license and realism, since Ovid appears to have embellished the portrayal of his exilic locale and its inhabitants with allusions to other descriptions of extreme conditions (Claassen, "Ovid's Poetic Pontus"). Finally, the autobiographic 4.10 paints a portrait of Ovid that is as interesting for what it omits as for what it includes. Whatever selection an instructor chooses to include, Ovid's *Tristia* is an effective capstone for a survey course on Latin literature through the Augustan Age.

Most interesting for me in teaching *Tristia* has been the variety of my students' responses to the poems. Some have difficulty getting past the depressing tone of the collection. Others want desperately to figure out the reason for Ovid's banishment and will try to steer the discussion in that direction. In any case, most students are skeptical about *Ars amatoria* as a reason for banishment. Some express disbelief at any suggestion of an anti-Augustan subtext in poems that are ostensibly pleas for forgiveness, but others express admiration for what they see as Ovid's refusal to bow completely to the emperor. Similarly, some believe that Ovid deserved banishment, if not worse; but others have sympathy and pity for him, even if they do not find the argument in book 2 entirely persuasive. In general, their reactions reflect the diversity of scholarly opinions, which confirms for me that it is fruitful to include *Tristia* in my syllabus.

From Ovid to Elvis:
Teaching Mythology in the Classical Tradition

Nikolai Endres

I assign Ovid's *Metamorphoses* in Mythology, an upper-level elective, which ranges from Ovid to Wotan. We look at Greek, Roman, and Norse myth, myth-making, and mythology from various perspectives (history, gender, archetypes), with interdisciplinary approaches (art, philosophy, music), and in the spirit of the classical tradition; by the end of the course, we have a deeper understanding of the origins, cultural significance, and continuing appeal of ancient mythology.

Students from departments all over campus take this course. As a result, they contribute varying backgrounds and multiple perspectives to the subject. When I ask them on the first day of class why they signed up for Mythology, their answers show various interests: classical literature in general, mythology in popular culture, understanding archetypes, or myth as propaganda. Frequently, I find, students bring a Jungian expectation to the course (creation and doom, gods and mortals, quest and change), which I am happy to meet.[1] Although we spend only two weeks on Ovid, *Metamorphoses* functions as a core or hinge for the entire course. In what follows, I describe both how I teach *Metamorphoses* and how I return to the epic's themes throughout the semester and relate them to other works on the syllabus.

We consult the following primary sources, which I group under separate headings:

> Divine Origins: Hesiod's *Theogony*, Plato's *Symposium*, and Genesis
> Strange Transformations: Ovid's *Metamorphoses*, Franz Kafka's *The Metamorphosis*, and Eugène Ionesco's *Rhinoceros*
> Tragic Entanglements: Aeschylus's *The Oresteian Trilogy*, Jean-Paul Sartre's *The Flies*, and Eugene O'Neill's *Mourning Becomes Electra* (film)
> Monstrous Passions: Euripides's *Hippolytus* and Jean Racine's *Phaedra*
> Dionysian Frenzies: Euripides's *The Bacchae* and Thomas Mann's *Death in Venice*
> Germanic Superpowers: *The Nibelungenlied* and Richard Wagner's *The Ring of the Nibelung*[2]

Why a pairing of Ovid, Kafka, and Ionesco? Other options are abundant: Apuleius's *The Golden Ass*, Edmund Spenser's *The Faerie Queene*, William Shakespeare's *A Midsummer Night's Dream*, Mary Shelley's *Frankenstein*, George Bernard Shaw's *Pygmalion* (or the musical *My Fair Lady*), T. S. Eliot's *The Waste Land*, Ezra Pound's *Cantos*, Hermann Hesse's *Pictor's Metamorphoses*, Salman Rushdie's *The Satanic Verses*, John Updike's *The Centaur*, or the Japanese animated feature narrated by Peter Ustinov, *Winds of Change* (1978). The shortness of Kafka's and Ionesco's pieces recommends them. More important, exile, the loss of one's home and identity, unites the three writers. "I feel out of place in life, among people," Berenger says in *Rhinoceros* (Ionesco 19). Kafka in Prague was displaced too—German-speaking, Jewish, sexually embattled, he was in a predominantly Austro-Hungarian, anti-Semitic, and heterosexual environment. Ionesco left his birthplace, Romania, and settled in France. Ovid, increasingly an outsider in the Rome of family values, was exiled by Augustus to Tomis (now Constantia), though after Ovid had completed most of his epic. Exile also evokes themes such as alienation and tyranny, past and present, distance and proximity, all of which we study over the course of the semester. Finally, hints of Augustan propaganda hit close to home. Does not all literature intend to effect change? And if so, how does it subvert the dominant political ideology?

First a general observation about particular teaching challenges: *Metamorphoses* is long, with about 250 stories that often run into one another or transition weakly and thus make for a rambling whole; has an elevated tone (perhaps the result of its being poetry); is written in a mixed genre; and features a large number of characters ranging from Chaos to Cleopatra and from Apollo to Augustus ("Do we need to know *all* of them for the final?" frustrated students often ask), which makes it, indeed, a masterpiece worthy of Daedalus, who "tricks the eye / with many twisting paths that double back" (253; *Met.* 8.160–61). To diminish the problem of length, I focus on books 1, 3, 6, 8, 10, and 13–15 (about half of the full text); for the rest, I provide summaries (e.g., Fantham, *Ovid's* Metamorphoses 157–66). I also hand out a list of multiple names for Ovid's characters (e.g., Diana/Phoebe/Cynthia). To make sure students keep up with the assignments, I have short reading quizzes or—which is more fun—I write the names of famous figures (Pygmalion, Actaeon and Diana, the Sibyl) on note cards and have students "play" the episode to the class. Regarding Ovid's digressions, I hold off an explanation until we get to Wagner, who abandoned traditional divisions of opera in favor of the leitmotif; I explain that Ovid too employs recurring themes (*variatio*). Finally, I focus discussions on clearly defined topics.

Naturally, we begin with creation—as does Ovid. What is created in the texts we have read? Why is it created? Why are human beings obsessed with origin(s)? Students always answer perceptively: "Knowing where we come from is part of knowing who we are." Is creation ever in peril? Do we ever fail to return to sources? Students eagerly recount all the paradises they have lost. And inevitably these days, someone mentions the creation-versus-evolution controversy, which I put to good use. In Ovid, do we have an omnipotent creator, an intelligent designer, or a form of exfoliation? Actually, is not the shaping of changes a related term for evolution? We also do not overlook the many anomalies in Ovid's account, which are paralleled by the *two* contradictory creation scenarios in Genesis.[3] True to our cross-cultural and ahistorical approach, I then give short lectures on the *Epic of Gilgamesh*, Snorri Sturluson's *Prose Edda*, Native

American stories from the southwestern United States collected by ethnographers, and African oral tales (Thury and Devinney 23-95; Morford and Lenardon 102-09). We realize that Genesis is hardly the only account, that the prelapsarian paradise, the flood, the second covenant, and the hero-king recur as indelible fantasies. Creation is an archetype, but different cultures place emphasis on different aspects of it, such as the status and value of gods and mortals.

When we get to the Nibelung myth, Ovid's gods can be compared easily with the Norse deities, who have many of the same characteristics: the philandering husband, the jealous wife, the favorite daughter, the trickster, father-son conflict, incest. Wagner too begins with the creation of the world, but unlike Ovid ends with an inferno of fire and water.[4] In groups, students trace conflicts among gods, such as Mars and Venus versus Vulcan, Apollo versus Cupid, or Juno versus Jove; Wotan (Odin) versus Fricka (Frigga, upholder of the sanctity of marriage), Odin versus Erda (matriarchal earth goddess), Odin versus Loge (Loki, god of fire). How much reverence does Ovid show his gods? Students quickly pick up on the Roman divinities' political and often comic aspects. What are the gods' limitations? Even Jove cannot "undo what any other god has done" (90; *Met.* 3.336–37); as Jove tells his fellow Olympians, even the highest gods must succumb to the Fates (306; *Met.* 9.427–38). Like Ovid's Parcae, Wagner features the Three Norns, who reign supreme in both Roman and Norse myth. Wotan, though guardian of pledges, violates his promises to the giants Fafner (Fafnir) and Fasolt, and now only a hero can save the gods: "We need a man / who lives without our protection, / who is free from the rule of the gods. / He alone / can accomplish the deed, / which, although it will save us, / the gods are forbidden to do" (*Ring* [1976] 101). Erda prophesied the waning of the gods as early as "Das Rheingold," and an imminent *Götterdämmerung* hints at the gods' inadequacy to sustain religious feeling among humanity.[5] Since we generally study this near paper time, students contrast Ovid's and Wagner's deities with the Christian god; in five pages, they need to synthesize specific biblical passages with passages from *Metamorphoses* and the *Ring*.

We then discuss the interaction between gods and mortals, one of Ovid's main narrative driving forces. What distinguishes them? Do they love or loathe, hate or help each other? Students look at various "love" triangles—for example, Artemis-Hippolytus-Aphrodite or Wotan-Siegfried-Brunhild (Brünnhilde in Wagner). Since American culture is steeped in religion, students also take great interest in the individual and the universal. Are mortals ever superior to the gods? Are the gods capable of love, of humility, of forgiveness (all qualities attributed by students to the Christian god)? Bacchus, for once, sides with Midas: "The gods are capable of kindness: since / King Midas recognized that he had sinned, / Bacchus restored his former state to him" (364; *Met.* 11.134–35). But what happens to Niobe's children reeks of total annihilation, and Minerva destroys Arachne simply because she cannot tolerate a human rival (or, as some students feel, simply because she does not like her). On what note does Ovid end his epic? Is Rome destined for greatness or will it follow other fallen cities? Is

Jupiter an attractive "ruler" for Rome? Has Ovid elevated himself to an immortal, a god: "my name and fame are sure: I shall have life" (549; *Met.* 15.878–79)? Students never fail to note the irony in Ovid's crossing the very boundary that topples so many of his human artists. In Kafka, although we find an essentially godless universe, Gregor's father throws apples at his son, "nailing" him as if to a cross, and leaves a visible "memento" (1661). The Old Testament god seems as capricious as Ovid's gods, for Gregor—the scapegoat?—never finds out what his sin is. How scary that he, equipped with full reason, does not once question why he wakes up as a bug; as is typical in Kafka, he is condemned without a trial.

Next is the nature of metamorphosis. What exactly is transformed? Does the change/punishment reflect the sin/crime (a form of Dantean *contrapasso*)? Arachne, the spider, pays for her transgressive weaving; Anaxarete has a heart of stone and is changed accordingly; Narcissus still admires his complexion after he is transformed into a flower; Lycaon has been a savage and predatory wolf (*lykos*) all along; the Myrmidons retain the thriftiness of ants. I encourage students to recall other transformations. In fairy tales, characters turn into ugly toads or hideous beasts (punishment) or into stately princes or beautiful maidens (reward). Change in the end, one could argue, is no change at all. Metamorphosis results in clarification, in showing one's true colors. Here I invite students to transform some of the greatest "villains" of all time into appropriate objects that bring home their crime. During this activity, "we've never had more fun" echoes throughout the classroom, with the great Ovid himself turning into the ever shape-shifting chameleon. Later we repeat the same exercise for Siegfried, Kriemhild, Hagen, and Brunhild in the *Nibelungenlied*. Into what would Ovid have metamorphosed them? Kriemhild, for example, ends up as a wolf, butcher, or headless Mother Death.

Kafka stands Aristotelian mimesis on its head, for Gregor Samsa's metamorphosis is something that could not have happened—but did. Harking back to Ovid, I ask why the insect is a particularly fortunate metaphor for Gregor. Students realize that he was an "insect" long before he turned into one; around his father, in his room, at work—he was constantly in a horizontal, in other words, spineless, position. Or, when he is tugging at his sister's skirt and apparently attempting to seduce her, is that not suggestive of incest? Well, only if he is not an insect, for incest is a cultural taboo among human beings but prevalent in the animal world. Are there insects that we find cute? Grete Samsa is compared to a butterfly at the end of the story. The three boarders, on the other hand, show traits of parasites, eating huge amounts of food and not paying for rent; moreover, like wolves, they live in a pack. When we read Ionesco's play, we collect on the blackboard the rhinoceros's most prominent characteristics (initially, Ionesco had contemplated sheep—would they have been preferable?): militant, aggressive, equipped with a deadly weapon, always charging straight ahead, moving at maximum speed, trampling the weak, systematically eradicating anything in its way. The rhino is the perfect Nazi, we conclude. Also, as a kind of dinosaur animal, the rhinoceros is prehistoric, atavistic, impervious—all qualities that sum up fascism's precivilized, or prehuman, social Darwinism, what Jean calls "the law of the jungle" (Ionesco 67). For exactly these reasons, the rhino's origins can never be explained in the play. As in Ovid and in Kafka, it is not until Ioneso's characters have turned into rhinos that we recognize their herd mentality.

Then we turn to the general problems associated with transformation, such as free will and coercion or regress and progress. I e-mail discussion ideas to the class. What kinds of change confront Ovid's characters? Acheloüs tells Theseus, "some who have suffered change, always retain / their newly given shape. But there are some / who have the power to take on many forms" (277; *Met*. 8.728-30). What are the effects of change? Is the story of Baucis and Philemon the only positive change? How about the apotheosis of Hercules? Why is a sex change necessary in the Iphis-Ianthe story for a happy ending? Can we ever draw a clear line between man and animal in *The Metamorphosis*? Whose metamorphosis is Kafka really referring to, Gregor's or the family's? What do we make of the mass transformation of a peaceful community in *Rhinoceros*? Why are people so eager to change? Even Monsieur Papillon, that gentlest of creatures, jumps on the rhino wagon. Unlike Ovidian metamorphosis, rhinoceritis is clearly a choice here. Why, as Ionesco seems to be saying, can only a weak person resist change? In groups, students probe the role of logic, culture, morality, academia, love, and religion in *Rhinoceros*. Is Berenger better or worse off as the only human being left? Could (useless) defiance be as absurd as (strict) conformism? This unit really engages students, for it drives home fundamental civic concerns about responsibility and victimization or reason and faith, issues of human agency that were as pressing to Ovid as they are to us.

Interdisciplinary activities follow: I photocopy poems from Nina Kossman's *Gods and Mortals: Modern Poems on Classical Myths*, which we compare with Ovid (e.g., William Butler Yeats's "Leda and the Swan," Thom Gunn's "Philemon and Baucis," W. H. Auden's "Ganymede," Frank O'Hara's "Jove"); then I hand out a famous name or story from Ovid (Orpheus and Eurydice, Narcissus and Echo, Ajax and Ulysses) and ask students to write a short poem, without explicitly naming the central characters, so that the class can divine the allusion. On the Web, in one of the many illustrated editions of *Metamorphoses*, or in Jane Davidson Reid's *Oxford Guide to Classical Mythology in the Arts*, students search for visual representations of the assigned story or, if artistically gifted, draw or sketch it; since Ovid is one of the most visual poets, students enjoy putting *Metamorphoses* on the canvas or the screen. In the library's music collection, they track down musical renderings; a student once even reenacted Ovid's creation using Wagner's famous E flat major on the double basses at the beginning of the *Ring*. Last but not least, supervised research in the library leads to reports or papers on Ovid and early imperial literature, myth, gender and sexuality, *Nachleben*, and much more.[6]

Having engaged with Ovid in great detail, students soon see myth everywhere. Every time I teach the class, they voluntarily share their enthusiasm.

We therefore finish with metamorphosis in our culture: plastic surgery, extreme makeover shows (remember Ovid's new and improved Hippolytus?), flip-flopping politicians, or gender ambiguity (such as Michael Jackson, whom students often regard as a "hermaphrodite" or as a modern-day Tiresias). I ask students to bring to class advertisements based on mythology and explain them in *PowerPoint*: Gianni Versace, Joop!, or Giorgio Armani; the logos for Rémy Martin, Hermès, or American Express; companies with mythological names, such as Medusa Cement, Vulcan Steel, Argus Security, or Nike (see also Hartigan). Yet sometimes I need to temper my students' zeal a bit, for in some cases, the uses of myth seem dubious: the ship *Titanic*, the Tennessee Titans football team (Hesiod's Titans lost), Trojan condoms (the Trojans lost through the insertion of a foreign object, and nowadays there is the Trojan virus that contaminates one's computer), calling someone an Adonis (to quote Ovid on the flower: "And yet Adonis' blossoms have brief life: / his flower is light and delicate; it clings / too loosely to the stem and thus is called / Anemone—'born of the wind'—because / winds shake its fragile petals, and they fall" [356; *Met*. 10.737–39]), Midas car repair (one would not actually want one's vehicle at the shop to turn to gold or into a lackadaisical ass), the cleaner Ajax (Ajax's death was decidedly messy [Mandelbaum 445]), or the incongruously named porn star Penelope. Sometimes, without an awareness of myth, an ad comes across as outright nonsense. I circulate the advertisement for Paloma Picasso's perfume Minotaure (see "Paloma Picasso's 'Minotaure'"), which shows a beautiful, muscular hunk, his head thrown back, in a provocative pose; the picture cuts off just below his waistline, with the bottle of perfume hiding the man's most prized possession. But who wants to purchase something with a name that recalls a bovine animal and the smell of a malodorous ox? However, if we consider the myth, we remember that the Minotaur has two halves. In the ad, only his "human" half is visible. Which man does not want his other half to be as potent as a bull?

Students next have a good time creating their own advertisements drawn from Ovid: the choice fish Neptuna; Daphne, the new tree fertilizer; an MLA caucus for Jargonauts; the radically enhanced fertility drug Salmacis 2; a psychedelic drug that moly-fies; the Protean Party for politicians of all shapes and colors; the gift shop Pandora; the law-firm Wotan & Loge; the running shoe Crane; or (my favorite) the journal *Pierides* for college professors. Some of the most popular movies of the past few years incorporate myth, such as *Pretty Woman* (1990), in which Julia Roberts plays the Pygmalion-like creation of Richard Gere's character. Ovid's hectic, fickle, fast-paced, continually evolving world—what Italo Calvino terms Ovid's "rapidità" (qtd. in McLaughlin 105)—is only too familiar to us: cell phones ringing, e-mails popping up, airplanes taking off, people multitasking. On the other hand, myth is indomitable, ineffable, invincible. Who or what are the myths of our time? Students adduce sports heroes (such as Magic Johnson, in itself a mythic name), Princess Diana (who died being *hunted* by paparazzi), Osama bin Laden (who, like Cronus's archrival Zeus or the Cyclops, lives in a cave or the underworld), 9/11 firefighters (who braved Herculean labors), Marilyn Monroe (the candle in the wind, whose wings of wax—or skirts of wax—melted when she flew too close to the sun), and of course the perpetually young Elvis (death becomes him, so to speak). We discuss what change(s) they have undergone. Are they fragile or stable myths? Have they been appropriated for political or social propaganda?

The final exam attempts to pull our readings together. Students write on the following topics:

1. The past, since it has already happened, maintains a profound influence on people's lives in the present. Discuss the past (history, time, memory, guilt, sin, heredity) in the *Theogony, Metamorphoses, Oresteia,* and *Mourning Becomes Electra.*
2. This semester we encountered a lot of animals: hideous monsters, sturdy horses, ugly vermin, feisty flies, adorable lion cubs. Look at these beasts in the *Metamorphoses, Oresteia,* and two other texts of your choice. Are they symbolic? Is there ever resolution or resistance?
3. What is myth? What can we know about myth? What does it contrast with in many of the books we read this semester? Why does a mythological version of history involve perpetual destruction and renewal? Is myth ever discarded in the end? If so, in favor of what?
4. We have seen various outcasts/aliens. Identify at least four such characters and explain how each reacts to his or her lonely lot. Negatively, positively, indifferently, hostilely? Do they fight for a common good? Are they ever reintegrated into a functional community at the end?
5. Compare the depiction of love and sex, marriage and adultery, chastity and fantasy in the *Symposium, Metamorphoses, Hippolytus* or *Phaedra,* and *Nibelungenlied.* What are the problems? Are they resolved in the end? What is the role of myth here?

I remain pleased with this approach, which combines classical and modern literature, ranges widely over cultures and histories (including neglected ones such as Native American and African), shows Ovid's continuing appeal, incorporates interdisciplinary activities that advance active learning, and, I daresay, offers a tentative blueprint for a course that students really enjoy.

NOTES

[1] If necessary, I lecture briefly on Carl Gustav Jung, whose ideas were clearly influenced by Ovid; see, for example, Morford and Lenardon 3–26.

[2] For *The Ring,* students can read the libretto or watch (parts of) the performances recorded in Bayreuth (Wagner, *Ring* [2005]) and in New York (Wagner, *Ring* [2002]); for a convenient plot synopsis narrated and sung by Anna Russell, consult her *(First) Farewell Concert.*

[3] We compare Genesis 1.26–27 (man created last) with 2.7 (Adam created) and 2.19 (animals created after Adam), and 1.27 (man and woman created equal) and 2.22 (Eve created from Adam; if not inferior, certainly secondary).

[4] We also know that during the composition of *The Ring*, Wagner read Aeschylus's *Oresteia* to immerse himself in the gravity of the subject matter; see Ewans. I usually ask a student to give a report on Wagner's engagement with Greek tragedy.

[5] "Das Rheingold" is part 1 of *The Ring*; the other parts are "Die Walküre," "Siegfried," and "Götterdämmerung."

[6] See, for example, several essays in Hardie, *Cambridge Companion to Ovid*; Christopher Martin, *Ovid in English*; Miles; Morford and Lenardon; Warner; Ziolkowski.

Reading and Teaching Ovid's *Amores* and *Ars amatoria* in a Conservative Christian Context

M. L. Stapleton

I taught for many years at a midsize state university in the American South. The courses I offered included sophomore surveys of pre-Enlightenment world literature in translation designed for the general student as well as classes devoted to early modern British authors for English majors and minors who planned to become public-school teachers. The institution is located in a community of fifteen thousand, which doubles in population with the students included, most of whom hail from the exurbs of the two major metropolitan areas three hours from campus in different directions. The town itself features eighteen Baptist churches along with an approximately equal number belonging to other Protestant denominations. It is also the seat of the only county within a one-hundred-mile radius in which one may legally buy alcoholic beverages. Those who read English translations or paraphrases of Ovid with me in these somewhat unlikely circumstances were not classics majors, nor did they enter my courses with an abiding interest in the ancient world or literary study. By and large, they were there merely to fulfill a requirement.

This environment poses special problems for the instructor who teaches material with erotic content, such as *Ars amatoria*. Some students of a conservative Christian bent, like the devout in other cultures, express puzzlement and outrage when class texts do not reflect or validate their perspectives. Many have no idea that the Bible has historical, artistic, and editorial traditions or that scriptural literalism is itself a type of theology. Most find medieval religious literary conventions incomprehensible and hypocritical: they are surprised that lyrics addressed to the Virgin and to the domina of *fin' amors* may draw mildly sexual imagery from the same wellspring; that some cathedral schools used *flores* (lines excerpted for memorization and study) from *Ars amatoria*, a few quite graphic (Hexter, *Ovid and Medieval Schooling* 72, 77) and that the first partial English translation of *Ars* was a book of precisely this type, *The flores of Ouide de arte amandi with theyr englysshe afore them* (1513); that Petrarch could be a practicing Christian who nonetheless admits in a poem that his passion for Laura outweighs his sense of the Passion during Good Friday Mass; and that Petrarch's fourteenth-century French contemporary, the author of the *Ovide moralisé*, allegorizes the brief account of Jupiter, Danaë, and Perseus in *Metamorphoses* as typological precursors of the Holy Ghost, the Blessed Virgin, and the baby Jesus. At the same time, to stereotype these students as intolerant is of no pedagogical value and therefore downright counterproductive. Actually, many Bible readers, as a result of their studies, have learned valuable inter- and intratextual hermeneutical skills unknown to their peers: the ability to read texts closely; a tolerance for simultaneous and contradictory interpretations within a literary work; a patience for allowing meanings to manifest themselves gradually to the individual; and the knowledge that communities of readers together negotiate and make meaning. They know, therefore, that group discussion of literary texts is necessary and exhilarating.

Other problems, certainly not peculiar to this student population, are gender related. No instructor would wish for his or her praise of Ovid's subtle poetics in *Ars* to be mistaken for an endorsement of the rogue masculine ethos of seduction or for the work to be misunderstood as entirely about physical love. The conscientious female professor would not wish to appear to be inviting inappropriate attention. An ethical male professor would want to use tact to avoid creating, however inadvertently, a classroom atmosphere that some female students might perceive as hostile to them.

Yet the greatest pedagogical problem may well lie with the nagging perceptions that even the most dedicated faculty members may find themselves sharing with their less conscientious peers. That is, students who take a course for compulsory distribution credit should not be condescended to because they are not convinced of the value of learning for learning's sake, an attitude that professorial negativity only exacerbates. Many of the young men and women I taught were products of test-oriented public school systems with rigidly unimaginative curricula that were just inches from violating church-state separation, whose governing boards, with the happy endorsement of the communities they served, firmly committed their budgets to football instead of academic programs or teacher salaries. Many had parents who had not encouraged them to become independent readers in their formative years.

Empathy, patience, and humility are therefore required for one professing Ovid in such an environment, and for other reasons besides those above. My students were often forced to learn in an academic milieu in which virtually everything has been predetermined—"radical determinacy," if you will, which stifles the critical thinking so crucial to independent learning. The only writing model that the members of a given class might have previously learned is the reductive tripartite-list thesis that fuels the mechanical five-paragraph essay. The sole reading model: learn the plot of the "story" (a term that can also mean "play" or "poem") and summarize it so that the act of meeting the page with the eyes can be verified. Students must sometimes also unlearn more pernicious educational vices, conceptual in nature: the idea that moral questions are simply solved and unambiguous—for example, that adultery is always wrong; that writers always have a hidden message that they alone know, which the instructor, as the sole authority in the classroom, should reveal; that, if the notion of radical indeterminacy one proposes as a counterweight to their previous experience is truly operational, the validity of everyone's opinion, including the instructor's, is arbitrary; and, most important, that a student should finish a given academic task as hastily as possible because it is at best boring, at worst worthless.

I concluded that my primary task was not to promulgate the study of Ovid per se to those who elected my courses or to prepare them for elite academic careers. My ethical perception of my job dictated that I use any means to encourage critical thinking and to teach analytical-argumentative writing skills. Assigning texts that were controversial and even offensive to some of my students was salutary for these purposes. My approach was broadly heuristical, learning by discovery: large-class discussion, group work, student presentations, and writing, writing, writing.

The Ovid of *Ars* (the *praeceptor Amoris* ["teacher of love"]) and of *Amores* (the *desultor Amoris* ["circus rider of love"]) provides a paradigm of writerly indeterminacy in any language, eminently useful as a teaching tool. How does one resolve the early statement of the *desultor* that he is not a circus rider of love (*Amores* 1.3.15) with his subsequent revelations (e.g., 2.4) that this is exactly what he aspires to be? He seems to follow much of the advice that the *praeceptor* offers both men and women in *Ars*, which proves disastrous for his attempt at a love life. Some of the material in this latter text contradicts itself or otherwise cancels itself out. How much efficacy, then, does the sage counsel of the learned doctor actually have? Many medieval writers, most notably Chaucer and Jean de Meun, speak reverently of *Ars* as a trustworthy, even infallible, guidebook to love, a position that few moderns would be likely to hold. Does this suggest that people from the distant past read differently? Did Ovid actually "mean" any of this? Is he the same person as the *praeceptor*? Although such questions may appear naive and jejune to those steeped in the lore of the critical site, they can be fresh and invigorating to the novice, especially when he or she is challenged to find textual evidence as support for arguments that must be logically structured to be credible for an academic audience.

That Ovid might not be writing autobiography or expressing his own deeply held opinions surprised my students, especially when I made available to them his famous disavowal of *Ars* from Tomis (*Tr.* 2.353–58): "I assure you, my character differs from my verse (my life is moral, my muse is gay), and most of my work, unreal and fictitious, has allowed itself more licence than its author has had. A book is not evidence of the writer's mind, but respectable entertainment; it will offer many things suited to charm the ear" (Ovid, Tristia [trans. Goold] 81). They asked why a writer should not be what he writes. Isn't this just special pleading, considering the circumstances? We discovered that they shared some critical perceptions with early commentators: "Of Ovidius Naso his banishmente, divers occasions be supposed, but the common opinion and the most likely is, that Augustus Caesar then Emperour, reading his bookes of the art of loue, misliked them so much that hee condemned Ovid to exile" (Churchyard, title pg. verso). This critic, like my students (and Augustus), identifies a writer with his work, especially that composed in the first person. What such a writer writes about might not have really happened but in some sense must be true. As a result, he bears responsibility for what he says and must accept the consequences of self-expression. Therefore, the named object of affection in the *Amores* must also be real, albeit pseudonymous, a concept that the commentator E. K. in Edmund Spenser's *The Shepheardes Calender* (1579) explains:

"Ovide shadoweth hys love under the name of Corynna, which of some is supposed to be Julia, the [e]mperor Augustus his daughter, and wyfe to Agryppa" (*Yale Edition* 34–35). Students resisted the concept of the persona, despite the evidence of the anguished statement of Ovid from exile. "Corinna" was a real person, and her admirer's love for her was true. My students suggested that there was no other reason to write about her.

Some moralized that a poet whose verses recommend adultery and celebrate sexual freedom deserves to endure the consequences, regardless of subsequent, convenient disavowals. We should judge writers on what they say and surmise what they think in consequence of their professed ownership of a text. Although I did not think it my duty or place to challenge my students' moral tenets, such a reductive argument struck me as worth answering, in one case with an essay assignment. If I, the instructor, ask you to choose a passage from *Ars amatoria* to analyze in a short paper, and then circulate the finished product to your peers, should they be able to make assumptions about your character and morality, based on the excerpt you select and your analysis of it? Would it be fair to say that your piece of the poem can be read as a kind of horoscope, revealing something secret and unknown (even to yourself) about you?

Naturally, I did not expect such discussions and writing prompts to produce a result from students that would magically convert them to a liberated and capacious position about life and literature. Indeed, I would have been disappointed if their textual interpretations had interacted with my criteria like the ingredients of a foolproof recipe, producing a pan of twenty-four perfectly symmetrical brownies. I hoped for some outrage. Some students applied themselves with enthusiasm, and others resisted. Some produced good essays, and some did not. Yet the act of thinking itself and the writing process were valuable, I hope, to them, because the assignment was immensely valuable for me as germane experience for future intellectual challenges. This constitutes the real usefulness of confronting, through writing and discussion, a complicated text such as *Ars*. The instructor may learn how to be a better teacher for his or her future students.

This Ovidian exercise in indeterminacy can also be useful in the English literature classroom. In an early modern survey course, it seems criminally negligent not to remind students that a syllabus of canonical texts constitutes only one interpretation of the period. They need to know about other authors besides Shakespeare; other forms of writing besides sonnets and tragedies; and other writers from different epochs and cultures whom the syllabus authors read, imitated, and emulated in the complicated nexus that we call intertextuality. To enable my students to explore these issues and broaden their perspectives as well as my own, I explain and illustrate one motif that Ovid repeats in three texts in different forms: the secret seduction of a married woman in front of her husband, which includes the humorous device of writing on the table in wine. The *praeceptor amoris* explains his strategies for executing this feat in *Ars amatoria* (1.571–72); the *desultor amoris* recounts his performance of it in

Amores (1.4 and 2.5.17); Helen chides Paris for the same behavior in *Heroides* (17.75–90).

The first exercise asks students to compare these repetitions and to note certain differences. Is Ovid's *praeceptor* serious about this as a romantic strategy? How successful, ultimately, is the *desultor* in his adulterous relationship with Corinna, especially in his use of this device? Why should Ovid also ventriloquize himself as a female speaker—Helen of Troy, no less—and then have her show mild disapproval of the same behavior? How do we square these conceptions of morality—not so different from those of Augustus, as legend has it—with our own? Again, I did not expect simple answers to such difficult questions. I just wanted my students to see that authors are not always consistent in their ideas and opinions and, more radically, that this does not often matter to them.

After we discovered the immense ambiguity beneath what seems to be a simple problem or question of influence, we turned to Spenser's very obvious, even showy manipulation of all three Ovidian uses of the material in the 1590 version of *The Faerie Queene* 3.9–10. His allusively named adulterers, Paridell and Hellenore, carry on in front of her husband, the despicably possessive and jealous Malbecco, who is conveniently (from his wife's perspective) blind in one eye. Spenser knows that adultery is wrong, too, yet does not entirely castigate Paridell as he seeks "to intimate / His inward griefe, by meanes to him well knowne" with "all that art he learned had of yore" (29), ostensibly the advice of the *praeceptor*:

> Now *Bacchus* fruit out of the silver plate
> He on the table dasht, as overthrowne,
> Or of the fruitfull liquor overflowne,
> And by the daunting bubbles did divine
> Or therein write to lett his love be showne;
> Which well she redd out of the learned line,
> A sacrament prophane in mistery of wine.
> (3.9.30)

The Protestantism of the students at my former institution tended to prevent their recognition of the significance of this final line, which was potentially blasphemous to a pious Roman Catholic. Yet they certainly noticed how Hellenore then very suggestively spills her own wine in her lap, not so much quenching her ardor as demonstrating the futility of cooling it off, "Shewing desire her inward flame to slake" (31), obviously aroused by Paridell's deployment of *Ars*. She later deserts her husband and, after her lover abandons her, takes up with a herd of satyrs who proceed to enjoy her with her full cooperation, which her cuckolded mate secretly witnesses as he pursues her (3.10.43–53). I then ask students to write an essay in which they consider two problems: How does Spenser transmute his profane material, and to what purpose? Why does he, a Christian author in other contexts, use it so approvingly? He shows an amusingly critical, even heartless, attitude toward Malbecco and does not seem to condemn Hellenore, as an observation by Helen C. Gilde implies: "there is nothing perverted about her sexuality—only about what causes her to express it in such ways" (235).

A seventeenth-century survey course could feature a less-specific conjunction of *Ars* with English literature. I found some success with the type of poetry classified under the carpe-diem tradition, which exemplifies the aforementioned rogue masculine ethos of seduction: John Donne's "The Flea" and "Elegy: On His Mistress Going to Bed"; Thomas Carew's "A Rapture"; Andrew Marvell's "To His Coy Mistress." These authors, thoroughly steeped in Ovid's erotic works, fashion speakers who adopt the amorality of the *praeceptor* and *desultor*. However, instead of facetiously addressing a group of ignorant pupils in the ways of love or recounting their experiences to a neutral third party as their classical predecessors do, the speakers directly address women with amorous condescension and supercilious logic to persuade them to feel privileged in submitting to the advances, as in *Ars amatoria* 3. An assignment can be crafted using virtually any section of *Ars* or any one of the poems in *Amores* as a prompt to explore how writers such as these emulate their predecessors.

Just as instructive is to ask one's students to go back a half century and read the soon-to-be canonical Isabella Whitney's "The admonition by the Auctor, to all yong Gentlewomen: And to al other Maids being in Loue":

> Some use the teares of Crocodiles,
>   contrary to their hart:
> And yf they cannot always weepe,
>   they wet their Cheekes by Art.
> Ovid, within his Arte of loue,
>   doth teach them this same knacke,
> To wet their ha[n]d, and touch their eies:
>   so oft as teares they lacke.
> Why have ye such deceit in store:
>   have you such crafty wile:
> Lesse craft the[n] this god knows wold soone
>   us simple soules begile.
> And wyll ye not leave of: but still
>   delude us in this wise:
> Sith it is so, we trust we shall,
>   take hede to fained lies.
>   (W[hitney], sig. A6)

This example was particularly piquant for many of the students in a course I once taught who were, like Whitney, young women reared in morally conservative households, themselves the objects of unsolicited masculine attention. This author had enough Latin to read *Ars* and identifies herself as a recipient of exactly the same kinds of blandishments that carpe-diem poets proffer. Some of my readers found Whitney's sarcasm amusing. Men who use *Ars* as a guidebook for the seduction of impressionable, love-starved maids deserve to be mocked, because their prey would be seduced just as easily with less effort. Some feminine voices, my students were pleased to discover, were raised against the monolithically masculine poetical beast.

Some of my students still resisted the idea that a text such as *Ars* is worthwhile or appropriate material precisely because it contains sexual content, even when presented with maximum professorial caution and empathy, and for one good reason that may be invisible to professors reared in different times and under different circumstances. Some students today have learned that sex is the most important thing in the world, an idea promulgated, somewhat contradictorily, by a strict or fundamentalist religious upbringing on the one hand and celebrity-driven popular culture on the other. They may feel pressured to participate in sexual congress to gain the love of their peers but take pledges of abstinence to ensure the love of their parents. To them, Ovid's intimations that the physical component of sexuality can be comical and supremely unimportant may sound subversive indeed. For one teaching his erotic poetry in this milieu, then, it is advisable to cull one of the *flores* that Renaissance schoolboys knew from *Metamorphoses* and to use it as an emblem: "ars adeo latet arte sua" 'so does his art conceal his art' (10.252).

Ovid and His Human Animals
Frank Palmeri

The last decade has seen the development of courses on human beings and other, nonhuman animals that pay particular attention to continuities or intersections between such animals and human beings and that explore the meaning of and attitude toward hybrid states, or creatures combining human and animal characteristics. Both Charles Darwin's writings and Ovid's *Metamorphoses* can serve as foundational texts in such a course. It is also useful to introduce early in the semester the argument of the anthropologist Mary Douglas in *Purity and Danger* that the attitude and behavior of human beings toward different species of animals depend on the extent to which the animals fit neatly into cultural categories; those animals that do not present category problems are often considered clean, suitable to eat, and unproblematic to use, whereas ambiguous or hybrid beings carry a dangerous charge that makes them objects of fear and revulsion, subject to taboos including prohibitions on their use or consumption, as well as objects of fascinated reverence and sites of great cultural significance.

Other works that can be studied in such a course include Michel de Montaigne's *Apology for Raymond Sebond*, Descartes's letters and other writings on animals as unfeeling machines, book 4 of Jonathan Swift's *Gulliver's Travels*, Julien Offray de La Mettrie's *Man a Machine*, H. G. Wells's *Island of Doctor Moreau*, and Peter Singer's *Animal Liberation*.[1] Still, however much the other readings and visual materials may be altered, it seems to me that, along with Darwin's *Origin of Species* and *Descent of Man*, Ovid's *Metamorphoses* remains essential for such a course because both Darwin and Ovid think through and represent continuities between human beings and other animals in ways that innovatively fall outside widely reigning taboos. In Darwin's account, these continuities result from developments that take place through immense stretches of geological time, thousands of generations and millions of years; in Ovid's narrative, the transformations that produce such commonalities occur in a matter of minutes or seconds.

The parts of *Metamorphoses* that are most important and relevant for such an approach include books 1–6 and 15. In particular, in the first books of the poem, the class may focus on the agents and the reasons for transformations from human to animal forms, the poet's descriptions of the moments or process of transition, and his implicit attitudes toward animals and human-animal mixings. The students soon perceive that a god or goddess is responsible for most of the transformations from human to other forms in the opening books of the poem and that transmutation often serves as a punishment of the human being, whether it is morally justified or not.

The story of Lycaon (book 1) presents perhaps the least complex and ambiguous kind of transformation, since an extensive continuity exists between the human king who violates fundamental laws by killing and eating a hostage (and planning to murder a guest) and the wolf, who is regarded as a bloody and frightening killer. Almost all of us feel that Lycaon's punitive transformation is justified and that there has been a transformation merely of external form because the king was already a hybrid, a wolf in human shape, before Jove visited him. After his transformation, the king has been placed where he deserves to be—outside the fold of human morality and civilization. The wolfish man has become more thoroughly the wolf his actions have already shown him to be. Such morally unproblematic transformations executed by a deity do not differ widely from the numerous aetiologic narratives in the poem that account for the origin and the nature of a species—usually a plant instead of an animal—often as a metonymy or a memorial for a human being after death. Such transformations occur in the examples of the Narcissus flower and the mulberry, whose purple fruit and roots commemorate the bloody death of Pyramus (book 4).

Such simple transformations of bodily form that reveal the animal (or plant) nature inside are exceptional, however. Although some discernible element of continuity of character, mind, or skill persists to link a human figure and an animal species, the narratives and the reasons for the transformations in Ovid usually possess greater complexity than the emblematic translation of a human being already possessing animal traits to an animal alone. Some transformations of human beings into animals occur for reasons that remain unexplained; for example, it is not clear why Cadmus and Harmonia, at the end of their lives, become snakes. Significantly, however, "even to this day / that pair do not flee men and don't attack. / Mild serpents, they remember who they were" (113; 4.602–03).

In addition to being a punishment, a metamorphosis can serve as a gift, a boon that may have been prayed for in a time of danger. Although those who receive such favors often are transformed into species of plants, not animals, the narratives of metamorphosis both as favor and as punishment revolve around sexual desire (in a god), resistance to his assault (by a young woman), and jealousy (of a goddess). It is important for students to note the two most striking examples of metamorphosis as boon, both of which occur in book 1: Daphne, fleeing Apollo, beseeches her father to change her form and deprive her of her beauty. In answer to her plea, she becomes a laurel tree, escaping Apollo, although the tree retains a beauty of its own (24; 1.544–52). Similarly, just as Pan catches up with the nymph Syrinx, she is transformed, as she has prayed to be, and becomes a handful of reeds (31; 1.700–06). Both young women are changed into immobile plants but retain their beauty, and that beauty is appropriated or sublimated for a cultural purpose: the laurel, now sacred to Apollo, will crown the victors in the Olympic games; and because of the mournful sound the reeds give out when Pan sighs over the loss of the nymph, he binds them together to make the first musical instrument. The transformation from a human to another form of being may mark, then, the establishment of a cultural institution or an accomplishment.

Among the most striking and memorable of the transformations in *Metamorphoses* are those that occur when Jove succeeds in forcing himself on an innocent young woman, who is then transformed as a punishment demanded or caused by Juno. Neither Io nor Callisto is guilty of any willed transgression, and each has already been a victim of Jove's assault; nevertheless, both are changed into animals by Juno's spiteful jealousy. Io does not entirely lose her beauty as a cow, although Callisto is changed into a more wild and dangerous animal, a bear. The pathos for both characters, however, depends on the retention by each of an unchanged mind (like the snakes who were once Cadmus and Harmonia; see, for example, the poet's statement concerning Callisto [56; 2.488]). Possessing a human mind in an animal form, these women have become hybrids: Io remains aware of her identity, but she is unable to identify herself to her father by speech. In the form of an animal, she is unable to make her feelings known through her expressions and tears and can only make her human side known by tracing a line and a circle in the sand with her hoof, thus writing her name in the sand (29; 1.647–50).

The pathos of possessing a human identity, mind, and emotions in an animal form reaches perhaps its sharpest form in Callisto, who loses her human son soon after giving birth to him and then lives more than fifteen years in the forest, her ursine body carrying a human mind and emotions. Her mute condition persists to the day when she sees a hunter in the forest who resembles her son:

> She froze, surprised; she seemed to recognize
> her son. And Arcas drew back, terrified:
> her fixed eyes stared and stared—he did not know
> just who that she-bear was; when she gave signs
> of drawing closer, Arcas poised to pierce
> her chest with his death-dealing shaft . . .
> (57; 2.500–05)

Callisto finds herself in a position comparable to Io's: living in an animal body, she wants to communicate her human identity and relation to a human being who is also her closest kin. The female bear recognizes her relation with the human, but the boy knows nothing of the human identity embodied in this bear. Only the direct and immediate intervention of Jove prevents the unwitting matricide that would follow from this nonrecognition. Jove's second transformation of Callisto celebrates the kinship of mother and son by changing them into Ursa Major and Minor. The stories of the transformations of Io and Callisto imply that other animals whom we may not recognize as having emotional capacities equivalent to ours in fact possess such capacities, such feelings. The inability of untransfigured animals to speak may not mean that such animals and human beings do not share a deeply comparable emotional and cognitive life.

The story of Actaeon reinforces this implication of continuity between human and nonhuman animals (book 3). The male Actaeon is defined as a hunter, who (like Callisto, another hunter) offends Diana, goddess of the hunt. When his outward form is changed into that of a stag, he too retains his mind, feelings, and identity. He remembers the names of all his dogs as they chase him, but, being unable to use a human voice to identify himself, he cannot prevent them from taking him down. (His position parallels that of Callisto facing the son who is about to hurl his javelin at her.) He learns quickly to feel the mortal panic and the sudden violent death that he inflicted on the stags that he hunted. Although his offense is not willed, there is something appropriate in the reversal: all hunted stags have never been human and possess no mixture of human traits yet have almost certainly felt the same emotions, the same panic that Actaeon does in their flight and in the moment of their death. Through such stories, Ovid is able to suggest that nonhuman animals experience emotions closely comparable in kind and intensity to those of human beings.

The story of Arachne (book 6) is important for offering an insight into the poet's sympathies not only with the young women assaulted by lustful gods but also with animals who may feel what they cannot say, at least to human beings. Arachne is emphatically not descended from gods, kings, or aristocrats, and yet by virtue of her talent and hard work, she becomes the most skilled weaver in the world. After the poet has described the pictures woven by Arachne and Minerva for their contest, he makes it clear that the mortal woman's is the superior in craft and art, as well as the more truthful; not even Minerva or Envy can find fault with her work. Still, Arachne is punished by the angry goddess for having the presumption to challenge a divinity, but she is allowed to live in altered form as a spider.

Because of her truthfulness, technical skill, and courage in telling many of the same stories that Ovid has told of the rapes of young women by deceitful gods, Arachne has been considered a figure for the author and a hero of the poem (Leach). In making a hero of a spider who retains the same superlative skill she possessed when she was human, and the same unbowed spirit, Ovid revises the attitude that human beings usually exhibit toward arachnids. His representation may seem to contradict Douglas's argument that anomalous creatures—which are suspended between air and land, which scuttle or slither instead of moving on all fours, or which combine human and animal traits—provoke abhorrence. But Douglas also points out that in many societies, an animal that is dangerous and forbidden is ritually killed once a year and eaten by its initiates so that they can appropriate its power—to make women fertile, to bring good fortune, or in some way to save the community (Douglas 206–08). Such an animal functions as a "benign monster" whose combination of opposed categories can bring blessings (208), and who even volunteers to be killed. Analogues to such animals include Oedipus, who experiences the extremes of human status, ranging from the highest as king to the lowest as violator of the incest taboo; he almost reaches the divine, but he is also like an animal. Oedipus has the power to bring a curse on the city of Thebes, but he can also lift that curse by leaving the city. Similarly, a spider or a serpent need not be considered only abhorrent or repulsive but may also be a culture hero: Arachne, for example, inhabits dark and unfrequented places as a poisonous insect but embodies the storytelling skills, honesty, and integrity of the poet.

Arachne is punished by Minerva for accurately assessing her own skill as greater than Minerva's, and she therefore shows insufficient respect for the divinity. The daughters of Minyas are punished for a similar offense: denying the divinity of Bacchus (book 4). Instead of joining in the festival in his honor, they stay inside, weaving and telling stories, and are consequently transformed into bats, who avoid the light and the company of other diurnal creatures, such as human beings (125; 4.391–415). Here, the element of continuity is strong, as the squeaking of the bats replaces the words that indicated their disrespect for Bacchus; however, the stories the bats tell are repeated by the poet, so they also become parts of Ovid's narrative. In fact, Ovid restores the voices of Minyas's daughters; their voices and the stories they tell in Ovid's own poem constitute a monument that memorializes them, just as the laurel and the pipes memorialize Daphne and Syrinx. Minyas's daughters direct their stories not to the gods but to one another, to other human beings, as does Ovid, and the stories of Ovid coincide with those of Minyas's daughters.

The stories told by Arachne and Minyas's daughters reveal the transgressive nature of storytelling as a distinctively human activity. Moreover, Ovid aligns himself with both Arachne and Minyas's daughters: all these narrative artists are weavers (Arachne and the daughters of Minyas weave textiles; the daughters and Ovid weave overlapping texts), and all of them exhibit a skeptical, irreverent attitude toward the sexually predatory, jealous, cruel, and vengeful divinities.[2] Ovid thus aligns himself with mortal women victimized for their beauty or their storytelling; he aligns himself as well with the low, scorned, and disparaged animals, such as spiders and bats, into which they are transformed.[3]

Finally, Pythagoras's long speech as reported to Numa by the old man of Croton in book 15 provides another important point of reference for a course on animals and their relationships to human beings. In this speech, Pythagoras makes one of the earliest and most well-developed arguments in the Western tradition for abstaining from the consumption of meat, maintaining among other considerations that eating dead animals makes the stomach a grave in which the processes of decomposition take place, corrupting and poisoning the system of the meat eater. This line of thought is later pursued by Plutarch in "The Eating of Flesh" and by Percy Bysshe Shelley in his "Vindication of Natural Diet." In addition, Pythagoras uses arguments drawn from the doctrine of metempsychosis to point out that the body of the cow one slaughters and eats may be inhabited by the soul of one's grandfather. Therefore, meat eating involves not only the possibility of cannibalism but also a lack of proper respect for beings who may be one's ancestors. Why should such risks of offending be taken, especially in pursuit of a kind of food that is not necessary and is probably harmful? Finally, Pythagoras's speech is significant for the way it summarizes Ovid's vision of the continuities among all beings, and indeed among all material forms. Human beings can change into bears and spiders or rocks and plants because all things change form; all is in constant flux. This is the burden of Pythagoras's paean to change, transformation, metamorphosis—a vision of the plasticity of forms, a vision that, although it concerns a much briefer lapse of time, reveals a remarkable convergence with Darwin's vision of the indefinite variations and transformations of the kinds of life over a span of thousands of generations.

Douglas points out that most members of most societies regard with horror and revulsion those animals whose characteristics combine features from different culturally constituted categories: animals that have wings but do not fly or that move on land but do not have feet. Through the long speech of Pythagoras and through his sympathetic depiction of beings with animal bodies but human minds and emotions, Ovid distances himself from those who consider such anomalous or hybrid animals frightening abominations. In this speech, and in the stories of Arachne, Minyas's daughters, Callisto, Io, and Actaeon, Ovid's attitude can be placed in alignment with that of Montaigne, La Mettrie, and Darwin: instead of condemning and seeking to extirpate the "bestial" elements in human beings, these thinkers acknowledge and even embrace not the identity but the continuities between the consciousness and emotions of human and nonhuman animals.[4] Moreover, the representation of animals in *Metamorphoses* demonstrates that Ovid does not subscribe to a hierarchy of being, with animals at the bottom, deities at the top, and human beings in between. Rather, the relations among exemplars of these three realms are mixed and horizontal, and the differences between them are neither fixed nor clear. Such continuities give rise to and follow from the unending transformation of which Ovid's Pythagoras speaks: it constitutes the ground out of which definite forms and individuals emerge for a time, before they return to their less-differentiated form, dissolving or adapting to become another individual or species.

NOTES

[1] I do not include in this list animal fables by Aesop or others because fables most often do not focus on the lives or treatment of animals but instead offer an allegory of human affairs. I argue, however, that a few self-critical fables by Aesop, Jean de La Fontaine, Jonathan Swift, and especially John Gay question this anthropocentric presumption (see Palmeri).

[2] I am thus in agreement with W. R. Johnson's argument that Ovid's *Metamorphoses* embodies a counterclassical sensibility or aesthetic that constitutes a political critique of Augustus's program to reinvigorate the classical artistic modes and traditional, patriarchal values. See Rosati for the relation between weaving and storytelling in Ovid.

[3] Inability to speak also functions as a distinctive marker of human-animal hybridity in other works that may well figure in a course on human beings and animals, for example Montaigne's *Apology for Raymond Sebond*, Wells's *Island of Doctor Moreau*, and Angela Carter's *Nights at the Circus* (in the last, individuals of two species, pigs and chimps, possess the ability to write, like Io).

[4] Darwin points to continuities between human beings and other animals not only in the *Origin* by implicitly regarding human beings as subject to and produced by the same process of natural selection that has shaped all other species of life on earth. He also traces continuities between the intelligence and emotional capacities of human beings and highly social animals in the *Descent of Man*. Elsewhere, he argues that human beings share almost all their significant facial expressions with other animals and that the meaning of such expressions remains the same in human beings and nonhuman animal species (*Expression*).

Teaching Medea to Freshmen:
Ovid, Thematic Criticism, and General Education

Ronald W. Harris

Ovid has much to offer students and instructors in general education courses. After all, Ovid's influence is pervasive in much of the literature, dance, music, and visual arts of the modern era—the kinds of things normally taught in general education courses. Yet even if students have some acquaintance with classical mythology, they typically know little about Ovid. Ovid's invisibility is a consequence not so much of neglect (though Roman studies often get short shrift in general education courses), as of departmental divisions of the literature curriculum. Introductory courses in literature and writing normally are taught in English departments, which organize their curriculum along national lines, British and American, with the rest lumped into "world literature." Even when students take an introductory course on the ancient world, they might get Homer, Plato, and the Greek tragedies but little in the way of Roman literature, save possibly some Vergil. Such curricular trends understate the importance of Rome in Western literature and work to isolate, in the minds of students, British and American literature from the larger field of Western literary history, where Ovid looms large.

Thematic criticism offers exciting ways to reincorporate Ovid into the curriculum in literature courses, as well as in writing courses, whether they are first-year composition or writing-across-the-curriculum courses at any level. Here, thematic criticism refers to the study of literature's subject matter, its *Stoff*, or content.[1] In this sense, thematic criticism becomes a vehicle for investigation into the processes and interrelations of literature. Moreover, while thematic criticism usually exposes students to a wide range of texts, the purpose of such study is not merely to catalog examples but to investigate the uses and abuses of literary representation. Nor is the purpose of such study necessarily one of literary history, though that is indeed possible. Rather, in the words of Susan Bassnett, comparative study of theme "opens up windows into differing moments of cultural history, exposing not only the overt details of what readers chose to read, but also the underlying assumptions encoded in each text" (137). The subject of study is no longer Ovid or *Metamorphoses*, for example, but a specific and particular theme or figure, of which Ovid provides just one or two examples. Although such a focus often seems counterintuitive to discipline-based specialists, it is quite in keeping with the curricular goals of most general education courses, which are intended to establish foundations for lifelong learning, civic participation, aesthetic appreciation, and engagement in the world. Many if not most literature, writing, and humanities courses aimed at first- and second-year students are already organized by theme or topic, around issues like identity, the self, the monstrous, the unthinkable, and so on, any one of which is amply represented in brief passages from *Metamorphoses*.

My thematic units often ask students to explore what Siegbert Prawer calls "the literary representation of *named personages* from mythology, legend, earlier literature, or history" (100). Study of a named personage offers an opportunity for diachronic study of a theme, helpful in a general education course, which typically covers several historical periods and geographic areas. Of course, Ovidian scholars are quite familiar with the kind of thematic criticism I describe. Several years ago, Stephen Hinds (who teaches classics at the University of Washington) described to me his Medea seminar, in which students read every available classical version of the Medea theme: those by Euripides, Apollonius of Rhodes, Ovid (selections from *Metamorphoses*, *Heroides*, and the fragments of his tragedy, *Medea*), Seneca, and Valerius Flaccus, among others. His students study the Medea theme in its classical context (including extensive readings in Greek and Latin), and each selection provides insight into classical literature and scholarship. I've since adapted Hinds's Medea seminar in a variety of ways, typically as a discrete unit on this named character, in courses including introductory literature and writing, classical mythology, Renaissance literature, and classical backgrounds. The named personage varies from class to class (sometimes Medea, other times Lucretia or Helen of Troy), depending on the specific needs of the course. And since most of my teaching has been in English departments, I've shifted the focus of study away from the ancient world to the modern world and its interactions with the classics. Almost all the readings are in good, modern translations, though I try to get the students to look at some Greek and Latin, in hopes that they'll become intrigued enough to sign up for a language class.

In a general education course that emphasizes student writing, I develop one or more three-to-four-week units on named personages. As an example, I describe one way of organizing a Medea theme–based unit, selected here for several reasons. First, the Medea theme is well documented. Recent books by Emma Griffiths and by James Clauss and Sarah Iles Johnston provide ample critical material for instructors who want to plan and carry out a unit on Medea. Second, the infanticide taboo is one likely to engage (and enrage) students, in productive ways. Certainly, studying this topic gives students a complex view of "the classics" and helps students move beyond the kinds of moralizing that too often substitute for public debate. Serious consideration of the infanticide taboo requires that students consider just why kinslaying might be possible, even logical, and what that says about such categories as the unspeakable, the unthinkable, and the monstrous. Thematic study of Medea also asks students to consider related issues, including what Gayle Rubin called "the traffic in women," which offer insight into contemporary debates over the nature and definition of cultural terms such as marriage and kinship. Ancient culture is different, but the terms remain contested.

My starting point is not a classical text but newspaper accounts of the "modern Medea," a mother who kills her young children. The accounts typically allude to the myth of Medea, who becomes reduced to her act of infanticide. The complex and complicated set of circumstances and motives that might induce a mother to kill her child or children become elided. In turn, the elision of context, with no attempt to comprehend or explain the behavior, produces something monstrous. In these sensationalized newspaper accounts, Medea becomes untethered from any historical or cultural contexts and instead becomes synonymous with a woman who has killed her children; that woman thereby "becomes Medea," to paraphrase Seneca the Younger.[2] With advanced students, I might supplement newspaper accounts with Roland Barthes's definition of myth as "stolen speech" (125) or Louis Althusser's discussion of ideology as a form of misrecognition (174), but in introductory courses it is often more useful to approach Medea through the infanticide taboo.

The taboo is so powerful that students initially have difficulty speaking about it rationally. As Barbara Johnson puts it, "When a woman speaks about the death of children in any sense other than that of pure loss, a powerful taboo is being violated" (198). Still, the mere discussion of infanticide in analytic terms goes far in breaking down that discursive barrier. Adrienne Rich argues that infanticide has historically been common in the West. Her claim should come as no surprise to classicists, who know that infanticide was not uncommon in Greece and Rome. Rich's controversial chapter from *Of Woman Born*, "Violence: The Heart of Maternal Darkness," explores the social implications and cultural logics of infanticide, by all means unsettling territory. Sometimes I assign Rich's chapter to advanced students, but for first-year students I usually summarize the main points of her argument to provide some starting points for students' own investigations. The taboo against infanticide then initiates exploration of the meaning and construction of culture, for which the Medea theme (not necessarily the same as the Medea myth) is the vehicle. By reading modern and ancient versions of the Medea motif, students gain greater understanding of the complexities of social life, culture, gender, and convention. Once students begin to consider Medea in a larger context, they moralize less, and they begin to analyze the figure in the light of specific texts.

Many students want to assume that representations of Medea are static throughout history and uncomplicated, and Ovid's *Metamorphoses* is an excellent place to show them that literary representations of named persons can vary widely even in the same text. As Carole Newlands argues, in *Metamorphoses* Ovid provides two traditions of Medea—as lover and as witch—without making any attempt to reconcile them ("Metamorphosis"). Hence, *Metamorphoses* itself helps students identify inconsistencies and contradictions and then try to make sense of them. Ovid asks us to notice and account for the complications too easily overlooked or ignored if the instructor presents "the classics" or "the classical tradition" in courses as stable monoliths against which we can limn modern art and culture. Once students begin to look for differences as well as similarities, they tend to enjoy identifying inconsistencies in characters or settings from one version to another. These identifications, in turn, become bases for further inquiry and reflection.

Choice of texts really depends on what an instructor wishes to emphasize.[3] The particular course and its specific pedagogical requirements dictate how many representations of Medea I include. I almost always teach the two major selections from *Metamorphoses*, to illustrate the complexity of Medea. Representations of Medea are many and varied. For example, if students read the fourth ode of Pindar's *Pythian Odes*, they find an image of Medea as an exotic, barbarous, Eastern other, in contrast to Jason's civilizing Hellenism. Euripides's *Medea* offers an image of Medea as a colonial subject who mimics her colonial oppressor's (Jason's) rhetoric, methods, and ways of thinking in order to destroy her enemies, "fully transcending—and eradicating—her own once-limited identity as woman, wife, mother, mortal" (Boedeker 148). Seneca's *Medea* attempts to rationalize her behavior in the face of an absolutely impossible position, the loss of family and identity, in which her slaying of her children and of Creusa offers Jason the opportunity to lose all, like Medea, and reside in a world alone and without hope. Although Ovid's *Heroides* is rarely taught in any but the most specialized undergraduate courses, its epistolary form is well suited for use in writing classes, and particularly useful for teaching students to read "against the grain" of a text (Bean 140–43; Elbow 147–90). The Medea of *Heroides*, letter 12, uses language as a weapon against Jason, her addressee, as she rationalizes her decision to kill the children, and Ovid's art seduces the reader into almost accepting Medea's arguments. Students become disconcerted when reminded that they are reading Medea's letter to Jason, a letter that furthers a particular agenda and resorts to self-serving arguments. When these selections are read together as a unit, students quickly see that literary representations of Medea offer ways to talk about human problems. Medea, as an outsider, becomes representative of those problems, and, through her character, students develop a broader vocabulary to describe their own world.

My use of Medea as a "named personage" is fairly narrow, because I want to illustrate as simply as possible the ideas that studying her might engage. In fact, it is easy enough to enlarge this unit on Medea to include representations of Dido; Cleopatra; Sethe (from Toni Morrison's *Beloved*); or even Sethe's historical analogue, Margaret Garner, whose story is amply documented by Steven Weisenberger. One could also study modern productions of the Medea plays by Euripides or Seneca, taking into account the lessons of Edith Hall and Fiona Macintosh, who analyze modern versions of the classics in modern productions of classical plays. These interpretations not only provide insight into the classical world but also help us understand the historical and historicized transmission of the classics and the transformation and translation of classical culture in the modern idiom.

Regardless of the course and the level of students taught, my thematic units provide ample opportunity for students to write. Even in literature courses, the reading and writing assignments are thoroughly integrated. For first-year students, a typical integrated writing assignment might include a sequence of formal and informal writings, beginning on the first day of the unit and concluding a few days after we finish the in-class portion of the unit. Although I evaluate some of their work, the focus of student writing is to provide students room to explore and investigate.[4] The assignment asks students to analyze representations of Medea in individual texts, compare several texts, and generalize about the function of the Medea theme in culture. The writing assignment begins with informal, ungraded, one-page response papers that students prepare for each class meeting. I always provide a prompt, which serves as a kind of reading guide. For example, as students read the Medea passages in *Metamorphoses* 7, the writing prompt asks them to consider why the youth potion works on Aeson and the old ram but not on Pelias. In response, students are obliged to consider not only the nature of magic but also Ovid's representation of Medea as a witch. As students prepare their one-page responses for each class, they also begin to draft their longer assignment, which asks them to expand and elaborate on those responses.

The formal writing assignments build on the informal writings and ask students to move from exploration toward tentative conclusions. After students have studied and written on several versions of the Medea theme, I ask them to compare several texts. I often ask them to write two comparisons, one of a classical and a modern text and one of a literary and a nonliterary text. The process of comparison provides historical and formal perspective on infanticide and offers students the opportunity to explore other issues they have identified in their study of Medea. Finally, I ask students to synthesize what they have learned by considering the original issue, infanticide, and the place of Medea in culture. Here, students usually offer complex analyses of the figure of Medea and of her position as a representation in modern culture. In particular, the moral complexity of Medea's story causes students to rethink simplistic newspaper references to her in relation to infanticide and to question their own initial responses to the newspaper accounts. Infanticide becomes enmeshed in complex social circumstances, still horrible but not necessarily monstrous. In attempting to understand, rather than to moralize, students expand their view of their world as a result of their encounter with Medea's particular kind of otherness.

The thematic course I've designed suggests strategies for teaching Ovid in the general education curriculum. Thematic criticism also can be used to reintegrate meaningful study of the classics into the introductory literature class, building on the exciting scholarly work being done in the classics. When students have the opportunity to read Ovid and other classical writers comparatively, they begin to see the classics as a fascinating site of lively debate, a far cry from popular representations of classical literature as the locus of abstract values, unclouded by the complexities of daily life, which ought to be admired and emulated. For students, these popular representations of the classics fall away quickly when they come face-to-face with what scholarship in the classics tells us about the ancient world. Students immediately discover that contradictions abound. As Page DuBois puts it, the Greeks "not only invented philosophy and democracy and the jury system, but also kept slaves and excluded their women from political life. Their culture was diverse and heterogeneous, and we need a fuller sense of all that it offers to contemporary readers." To counter overly simplistic representations of the classics, DuBois suggests that reading Sappho "might allow us to see the diverse, vivid, complicated, and contradictory beginnings of Western civilization" (*Trojan Horses* 22). A similar argument might be made for reading Ovid.

Ovid's poems, particularly his *Metamorphoses*, are messy. His stories about the Greeks and their gods do not hold out the promise of continuity, stability, and decorum but depict scenes of upheaval, unfairness, whim, and caprice. By reading Ovid, students begin to find that the ancients

> are fascinating because they are not like us, because, although we owe to them some of the institutions through which we organize our culture, they did it all quite differently, and therefore offer us differences from ourselves, other voices, latent traces of features of their culture filtered and edited out through centuries of interested inheritance.
> (DuBois, *Trojan Horses* 137)

Teaching Ovid comparatively requires an adjustment of attitude toward Ovid, toward one's students, and toward one's own role in the classroom. When I teach Ovid, I often find myself not so much an authority as a fellow traveler with students, as we inquire and explore Ovid's contradictions. These contradictions (in texts, between texts, between ancient and modern) create a fragmented view of the world, which in turn encourages students to adopt a more complex view of the classics. Initially, it may seem counterintuitive to present a fragmentary view in a general education course, where the goal is to solidify a student's understanding of the world. In practice, general education courses often survey a body of knowledge, hitting some high points while eliding gaps and fissures in the field. Ovid's artistry reveals the mechanics of literary meaning, calling our attention to contradictions not only in his texts but also in the world, encouraging us to confront our necessarily fragmentary knowledge of the world. When they work with these fragments, students continue along their path of learning, and, although Ovid refuses to play the part of Dante's Vergil, he prompts the kinds of questions that will propel us forward.

NOTES

[1] In the broadest sense, my approach is comparative, but I want to maintain focus on the concept of thematics (also called thematology, or *Stoffgeschichte*), one of the traditional modes of comparative literature. Other, sometimes overlapping, concepts for comparison (translation, genre, period or movement, influence, reception, interarts comparison) also offer promising avenues for the study of Ovid. Comparative literature handbooks routinely discuss the concepts, along with their applications and limitations. See, for example, recent handbooks by Bassnett; Prawer; and Weisstein.

[2] *Medea*, line 910: "Medea nunc sum" 'Now I am Medea.' Cf. line 171: "Medea . . . fiam" 'Medea I shall become.'

[3] Medea figures in a number of interrelated episodes. Griffith surveys the field; Graf (22) identifies five primary episodes that compose the tradition; and Hinds, "Medea in Ovid," investigates Medea's identity as an "intertextual heroine," locating the thematic center in *Heroides*, letter 12. Modern examples of the Medea figure (as well as other "named personages") are too numerous to list. Exhaustive bibliographies are provided by Jane Reid; Jeanetta Boswell; Elisabeth Frenzel; and Donald Poduska. Practically any college-level mythology textbook cites the more familiar texts and reproduces visual images.

[4] As a rule, my integrated writing assignments do not culminate in traditional student essays, though traditional essays are possible, if that's the aim of the course. Rather, I design the sequence of formal and informal writing assignments to help students learn about literature. While it is true that the assignment I describe does not require students to sustain a lengthy argument, a separate skill, it does require a sustained engagement with the texts and concepts we study in class, which is my goal in a literature course.

POLITICAL OVID

Always Hopeless, Never Serious: Wit and Wordplay in Ovid's *Amores*

R. W. Hanning

Ovid is one of the great, and foundational, comic poets of European tradition. Like many of today's comic performers, such as stand-up comedians and late-night talk-show hosts, Ovid found inspiration for his wit in the complexities and frustrations of human relationships, as well as in the inevitable gaps between institutional ideals and ideologies, on the one hand, and the foibles, follies, and hypocrisies of social and political reality, on the other. Above all, in his comic writings—and in many parts of his less overtly or completely comic poems, such as *Heroides* and *Metamorphoses*—Ovid communicates his amusement at (and often, I believe, his sympathy for) the disappointment and impotence (literal and metaphoric) that result from hopes dashed, aspirations thwarted, and self-esteem mocked in our encounters with life.

In this essay I examine some examples of Ovid's comic art as instantiated in *Amores*, a three-book collection of fifty poems composed in elegiac couplets. At first glance, the main (though not exclusive) subject of *Amores*—and object of its comic vision—appears to be its narrator's experience of erotic desire and varied, often discouraging dealings with the woman or women who are the object or objects of that desire. (The special object of his affections is the *puella* Corinna, but she is far from his only *amor*; see *Amores* 2.4, 2.8, 2.10.) As Barbara Weiden Boyd (*Ovid's Literary Loves*) has convincingly argued, however, the narrator as lover is only one of *Amores*'s two main subjects, the other being the narrator as poet, applying his love affair with language and poetic traditions to the kaleidoscopic phenomenon of love. Also worthy of note is the collection's intermittent, multifaceted enagement with Augustus, since 31 BCE the undisputed, though not fully declared, ruler of Rome and her empire.

Like any good poet (or comic writer), Ovid was intoxicated by the possibilities offered by language as the medium of his idiosyncratic vision. Above all, language invites wordplay: double entendres, parodies of established texts and discourses, and the exploitation of rhetorical tropes and figures such as alliteration, irony, and metaphor. The text of *Amores* crackles and coruscates with all these verbal tricks, many immediately obvious, others identifiable with such excellent aids as J. N. Adams's helpful handbook on Latin sexual vocabulary and J. C. McKeown's scholarly commentary on *Amores*.

Amores is rife with sexual innuendo and metaphor. In the sixth elegy of book 1, an example of the *paraclausithyron* (a complaint by the lover at the portals of his *puella*'s house), the lover's pleas that the door be opened and his threats to break it down gain comic force from the door's status as a metonymic displacement of the opening that the lover really desires. When the narrator asks the *ianitor* to open the door just enough for him to slip in sideways, since "my long [bondage to] love has slimmed me down to do things like this, / making my *membra* suitable by taking away the flab" ("longus amor tales corpus tenuavit in usus / aptaque subducto pondere membra dedit" [1.6.5–6]), the humor of his request arises from both the bizarre image of skewed (lateral?) sexual intercourse ("membra" can refer generally to the body or specifically to the penis) and the literalization of the lyric commonplace that unrequited love makes a suitor waste away.[1]

Amores 1.9 draws an extended parallel between the lover's life and that of a soldier—a comic reversal of the conventional (and poetic) wisdom that opposes the former's "otium" 'leisure, sloth' to the latter's "negotium" 'responsible, public action'—in which doors guarded, besieged, and broken inevitably figure (1.9.7–8, 19–20), along with these deliciously innuendo-laden lines (1.9.25–30):

> Nempe maritorum somnis utuntur amantes,
>   et sua sopitis hostibus arma movent.
> custodum transire manus vigilumque catervas
>   militis et miseri semper amantis opus.
> Mars dubius nec certa Venus; victique resurgunt,
>   quoque neges umquam posse iacere, cadunt.

> Obviously, lovers take advantage of sleeping husbands brandishing their
>   weapons while the enemy lies senseless.
> It's always the task of the soldier and the unlucky lover
>   to get past a band of guards or troop of sentinels.
> There's no sure thing with either Mars or Venus; the defeated rise again,
>   and things you deny could ever collapse do indeed fall down.

This more or less literal translation occludes the fact that "arma" is a widely attested euphemism for the penis and that the "opus" of the lover can refer to the sex act, achieved in this case by getting around the "manus," or legal (and thus sexual) authority of the husband over his wife (Adams 21, 57, 157). The bedroom resonance of the imagery of rising again and unexpectedly falling needs no further clarification.

Many moments in *Amores* integrate sexual wordplay into the language of paradox and hyperbolic melodrama, as in this passage from 2.9B,[2] where the narrator commands Cupid to conquer him anew (2.9B.35–38):

> Fige, puer! positis nudus tibi praebeor armis;
>   hic tibi sunt vires, hac tua dextra facit;
> huc tamquam iussae veniunt iam sponte sagittae—
>   vix illis prae me nota pharetra sua est!
>
> Transfix me, boy! I stand here, exposed and naked with my weapons thrown down;
>   here's a target for you, a place for your good right hand to strike;
> here come your arrows into my heart, of their own accord but as if taking orders—
>   thanks to me, they hardly know their own quiver!

"Armis," "vires," and "sagittae" all have phallic connotations, but the passage's comic force also derives from the "hic . . . hac . . . huc" progression, the self-lacerating invitation of "Fige, puer!," and the delightful conceit that the arrows are kept so busy striking him that, like soldiers constantly in foreign wars, they can hardly remember their homes.

One area within *Amores* where Ovid presumably knew that he was playing for high stakes is the poem's presentation of situations that refer, or appear to refer, to the person and policies of Augustus. For example, 1.2 dramatizes the narrator's realization that he is in love, and thus in bondage to Cupid, who rides in an obviously Roman triumph, accompanied by his victims and his followers, while the crowd acclaims him (1.2.23–36). The narrator's description concludes with the observation, "with such warriors as these [including *Error* and *Furor*], you conquer both men and gods; / if you lacked this support, you'd be deprived [of your power]" ("his tu militibus superas hominesque deosque; / haec tibi si demas commoda, nudus eris" [1.2.37–38]). Beyond the obvious joke that Cupid is already, in Roman iconography, literally "nudus," are we to read these lines as an indirect suggestion that Augustus is a bullying conqueror who would be exposed ("nudus") as considerably less than the great princeps were it not for the army whose loyalty he has so assiduously cultivated, in good part by offering them "commoda" ("fringe benefits, retirement bonuses") after the completion of their military service? (Ovid jokes about these "commoda" in *Ars amatoria* 1.131–32.) The implication remains, even though the poem ends with the narrator asking Cupid not to tyrannize over him since he has surrendered, urging the god, "follow the example of your kinsman Caesar's [i.e., Augustus's] successful campaigns— / he protects his defeated enemies with the very hand that beat them" ("adspice cognati felicia Caesaris arma— / qua vicit, victos protegit ille manu" [1.2.51–52]).

On a different level, in 1.8, an old bawd called Dipsas, in the course of urging the narrator's *puella* to take rich suitors, not poor poets, as lovers, hails the goddess of love as Rome's new patron deity: "now Mars keeps men busy in foreign wars, / but Venus reigns in the city of her Aeneas" ("nunc Mars externis animos exercet in armis, / at Venus Aeneae regnat in urbe sui" [1.8.41–42]). The characterization of Rome as a city governed not by Mars—in other words, by the martial, muscular Republican virtues now revived under Augustus—but by Venus (the word *Venus* can refer to love in general, but also to sexual intercourse) hardly accords with the intent of the Augustan *Lex Julia de adulteriis coercendis* of 18 BCE, which restricted men (at least those of the upper classes) to sex outside marriage only with prostitutes and "lenae" 'bawds' and threatened adulterous women of all other groups with draconian penalties (McGinn; Gibson 25–37).

More directly (albeit comically) abusive of Augustan moral legislation are *Amores* 2.19 and 3.4: in the first, the poet angrily instructs the *vir* of his *puella* to place her under heavier guard—if not in his own interest, then in that of the lover, so that the lover will want her more; the poet's characterization of the insufficiently protective husband as, in effect, a pander ("quid mihi . . . cum lenone marito" [2.19.57]) constitutes a direct, jokey allusion to the *Lex Julia*, according to which a husband was liable to the accusation of pandering if he did not divorce his adulterous wife and refer her case to a special morals court. Then, in 3.4, the Ovidian surrogate reverses field, attempting to persuade a "durus vir" ("strict husband") that there's no point in his guarding his *puella* too closely, since such restrictions are unnecessary for a good woman, unavailing for a faithless one. Did Augustus read these elegies? Was he amused, or shocked? Could they have played any role in Ovid's eventual relegation to a Black Sea port? At this distance, we cannot know; we can only chuckle.

Can one speak of large themes that lend overall coherence to *Amores*? One such, I believe, involves the presentation of the narrator as a poet prone to the dictates of erotic desire who appears rarely to be in control of his life as either poet or lover. This quandary, treated comically in many of the collection's elegies, recalls an old joke purporting to capture the essential difference between Germany's earnest efficiency and Austria's cheerful disorganization: in Berlin (as, e.g., in *Aeneid*), the dictum goes, things are always serious but never hopeless, while in Vienna (or, *mutatis mutandis*, in *Amores*) things are always hopeless but never serious.

This comic hopelessness manifests itself brilliantly in the collection's opening poem, which boldly announces an epic subject of potentially Vergilian scope (its opening word, "arma," echoing that of the *Aeneid*), observing the traditional

Roman decorum of meter and genre: "Arms and violent wars I was ready to relate in weighty verses, with form fitted to contents" ("Arma gravi numero violentaque bella parabam / edere, materia conveniente modis" [1.1–2]). But both the content and form suffer almost immediate deflation; the third verse, confirming the poet's commitment to appropriate meter ("par erat inferior versus"), is rudely interrupted, it would seem, by a god's intervention: "Cupid is said to have laughed and stealthily stolen one foot" ("risisse Cupido / dicitur atque unum surripuisse pedem" [1.1.3–4])—from the "inferior versus," the second line.

There are actually three jokes here at the poet's expense: merely out of a malicious sense of fun ("risisse"), a god can override his professed poetic goal; the poet isn't in sufficient control of his situation to know exactly what happened to him ("risisse Cupido / dicitur"); and, in any case, his intention to compose an epic in its proper meter subverts itself even before Cupid can: the "inferior versus" proclaiming itself in possession of "materia conveniente modis," far from being "par," is already a pentameter!

The outraged poet charges Cupid with meddling where he has no right to and in effect violating divine as well as poetic decorum: "we're the Muses' followers, not yours" ("Pieridum vates, non tua turba sumus" [1.1.6]), he contends; what would happen to the world if Venus and Minerva, Ceres and Diana, or Apollo and Mars exchanged the attributes that define their respective powers and spheres of influence? Anger quickly gives way to apprehension: is Cupid making a massive power grab, seeking to expand his already great empire—and have Apollo and the poets Apollo patronizes lost their autonomy (1.1.15–16)? These lines contain both humor at the expense of the self-proclaimed exalted status of poets ("vates"), here referred to as the "Muses' mob" ("turba"), and, I would argue, an oblique comment on the consequences of Augustus's seizure of absolute power, however disguised as the renovation of the Roman Republic, which in fact compromised the autonomy and prerogatives of the Senate and all other traditional stakeholders in the power of the state.

The poet's complaint that, thanks to Cupidian intervention, the strong epic beginning of his verse has been attenuated ("cum bene surrexit versu nova pagina primo, / attenuat nervos proximus ille meos" [1.1.17–18]) alludes ironically to the traditional charge of effeminacy leveled against love poets and their verse by partisans of a more austere, heroic poetic art: the elegiac couplet, however erect ("surrexit") in its first line, flops in its second. ("Nervos" is yet another popular synonym for the penis [Adams 38].) Then, by confessing that he has no appropriate subject matter (1.1.19)—in other words, no object of sexual desire, masculine or feminine (20), about whom he might write in elegiac couplets—the poet creates a fateful opening for Cupid: wilfully interpreting a complaint over his indecorous interference as a plea for his erotic assistance, the god chooses an arrow from his quiver and impales the poet with it, in two lines of Ovidian word painting that brilliantly capture the effort involved in a small boy's stretching taut a big bow and finally letting fly its shaft: "lunavitque genu sinuosum fortiter arcum / 'quod' que 'canas, vates, accipe' dixit 'opus!'" The slow, sinuous imagery of the hexameter ("lunavit . . . sinuosum" [1.1.23–24]) gives way in the pentameter to a staccato rhythm that reproduces with each successive accent (*cànas, vàtes, àccipe, dìxit*) the backward tug of the bowstring; on *"òpus"* (slang for sexual intercourse), the arrow is let fly and all but simultaneously thuds into the heart of its target.[3] What's left for the stricken poet is admission of his painful defeat—"wretched me! I'm burning up, and Love now reigns in my [hitherto] empty heart" ("me miserum! . . . / uror, et in vacuo pectore regnat Amor" [1.1.25–26])—a farewell to the now-foresaken epic subject and meter (28), and an instruction to his Muse henceforth to compose in the eleven metrical feet of the elegiac couplet (30).

Ingeniously adapting the elegiac theme of the *recusatio* (the poet's refusal to abandon elegy for more serious subjects), Ovid here invents a dystopian form of poetic inspiration—the hopelessness of trying to compose on a noble, elevated theme when the god of love has other plans for you. Not being satisfied to parody in this way the notion that love poetry results from passion instead of calculation (or, to use the poet's own terms from *Remedia amoris* [*Remedies for Love*] 10, "impetus" instead of "ratio"), Ovid also directs his wit at the conventional hierarchy of genres, in effect inverting the process whereby the choice of topic dictates the choice of meter: only after having stolen a poetic foot from the bard's would-be epic verse does Cupid justify (or, in poetic terms, make decorous) this sneaky theft by invading and occupying his victim's hitherto loveless heart ("vacuum pectus"), like some ambitious Roman general.

The comic spectacle of lost control in *Amores* 1.1 reappears in the first elegy of book 2, which restates the poet's inability to devote himself to more-serious subject matter. This time, however, the vagaries, instead of the onset, of love upset his plans, and elegy's power, not Cupid's, is on display. The poem begins boastfully, the poet offering ironic tribute to his own fame as an elegist in a marvelously epigrammatic pentameter: "Ille ego nequitiae Naso poeta meae" 'I'm that [very] Ovid [you've heard about], the poet of my own worthlessness/idleness/wantonness' (2.1.2)—the noun "nequitia" can carry all these meanings, thus conveying, as it mocks, the connection of the elegy with lack of public value, with *otium*, and with sexual indulgence.

Once he undertook a mythical epic, however—continues Ovid—narrating the war of the earthly giants against the Olympian gods, and "just as I was about to have Jupiter hurl defensive thunderbolts at his enemies, *clausit amica fores*" ([2.1.15–17]). Through the brilliant comic stroke of these last three wholly unexpected, sexually suggestive words—"my girlfriend slammed the door [on me]"—the poem signals a sudden crisis in the poet's personal situation and, simultaneously, a drastic but unavoidable alteration of his poetic agenda, described with comic urgency and superlative Ovidian wit: "I put aside the lightning and Jupiter with it; Jupiter himself fell [sc., like a lightning bolt] out of my thoughts. / Forgive me, Jupiter; your weapons were of no help to me; / that closed door was a greater thunderbolt than [any of] yours" 'ego cum Iove fulmen omisi; / excidit ingenio Iuppiter ipse meo. / Iuppiter, ìgnoscas! nil me tua tela iuvabant; / clausa tuo maius ianua fulmen habet' (17–20). Elegy alone, not epic, will soften the hard-hearted door (2.1.22); hence there's nothing for it but to say, "farewell, famous names of heroes; your influence is not what I need now" ("heroum clara valete / nomina; non apta est gratia vestra mihi" [2.1.35–36]). Lurking behind this playful statement of *epos interruptum* and the hopelessness of resisting love's generic imperative there may be a more serious Ovidian meditation on the relative importance of personal and sociohistorical values (represented, respectively, by elegiac and epic-mythological poetry) in the life of the polity: there comes a time, *Amores* 2.1 hints, when individual needs and desires cannot (or can no longer) be subordinated to the demands or edicts of the state, the *res publica*. Seen in this light, the poem could be construed as expressing muted resistance to Roman imperialism or Augustan attempts to regulate the sexual and marital lives of at least the elite classes.

As with issues of poetic vocation, so in representations of love and its crises Ovid often exploits hopelessness for comic effect in *Amores*. In 1.4, the poet reports his anguish on the occasion of attending a banquet at which not only his *amica* but her *vir* will be present, rendering impossible open affection between the lovers. The body of the poem recounts the strategies and pleas, addressed to the beloved, by which the poet-lover attempts to deny, or at least mitigate, the obvious hopelessness of his situation; the ingenuity and complexity of these efforts generate pathetic comedy because of their obviously foreordained futility, a futility already acknowledged in his first suggestion: "come to the banquet before your *vir*" ("ante veni, quam vir"), he proposes, only to add, "I don't see what we can accomplish if you do come first, but come anyway" ("nec quid, si veneris ante, / possit agi video; sed tamen ante veni" [1.4.13–14]).

A succeeding litany of coded signs for the lovers to exchange—"excipe furtivas et refer ipsa notas" (1.4.18)—including raised eyebrows, words written in wine on the banquet table, cheeks touched, rings twisted on fingers, and earlobes tugged, grows funnier as it exfoliates (1.4.19–26). Even the poet's dire threat to make a scene if his *amica* submits to her *vir*'s hateful embrace—"if you grant him kisses, I'll reveal myself as your lover and insist, 'those kisses are mine!'" ("oscula si dederis, fiam manifestus amator / et dicam 'mea sunt,'" [1.4.39–40])—quickly subsides into mute acquiescence and dread (1.4.41–42). The trouble is, he admits, he has in his day done so many things "concealed by garments" that he is worried—"I'm tortured by fear of the example I've set [in lovemaking]" ("exemplique metu torqueor ipse mei" [1.4.46])—a line that gains comic force by postponing to its very end the source of the tormenting example—himself!

Powerlessly contemplating the sexual liberties the *vir* will take with the *amica* behind closed doors that night, the poet begs his beloved to yield only grudgingly and without pleasure; and then, with an unexpected turn, a final couplet offers profound, albeit humorous, insight into how we deal with the hopelessness of thwarted, jealous desire: "but nonetheless, whatever may happen tonight, / tomorrow deny to me in a steady voice that you gave in [to him]" 'sed quaecumque tamen noctem fortuna sequetur, / cras mihi constanti voce dedisse nega!' (1.4.69–70). In other words, I can't deal with the truth; just tell me what I want to hear.

The narrator's preference for lies over truth as a hedge against unhappiness (cf. 2.13.6, "est mihi pro facto saepe, quod esse potest" 'I often substitute what might be for what is'), and the twists and turns of outlook that dramatize his attempts to escape hopelessness appear again in 2.11, where the narrator, seeking to prevent Corinna from undertaking a sea voyage, advises her to listen to and be persuaded by the tall tales people love to tell about the sea's dangers, since no one gets hurt by believing such lies (21–22). Anticipating, in yet another implicit admission of hopelessness, that his words will fall on deaf ears or, as he puts it, will be carried away on the sea winds (33), he falls back on imagining instead their blissful reunion (45–46) and a seaside banquet, over which Corinna will regale him with her own tall tales of hardships endured and steadfast devotion to him. To all of which, with a lover's credulity, he will respond as earlier he wished her to: "omnia pro veris credam, sint ficta licebit— / cur ego non votis blandiar ipse meis?" (53–54); that is, why bother with the truth, when fictions are so much more satisfying, especially in love?[4]

Finally, in 3.4, as already noted, the narrator, in defiance of Augustan moral legislation, seeks to persuade his *puella*'s *vir* not to guard her too closely. But his arguments—difficulty of access only makes the object of desire all the more attractive, harsh constraint will only increase a woman's desire to defeat it—give way at line 37 to a very different strain: the overly protective husband, he claims, is merely "rusticus," a country bumpkin who doesn't understand the mores of Rome: if you'll just lift your guard on your lady ("indulge dominae"), the lover insists, good things will happen to you: "thus you'll always have a place at the young people's banquets and notice many [gifts] around the house that you never gave (your *puella*)" 'sic poteris iuvenum convivia semper inire / et, quae non dederis, multa videre domi' (3.4.47–48). This concluding couplet seems to allude to the situations depicted, respectively, in 1.4 (flirting at the banquet) and 1.10 (accepting presents from rich men in return for sexual favors), which, like this one and many others, stand out as beacons shedding abundant light on the always hopeless, never serious (at least not on the surface) world of *Amores*.

NOTES

[1] All translations are my own.

[2] A separate poem from 2.9A, as Boyd has demonstrated ("*Amores*").

[3] See McKeown: "The effect of delaying this emphatic word [*opus*] here is to suggest the tension as Cupid draws back the bowstring and then shoots at, or hits, Ovid" (2: 26).

[4] See McKeown's pointed reading of 2.11.54: "Why should I not indulge the fond fancy that what I long for is true, even if it is not?" (3: 260).

Transforming Exile: Teaching Ovid in Tomis

Matthew McGowan

Exile transformed Ovid from a popular love poet, playwright, and epicist to a banned poet of lament, and the experience of banishment he represents in *Tristia*, *Ibis*, and *Epistulae ex Ponto* has been crucial to shaping his legacy in the tradition.[1] In recent years, Ovid's exile has come to dominate that legacy and continues to inspire essays, novels, and poems from contemporary writers of the highest order. In the current boom, one could readily assemble enough material to build an entire course on the literary reception of the poet's exile. In the present essay, however, I attempt to synthesize my own experience teaching an undergraduate survey, Exile Literature from Antiquity to the Present, and a course titled The Classical Tradition in Contemporary Fiction and Film. In both cases, I also used selections from *Metamorphoses*, although my focus here is on the reception of Ovid's exile among the contemporary poets Seamus Heaney and Derek Mahon, from Northern Ireland; Derek Walcott, from the island of Saint Lucia; and the Canadian Anne Carson. I also touch briefly on Osip Mandelstam's poem "Tristia," which sets the stage for much of the twentieth century's reception of Ovid's exile. My focus throughout is thematic: exile is understood here as a geographic and an existential condition that Ovid himself shapes and that modern poets continue to transform in the interest of their own art. I aim to show that such transformation is important both for what it tells us about the concerns of contemporary poets and for insights into Ovid's exile poetry itself.

To introduce Ovid's exile poetry, I use *Tristia*, books 1 and 2, and book 4, poem 10 (Ovid's autobiography in verse), because *Tristia* is the most popular work in the exilic tradition and because the repetitive nature of the poetry in *Tristia* invites a kind of interpretive synecdoche: a select part can be applied to understanding the whole. Over the course of *Tristia*, book 1, Ovid uses the details of his journey to construct an exilic persona that holds for the rest of the collection. In the first poem, for example, the book itself is addressed in the opening verses: "Little book . . . you're off to the City / without me, going where your only begetter is banned!" (P. Green, *Ovid: The Poems*). The physical book makes the poet's presence felt at Rome—an unexpected presence in absence—which Ovid emphasizes throughout the collection by imagining these poems as fictional letters. The very form of the letter reveals the paradox of his punishment: the emperor Augustus requires Ovid's absence from the city by law, even as the poet re-creates his own presence there through his poetry (P. Miller 224). In the second poem of book 1, Ovid bemoans his trials at sea, a theme revisited three more times in this book (poems 4, 10, 11), in which he develops the oft-repeated claim about the deterioration of his poetic power in exile.[2] He also writes a farewell to the city of Rome and his family (poem 3) and sends verse epistles to his most frequent correspondents: true friends (poems 5, 7), a false friend whom he verbally abuses (8), and his wife (6). Book 1 contains in miniature the most prevalent themes of the exile poetry: presence in absence, the physical hardship and mental anguish of (going into) exile, and the appeal to his wife and friends to sue on his behalf at the Augustan court for a reprieve or at least for a transfer to a more agreeable place of exile.

Ovid's place of exile was Tomis, an ancient Greek port town on the western coast of the Black Sea, in what is now Constanţa, Romania. The poet's description of it in *Tristia*, book 2, is typical of the exile poetry in general: "Here / is the ultimate torture for me, exposed amid foes, . . . beyond here lies nothing but chillness, hostility, frozen / waves of an ice-hard sea" (P. Green, *Ovid: The Poems*; *Tr.* 2.186–87, 195–96). The true antagonist of *Tristia*, book 2, however, is neither the climate nor the barbarians but the emperor himself, before whom Ovid mounts an elaborate defense of his poetry in the form of a lengthy personal letter. Of course, the letter's publication explodes the fallacy of intimacy it attempts to create, and the reading public is privy to the disclosure here that Augustus decreed Ovid should be "relegated" on two charges: a poem and a mistake ("duo crimina, carmen et error" [2.207]). The poem was most likely *The Art of Love* (*Ars amatoria*), a didactic experiment on the art of courtship and amatory intrigue, which seems strangely to have aroused the ire of the emperor some six years after its completion in 2 CE.[3] Ovid's refusal to reveal his mistake has given rise to much scholarly (and nonscholarly) speculation: some posit that it was political, others that it involved some sexual indiscretion, and still others that the exile itself was a poetic fiction.[4]

Students enjoy this kind of literary detective work and find themselves drawn in by the "mystery of Ovid's exile." More important, they have a chance to observe in *Tristia*, book 2, a key feature of Ovidian poetics: by likening himself to persecuted mythical figures such as Telephus, Actaeon, and Odysseus, the poet maps onto myth his experience of punishment at the emperor's hands. On one level, this belongs to Ovid's attempt to construct a poetic persona with "mythic" status, a new addition to an illustrious literary tradition of which the poet was intent on becoming an integral part. On another, he bears witness through myth to his own status as a persecuted artist and enshrines an image of the princeps as an autocrat whose anger knows no bounds.

While critics have continued to focus on the historical reasons for Ovid's relegation, a long tradition of poets has taken him at his word and readily identified with his predicament there (Ziolkowski 105). In Ovid's representation of exile, for example, they are willing to see both the physical hardship of life in a harsh climate among Latinless barbarians *and* the psychological trauma brought on by the forced separation from family and friends and the imminent fear of dying on foreign soil. Ovid's personal suffering has become an existential problem in the contemporary tradition, which is ready to accept his exile as both a physical reality and an imagined one, a poetic place of genuine sorrow and a metaphor for the marginalization of his poetry from Rome by Augustus.

Perhaps the best example of how Ovid re-creates the experience of exile and in turn shapes its legacy can be found in his autobiographical poem, *Tristia* 4.10.

The poem opens with an appeal to posterity: "Who was this I you read, this trifler in tender passions? / You want to know, posterity? Then attend." The appeal calls to mind an earlier passage in the collection: "I who lie here, sweet Ovid, poet of tender passions, / fell victim to my own sharp wit. / Passer-by, if you've been in love, don't grudge me / the traditional prayer: 'May Ovid's bones lie soft!'" (*Tr.* 3.3.73–76). This passage is written as the self-composed funerary epitaph of the poet, a so-called speaking inscription of a familiar type for the meter of elegy in antiquity. Ovid plays on the associations of the elegiac genre with the epitaph throughout his poems from exile, which he repeatedly likens to a form of death.[5] This is a common theme in exile literature in antiquity, where the loss of family, city, and fame amounts to the loss of identity itself. In *Tristia* 4.10, Ovid faces that loss by appealing to posterity at the outset and closing the poem with a claim to the immortalizing power of poetry to preserve both his name and a direct account of his suffering: "So if there's any truth in poetic predictions, even / should I die tomorrow, I'll not be wholly earth's" (129–30).

The power of poetry to immortalize its subject had been a concern of Ovid's since his first published collection, as seen in *Amores* 1.15 and 3.15, and receives its most famous treatment in the coda to *Metamorphoses*: "the fatal day (which has / only the body in its grasp) can end / my years . . . [but] my lines / will be on people's lips; and through all time— / if poets' prophecies are ever right— / my name and fame are sure: I shall have life" (549; 15.874–79). The poet effectively fulfills this claim in *Tristia* by implying that exile has in fact ended his life while his disembodied voice from Tomis continues to be heard in Rome. Moreover, the claim to immortality allows Ovid to establish the enduring power of poetry over the transient temporal power of the emperor. Ovid's poems of exile thus offer an ongoing challenge to the historical circumstances that made his banishment possible.

This relates to what Seamus Heaney has called the "redressing effect of poetry." Heaney developed this idea for his opening address as professor of poetry at Oxford, "The Redress of Poetry," in which he defines poetry as fundamentally informed by "the idea of counterweighting, of balancing out the forces, of redress—tilting the scales of reality towards some transcendent equilibrium" (3). Heaney's remarks not only make students think about the place of poetry in contemporary society but also provide a hermeneutical framework for interpreting Ovid's appeal to posterity in *Tristia*. Using Heaney, students can look beyond the conventional claim to the immortality of verse and confront the trauma of personal experience revealed in these poems. Indeed, Ovid responds to the painful predicament of exile by calling on his readers, both then and now, to take note. He seeks through poetry to redress the forces of history and to provide an enduring counterweight to the burden of physical banishment by challenging the power of the emperor to silence his voice at Rome. Reading the exile poetry in the light of Heaney's idea of poetic redress forces students to consider whether Ovid's fate is peculiar to his personal circumstances in

Augustan Rome or whether exile (and its alternative, death) is a possibility that threatens all poets from Homer to Heaney.[6]

In the poem "Exposure," from his breakthrough collection *North*, Heaney had already invoked the exilic Ovid while contemplating his own self-imposed exile from his war-torn home in Northern Ireland. He writes:

> How did I end up like this?
> I think often of my friends'
> Beautiful prismatic counselling
> And the anvil brains of some who hate me
>
> As I sit weighing and weighing
> My responsible *tristia*.   (72–73)

Heaney relates his poetry to Ovid's here in establishing for himself a place of intellectual refuge, in which he becomes "an inner émigré . . . a wood-kerne / Escaped from the massacre." In learning that a "wood kerne" is a wild Irish foot soldier, students can consider how Heaney's idea of inner exile depends on and in turn elucidates Ovid's sad songs.

Heaney's *"tristia,"* however, have evidently been filtered through one of the most profound influences on his work, the Russian poet Osip Mandelstam. Even before he was sentenced to exile and the gulag by Stalin, Mandelstam had identified with the exilic Ovid in his four-stanza poem "Tristia" (1918). This poem is a reflection on sadness as an existential condition; it is not itself a lament but, in keeping with the poetics of Ovid's *Tristia*, a celebration of the power of poetry to endure time and the whims of fortune. The poem opens, "In night's bare-headed laments / I've learned the science of farewells," and clearly aligns itself with the arts of lament and farewell that characterize *Tristia* (Podossinov 1065). But sorrow here is a rhetorical posture for Mandelstam—as it was for Ovid in exile—which aids him in finding the most suitable language for reproducing his experience of life:

> Oh the thin, thin foundation of existence,
> the poverty-struck language of joy!
> Everything's been told before, everything will happen again,
> and all that's sweet is the instant of recognition.   (102)

Mandelstam discovered that "instant of recognition" in Ovid's exile poetry and aptly appropriated a title from it for this poem. In the poem he yields to existential reverie, which leads to a seemingly whimsical close in the final stanza: "So be it: . . . / Battles work out our fate, only battles, / but they can die, if they want to, while casting fortunes" (103). The cruel whim of fortune no doubt touched the poet personally during the social upheaval of early-twentieth-century Russia, and he turned to the exilic Ovid to shape his response. Mandelstam seems to suggest here that the art of poetry can mitigate the drastic effect of forced parting and its concomitant tears: men may die or have their fortunes altered by other men, but they can be knowable across generations through the recognizable expressions of poets at work.

Like Mandelstam, the Caribbean poet Derek Walcott has recognized in the exiled Ovid a source for shaping a response to personal suffering and finding a poetic voice of his own. In the poem "Hotel Normandie Pool," from his collection *The Fortunate Traveller* (1981), Walcott reflects on a dramatic life change: "the disfiguring exile of divorce" (441). In doing so, he summons Ovid as "the master" to "a small, suburban tropical hotel, its pool pitched to a Mediterranean blue" for conversation about the order of poetry (442). Like most of Walcott's work, this is a difficult poem, and I have had little success in selling it to undergraduates. Nevertheless, I include it here because it is an important moment in the ongoing reception of Ovid's exile from a modern master, whose abiding themes Heaney has defined as "language, exile, art" ("Language" 10).

At the appearance of Ovid by the poolside of the title, Walcott imagines that "corruption, censorship, and arrogance / make exile seem a happier place than home" (442). The inversion of Ovid's professed yearning for home in the exile poetry rings true here, no doubt for the modern poet but also for the Roman. Walcott has effectively removed the surface layer of sadness from Ovid's laments to reveal a subtext in which at least the potential for happiness exists. In the guise of a transplanted tourist, "a sandalled man . . . with sunglasses still on" (441), Ovid catches sight of his modern counterpart and addresses him:

> When I was first exiled,
> I missed my language as your tongue needs salt . . .
> till, on a tablet smooth as pool's skin,
> I made reflections that, in many ways,
> were even stronger than their origin.   (443)

Walcott, the paradigmatic poet of exile among moderns, is channeling Ovid here to find his own voice, which he defines as a matter of *practice*, not of place, not even of language: "the beaks of needling birds / pricked me at Tomis to learn their tribal tongue, / so, since desire is stronger than disease, / my pen's beak parted till we chirped one song" (444). In Walcott's poem Ovid's industry turns the misfortune of exile into a powerful source of individual resistance:

> Campaigns enlarged our frontiers like clouds,
> but my own government was the bare boards
> of a plank table swept by resinous pines
> whose boughs kept skittering from Caesar's eye
> with every yaw. There, hammering out lines
> in that green forge to fit me for the horse,
> I bent on a solitude so tyrannous

against the once seductive surf of crowds
that no wife softens it, or Caesar's envy.   (444)

The resinous pines, yaws, and surf so familiar from Walcott's verse have a transformative effect on Ovid's words: the voices of the two poets have become one, and the "wife" (whether Ovid's from the exile poetry or, more likely, Walcott's own) has been relegated by a kind of "conspiracy of solitude" between the poets, whose art now trumps even the tyranny of Caesar.

Before leaving the pool (and the poem) Ovid turns to warn Walcott:

Romans—he smiled—will mock your slavish rhyme,
the slaves your love of Roman structures, when,
from Metamorphoses to Tristia,
art obeys its own order.   (444)

The "Romans" here represent the European poetic tradition, at once burdensome and necessary to the postcolonial poet, who requires its form but can never truly belong to its fraternity. Of course, Walcott relishes such conflicted solitude; it is what defines the intellectual exile of the modern artist and makes this poem so successful. And yet he undercuts any chance of self-congratulation at having transformed the Roman poet into a flaccid European on a Caribbean vacation by having Ovid's words echo after his parting: "to make my image flatters you." The poem ends, then, not unlike the close of Heaney's "Exposure," at a distance from the "invisible, exiled laureate, where there's no laurel," in a world that grows darker but manages to remain vivid: "Dusk. The trees blacken like the pool's umbrellas. / The mangoes pitch from their green dark like meteors. / The fruit bat swings on its branch, a tongueless bell" (445). Again, this is demanding verse and perhaps not to the taste of many undergraduates, but it grows clearly out of the world of Walcott's exile, a place that Ovid's *Metamorphoses* and *Tristia* have helped shape but whose mood sways comfortably in the Caribbean breeze.

While Heaney and Walcott strike a suitably melancholy tone in reshaping Ovid's exile, Derek Mahon and Anne Carson remain alive to finding Ovid at play (*poeta ludens*) in the exile poetry, and their efforts are perfectly in keeping with the morbid levity often found there. Of course, Mandelstam's existential yearning informs the work of all the poets mentioned here, but that does not prevent Mahon and Carson from having fun and enlivening a potentially dour topic of study in the classroom.

In "Ovid in Tomis" (1982), Mahon lets the ancient poet himself narrate in a tone that is slightly flippant but dispassionate and devoid of bitterness. The poem begins by collapsing past and present: "What coarse god / Was the gear-box in the rain / Beside the road?" Ovid's own puzzlement is also that of the reader, who later becomes aware that this poem presents exile as metamorphosis. When the narrator notes, "It is so long / Since my own transformation / Into a stone" (37), the reader familiar with Ovid's exile poetry stops short at the fittingness of the image, only to find that he is speaking here of his own statue in modern Constanța: "A handsome city / An important port . . . / [with] even a dignified / Statue of *me* / Gazing out to sea" (38–39). As Hugh Haughton has noted, Mahon constructs here "a posthumous literary metamorphosis of poet to statue, banished intellectual to civic monument" (157). When Mahon has Ovid "meditate upon / The transience / Of earthly dominion, / The perfidy of princes" (39), he reminds the reader of the dynamic tension between poet and prince in *Tristia*, especially book 2, where the transcendent power of poetry confronts the transient power of the princeps.

Mahon's Ovid, however, is consummately modern, a persecuted artist and contemporary intellectual recognizable from Walcott's poem: "I know the simple life / Would be right for me / If I were a simple man" (40). Indeed, an urbane modernity seems to characterize the poet in the contemporary consciousness and the Ovidian tradition generally (S. Brown, *Metamorphosis* 227). Mahon uses the figure of the exiled Ovid to reflect on the place of poetry in a modern world beset by alienation and human apathy:

> The Muse is somewhere
> Else, not here
> By this frozen lake—
>
> Or, if here, then I am
> Not poet enough
> To make the connection.   (41)

Mahon wryly honors Ovid's claim to the deterioration of the quality of his verse in exile and, at least on the exterior, gives in to the existential resignation so palpable there. For him, the exiled Ovid is in fact a contemporary poet whose marginality is not in doubt:

> Better to contemplate
> The blank page
> And leave it blank
>
> Than modify
> Its substance by
> So much as a pen-stroke.   (42)

But Mahon is also aware of the fundamental principle of Ovidian transformation that drives *Metamorphoses*: change in shape is an exterior event and does not affect inner essence. The physical form of the piece of paper in the poem, "Woven of wood-nymphs," makes this clear. That the blank page "speaks volumes / No one will ever write" does not diminish its importance but merely transmutes what is observable into pure thought (42): the physical becomes metaphysical, as Ovid's *Metamorphoses* teaches. Mahon's ostensible apathy toward the poetic act is ultimately undercut by the existence of the poem itself. If his final gesture, "I incline my head / To its candour / And weep for our exile" (42), is one of existential resignation induced by a modern person's sense of alienation from the society in which he or she lives (Ziolkowski 129), it is also a compelling show of solidarity with Ovid and every poet-artist ever to be "exiled" to the pages of books.

I end this survey of recent transformations of Ovid's exile with the Canadian classicist and poet Anne Carson, whose writing aims in large part at refiguring the classical world and its literature in a contemporary, feminist idiom. From a series titled "Short Talks" in the volume *Plainwater*, the prose poem "On Ovid" conjures up the poet in exile: "I see him there on a night like this but cool, the moon blowing through the black streets." The adjective "cool" is a translation of Ovid's *frigidus* used to describe the climate of Tomis, which the word "black" reminds the reader is to be found on the Black Sea. As in Mahon's poem, "The radio . . . on the floor" collapses past and present, and this collapse reveals in both poets a desire for a commonality of experience and purpose with Ovid. That the radio "blares softly" springs entirely from Carson's art, which thrives on jarring contrasts and logical incongruities. She notes playfully that "people in exile write so many letters," and in so doing calls attention to the importance of form in Ovid's poetry of exile.

The reader is meant to pause after the next sentence: "Now Ovid is weeping," which is the shortest sentence at the very center of this very "short" text. Its placement and laconic simplicity draw attention to the emotional center of Ovid's "sad songs" (*Tristia*): tearful sorrow. Carson (like Ovid) is no sentimentalist, and she quickly points out that this is a rhetorical pose: "each night about this time he puts on sadness and goes on writing." Part of that pose also involves Ovid's learning "the local language (Getic), in order to compose in it an epic poem no one will ever read."

Carson's "Short Talks" thus closes on a pathetic note reminiscent of the musings on poetry's place in contemporary society found in Heaney, Walcott, and Mahon and already present in Mandelstam's "Tristia." Carson no doubt laments the marginalized status of poetry in the postmodern era, but by continuing to write she confirms its power to endure—albeit in different form. By reshaping Ovid's exile to fit her perceptive, humorous, and deeply intelligent art, she also sheds light on the humor, rhetoric, and profound emotional center of Ovid's own poetry. In a sense, she honors his wish to live on after death from the final verses of *Metamorphoses*: "legar . . . vivam," 'I shall be read and have life!' Carson has read Ovid, and her reading has enlivened his verse for us and, I hope, for our students.

NOTES

[1] Ziolkowski is essential reading for those interested in the Ovidian tradition, and this study is greatly indebted to his survey, especially part 2, "Ovid and the Exiles."

[2] Several recent studies have shown a disjunction between what Ovid says (amounting in paraphrase to "my poetic skill has deteriorated in exile") and what a close reading reveals to be the case (to summarize recent developments in scholarship, "these poems are as successful as any in the Ovidian corpus"). See Gareth Williams, "Ovid's Exile Poetry" 357–60 and *Banished Voices* 50–99; Claassen, "Meter"; and Nagle, *Poetics* 109–20—all authors on "deterioration" as a motif.

[3] On *Ars* as one of the contributing causes of his exile, *Tr.* 1.1.67–68; 2.212; 2.345–47; 2.539–46; 5.12.67–68; *Epistulae ex Ponto* 2.9.75–76. The poem was subsequently banned from Rome's public libraries (*Tr.* 3.1.59–82; 3.14.5–8).

[4] On the silence he must keep regarding his *error*, *Tr.* 2.207–08; 4.10.99–100. There are digestible surveys of the different theories in Thibault and in Verdière; cf. P. Green, "*Carmen et error*"; Goold, "Causes"; and Knox, "Poet." For a summary of the *Fiktionsthese*, see Chwalek 28–31.

[5] On the recurring theme of exile as equivalent to death, see Claassen, *Displaced Persons* 239–41 and 239n37; Gareth Williams, *Banished Voices* 12–13; Nagle, *Poetics* 23–35.

[6] The punishment of exile became so common in antiquity precisely because it was viewed as an alternative to execution; see Grasmück 146.

Teaching the *Really* Minor Epic: Literature, Sexuality, and National Belonging in Thomas Edwards's "Narcissus"

Jim Ellis

The Ovidian literature that I most frequently address in the classroom is the epyllion, or minor epic, usually in the context of an upper-level or graduate course devoted entirely to the genre. The genre has a conveniently short life span (the 1590s), which is roughly coterminous with the Elizabethan vogue for the sonnet sequence. Not only that, it is confined to a particular milieu: the poems were, for the most part, written by and for the students of the Inns of Court in London, the training ground for ambitious young men of the kingdom. My interest in the genre is exploring the cultural work performed by these poems. The minor epic typically spins out twenty or thirty lines of Ovid into nine hundred lines of flashy rhetorical verse, most often concerning the transformation of youths. How are these poems about the metamorphoses of young men speaking to a group of ambitious humanists and lawyers at the center of a changing culture? In my book on the genre, I argue that they are reimagining male subjectivity and sexuality in response to a new version of England that is coming into being.

Along with the major examples of the genre, such as John Marston's "The Metamorphosis of Pigmalions Image," William Shakespeare's *Venus and Adonis*, and Christopher Marlowe's "Hero and Leander," I teach lesser-known poems such as Thomas Edwards's "Narcissus" (1595). Edwards's poem is useful for a number of reasons. Teaching a lesser example of the genre can be an apt way of clarifying what might be at stake in the more famous poems. Whereas great works of art tend to transform or transcend generic constraints, lesser works often adhere fairly closely to generic norms. More important, Narcissus is the genre's favorite example of failed masculinity, a negative exemplum frequently proffered to the youthful protagonists of other poems. Venus warns the recalcitrant Adonis, "Narcissus so himself himself forsook / And died to kiss his shadow in the brook" (161–62); the men of Abydos ask Leander, "Why art thou not in love, and lov'd of all? / Though thou be faire, yet be not thine own thrall" (89–90). Narcissism is connected in the genre to a range of inappropriately directed desires, but most centrally to the youth as the object of desire, whether his own or another's. Narcissism thus figures in the epyllion as a developmental danger: unless desire is directed outward to an appropriate object, the youth will never be transformed into a man. In addition to providing an opportunity to investigate a key myth for the genre's theory of male subjectivity, many of the strange additions that Edwards makes to the myth allow us to address a number of critical debates concerning early modern male sexuality, including theatrical cross-dressing, effeminacy, male friendship, and sodomy. A final attraction of the poem is that it is not without its own merits and pleasures: it displays flashes of wit and poetical sophistication, and it is one of the most engagingly weird versions of the Narcissus tale in early modern literature.

The minor epic is a self-consciously literary genre, and this poem in particular seeks both to position itself within a genre that includes the more famous examples by Shakespeare and Marlowe and to position the genre within a national literary landscape. The poem begins by self-consciously addressing Petrarchan mistresses: "You that are faire, and scorne th'effectes of loue, / You that are chaste, and stand on nice conceites . . ." (1.1–2). Similarly, the envoy that concludes the poem ends with the wish that England might produce another Vergil. These bracketing allusions signal the two major genres against which the minor epic typically defines itself. When the genre turns satiric, its target is most often the Petrarchan poet, who is typically characterized as an immature (and ultimately narcissistic) youth in love with the idea of love. The Ovidian poet, by contrast, has a healthy and amoral interest in sex. Specifying the relation between the epic and its minor cousin is a little more difficult. What can be argued is that like most epics, epyllia promote an exemplary male subjectivity that is linked to a newly formed community, although in the epyllion this is proposed in comic rather than heroic terms.

One benefit of looking at this poem is that it allows students to see very clearly the connections between literary debates and larger cultural issues: is the satire of Petrarchan poetry simply a matter of literary fashion, or are there extraliterary questions at stake? Does a mock epic still engage with the political concerns of the epic, and does it address the nation and national belonging from the same perspective? The poem is useful for the way it can be used to explore and draw connections between current critical discussions of gender and sexuality in the period and studies of nation formation.

In practical terms, I proceed to read the poem rather methodically. We look first at the story of Narcissus in Ovid, to establish the major outlines of the story. Ovid's poem carefully specifies Narcissus's age ("when he reached his sixteenth year, Narcissus— / who then seemed boy or man—was loved by many" [91; *Met.* 3.351–53]) and suggests that Narcissus is suspended between two developmental states. The progress from youth to man is in fact the central metamorphosis that the genre is interested in, a progress that is seen as neither natural nor inevitable. We note his attractiveness to both genders ("both youths and young girls wanted him" [91; *Met.* 3.353]), his rejection of all admirers, the dialogue with the nymph Echo, the spurned male admirer who calls on Nemesis, and finally the events at the pool and the resultant metamorphosis: "I burn with love for my own self: it's I / who light the flames" (96; *Met.* 3.463–64).

We then look at Arthur Golding's 1567 English translation of *Metamorphoses* and notice the particular terms he uses to frame the relation between Narcissus and his image:

> O pierlesse piece, why dost thou mee thy lover thus delude?
> Or whither fliste thou of thy friende thus earnestly pursude?
> Iwis I neyther am so fowle nor yet so growne in yeares,

> That in this wise thou shouldst me shoon. To have me to their Feeres,
> The Nymphes themselves have sude ere this. And yet (as should appeere)
> Thou dost pretende some kinde of hope of friendship by the cheere.
>
> (74; 3.570–75)

Golding uses the discourse of Renaissance male friendship, which allows us to note both the inevitable changes that result in translating a text from one culture to another and the historically and culturally specific nature of sexuality. Here is a useful place to address Alan Bray's groundbreaking work on early modern anxieties surrounding the conceptual confusion between sodomy and male friendship, anxieties that Bray links to a changing social order and class structure.

Having established the outlines of the myth and the cultural adaptations of its translation, we turn to the English poem. The form of "Narcissus" is in fact closer to a complaint than the more usual narrative form of the epyllion, featuring a ghostly Narcissus returning from the underworld to tell his story to the narrator, and Edwards uses the same stanza form as that of *The Rape of Lucrece*. The essentially comic tone of the narrator, however, with his lewd observations on his own life, and Edwards's continual allusions to and citations of Marston, Marlowe, and Shakespeare, make it clear that this poem sees itself as occupying the terrain of the minor epic rather than the complaint. (Alternatively, it could be argued that this shows the looseness of this particular generic boundary; some scholars argue that the generic category of epyllion is an entirely modern invention.)

We use the readings of Ovid to identify the elements of the story that Edwards has retained, altered, or removed and to speculate on the point of the differences. As in Ovid, the young Narcissus is a supremely beautiful youth. In this poem, however, he has only female admirers, who pursue him relentlessly: "How many times have I been luld a sleepe, / In Ladies bowers, and carried to and fro, / Whilest but a stripling" (14.1–3). The ghostly Narcissus observes in an Ovidian fashion about his immature self: "Had Priapus Narcissus' place enioy'd / He would a little more have done than toy'd" (14.6–7). Although the male admirers have been removed, there remains a good deal of attention to Narcissus's fatal attractiveness, which culminates in an extraordinary outburst:

> Would some good man had massacred my face,
> Blinde stroke my eies, as was my hart thereto,
> Dasht in my throate, my teeth, done some disgrace,
> For with my tounge some say they were undoe.
>
> (12.1–4)

The violence of this passage suggests that the poem sees the beauty of youths as an almost irresistible attraction that can only be countered with considerable force.

This anxiety about the dangerous and irresistible beauty of male youths (to men and women alike) echoes the fears that Stephen Orgel locates in antitheatrical tracts about the seductiveness of boy actors ("Nobody's Perfect"). In an extended condemnation of these transvestite players, for example, John Rainolds writes that "experience sheweth . . . that men are made adulterers and enemies of all chastitie by comming to such playes . . . [and] that an effeminate stage-player while hee faineth love, imprinteth wounds of love" (18). There is no suggestion that these good men are fooled by the costumes; on the contrary, Orgel argues that "the attraction of men to beautiful boys is treated as axiomatic" in the literature (16).

The various flirtatious games and love debates taken up between Narcissus and his female admirers are detailed in a number of stanzas before the ghostly Narcissus invites Adonis and Leander to come and commiserate with him. These are recognizably Shakespeare's and Marlowe's creations. Leander, for example, shows up naked, as he does to Hero's tower, and reference is made to Hero's comic outfit in Marlowe's poem:

> Welcome Leander, welcome, stand thou neere,
> Alacke poore youth, what hast thou for a pawne,
> What, not a rag, where's Heroes vale of lawne?
> Her buskins all of shels ysilvered ore?   (26.3–6)

Adonis is given the epithet "thrice faire" (24.2), echoing Venus's initial salute in Shakespeare's version of the story. These evocations of an English Adonis and an English Leander work with the poem's larger interest in asserting the existence of a national literary canon.

After the address to these fellow tragic youths, Narcissus turns back to his story, at which point the familiar narrative should begin. But instead of encountering Echo while hunting deer, we find that Narcissus, still sporting with the maidens, has now taken to cross-dressing like the Elizabethan boy actors:

> I tooke the Iewels which faire Ladies sent me,
> And manie pretie toies, which to advance
> My future bane, unwillingly they meant me,
> Their whole attire and choice suites not content me;
> But like a lover glad of each new toy,
> So I a woman turned from a boy.   (44.2–7)

This metamorphosis is, as far as I know, unprecedented in versions of the Narcissus myth, and it makes literal the genre's assertion that the narcissistic youth often plays the part of the Petrarchan mistress. This change in the story is presumably a response to the anxieties that have removed the male admirers from the tale, so that we will not have a youth wooing a youth (although the result is, if anything, more outré). Narcissus subsequently falls in love with his own image *as a woman* in the pool.

This critique of the effeminizing qualities of Petrarchan poetry parallels antitheatrical anxieties about boys dressing as women on the stage, and this association is reinforced when in the extended wooing of his own image we see Narcissus referring to himself as an actor. The connection between cross-dressing and Petrarchanism is further solidified when Narcissus, dressed as a woman, sings "soveraigne sweet Sonetto's to loves mother" (46.4). "Lead by [his] attractive Syren-singing selfe" (50.1), Narcissus falls in love with the fabricated image of a woman in the brook by mistaking his own voice for the image's: "His owne conceit with that of his did fire him" (49.6). In Marston's poem, the satirical point is that the sculptor Pygmalion, like the Petrarchan poet, falls in love with a creature of his own imagination, and not a real woman at all. Here, much the same point is being made: the Petrarchan mistress is essentially a projection or reflection of the immature Petrarchan poet's own fantasies, which have little to do with actual flesh-and-blood women. He is seduced by his own naive ideas about love.

In this version, Narcissus falls in love initially not with his image but with his voice; the image he sees in the water is himself in drag; and he never seems to realize who it is he's fallen in love with. The male admirer who calls on Nemesis is removed, like all the other male admirers in the story, and Echo's role is reduced to complaining to the gods about "a boy uniust, cruell, unkinde" (92.2). The gods intervene (how is unclear), and in the penultimate stanza Narcissus meets his end:

> This done, amaine unto the spring I made,
> Where finding beautie culling nakednes,
> Sweet love reviving all that heavens decaide,
> And once more placing gentle maidenlikenes,
> Thus sought I favour of my shaddowed mistres;
> Imbracing sighs, and telling tales to stones,
> Amidst the spring I leapt to ease my mones.
> (93.1–7)

Given this last crucial change—that Narcissus never realizes whom he is wooing—the question in class always becomes, If this is no longer a story about narcissism, then what is it about? Or, alternatively, how is it still a poem about narcissism? This is where I draw attention to some of the isolated elements that have surfaced in the discussion and get the class to draw them together: the references to English poets, the demonization of Petrarchan poetry (Narcissus as sonneteer), the anxieties about the beauty of youths, and the removal of the male admirers.

The envoy offers some help in sorting the poem out. It is nearly impossible to match the moral it offers to the story we've just heard: "men are fleeting, . . . women's shewes are pelfe, / And their constancies as flowers" (1.3.5–6). This insufficient conclusion, however, might be part of the comedy, much like the comically inadequate conclusion to Marlowe's digression in *Hero and Leander*. The greater part of the envoy is devoted to sketching out a national literary canon, often naming poets by their most famous poetic creation. Spenser ("Collyn") is given pride of place, followed by Sidney, Samuel Daniel ("Rosamund"), Thomas Watson ("Amintas"), Marlowe ("Leander"), and Shakespeare ("Adon"). He makes reference to another poet, potentially greater than them all, but it is difficult to guess to whom he is referring. The point of this calling of the roll is both to assert that there is a national poetic canon and that this national canon has a political role to play:

> What remaines peerelesse men,
> That in Albions confines are,
> But eterniz'd with the pen,
> In sacred Poems and sweet laies
> Should be sent to Nations farre,
> The greatnes of faire Albions praise.
> (12.1–6)

England's poets should be "audacious proude" (13.1), while at the same time recognizing that "[e]verie stampe is not allow'd" (13.3)—particularly, one assumes, the effeminizing stamp of Petrarchan verse. He ends by suggesting that poets should be offered "due honor and . . . praise" (15.2) and by expressing the following hope: "Then thus faire *Albion* flourish so, / As Thames may nourish as did *Po*" (15.5–6). The reference to the Po River is presumably to the Mantuan Vergil;[1] the hope is that given the right encouragement, England will produce its own epic.

Edwards's interest in a literary nationalism that results in a literary imperialism—"Poems and sweet laies . . . sent to Nations farre"—is thus linked to the familiar Elizabethan wish to be the heir of imperial Rome. Edwards's sincere alignment of the poem with epic desires leads us to interrogate the relation between these desires and the Ovidian narrative that has come before. How might this comic complaint and its burlesque of Petrarchan verse be consonant with imperial ambitions? One answer is that the Ovidian voice connects the poet to imperial Rome, if not through the Elizabethan era's most esteemed author Vergil, then at least through the more-greatly-loved Ovid. Petrarchan poetry, on the other hand, is connected to contemporary Italy, in a genre where *Italianate* is a virtual synonym for *sodomitical*.

Equally important, the epic and epyllion have in common the positing of an exemplary subject. In the case of the epyllion, the exemplary subject is not the hero of the narrative, who is generally a negative exemplum or failed subject, but rather the narrator. The Elizabethan version of the Ovidian voice is urbane, fashionable, witty, rhetorically sophisticated, and cynical about desire. Unlike the Petrarchan poet, who masochistically (and, suggests the poem, narcissistically) flaunts his subjection to the woman and to desire, the Ovidian narrator is beyond desire, or has at least sufficiently mastered his own desire to find all desire comic. This opposition is especially clear in this poem, with its two incarnations of Narcissus: the naive Petrarchan protagonist and the suave and worldly Ovidian narrator. In a culture where rhetoric was seen as the foundation and hallmark of civilization as well as the supremely important skill for the ambitious, the Ovidian voice is the voice of power.

NOTE

[1] Alternatively, the reference could be to Ariosto, whose *Orlando furioso* is to some degree a dynastic epic for the Este family of Ferrara. In that case, the emphasis would shift from continuity with the past to competition in the present.

Teaching the Ovidian Shakespeare and the Politics of Emotion

Cora Fox

Introducing students to the relation between works by Ovid and Shakespeare means exposing them to versions of Shakespeare they may not recognize. Although many of Shakespeare's plays are filled with local allusions to Ovid, creating a syllabus including the works that engage more broadly with *Metamorphoses* (primarily, among other works by Ovid) illuminates aspects of Shakespeare's work that have been the focus of exciting recent scholarship but that are not often reproduced in popular Shakespeare on or off the stage. Ovid is the source, for instance, for various evaluations of the relation between individual interior experience and larger systems of authority, which is an obsession of Ovid's poem and Shakespeare's works as well. Ovidian tales underlie models of revenge in some of Shakespeare's plays, most notably *Titus Andronicus*, and Ovidianism in these plays works to define the emotional status of the revenge figure and his or her ethical relationship to the larger social world. Similarly, many of the comedies are filled with the language of metamorphosis as the trope for love or desire, but with the Ovidian twist that the transformative experience is violent, uncontrollable, and often dangerous to a civilized society. Violence in general, its nature and origins and the problem of how it can be channeled and controlled in a culture, is a central question of *Metamorphoses* and one that Shakespeare returns to again and again. But even before students encounter this complexity, just highlighting how Shakespeare's plays are informed by an Ovidian aesthetic and ideology runs counter to the way the bard is constructed as an original and solitary genius. A class focusing on the Ovidian Shakespeare is exciting and can teach students about intertextuality and the nature of literary and cultural production by showing them, rather than telling them, how language and ideas work.

I teach this course as an advanced undergraduate special-topics course, and although most of the students who take it are English majors, there are always students from other majors taking the course for general humanities credit. Some of the students come into the class having read some Shakespeare or some Ovid, but only a few have a great deal of knowledge about either author, and some have never read either (beyond high school Shakespeare and sometimes Edith Hamilton). All have heard of Shakespeare, but many have never heard of Ovid. Given these conditions, it is surprising how quickly sophisticated discussions have developed in this class, and I attribute this to the fact that, when approached together, the works enlighten one another and encourage students to make subtle, nuanced connections immediately. Reading Ovid, the students often discover their own Western mythological tradition, and I point out the ways *Metamorphoses* itself is self-consciously intertextual; reading

Shakespeare they get to experience what it is like to be "in the know," listening in on a dialogue between the works of two great authors.

Although I would love to teach all of *Metamorphoses* in this semester-long course, I do not; however, I do ask students to read significant portions of the poem and whole books rather than single tales. I devote the first two or three weeks to *Metamorphoses* and to a brief introduction to theories of intertextuality. I have students read *Metamorphoses* books 1, 2, 3, 6, 10, 11, and 15, in the translation by Allen Mandelbaum. We discuss Ovid's larger purposes and ideological investments in these first two weeks, and then we return to some tales in more detail as we work through Shakespeare's engagement with them in the plays. I also assign at least one introductory chapter from Graham Allen's volume in the New Critical Idiom series, titled *Intertextuality*. Some theoretical grounding helps students get beyond reading only for allusions and prepares them for the broader ways we will discuss the works themselves. In addition, as recommended reading I encourage students throughout the semester to read some of the excellent scholarship on Shakespeare and Ovid, often chapters from Leonard Barkan's *The Gods Made Flesh*, Jonathan Bate's *Shakespeare and Ovid*, Heather James's *Shakespeare's Troy*, or Lynn Enterline's *Rhetoric of the Body from Ovid to Shakespeare*. An analysis of one of these critical approaches is often a short writing assignment in the course and provides a methodological model for how to work with these texts.

And how does one choose which plays by Shakespeare to teach? I list below the plays I select and how I link them in class to certain stories, but then I focus on one strain of Ovidianism in *Titus Andronicus* that is particularly enlightening and exciting for students to discover, and I describe how I incorporate Mary Zimmerman's *Metamorphoses: A Play* into the conclusion of the course. This list and the tales I refer to are subjective evaluations of which plays are the most Ovidian in Shakespeare's canon and which tales in Ovid are most crucial for reading those plays. Just as there are many Ovidianisms circulating in the literature of the early modern period, Shakespeare's Ovidianism is characterized differently by each critic who chooses to risk such characterization. It is also regrettable that I have not included Shakespeare's poetry in this course, and I intend to remedy this in future iterations. The plays I teach, alongside the tales I suggest students reread before class, are listed below:

> *Titus Andronicus* and Actaeon (3.138–252), Philomela (6.424–674), Hecuba (13.399–575)
>
> *Two Gentlemen of Verona* and Salmacis and Hermaphroditus (4.285–388), Erysichthon (8.738–878)
>
> *A Midsummer Night's Dream* and Pyramus and Thisbe (4.55–166), Midas (11.85–193)
>
> *The Winter's Tale* and Proserpina (5.346–571), Pygmalion (10.243–97), Arachne (6.1–145)

Cymbeline and Philomela (3.138–252)
The Tempest and Medea (7.1–403, along with Medea in *Heroides*, poem 12)

As this list suggests, the links between the plays and Ovid's tales are sometimes made through direct allusions, but they are primarily thematic, and by the time we reach *Cymbeline*, a play infused with Ovidianism without any strong links to a particular tale (except for the telling moment when the play highlights Philomela's rape in relation to Imogen's experience), the students have usually learned to read the two works as true intertexts, looking for thematic and ideological dialogues and negotiations of cultural values. This list leaves out many plays that also engage with *Metamorphoses*; *Hamlet*, for instance, always comes up in discussions, although I do not assign it, partly because it is given enough attention in other courses.

Within this structure, *Titus Andronicus* makes an excellent introduction to the course because it so insistently and allusively comments on Shakespeare's Roman literary heritage. The story of Lavinia's rape and mutilation (her tongue is cut out and her hands are cut off) is a gruesomely self-conscious repetition of Tereus's rape of Philomela in *Metamorphoses*, in which her tongue is cut out and she reveals her rapist by weaving a tapestry. Famously, it contains the only scene in Shakespeare's works where a physical book is brought on stage and identified, and this book is *Metamorphoses*:

> TITUS. Lucius, what book is that she tosseth so?
> BOY. Grandsire, 'tis Ovid's *Metamorphosis*;
>   My mother gave it me.
> MARCUS. For love of her that's gone,
>   Perhaps she culled it from among the rest.
> TITUS. Soft, so busily she turns the leaves!
>   *Helps her.*
>   What would she find? Lavinia, shall I read?
>   This is the tragic tale of Philomel,
>   And treats of Tereus' treason and his rape—
>   And rape, I fear, was root of thy annoy.
> MARCUS. See, brother, see: note how she quotes the leaves.
> TITUS. Lavinia, wert thou thus surprised, sweet girl,
>   Ravished and wronged as Philomela was,
>   Forced in the ruthless, vast and gloomy woods?
>   (4.1.41–53)[1]

"Quotes," as Jonathan Bate points out in his notes to his edition, carries the more general sense of "observes" but preserves the specific sense of citing a particular passage of literature (214n50). The word used here carries a broader significance as a revelation about the nature of characterization in the play.

Lavinia can "quote" her own identity, but such recognition belongs not only to her but also to the male characters, who see their own implication in the literary narratives constructing the entire action of the play. In fact, as many critics have pointed out, Lavinia has already been repeatedly compared with Philomela by her rapists and their instigator, Aaron, and her uncle Marcus has already made the comparison himself before this scene.[2] The scene, therefore, is a moment of overdetermined intertextuality, drawing attention to the way the play and its characters have been locked into an Ovidian intertextual narrative. Titus even curses the fictional setting in which this event took place: "Ay, such a place there is where we did hunt— / O, had we never, never hunted there!— / Patterned by that the poet here describes, / By nature made for murders and for rapes" (4.1.55–58). Not just the characters but the setting for their destruction is "patterned" after Ovid.

The final scene, and the culmination of the double revenge plot of the play, reinforces this self-conscious intertextual relation between Shakespeare's work and Ovid's narrative of Philomela and Procne's revenge. Titus has captured Lavinia's rapists, the sons of the evil Tamora, and he prepares them to be served as pasties at the concluding cannibalistic feast for their mother:

> This is the feast that I have bid [Tamora] to,
> And this the banket she shall surfeit on,
> For worse than Philomel you us'd my daughter,
> And worse than Progne I will be reveng'd.
> (5.2.192–95).

In these lines, Titus regenders himself as a female revenge figure, assuming the role of Procne, Philomela's revenging sister (who serves Tereus his son at dinner as punishment for his crimes against her sister). The play uses this Ovidian female-revenge narrative to construct a complicated analysis of suffering and to show how an immobilizing grief can be turned to action. Titus self-consciously suffers as Procne suffers, his daughter suffers as Philomela suffers, and overall the play uses the feminized position of impotence to comment on general and political abuses of power, just as Ovid does by repeatedly referring to Tereus as a Thracian "tyrant" (6.436, 549, 581).

The play's dialogue with *Metamorphoses* goes deeper than this self-conscious set of allusions, however. The other Ovidian female figure alluded to twice in reference first to Tamora and then to Lavinia is Hecuba. Tamora's son hopes in the opening scene of the play that his mother will be able to model her revenge on Hecuba's:

> The self-same gods that arm'd the Queen of Troy
> With opportunity of sharp revenge
> Upon the Thracian tyrant in his tent
> May favor Tamora, the Queen of Goths

(When Goths were Goths and Tamora was queen),
To quit the bloody wrongs upon her foes.
(1.1.130–41)

Then, in the scene analyzed above, Lavinia is also associated with Hecuba, in a misreading of her frenzy to get hold of her nephew's school copy of *Metamorphoses*:

> MARCUS. Canst thou not guess wherefore she plies thee thus?
> BOY. My lord, I know not, I, nor can guess,
> Unless some fit or frenzy do possess her;
> For I have heard my grandsire say full oft,
> Extremity of griefs would make men mad;
> And I have read that Hecuba of Troy
> Ran mad for sorrow. That made me to fear,
> Although, my lord, I know my noble aunt
> Loves me as dear as e'er my mother did.
> (4.1.15–23)

Lavinia's sorrow, the boy worries, may turn her into another Hecuba, so she, like Tamora, might assume the role of violent revenger. The boy has learned from his grandfather, Titus, that extreme grief can lead to violent madness, but his ultimate authority is this Ovidian story, and it is more powerful than the characterization of Lavinia as a nurturing mother figure. She is instead, according to this well-read child, a potentially destructive revenger.

These two allusions to Ovid's Hecuba are especially interesting because they point to two different ways to read this particular Ovidian narrative and suggest the ways *Titus* explores the morality of revenge through Ovidianism. Tamora's son, Demetrius, reads Hecuba's tale as a tale of revenge successfully accomplished. For him the narrative is a model of how to seize an opportunity for at least a limited kind of power. For Marcus and the younger Lucius, however, the tale is about the madness brought on by extreme grief. For the boy, at least, the possibility that Lavinia might become the revenger is threatening because it means she might be violent and this violence might be indiscriminate. These two Ovidian allusions, presented by male characters from such different perspectives, point to the dialectical nature of Shakespeare's engagement with this tale in Ovid as well as with the form and ethics of the revenge plot. When Shakespeare alludes to Hecuba, he raises the entire problem of how extreme emotion might be expressed, and, by associating both Tamora and Lavinia with the same Ovidian figure of sorrow, he encodes Hecuba's grief as a particularly feminized grief, one caused by impotence in the face of extreme disparities of power.

The action and evaluation of revenge, therefore, are both modeled on Ovid's tales of Philomela and Hecuba, and the play encourages a comparison of these figures in *Metamorphoses*. This is where a larger comparative analysis of *Metamorphoses* in relation to the play is most revealing. Not only are these two figures linked in the violent action of revenge, but Ovid's poem links their emotional states in the moments leading up to the revenge. Their internal states of suffering are the generative source of agency, whether it is positively or negatively valued. Procne's pain is described in the following way:

> . . . dolor ora repressit,
> verbaque quaerenti satis indignantia linguae
> defuerunt; nec flere vacat, sed fasque nefasque
> confusura ruit *poenaeque in imagine tota est*.
> (6.583–86; my emphasis)[3]

And Hecuba, when she finds Polydorus's body and turns to take revenge on Polymnestor, responds similarly:

> Troades exclamant; obmutuit illa dolore,
> et pariter vocem lacrimasque introrsus obortas
> devorat ipse dolor, duroque simillima saxo
> torpet et adversa figit modo lumina terra,
> interdum torvos extollit ad aethera vultus,
> nunc positi spectat vultum, nunc vulnera nati,
> vulnera praecipue, seque armat et instruit ira.
> qua simul exarsit, tamquam regina maneret,
> ulcisci statuit *poenaeque in imagine tota est* . . .
> (13.538–46; my emphasis)[4]

Although Mandelbaum translates the crucial and identical phrase in Latin differently in these two tales (Procne is "imagining / both licit and illicit penalties / she could inflict" and Hecuba "images / harsh punishment"), both characters are described as experiencing a specific, highly visual, and imagistic emotion at the moment that they turn into revengers. Before their final metamorphoses, Procne and Hecuba express the extremity of their suffering through highly rhetoricized laments, and at the moment in which their imaginations can picture nothing but revenge, they accomplish acts of excessive violence. The formulaic phrase in Latin suggests that this kind of excessive emotion is more broadly considered to be essential to their assertion of agency, and it is this narrative of their agency that deeply informs the representation of revenge that students encounter in *Titus*.

Titus, as the revenger of Shakespeare's play, follows an analogous trajectory, grieving for most of the play, and then finally accomplishing a spectacularly violent revenge. The play's Ovidianism, therefore, models how subjects can seize agency in moments of extreme grief. When Titus is pushed to the limits of human suffering, he joins Hecuba and Procne in the feminized role of the impotent victim who is transformed through a mysterious internal process into a revenger. Emotion is here the cause of action, however ethically ambiguous, after the period of mute grief, and the play speaks through Ovid to the complexities of suffering and its repercussions for both the individual and the society in which he or she must participate.

Ovidian and then Shakespearean cultural narratives about the social consequences of extreme grief thus begin the course, and we end the semester with a contemporary dramatic adaptation of Ovidian stories in Zimmerman's *Metamorphoses: A Play*, since it addresses those same Ovidian questions about sorrow and the social world. Zimmerman's play, first produced by Chicago's Lookingglass Theater in 1998, went to New York's Second Stage Theater in October 2001 and then Broadway in 2002, where it earned Zimmerman a Tony for best direction in that year. In a culturally remarkable coincidence, the play arrived in New York shortly after the terrorist attacks of September 11, 2001. Ben Brantley, reviewing the play for the *New York Times* in a piece called "How Ovid Helps Deal with Loss and Suffering," describes intense audience reactions to what he characterizes as the play's focus on suffering, noting that "sorrow is a fugue in Mary Zimmerman's *Metamorphoses*" and gushing that the play is "speaking with a dreamlike hush directly to New Yorkers' souls." As this review indicates, the play is an important artistic artifact, serendipitously in harmony not just with the communal and individual suffering of New Yorkers, but also with the cultural climate in which the events of September 11 and their aftermath unfolded, a moment in history that continues to have profound and obvious effects on the domestic affairs of United States citizens and the foreign policies of the nation.

I assign both Zimmerman's play and Brantley's review in the final week of the course, and we focus our discussion on how Ovid's analysis of grief is transmuted by Zimmerman and what the review of the play reveals about that critical cultural moment in United States history. Student readers, like most audiences of the play, find the play particularly moving and beautiful, and they enjoy the modern adaptations of the Ovidian stories that have become familiar over the course of the semester. They are quick to point out, however, that even Zimmerman's selection of tales tends to mitigate the highly critical stance Ovid's poem takes toward all figures of authority, and particularly rulers and gods. With characters like Midas, Myrrha, Orpheus, Alcyone, Pomona, and Phaethon as foci, Zimmerman's play avoids the most violent representations of the gods and narrows in instead on human beings and their misguided points of view or doomed relationships with one another. She also changes the tone of Ovid's tales significantly by providing a sort of narrative of grace, ending with the tale of Baucis and Philemon and the survival of love. The play, therefore, as students often argue themselves, is markedly less political in the narrow sense than is Ovid's poem—less critical of structures of authority, less invested in representing injustice as often causeless and unmitigated, and less topically interested in present-day rulers, as Ovid repeatedly is in Augustus in *Metamorphoses*. Although suffering permeates the social world created by Zimmerman, it is not directly caused by structures of authority and the individuals who have power, as it often is in Ovid and Shakespeare. There is no wronged avenging hero ridding Rome of an evil empress, as in *Titus*, and no Pygmalion-like artist to redeem the tyrant, as in *The Winter's Tale*. Instead, Zimmerman's play focuses on art and myth as archetypal abstractions that are important because they exist seemingly outside such impermanent societal structures. But what does the play's ostensibly apolitical stance mean about the culture that produced it? What does it tell us about United States culture when set in contrast with Shakespeare's England? Our class discussions zero in on fundamental questions about the role of art in any society, and they demand that students ask what it is that the play reflects in United States culture in the period of and after September 11.

To further discussion of these issues, I incorporate Brantley's review, which praises the play as an especially effective cathartic release for New Yorkers, and in which his own rhetoric becomes highly emotional:

> For New Yorkers today who encounter the same recorded visions of terrorist destruction whenever they turn on their televisions, Ms. Zimmerman's portrayal of tragic scenes repeated has an anxious and immediate familiarity. But there is balm in Ovid's world, as Ms. Zimmerman presents it. Those images from television stay the same; metamorphosis occurs in the human imagination. There can be artistry and solace in remembering.

Although this version of metamorphosis as an imaginative salve can certainly be found in Ovid's poem, the other versions crowd it out as an answer to the social problems of suffering and violence. Metamorphosis in Ovid is too often a punishment or a permanent state of misery to be a solace. Brantley's review, then, and to a great extent the play it describes, reveal the cultural fantasy that what he terms a "personal mythology" will be enough to counter the social consequences of grief and violence. Brantley concludes:

> Ms. Zimmerman makes an ardent and eloquent case for the importance of a personal mythology that gives order to the chaos of suffering. The final tale of Baucis and Philemon, a couple whose only prayer is that they not die apart, leads to the evening's concluding scene. Candles are lighted, whispered words are repeated into the darkness and, for one delicate moment, it seems that love has truly conquered death.

The beauty of the play and Brantley's vision of its final moments beg the questions he raises earlier in the review. Is remembering or abstracting enough? What is the social purpose of myth? What does a society do with suffering? In *Titus*, the result of individual grief is powerful but violent. In Zimmerman, as Brantley points out, acceptance seems to be the goal, but at what cost? Is it enough to acknowledge that love can conquer death for just that moment or is that a relinquishing of the more ethical possibilities for communal power found in grief?

Facilitating student access to details of Shakespeare's dialogue with Ovid and then allowing them to read a play such as Zimmerman's that reflects a culture closer to home helps them begin to grasp questions of culture that are central to Ovidianism—often such difficult and unstated ones as those surrounding definitions of agency, emotional expression, and the role of art in human societies, not to mention questions of gender. Students finish the course admiring Shakespeare's keen readings of his favorite poet, but more important, they witness and evaluate the ongoing process of negotiating the relation between the internal life of the individual and cultural systems of authority. Ovidianism both grounds and unleashes this investigation in Shakespeare's plays, and then, as students notice, a different one in Zimmerman's play from just a few years ago. Students, who as citizens of a democracy can participate in these cultural negotiations, learn to recognize a complex, intertextual, Ovidian Shakespeare and feel the force of Ovid's politics of emotion as it reverberates through history and into our own time.

NOTES

[1] All quotations from *Titus Andronicus* are taken from the Arden Shakespeare edition by Jonathan Bate.

[2] See Bate's introduction to the Arden edition (29) and his *Shakespeare and Ovid* for a full discussion of the tale of Philomela as a pattern for the play's action. Thompson also explores the play's reliance on the narrative of Philomela's rape and its revisions.

[3] Mandelbaum translates: "She does not speak: her mouth is blocked by grief. / Her tongue seeks words of scorn to match her wrath / but does not find them. Nor does Procne weep: / she sinks into herself, imagining both / licit and illicit penalties / she could inflict; revenge is what she needs" (200).

[4] "The Trojan women wail, but any tears / and words of Hecuba are checked by grief: / she cannot speak. As mute as stone, as stiff, / she's stunned; she stares at what lies at her feet, / and now lifts up her grim gaze heavenward, / and now stares at his face, now at the wounds / of her dead son as he lies there, outstretched. / But it's the wounds on which she's most intent; / it's these that fuel her anger, arm her wrath. / And once she is inflamed, she plots revenge / as if she still were queen: she images / harsh punishment" (Mandelbaum 451–52).

Reforming *Metamorphoses*: The Epic in Translation as a "Major Work" of the English Renaissance

Scott Maisano

> The more profoundly they see into the spirit of Ovid, the more their own originality is enabled.
> —Leonard Barkan[1]

It begins with Chaos. The class is laughing at two students' comments on the transformation of Daphne: the first has observed, "Apollo is the original tree-hugger," and the next, "Apollo gets wood!" I could be upset by the casualness, the anachronism, and, in the latter example, the sexual slang on display in these remarks; but I am secretly delighted. That's because, only a few weeks into the semester, I know two things that the students do not know at this point. First, the liberties they are taking with Ovid's epic are relatively innocent and innocuous by comparison with what the writers of the English Renaissance were willing, and able, to do. Second, Ovid, instead of being the victim of such ransacking and rereading of classical materials—not to mention lowly witticisms and puns—actually sets the gold standard for such indecorous transgressions. I am comforted, too, by the knowledge that my students are already blithely disregarding Arthur Golding's "Epistle to Leicester" and his "Preface to the Reader," which we have read in advance of books 1 and 2. Golding's letters of introduction are, as I hope to show, *purposely* insufficient as context for the poem. Indeed, the initial chaos and confusion notwithstanding, I would prefer my students to read the poem in the absence of any annotation rather than, as in most other undergraduate surveys of English Renaissance literature, to read an abundance of annotation in the absence of the poem.

In this essay I discuss my decision to select Golding's Elizabethan translation of *Metamorphoses*, edited by Madeleine Forey, as "a major text" in my course on English Renaissance literature at the University of Massachusetts, Boston. Although the greater Boston area is famous for its institutions of higher education—Harvard, MIT, Tufts, Brandeis, Boston University, and Boston College come immediately to mind—the University of Massachusetts, Boston, stands out from these other doctoral-granting, research institutions in one remarkable sense: we are a public school. So, when the private schools mentioned above announce major initiatives to increase the numbers of first-generation, nontraditional, and minority students in their entering classes, they are saying, I think, that they wish to be more like UMass-Boston. Meanwhile, my students—most of whom *are* the first in their families to attend college and many of whom are older, returning students—tend to be humble to a fault: they often underestimate their own academic preparedness and intellectual instincts. For that reason, I decided to require students to purchase the complete Elizabethan translation of Ovid's *Metamorphoses* with a specific exercise and a modest curricular reform in mind. I wanted my students to discover that they did not need editors' footnotes to understand what we were reading; indeed, in some cases, such editorial interventions were not helping them but holding them back. My students, I knew, were capable of creating better scholarly editions of Renaissance texts for themselves.

My approach in this class—little more, in truth, than heeding the Renaissance humanists' rallying cry of *ad fontes* or "to the sources"—was precipitated by a problem I had confronted in previous semesters. Students would mention that they felt they had to have prior knowledge of Ovid in order to understand half the material we were reading; they were constantly looking down at the footnotes to get the gist of a passage; and, as a result, the literature itself had become a series of cryptograms that needed only to be decoded. Worse yet, from the students' perspective, the decoding had always already been done for them: the answers were right there at the bottom of the page. For example, the footnotes to Ben Jonson's "Masque of Blackness" in *The Norton Anthology of English Literature* informed them that Deucalion was "[a] Greek analogue to Noah, as the survivor of a flood"; Phaëton was the "Son of Apollo the sun god, whose ill-fated attempt to drive the sun's chariot scorched the earth"; and Pythagoras was a "Mystical Greek philosopher, who taught men how to read writing on the moon" (*Norton Anthology* 1298–99). Once you understood those crucial details, they presumed, you understood the masque. Thankfully, of course, Ovidianism in the Renaissance is not nearly so simple. But it would do no good for me to tell them that; I had to show them, or rather, let them see for themselves.

Teaching Golding's translation, a work reduced to twenty-six lines in the *Norton Anthology*, as a "major work" of the English Renaissance brings to the fore all sorts of unexamined assumptions about both literary form and historical periodization. First, there is the age-old concern over whether Ovid is, properly speaking, an epic poet. Do the hundreds of stories and the disparate genres contained in *Metamorphoses* really constitute a singular work, an integral and aesthetic whole on a par with Vergil's achievement in the *Aeneid*? Beyond the questions surrounding Ovid's Latin text, however, are additional concerns regarding its sixteenth-century and seventeenth-century "Englishings." Should a translation count as British literature? Aren't the myths in *Metamorphoses* really the products of another place and another time? Do we want to cede space to Arthur Golding and George Sandys when there are figures such as Sidney, Spenser, Shakespeare, Donne, Jonson, and Milton to cover? Rather than sweep such questions under the rug, I chose to place them front and center this particular semester by beginning *in medias res*, with a look at the most famous book of the entire period—a book that just happens to be another loosely connected collection of ancient tales in translation, the King James Bible.

Actually, we did not look at the King James Bible per se, except for about ten pages of facsimile handouts; instead we started the semester by reading Adam Nicolson's *God's Secretaries: The Making of the King James Bible*. This affordable and accessible best seller provides a wonderful panoramic introduction to sixteenth- and early-seventeenth-century England and enables students to become acquainted with, even excited about, issues of translation, interpretation, and annotation as the debates over the proper appearance for an English Bible (including its Gothic, as opposed to roman, typeface) unfold against the backdrop of the wider culture. What was most significant about the English Bible, from John Wycliffe's translation to the Authorized Version, was not who was writing it, but who was reading it and how it was read. In theory, if not always in practice, the literate laity could suddenly see for themselves the Holy Scripture in their own language, free from the glossing and interpretations of clergymen. Though the heavily Latinate diction, ornate black-letter font, overall expense, and centralized authority of the King James Bible marked a retreat from the reformist zeal that had once sought to create a priesthood of all believers, the Authorized Version nonetheless carried the doctrine of *sola scriptura* to its logical extreme. James had specified in his instructions to the translators that the text should be as free from marginal notes as possible; his Bible would eliminate the commentaries and editorializing—the ready-made interpretations—that had been larded into the margins, for example, of the Geneva Bible. So long as reformist translators continued to print their explanations of biblical passages on the same page as the text itself, the English Bibles would appear, like the Roman Church, to be placing commentary—and hermeneutic tradition—on a par with Holy Writ. James's Bible, however, would have none of this.

After a couple of class sessions discussing the issue of tradition versus scripture as well as the anxieties over reading and reception with regard to various English bibles, I suggest that what the English Bible was to the Reformation, the English *Metamorphoses* was to the post-Reformation Renaissance. Indeed, the danger in translating Ovid's epic and thereby making it available to a larger audience was similar to the danger inherent in the vernacular Bible: there were right and wrong ways to read Ovid. If an uneducated reader simply picked up *Metamorphoses* and started to peruse it, he or she might be shocked or scandalized to find that a book used in grammar schools was chock-full of illicit pleasures. Thus there was a real need for a historical and moral awareness of the poem's intent before reading it; there was, as it turns out, a need for literary criticism.

Students, however, rarely prefer reading literary criticism to literature itself. To be sure, just as my students in previous semesters had felt frustrated by encountering only scholarly summaries and glosses of individual myths without any sense of *Metamorphoses* as a complete literary work, so too must students have felt four hundred years before them: students with names like Shakespeare, Spenser, and Jonson. The grammar school curriculum in the sixteenth century also doled out Ovid in carefully selected and predigested bites. The *Metamorphoses* proved especially teachable in such a curriculum because it supplied an embarrassment of riches for humanist schoolmasters who, pressed for time and resources, taught it not as an epic but as a florilegium of ready-made lessons in grammar, rhetoric, and natural as well as moral philosophy. Most school editions of *Metamorphoses*, therefore, consisted largely of commentaries that either identified the rhetorical tropes at work in a passage or specified the moral lessons to be drawn from it. Indeed, in 1531, it was still possible for Thomas Elyot to insist that the virtues of Ovid's *Metamorphoses* were, in Heather James's elegant paraphrase, "not to be found in the pagan verse itself but in the great commentaries that figuratively and literally grew around it" ("Ovid" 345).

So what prompted Golding to publish an English translation of the entire *Metamorphoses* in 1567, three years before even a Latin edition of the complete epic would be published in England? The opening couplet of Golding's "Preface to the Reader" quickly indicates that, the vernacular notwithstanding, his text is not for everyone: "I would not wish the simple sort offended for to be / When in this book the heathen names of feignèd gods they see" (23). Who, exactly, was Golding referring to as "the simple sort"? And more to the point: who exactly was Arthur Golding? What most surprised my students about Golding—especially those students who were natives to New England—was that, in the words of the *Norton Anthology*, he was "an ardent Puritan" whose numerous translations included "seven works of Calvin" (600).

Why had Golding, a puritanical Calvinist, been the first to translate a work of pagan mythology, especially one as sexually explicit as Ovid's *Metamorphoses*? In the "Epistle to Leicester" that prefaces the first publication in 1567, Golding draws moral examples from individual myths, but he largely ignores the long-standing tradition, perfected by the *Ovide moralisé* and Pierre Bersuire, in which the pagan pantheon—like the prophets and kings of the Old Testament—foreshadowed the ultimate truth of Christ and his teachings. Similarly, when Golding cites Philo Judaeus to the effect that Ovid's account of creation concurs with that of scripture, he is careful to confine such observations to his dedicatory material. Bersuire's commentary, by contrast, had "formed a close parallel to the book that followed it," a physical proximity that, as Ann Moss explains, "emphasized how much [Bersuire's] allegorization had in common with the language and methods of biblical exegesis" (66). Golding's editorial philosophy, with the exception of his introductory letters to Leicester and "the reader," is minimalist: he removes the apparatus of scholarly and moral mediation from both the poem and its surrounding borders. If the Geneva Bible can be characterized by its meddlesome marginalia, Golding—good Calvinist though he was—produced anything but a Geneva *Metamorphoses*. The absence of editorializing, however, left the reader free to get into all kinds of trouble. That, I think, was Golding's intention.

In a remarkable conclusion to his preface, Golding suggests that the onus of responsibility is on the reader, not the translator or editor, of *Metamorphoses*:

> If any stomach be so weak as that it cannot brook
> The lively setting forth of things describèd in this book,
> I give him counsel to abstain until he be more strong,
> And for to use Ulysses' feat against the mermaids song.
> (29)

Raphael Lyne, whose 2001 book on the early modern English *Metamorphoses* is an excellent resource for professors and advanced students alike, calls attention to this passage and notes that the "image of the concerned reader being advised by the translator to adopt Ulysses' defence against the sirens is a comical one: it comes close to saying, if you cannot approach this work properly, then avoid it" (*Ovid's Changing Worlds* 45). This seemingly comical image, however, contains more than a simple caveat to the reader. In these final lines, Golding is no longer outlining the contents of Ovid's epic; he is now imitating Ovid's precocious style, in which, as Garth Tissol reminds us, wit and humor are not ornamental but central to a reading of the poem. If we suppose, as Lyne himself does, that the "simple sort" of reader to whom Golding alludes in his first couple of lines refers to "those who had not received the benefits of a humanist education, and who did not keep commonplace books in which to structure and improve their thinking through judicious annotation" (42), then it seems unlikely that such a reader would even get the joke. Instead, such a reader would be tempted to read ahead, assuming that an account of "Ulysses' feat against the mermaids song" would appear in *Metamorphoses* itself. Thus, what looks to the educated reader like a caution against proceeding further turns out to be an inducement for the "simple sort" to turn the page—and to keep turning—until Ulysses himself appears, several hundred pages later, in book 13.

When Ulysses does finally show up in *Metamorphoses*, however, Ovid barely hints at—indeed he almost omits entirely—the ordeal with the sirens: we hear from Macareus, an erstwhile companion of Ulysses (who decided to heed Circe's advice and stay behind!), that "Circe told us all / That long and doubtful passage and rough seas should us befall" (419). That's all. There's nothing more. Ovid's narrative contains no indication of what transpired between Ulysses and the sirens, nor any hint about what lesson or example the reader could take from this mythic encounter. So, if he were truly concerned with his readers' sensibilities, why would Golding conclude his address to the reader with such a cryptic and dangerously misleading allusion? Where Lyne sees only a comical image—the reader, as Ulysses, being warned—I see the translator of this pagan poem positioning himself as Circe, as the person offering the unheeded advice to the insatiably curious Ulysses, and thus as someone with the power to transform men into pigs and unsuspecting nymphs into hideously deformed monsters. And yet, according to Golding, he is not to blame if men and women become brutish and coarsened as a result of reading Ovid's *Metamorphoses*:

> I know these [pagan] names to other things oft may, and must, agree,
> In declaration of the which I will not tedious be,
> But leave them to the reader's will to take in sundry wise,
> As matter rising giveth cause constructions to devise. (25)

In other words, readers are left to their own devices; and, ultimately, the "reader's will," not the translator's declarations, will determine the meaning of various passages and of the book as a whole.

This is where I take my pedagogical cue. In both Golding's *Metamorphoses* and the King James Bible, readers are handed a text completely out of context. The scholarly work of translation and interpretation, though necessary to create the text, has been stripped away from the final product. What remains is only the bare, plain text: the literary equivalent of the reformed church. Just as the "iconoclastic hammers and scraping tools" had been used to remove layer upon layer of elaborated and traditional interpretation from church walls (Duffy 4), so, too, had reform-minded editors undressed the margins of their books, leaving only white spaces in the margins where moralistic glosses and humanistic explanations had once stood.

We re-create these iconoclastic, reform-minded conditions in my classroom for a couple of days by setting aside the amply annotated *Norton Anthology* and looking, instead, at photocopies from Elizabeth Story Donno's *Elizabethan Minor Epics*, first published in 1963. The remarkable thing about Donno's book—an anthology of a dozen Ovid-inspired epyllia—is how closely it follows Golding's model from four hundred years earlier. Donno prefaces the collection with a wonderful twenty-page introduction that demonstrates the ubiquity of Ovid and the diversity of reactions to his major works in the period, beginning with Stephen Gosson's negative characterization of Ovid as an "amorous scholemaister" in 1579 and ending with Henry Reynolds's belated Christianizing of the Narcissus myth in 1632 (qtd. in Donno 1). Beyond those first twenty pages, however, Donno includes absolutely no annotation—no footnotes, no endnotes, no marginalia—to assist her readers with such difficult and obscure poems as Thomas Heywood's *Oenone and Paris*, Thomas Edwards's *Cephalus and Procris*, Michael Drayton's *Endimion and Phoebe*, and (the one my class read) Thomas Lodge's *Scillaes Metamorphosis: Enterlaced with the Unfortunate Love of Glaucus*.

Obviously, there was less concern in the early 1960s for making the curriculum at American universities accessible to first-generation, nontraditional, underrepresented groups; still, one wonders how undergraduates ever could have read such an edition. And yet Donno's confidence that these poems could be read without the elaborate editorial apparatus found in most twenty-first-century editions of Renaissance literature emboldened me and my students: we were, collectively, up to the challenge. After distributing photocopies of the poem—but *not* the introduction—to the entire class, I recommended that students consult the index of major figures located at the back of Forey's edition to find out where Scylla and Glaucus (as well as Isis, Thetis, Venus, Cupid, and other Ovidian names in Lodge's poem) appear in the epic. I advised students to read as much of *Metamorphoses* as they felt was necessary to create their own scholarly edition of Lodge's poem.

Instantly, there were disagreements about just how much context is necessary for an understanding and appreciation of Lodge's Ovidian homage. Plus, admittedly, there were a couple of complicating factors. First, Lodge follows Golding's erroneous translation and thus gives Glaucus's mother's name as Thetis, instead of Tethys, and thereby confuses (or conflates) two distinct characters in *Metamorphoses*. Should this unintentional transformation be included or discounted from the analysis? Does it matter if Lodge himself believed Thetis to be Glaucus's mother? Does her seemingly unrelated myth somehow play a part in this poem? Second, "Isis" in Lodge's epyllion actually refers to the River Thames at Oxford and not to Ovid's Egyptian goddess. But in the absence of annotation, only a couple of students made the connection to Oxford; meanwhile, those students who had read of the sex-change operation Isis performs at the end of book 9 were convinced that Lodge purposefully chose her rather than Circe (who does not appear in *Scillaes Metamorphosis*!) as the poem's resident genius or problem solver. The students insisting that Ovid's Isis has nothing to do with Lodge's poem noted that it is actually Venus and Cupid, a mother-and-son team, who come to the rescue of the distraught Glaucus and his mother in Lodge's account. "But what," countered one frustrated student, "has Venus to do with the story of Glaucus and Scylla in Ovid?" A group of students, specifically the ones who read books 13 and 14 in their entirety (rather than just the isolated narrative of Glaucus and Scylla), responded by noting that not only does Venus appear at the end of book 14 (the same book that *begins* with the story of Glaucus and Scylla) but she does so in order to apotheosize her son. But whereas Lodge refers to Cupid when he invokes "lovely Venus and her conquering Sonne" at the end of his elegiac love poem, the "conquering Sonne" in book 14 is not Cupid but Venus's *other* son, Aeneas. Is this substitution significant? The martial hero of epic is exchanged for the boyish cherub of romantic love? Again the class was divided.

Lodge, according to some students, probably knew the story of Glaucus and Scylla in isolation from the "little *Aeneid*" in which it appears in *Metamorphoses*. (Why *does* it appear there in Ovid's epic anyway? What *was* he thinking?) For others, the theme of mothers attempting to protect their male children is one that gets repeated throughout these two bloody, epic-minded books: Achilles's mother tries to prevent her son from going to war; the sufferings of Hecuba culminate in the discovery of Polydorus's body on the beach; Aurora cannot even feel sorry for Hecuba because she is too busy mourning her own lost son, Memnon, who died at the hands of Achilles. Perhaps Lodge, like Ovid, is protesting the Augustan (and Elizabethan?) ethos that would sooner make war than love; or perhaps Lodge is suggesting that love and war are not really so different after all and that "all is fair" in each. The in-class discussion was lively, spirited, and scintillatingly intellectual; and the resulting interpretations, I found, were simultaneously ingenious, implausible, and almost always inconsistent with one another. In short, my students made connections every bit as creative, unpredictable, and diverse as those made by Lodge, Shakespeare, Spenser, and Jonson. The students' responses were, as such, closer to the spirit of *Metamorphoses* (and more substantial in their analyses) than the simple and brief, if uniform and authoritative, glossing of individual myths that compose the footnotes and prefatory material in even the most trusted editions and anthologies currently on offer. Indeed, on returning to Jonson's inaugural "Masque of Blackness" after reading Golding's translation, students noted how Jonson's decision to postpone the promised metamorphosis of the Nigerian nymphs until his second masque made perfect sense in the light of the way Ovid uses a similar cliff-hanger technique to suspend the story of Phaethon—and thus the original mythological transformation of the Ethiopians—across books 1 and 2 of *Metamorphoses*.

When one is asked to teach an undergraduate survey course on the literature of the English Renaissance, the reasons for identifying the century and a half between Thomas More's *Utopia* and John Milton's *Paradise Lost* as a distinct literary-historical period can suddenly seem less obvious than they had when, as a graduate student, one first formulated a reading list and a critical problem within this oft-anthologized epoch. The defining features of the English Renaissance, or early modern period, are, like the shape-shifting Thetis herself, "difficult to grasp" in a single semester. Is there really a historical narrative here? If so, is it the narrative of print culture or Protestantism? the recuperation of the pagan gods or the centralization of political authority? self-fashioning or sonneteering? Or, absent a series of causal relationships that would lead the class from More to Milton, is there a thematic through-line perhaps? How is it that sonnets, allegories, masques, epyllia, elegies, essays, epics, romances, and even natural philosophy (Bacon's *Novum organum*, its outspoken empiricism notwithstanding, is awash with Ovidian mythology!) can be made to form a coherent whole? Ironically, I found that Ovid's *Metamorphoses*, with its own notoriously obscure and complex sense of narrative cohesiveness and thematic unity, enabled my students to get a firm, if fleeting, handle on the many issues and anxieties that characterize the period.

Chaos is come again. Just one semester after teaching the course on the English Renaissance, with the English *Metamorphoses* as a major text, I found myself teaching an upper-level undergraduate course on Shakespeare's early plays. I was especially hoping, in this course, to increase my students' appreciation, understanding, and enthusiasm for some of Shakespeare's lesser-known works, including *Titus Andronicus* and *The Comedy of Errors*. In an effort to shore up the legitimacy of *Titus Andronicus* in particular, I assigned Jonathan Bate's 120-page introduction to the third Arden edition of the play as well as his appendix that excerpts "the rape of Philomel" episode from Golding's translation of Ovid. Like Bate himself, I wanted a new generation of Shakespeareans to perceive *Titus Andronicus* as a "complex and self-conscious improvisation upon classical sources, most notably the *Metamorphoses* of Ovid" and thus not to dismiss it as an amateurish bloodbath (3). Bate's expansive introduction and copious, deeply learned footnotes in the Arden edition were, I thought, just the kind of critical supplement my students would need. One student, however, who had been in the English Renaissance course, decided to take issue with a seemingly minor point in Bate's introduction, concerning a character's name. Bate had written that "Virgil's Lavinia, the mother of early Rome, becomes [in Shakespeare's tragedy] the mutilated daughter of late Rome" (18). This student, however, wondered whether Shakespeare's Lavinia might not be named for Petrus Lavinius, the moralizing sixteenth-century commentator on Ovid's *Metamorphoses*, about whom he had read in Forey's introduction to Golding's text. I could not immediately fathom why Shakespeare would go to the trouble of naming a major character, Lavinia, after such a minor commentator, Lavinius. But, when pressed to explain the reasoning behind his question, the student noted that the "by-the-book" rape and mutilation of Lavinia (indeed, the details of the crime committed against her are related by bringing a copy of *Metamorphoses* on stage) might offer up a sort of "moralize this!" challenge to spectators and commentators of the play. Given that it is Young Lucius, a schoolboy, who possesses a copy of *Metamorphoses* in the play, it might be that Shakespeare was inviting his audience to think about what was being taught—and how it was being taught—in the new humanist curriculum of his day. A generation of students taught to extract tidy grammatical and moral lessons from a book of horrors might grow up to write plays like *Titus Andronicus*: bloodbaths that blinkered schoolteachers would later praise for their "complex improvisations upon classical sources." My student taught me that day something that I thought I had already taught him: sometimes the best way to convince students that a text is worth reading is to let them read it for themselves, without supplying all the trappings of expertise and explanation in advance.

NOTE

[1] Barkan here writes on Renaissance artists in *The Gods Made Flesh: Metamorphosis and the Pursuit of Paganism* (172).

Ovid's Genial and Ingenious Story of King Midas
William S. Anderson

The story of King Midas is familiar to most readers, and, although they may not realize it, they owe their knowledge of Midas's narrative to Ovid, whose genius and geniality have shaped it. There are several parts to the story of King Midas, but the best known is the skillful and ironic account of the "golden touch." Around that central narrative, Ovid includes others to account for the magical power that Midas acquired to turn things into gold at his mere touch; to describe what happened to the golden touch when Midas prayed to be rid of it; and finally, to show, in a sequel, how little he had learned from his first disaster and how he therefore earned himself a prize for stupidity, ass's ears. Ovid's sequence and genial language delighted his readers and hearers for nearly 2,000 years and inspired pictorial artists to illustrate the tale. In 1851, however, Nathaniel Hawthorne offered some changes in an attractive reworking of the central story: he is to be credited, I believe, with adopting as the title the phrase that I have already used, "the golden touch." Therefore, after giving background to Ovid's material and spending most of my time on his masterful account, I finish with the contribution of Hawthorne.

The story of King Midas is set in Phrygia, a region in ancient Anatolia, today in central Turkey not far from the capital Ankara. When the Greeks started telling stories about the Near East, it was often because originally there was a grain or more of historical truth behind their later fantasy. King Midas was indeed a real king of Phrygia (Roller). He lived at the end of the eighth century BCE; exerted considerable power during his reign; and therefore accumulated, like many kings, a large amount of wealth.

Early in the seventh century, his kingdom was invaded and destroyed by a savage people called Cimmerians, and Midas was killed. In the years of his prosperity, he had tried to extend his name into Greece, and he is supposed to be the first so-called barbarian to have made gifts to the Greek shrine of Delphi. Herodotus refers to a throne that Midas entrusted to the Corinthians to deliver to Delphi on his behalf (1.14.3). Nothing is today known of that throne, which was no doubt looted and melted down, but early in January 2002, an archaeologist from the University of Pennsylvania proposed the theory that a statuette of very precious ivory, found some years ago at Delphi, is Anatolian and datable to the time of Midas (Wilford). The wealthy king gave more than a throne to the Greek Apollo, it appears.

The Greeks of the eighth and seventh centuries were not politically organized and did not inhabit a land rich in gold, and they were so fascinated by accounts of Eastern gold that they tended to imagine it in mythical amounts. In less than a century after the death of Midas, he had become the epitome of colossal wealth, specifically gold, as we know from the Greek poet Tyrtaeus (frag. 12, line 6).

And already in Tyrtaeus a moralistic and chauvinistic theme was prominent: no truly honorable Greek male would choose the gold of the corrupt East over the virtuous bravery of Greece. Midas served Greek propaganda well, until the historian Herodotus in the fifth century offered other examples of rich, powerful, and doomed Eastern kings (Croesus, Cyrus, Xerxes), who effectively replaced the Phrygian monarch as paradigms. Meanwhile, other stories became associated with Midas, these of a more directly legendary nature. Illustrations on black- and red-figure pottery in the sixth and fifth centuries again and again depict a ruler, often identified as Midas, who takes as hostage (or guest) a drunken old man who is Dionysus's beloved teacher Silenus.

The first reference to the golden touch does not appear, however, until the fourth century BCE, in, of all people, Aristotle, in the discussion of riches in the first book of his *Politics*.[1] He knew a story according to which Midas had died or almost died in the midst of his wealth "because of his insatiable wish." These words assume that Midas had been given his wish, namely, to turn anything he touched to gold and that, as in Ovid, he could not eat or drink a thing before it turned to gold. The ass's ears, or what seem to be ass's ears, had already begun to appear on Midas's forehead in later representations of his connection with Silenus. The painters of course did not explain their drawings, and it took later storytellers to produce some explanation for these appendages. Ovid's version (*Met*. 11.85–193) is the best, in my opinion.

Thus, in the seven hundred years between the time of Midas and that of Ovid, a composite legend developed about this once-historical king. It reflected various aspects of Greek prejudice against the Near East and various moralistic themes dear to the Hellenic and later Roman minds. Ovid, fortunately, is not a heavy-handed moralist, and I have called his account genial and ingenious, to give due credit to his amiability and his artistic insights. He even characterizes Midas as "genially" hosting Silenus in the opening sequence of his story: that is the first time the adverb "genialiter" (11.95) makes its appearance in Latin. Midas is a king, yes, but he seems to be a decent person, not a sadistic tyrant, and there is no indication that he is wallowing in riches at the start. On the contrary, Ovid goes to considerable pains to describe him as a practitioner of the rites of Orpheus and a fellow devotee, with Silenus, of Bacchus. He respectfully and genially entertains Silenus for ten days, then travels to Lydia to restore the old man to his fond pupil Bacchus. In his initial ten lines, accordingly, Ovid has presented Midas in a favorable light: reverent, hospitable, a merry king somewhat like Old King Cole of our nursery rhyme.

Midas's Initial Delight

As I said, Greek art had pictured this part of the story without prejudice against Midas and without connecting it to the golden touch. Ovid uses it to explain how Midas gained that special privilege. To reward Midas's piety and hospitality to Silenus, Bacchus allows him to choose anything in the world and promises to grant the wish. Ovid's phrase is ironically significant: he calls it "the judgment or judicious decision of his gift" and adds the adjectives "pleasing but useless" ("optandi gratum, sed inutile . . . / muneris arbitrium") to prepare us for a poor decision by the simple-minded and delighted Midas (11.101–02).[2] Thus he transports his audience into a familiar fairy-tale situation: the reward gained through one or three wishes, the foolish choice (regularly for wealth), and the regret of the friendly god, which anticipates the miserable outcome of the wish granted to Midas. Without thinking of possible consequences, Midas blurts out, "Make whatever I touch with my body turn into yellow gold" ("effice quidquid / corpore contigero, fulvum vertatur in aurum" [11.102–03]).

We might imagine how a vase painter or a muralist could have represented Midas's progress from sheer unthinking pleasure with his golden touch to anxiety and then despair or how the nucleus preserved in Aristotle could have generated various Greek narratives before Ovid. But it is Ovid who creates and hands on to the future the immortal story. Once again, he is very genial toward poor Midas, never once labeling him a fool or a stupid Phrygian, as a Greek narrator might have done. Midas emerges as an ordinary folktale character, devoid of ethnic or racial features, no more kingly than any of us, just a little more foolish in his good luck than we perhaps would be. As Ovid puts it, "he goes off happy, delighted with trouble, a true hero-son of Berecyntian Cybele" ("laetus abit gaudetque malo Berecyntius heros" [106]). Ovid likes to call unheroic characters "hero" and to identify them through their mothers rather than what one would expect, through their fathers.[3] Thus, although he has adopted an epic form and freely resorts to epic motifs and language, the context prepares us for a signally unepic "hero" here.

Like many an epic hero, Midas possesses a special power, but that power does not reside in martial or regal might. What is worse, it proves to be a power over which he ultimately exerts no control. Thus, whereas at first he believes himself to be positively powerful and a beneficiary of his special touch, he realizes before the day is over that he has become a victim of that very power, which operates unchecked despite him. As Ovid describes the developments of the day, he plays with the major theme of his entire poem, metamorphosis itself, change in all its permutations. At the start, Midas tests his touch on the first available thing, a branch of a nearby ilex that is within reach. Ovid shows the marvel for Midas of this first metamorphosis, by the planned word order of his poem. "He plucked from an ilex a branch: the branch became golden" 'ilice detraxit virgam: virga aurea facta est' (11.109). Exactly in the middle of the line, the word "branch" '*virga*' is repeated, but, since Midas has touched it, it has ceased to be a branch and is metamorphosed into gold. Ovid repeats this rhetorical structure (polyptoton) when Midas picks up a rock and touches a clod of earth ("tollit humo saxum: saxum quoque palluit auro; / contigit et glaebam: contactu glaeba potenti / massa fit" 'He picked up from the ground a stone: the stone also paled to gold. / He also touched the dirt: at the potent touch, the dirt /

became a lump of gold' [11.110–12]). In the middle of each line, at the caesura, the useless things obey his touch and change to gold. He has become like a god, able to transform the nature of things; and, testing that power, Midas runs from one thing to another in what later tradition, typified by Hawthorne, imagined as the royal garden. Ovid does not define the place, and what Midas touches is only what anyone could touch in almost any region of the ancient world. What Ovid concentrates on is the delusionary pleasure of Midas with the first harmless trials of his power. He thinks he is free and able to use his touch like a god, when in fact he is running around like a child with a new toy gun. And the gold is dead and useless; indeed, it will soon threaten Midas's very life.

But Ovid wants to describe convincingly the godlike sensations of Midas, and so he resorts to mythological allusions. Midas wanders into a field where some ripe grain stands, ready for reaping. As Americans know from experience, or at least from the lines of our patriotic song, ripe grain is stereotypically "golden." Although Midas will touch it and change its substance, it will remain pretty much the same color. Ovid, however, calls the grain "the harvest of Ceres" (11.112). Ceres is the Roman goddess of agriculture, and implicitly Midas matches power with that of the goddess. He seems, at first thought, to have defeated and mastered her, robbing her of her grain and making it his gold. But this metamorphosis is symptomatic of the defectiveness of his apparently godlike power: he destroys the vital usefulness of the grain, which all people need for bread, and he gets instead a fundamentally ugly and useless piece of gold in the shape of an ear of grain. Passing on into an orchard perhaps, Midas picks an apple from a tree. Instead of saying now rather boringly that the apple turned to gold, Ovid resorts to another mythical allusion, inviting the audience in to appreciate the dubious miracle: "You might think," he writes, "that the Hesperides had given Midas that apple" ("Hesperidas donasse putes" [11.114]). Let me unpack that allusion. In the far west, normally imagined as the northwestern coast of Africa, was a special garden whose prized tree produced golden apples, watched anxiously over by a set of nymphs called the Hesperides, "the western women." But the gigantic Atlas also guarded it. The hero who did pluck the golden apples of the Hesperides was Hercules, carrying out for his hated stepmother, Juno, one of the many labors assigned him. Midas can momentarily be imagined as another mighty Hercules, and his delusion of power deceives him into some such fancy, but even if he can't, the audience should think the situation through more carefully. He has not picked the mythical golden apples, and no Hesperides have yielded to his mighty power. On the contrary, he has turned a golden delicious apple, so very luscious to eat, into an inedible lump of gold shaped like the original apple. My ideal audience would not have been taken in by this mythical exaggeration, even though the king is deluded. Once again, Midas has perverted the uses of an item of food, and he is too fascinated with his power to realize what is actually happening. Unlike Hercules, he can perform no heroic exploit on the basis of this golden apple.

After pausing to turn marble pillars into gold, Midas strolls or runs over to some water flowing from a brook or fountain: Ovid does not specify. "When he but rinsed his hands in running water, the water might have cheated Danaë" ("ille etiam liquidis palmas ubi laverat undis, / unda fluens palmis Danaën eludere posset" [11.116–17]). The juxtaposition of the two words for water emphasizes that the water, once touched, ceases to be water and has become gold. And the mythical allusion reminds us of how Jupiter elsewhere in Greek mythology approached Danaë as a shower of gold and raped her, thus becoming the father of Perseus. Again, when we unpack the allusion, Ovid points to the false power of Midas's magic touch and the uselessness of the gold he acquires. Jupiter turned himself into the golden shower to overpower the virginal resistance of Danaë and the fanatic guardianship of her father. His gold was potent indeed, in several senses of the word. After all, he sired Perseus on that occasion. Midas, on the other hand, has merely had water turn to gold in his hands. What can he do with that golden replica? He is not fooling anyone but himself, thinking himself powerful, but in fact lacking the most basic and necessary item for survival: water.

Midas's Disillusionment

Ovid has completed his narrative of Midas's initial reactions to his magic touch. The king could hardly grasp all that he had hoped; he is simply overjoyed, without a doubt that he is the happiest man alive, like a god in his power of transformation. Alas, the second phase of discovery now begins, to confirm the ironic meanings of those mythological allusions that I have just reviewed. Servants bring to him a fine private feast, including specially cooked bread, to help him celebrate his delight with his golden touch. However, as soon as he touches any piece of food, of course it turns into inedible gold. He starts by reaching for the bread, which Ovid describes in metonymy as "the gifts of Ceres" ("Cerealia . . . munera" [11.121–22]). This recalls what happened to the ears of grain belonging to Ceres earlier: Midas cannot now enjoy the beneficence of Ceres, cursed as he is by his potent touch, and the warm bread grows rigid in the right hand that had picked it up. So he turns his attention to the piled-up foods of the banquet. Whatever he took up to chew with an eager appetite ("avido dente" [11.123]) turned to a sheet of gold as his teeth chomped down on it. That is, the foolish appetite for gold frustrates the natural appetite for food and frustrates it so radically that Midas seems doomed to starve to death amid a growing pile of useless, inedible, and increasingly hated gold. (That is Aristotle's version of what happened to the king.) The final blow to the expected feast comes when Midas prepares to drink some wine. Ovid again resorts to metonymy and describes the wine ironically as the "originator of Midas's gift" ("auctorem muneris" [11.125]). When the king, however, attempts to take a sip of this vintage wine, Bacchus is no longer in it. The king has turned it into a rigid semblance of flowing gold, and Bacchus, once his patron, has been affronted by the golden touch. Midas's power acts without his control to destroy every living, pleasurable aspect of human existence and indeed threatens to destroy its master, Midas himself.

Until this threat of starvation, Midas has responded with uncomprehending delight to the various manifestations of his metamorphic powers. Now, unable to eat or drink, he reacts with astonishment and despair at this new power of his, which is obviously a curse. As commonly happens to characters in Ovid's poem, Midas becomes a victim of metamorphosis, though ironically this predicament is a result of the granting of his dearest wish. And so he becomes his own victim. His choice of the golden gift has spoiled all the natural gifts of existence. Ovid catches the paradox of the man, who is both rich and wretched ("divesque miserque" [11.127]), who hates what he had so recently prayed for. There is no way all that gold can relieve his hunger, even if Midas tried to buy more food, no way that water or wine can satisfy his growing thirst. To summarize Midas's plight, Ovid notes that the king is deservedly tormented by the gold he now hates. What can he do? He lifts up toward heaven his hands and arms, heavy and glittering with golden ornaments and rings, and he prays to Bacchus: "I have sinned. But pardon me, father Bacchus, and free me from this curse that seemed so attractive" ("da veniam, Lenaee pater! peccavimus . . . / sed miserere, precor, speciosoque eripe damno" [11.132–33]). Calling the golden touch a curse, Midas captures its essential evil and suggests the moral embedded in the tale: the true value of desires is determined by their utility; gold in immense quantities, answering every touch, is pernicious.

Bacchus responds favorably to Midas's pathetic prayer, because he feels kindly toward the king in his pathos and penitence. With the same Latin phrase with which he had originally granted the gift, he now dissolves it ("munera solvit" [11.104, 135]). He goes further. As every item on the king's body has been turned to the hated gold, Bacchus urges Midas to go up the Pactolus River near Sardis to its source in the mountains and there bathe and purify himself and wash away the pollution. When Midas does so, the golden power of his touch ("vis aurea" [11.142]) transfers itself from the man to the river, which seems now to have the power to turn the land where it flows into gold. Many nuggets were found in and near the Pactolus in ancient times, and the fields seem to grow gold. Thus, the golden touch has at last turned into something more ordinary and useful, the source of occasional lucky finds of gold.

Midas as Lover of the Countryside

It remains for Ovid to explain the ass's ears, which the early artistic tradition had assigned to Midas in connection with his reception of Silenus. Ovid decides to separate the ears entirely from the earlier situations he has portrayed and to make them an emblem of a new stupidity in Midas, a demonstration of his incorrigible and innate thickheadedness ("pingue ingenium" [148]).[4] In drastic reaction against the riches that he once prized, Midas flees court society and all its false glitter and takes to the woods and countryside and the companionship of the rustic Pan.

Changing one's environment does not change the man, as we know, and Midas carries along with him his essential lack of discretion and perception. This failure, says Ovid, will injure him as did his earlier choice of the golden touch. This time, he fails to understand the qualities of musical art and so deludes himself that the minor deity Pan, with his pipes, is the greatest musician in the world. Pan also thinks so about himself and accordingly challenges the supreme god of music, Apollo himself. There follows a contest in which the surprise loser is Midas.

Ovid has staged several contests between musicians and challengers, most commonly between human rash challengers and superior deities, like the Muses; and he has other fools rival the gods in weaving or in having the greatest number of children. In all previous instances, the daring human challenger loses and suffers punishment through metamorphosis. Marsyas was flayed alive for taking on Apollo earlier. In this case, Pan must of course suffer defeat: he is no match with his pipes against the lyre, and even his rustic attire presages his loss to the elegantly dressed Apollo. When he is judged the loser, however, he disappears unscathed from the story, and stupid Midas takes over his role as the punished one. The judge Tmolus wins unanimous assent to his verdict from the usual inhabitants of the countryside. Only one person disagrees, and that of course is Midas, the outsider, who claims that the decision is unfair (11.173).

Midas Condemned

When Midas dares to disagree with Tmolus, he is justly punished by Apollo, who quickly changes Midas's stupid human ears into the form that best represents his insensitivity: long, hairy, floppy ass's ears. This metamorphosis represents a well-known ancient belief and saying, that the ass can never appreciate the lyre (and indeed often brays at the lyre's music).

Midas is effectively marked with the emblem of his stupidity, for all to see and ridicule, unless he can contrive to conceal it. And that's hard: donkey's ears are very long, as Pinocchio found out. He resorts to an Eastern headdress called the "tiara" (11.181), a tall, pointed cap, not quite like a dunce's cap (though we might use that in a modern version). For some time, he manages to hide his shame. However, he needs to be shaved and barbered regularly, and inevitably his barber learns the dread secret. It puts the barber in a terrible predicament: he is bursting to share the secret with others, but he knows that such a revelation will cost him his life. The poor man cannot keep quiet, so he devises what he thinks will be the safest method of telling the story without speaking to anyone in particular. He digs a hole in the fields, then stoops down and whispers into the empty hole his information about the ears. Shoveling back the earth and filling up the hole again, he creeps quietly away. Unfortunately for Midas—we never hear whether the barber was punished for informing against the king—the nature that he had ignored now completes his disgrace. A grove of reeds starts growing from this hole seeded with the barber's data. When they grow tall and wave in the wind, the breeze wafting through them seems to pick up the whisper seeded in them by the man whom Ovid wittily calls their "farmer" ("agricolam" [192]). So the reeds, the substance from which Pan made his pipes, betray the secret and prove the shameful truth about Midas's ears.

Ovid has built up a complicated story with a system of metamorphoses: from the items turned to gold to the Pactolus River to Midas's simple delight with his gold to Midas's ears and finally to the barber's secret. However, his narrative seems to fall into two main parts featuring the foolish choice of gold, then the more seriously foolish preference for the shrill panpipes over the mellifluous sounds of Apollo's lyre. The theme word of the first part is "gold" or "golden" ("aurum," "aureus"); of the second, "ears" ("aures"). The connection between the parts of this diptych can be captured nicely in Latin, exploiting the similarity of the two terms: as Franz Bömer suggests, for example, we can call part 1 "Midas aureus" ("Golden Midas") and part 2 "Midas auritus" ("Midas with the Special Ears").[5]

Hawthorne's Midas

I conclude with a brief appreciation of Hawthorne's very readable and indeed quite memorable story "The Golden Touch," the second of six stories adapted from Greek myth in *A Wonder Book* of 1851. It was written early in that decisive period of creativity (1850–52) when Hawthorne published three great novels—*The Scarlet Letter, The House of Seven Gables*, and *The Blithedale Romance*. His popular retellings of Greco-Roman myths, many from Ovid, are not much read today, but one part of his story of Midas stirred so much admiration that it has often become amalgamated (often unconsciously) with the account of Ovid; I refer to the part he invented for Midas's daughter. She plays a special role in Mary Zimmerman's recent successful Broadway production, *Metamorphoses*. Ovid gives Midas no family or friends: he is a lone fool making poor choices and decisions on his own, at his own cost. And the worst penalty for him from the golden touch is the danger of starvation. But Hawthorne was writing for children and parents who in his Romantic era were awakening to the charm and pathos of children's stories.[6] A second innovation was the creation of a youthful narrator who is very different from the usually serious narrator that Hawthorne adopted for his adult *Twice-Told Tales*. This new narrator is Eustace Bright, a student of eighteen at Williams College, who enjoys captivating his audience of girls and boys and adapting the old stories for the high spirits of his young friends. In his first paragraph, therefore, Eustace introduces Midas, and then goes on: "And he had a little daughter, whom nobody but myself ever heard of, and whose name I either never knew or have entirely forgotten. So, because I love odd names for little girls, I choose to call her Marygold" (40)—an inspired choice of character and name. And clearly, in his diffident way, Eustace was announcing his bold addition to Ovid's cast.

Marygold makes all the difference to Eustace's account: she is the emotional center of his sentimental tale, which changes radically the tone of Ovid's genial tale. For Eustace, Midas is a kind of miser, possessing piles of gold but eternally dissatisfied with what he has. One day an unidentified stranger, emitting a golden radiance, visits him in his treasure room and offers to grant him his dearest wish. This stranger is clearly not Bacchus but seems to be the magical or divine power of gold itself. This is where the phrase "golden touch" becomes associated, I believe, with Midas, for he makes the same foolish choice as in Ovid. The stranger tells him that the next morning at sunrise he will possess the golden touch.

Sleeping very little that night, Midas anxiously waits for the first streak of sunshine, when he discovers from the weight and color of the bed linen that he has indeed been empowered. As he gets up and dresses, he notes some negative features of his touch: the pages of a book turn to gold and become illegible; his spectacles—which Eustace smilingly admits had not yet been invented—become impenetrable gold, a transformation that he "philosophically" accepts (47). Going outdoors into the garden, where fragrant roses are in full and lovely bloom, the unwise king turns every flower into gold and thinks that he has improved his garden vastly. Proud of himself, he goes into a breakfast fit for a New England family of 1851: trout, hotcakes, eggs, and coffee. And here is where little Marygold enters and plays her key role. She comes in from the garden "crying bitterly" (48), and, in answer to her father's query about the cause of her tears, she holds out one of the now-golden roses and proclaims it "the ugliest flower that ever grew" (49). Unimpressed with his child's judgment, her preference for natural over synthetic beauty, Midas urges her to eat her breakfast and starts on his. Of course, as soon as he touches any item of food or drink, it becomes inedible or undrinkable. This leads to a succession of ever-more-audible groans of frustration. Good little Marygold, concerned for her father, rushes up to hug him around the knees and comfort him in his distress, and she turns into a golden statue at his kiss. He addresses her tenderly, "but Marygold made no answer" (52). At last the reality of his curse is brought home to the foolish but loving king. The unnatural dehumanization of Marygold epitomizes his folly and the worthlessness of all his gold. The stranger suddenly reappears, and, when Midas calls the golden touch hateful, he allows Midas quickly to free himself from it and, with ordinary water sprinkled on the various items he has changed, to restore them to their original natural state. He of course first transforms Marygold back into her happy, affectionate, childish human self, and so, a wiser man and a better father, he lives, according to Eustace, to hold her children in his lap and tell them edifying stories.

I believe that Hawthorne's changes to Ovid's account were inspired and readily welcomed in his time. It is easy to imagine Queen Victoria reading and weeping over Hawthorne's Marygold, in the midst of her many children. But the Romantic notes and characters cannot simply be added to Ovid, for his is not a Romantic children's story. His geniality toward Midas is tolerant but unsentimental, and he lets the king hurt nobody but himself, to the verge of starvation. When in his more elaborate series of adventures Midas learns all too little from his golden touch, it is only right that his poetic stupidity be permanently punished with ass's ears. Exploiting the manifold thematic possibilities of metamorphosis, Ovid gradually distances us from an increasingly isolated King Midas. He does not, like Hawthorne, limit himself to the golden touch, nor does he play with his story by inventing obvious anachronisms and a spirited little daughter to focus on the king as a father. The sudden silence of Marygold is quickly reversed, and life and family love prevail, as Eustace Bright's young audience expects. Ovid allows no family members to soften the presentation of Midas. Elsewhere in the poem he has children tragically killed in front of their parents, indeed often killed by their parents with insane deliberation. But here Ovid presents the suicidal power of gold to destroy a greedy king who escapes but learns nothing.

NOTES

[1] *Politics* 1.3.16 (1257b): "A man with plenty of money may often lack the bare necessities for living. Yet it is absurd that wealth should be such that, though a man have a good amount of it, he dies of hunger, like the well-known Midas of the myth: because of the insatiable greed of his prayer, every item of food that was served to him became gold" (my trans.).

[2] Translations of Ovid are my own.

[3] One of my favorites is "Autonoeius heros" for Actaeon when he first becomes a timid deer (3.198).

[4] This and other kinds of stupidity serve as a basic theme for Apuleius's *Golden Ass*.

[5] I have tried to capture it in English (but I don't consider myself very successful) with "crass Midas" and "ass Midas." If anyone thinks up a good jingling pair of titles, I would be happy to use them, with full credit.

[6] Hawthorne defined his audience in the subtitle: "For Girls and Boys." Of more than a hundred stories that he wrote up to 1851, these are the only ones he designated for young people (the age of his own children).

GENDERED AND EMBODIED OVID

Sex and Violence in *Amores*

Paul Allen Miller

Sexual and gendered hierarchies rest on an at least implicit violence. In most societies, those deviations from expected norms that are perceived as threatening to the existing relations of sexual power are dealt with harshly. Whether the issue is gay bashing, domestic abuse, female circumcision, or the quasi legality of rape in many societies, in each case the common denominator that extends across time and space is the violence that inheres in and enforces these relations of power. Yet it is equally true that this violence, while omnipresent, is not on a day-to-day basis experienced as violence. The lived texture of normative sexuality, whether that of the ancient pederastic model, that of traditional marriage practices, or that of one of the innumerable varieties of concubinage practiced throughout history, is one of attraction, desire, and consent, even in the act of refusal.

The poems in Ovid's *Amores*, profoundly sophisticated works of art and intellectual refinement, perfectly embody this tension. On the one hand, its poems are filled with images of violence. Corinna is struck by Ovid (1.7).[1] Her slave is beaten and essentially raped (2.7, 2.8). She is assailed for having an abortion (2.13, 2.14). Love itself is compared to military service (1.9). The poet even invokes the officially sanctioned violence of the law in pursuit of his own transgressive desires (1.4). On the other hand, the poems themselves feel nothing like this. Their atmosphere is not that of a charnel house from the Marquis de Sade but that of the literary salon. Love is the province of a mocking Cupid, not Mars. His wounds and triumphs incite desire, not grief (1.2, 2.12). Even remorse can serve as a sophisticated aphrodisiac. Only the unrefined would object (3.4).

Amores, then, offers a perfect vehicle for teaching not only about ancient sexual and gendered hierarchies but also how the violence inherent in those norms is produced beneath the ruse of consent. As such Amores reveals as much about contemporary relations of sexual power as about those of ancient Rome. Such a reading is not a denial of these poems' wit or artistic power but is predicated on it. In the next few pages, then, I look at three representative sets of poems to examine how Ovid both unmasks the inherent violence that lies behind Roman sexual norms and simultaneously renders that violence acceptable and even enjoyable to a sophisticated and civilized audience of readers from both sexes. I look first at 1.4, on Corinna's relation to her husband, or "*vir*."[2] Then I examine the power relations portrayed in Ovid's sexual liaison with Corinna's slave, Cypassis, in 2.7 and 2.8. Finally, I examine 1.7, in which Ovid portrays directly the aftermath of his having struck Corinna.

In poem 1.4, Ovid, Corinna, and her *vir* are all to attend the same dinner party. Romans ate reclining on couches, normally with three guests to a couch. Such arrangements offered the enterprising lover countless opportunities for games of footsy, heavy petting, and more. In this poem, the poet appears in the standard elegiac pose of the "praeceptor amoris," or "love tutor," instructing Corinna in the art of adultery so that she may deceive her *vir*. In this poem's companion piece, 2.5, the poet is hoist on his own petard. There the very same hand signs, winks, and nods, which the poet here proposes as a lover's discourse to his beloved, are used against him.

Poem 1.4 begins with a series of double entendres in which Ovid contrasts his position with that of Corinna's *vir*, invoking both legal vocabulary and images of sexual violence:

> Will I then have to sit through dinner, only looking at my beloved
>   Girl? Will there be another who will enjoy being touched?
> Will she warm the lap of another whom she has snuggled up under?
>   Will he put his hands round her neck whenever he wishes?
> Do not be amazed that the radiant daughter of Atrax drove those ambiguous
>   Men to take up arms when they had finished their wine;
> My home is not in the forest, nor do my limbs adhere to a horse:
>   Yet I can scarcely keep my hands off you.   (1.4.3–10)[3]

The tone here is comic. We are invited to sympathize with the poet's plight of seeing his girl in the arms of another. At the same time, he compares himself to the drunken centaurs that ran riot at the wedding of Hippodamia and Pirithous. The gesture is grotesque and self-deflating. Corinna may be with her *vir*, but Ovid, like the half-man, half-beast centaurs, is a *vir ambiguus*, a phrase that simultaneously questions his masculinity and attributes to him a bestial and uncontrolled sexuality in the manner of a centaur.

In their battle with the Lapiths, an episode famously depicted on the Parthenon metopes, the centaurs were in fact intent on nothing less than ravishing the bride. Nor is this an isolated image of bestial rape in *Amores*. In 1.3, Corinna is asked to yield to the poet as Io, Leda, and Europa had yielded to the various animal disguises of Jupiter. The deployment of elaborate mythological discourse sublimates the implicit sexual violence in these scenes, which are in fact rapes, and can quickly cause us to forget what is actually at stake in 1.4: which of the two men has the right to treat Corinna as his sexual property?

This reference to a discourse of property rights is not mere feminist hyperbole. Ovid explicitly and directly employs the language of Roman property law in the text of the poem. This is made clear in line 6, "iniciet collo, cum volet, ille manum?" 'Will he put his hands round her neck whenever he wishes?' The phrase *inicere manus*, which on a first reading seems merely to refer to the physical placement of the man's arms round Corinna's neck in an embrace, in fact quotes a legal formula used by a plaintiff for claiming stolen goods as one's own in a court proceeding known as a *vindicatio* (Gaius 4.16; Daube 227; Kenney, "Ovid and the Law" 254–58; and McKeown's commentary on 1.4.6 at 2:81). Moreover, *manus* ("hand") itself was no insignificant term in the legal vocabulary regulating commerce between the sexes: in marriage, the possessor of *manus* is he who has power over the bride—the person under whose thumb she must ultimately live, be it her husband or father.

There is, then, a complex series of puns here, whose wit provides the poem's aesthetic enjoyment even as it both sublimates and highlights the sexual violence inherent in the poem's founding conceit. Thus, what at first seems a gesture of pure eroticism—the poet's rival can embrace Corinna whenever he wishes—contains within it another level of meaning: the *vir* can claim Corinna as his and demand his property rights whenever he wishes. The result of such a claim, however, is that Ovid becomes transformed into a *vir ambiguus* whose bestial lust and anger make him "scarcely able to keep his hands off" her ("vix a te videor posse tenere manus"), a phrase that simultaneously asserts a legal counterclaim, imagines an irresistible erotic attraction ("I just can't keep my hands off you"), and portrays a potential assault in the manner of a centaur. The last shade of meaning becomes clear in 1.8, where the poet is depicted as listening in as the elderly bawd, Dipsas, instructs Corinna on how to dun her lovers for expensive gifts. He exclaims:

> at nostrae vix se continuere *manus*
> quin albam raramque comam lacrimosaque vino
>   lumina rugosas distraherentque genas.
>
> (1.8.110–12)

> . . . and my *hands* were scarcely able to restrain themselves
> from tearing to shreds her thin white hair,
>   her eyes bleary with wine, and her wrinkled cheeks.

This passage, in which there is no possibility of an erotic interpretation, necessarily colors its earlier erotic counterpart. The very existence of an exclusively violent reading of the phrase "vix se continuere manus" means that the earlier erotic passage in 1.4.10, "vix . . . posse tenere manus," can never be reread outside this context. Law, violence, ownership, rape, and lovemaking momentarily become one in the act of laying hands on another. The implicit violence of 1.4's simile comparing Ovid to the centaurs here becomes explicit.

The key to interpreting this series of double entendres is to be found in 1.4.39–40. Here the poet's potential jealousy threatens to explode into the open. He will declare himself, at the dinner party, to be Corinna's "amator" ("lover") and explicitly assert his own property rights:

> If you kiss him, I will show myself a lover caught in the act
>   ["manifestus"]
> And I will say those [kisses] are mine and lay legal claim to them
>   ["iniciam manus"].

The irony, of course, is that as Corinna's *amator* and not her *vir*, Ovid has no such claim, and the phrase "amator manifestus" acknowledges as much since it is derived from the legal term *fur manifestus*, "a thief caught in the act." The irony of the thief laying legal claim to that which he has stolen is, of course, deliciously absurd, even as it simultaneously reveals the relations of property and violence that subtend the erotic.

In fact, Corinna's sole freedom is to give her kisses to a lover in secret ("furtim") as well as to the man who has legal claim to them:

> At night your man will lock you in, but I, soaked with sad tears,
>   Will follow you all the way to the cruel doors, as is my right.
> Then he will take kisses, then, he will take not only kisses;
>   What you give me in stealth, you will give him forced by the law.
>   (1.4.61–64)

Note, however, that Ovid's realm of freedom and transgression, that of the *amator* or *fur* as opposed to the *vir*, uses the same language of legal right and erotic violence as the *vir* whose eroticism is explicitly defined as pertaining to this realm. Ovid thus inverts the normal significations of Roman jurisprudence defining right and freedom as the transgression of the norms of sexual, legal, and property relations. This creates hilarity and an image of subversion and freedom from constraint even as it implicitly underlines Corinna's subjection to whoever can lay his hands on her.

In 2.7 and 2.8, the same set of virtuoso rhetorical strategies is used not only to legitimate sexual coercion but also to render it, together with torture, a source of enjoyment. On the level of plot, the story is anything but appealing. Yet students and other readers, myself included, are consistently amused both by Ovid's perverse rhetorical audacity and the sheer ingenuity of his poetic invention. In 2.7, Corinna suspects Ovid of having a liaison with Cypassis, the slave who fixes Corinna's hair. Ovid protests vigorously, arguing that Corinna frequently misconstrues his most innocent gesture as a sign of sexual commerce between him and another woman. Since Ovid has already instructed Corinna in 1.4 on how to use a series of seemingly innocuous gestures for covert erotic communication, and since in 2.4 he has blithely announced that there is no type of woman that does not appeal to his omnivorous sexuality, we in fact have every reason to suspect that all may not be as the poet claims.

The climax of his apologia comes in 2.7.21–22, when he claims to take offense at the notion that he could be erotically attracted to a body that had undergone the forms of torture and physical subjection that were a normal part of servile life:

> What free man would wish to enter into connubial Venus with a servant,
>   And to embrace a back scarred by the whip?

Ovid's argument is based on a double entendre that turns on legal terminology. Sexual relations between the free and servile population were, as in the antebellum American South, a regular and assumed part of daily existence. But Ovid here uses specifically the term *conubium*, which legally refers to a marriage and only later is used as a euphemism for sexual intercourse. The addition of the nominal modifier, "Veneris" 'of Venus', moreover, gives this particular formulation a distinctly erotic coloring. Ovid is a master of doublespeak. He says something both completely true and yet explicitly designed to deceive Corinna. It would, in fact, be impossible for a free man to marry a slave, and his argument that the mere suggestion of such a possibility would be repulsive to any free Roman would have been accepted without question by Ovid's readers. Yet the poet clearly wants Corinna to understand not marriage but sexual relations.

It is at this point that the detail of embracing the scarred and naked back of Cypassis assumes a key importance, condensing three different strands of meaning into a single image: first, the erotic superiority of Corinna. Her back is not scarred. This appeal to her vanity and her social superiority is designed rhetorically to clench Ovid's argument. Second is the erotic appeal of the image itself. Just as the word *conubium* presents two different sets of significations, depending on the point of view from which it is read, so does Cypassis's scarred back. The first emphasizes its ugliness and deformity, the second the visual and tactile sensation of Cypassis's naked back, as the poet's hands embrace and brush against the scarred flesh. The specificity of the image brings to life the moment of the erotic encounter in a fashion designed both to arouse and to repulse.

The third strand of meaning condensed into this image is that of Cypassis's complete erotic and physical subjection to the whims of others. This is a meaning that only becomes clear retroactively, after the reader has finished 2.7's companion piece, 2.8. While upon a first reading it is possible for the naive reader to believe that the poet has been unjustly accused by Corinna, in 2.8, when the poet turns to address Cypassis, the cynical nature of his rhetorical brilliance is revealed. The poet begins by congratulating himself before Cypassis on his successful parrying of Corinna's charge. He notes that his cool demeanor under pressure is all that saved Cypassis from a beating. After a brief digression, in which a variety of mythological precedents are offered to argue for why his earlier protest that no free man could be attracted to a slave should not be taken seriously, he argues that he is owed repayment for the successful defense he mounted against the charges Corinna had leveled against him and Cypassis:

> For my good offices then pay me back with a sweet reward,
>   Sleep with me today, dusky Cypassis.   (2.8.21–22)

When the slave who has just escaped being caught in her mistress's bed hesitates, Ovid threatens to blackmail her by revealing their sexual secrets. He will not only admit what he denied in 2.7 but also give details of times, places, and positions, sure to inflame Corinna's anger. For Ovid, the result would be the end of his liaison with Corinna, but for Cypassis it would mean at a minimum new scars on her back, torture, perhaps even death. The outrageous rhetoric and the sheer, perverse bravura of pairing these poems cannot help delighting the reader, even as this technical virtuosity masks what is really at stake in this scenario: Cypassis has no meaningful ability to consent. What we witness in 2.8 is the rape of a slave who must either submit in silence or face certain physical punishment: a realization that transforms our knowing smile into nervous laughter and our desire into awkward shame.

While in 1.4 Corinna is the victim of implicit violence and legal coercion, and while in 2.7 and 2.8 her servant, Cypassis, is subjected to the violence of slavery and the sexual subjugation that was its constant concomitant, in 1.7 Corinna herself is assaulted. In the poem immediately before that in which the poet threatens to tear the cheeks of the bawd Dipsas (1.8), he strikes Corinna with the same "manus" 'hands' that he can barely keep off her at the opening of 1.4. These are the hands that he will use to claim his stolen property rights later in the poem and that represent the legal authority that her father or her husband continues to wield over her even as an adult. Throughout *Amores*, these hands are very busy and seldom truly clean.

> Bind my hands (they merited chains),
>   Till my madness wanes, if a friend be present:
> For madness moved my heedless arms against my mistress;
>   My girl weeps, wounded by my insane hand.   (1.7.1–4)

Yet the poet's pretense to remorse need not be taken too seriously. It is part of the fun. We then immediately devolve into a series of mythological exempla in which the poet's "furor" is compared to the madness of Ajax and of Orestes. The distancing effect of the rhetoric of mythology allows the violence of the opening scene to be sublimated into a moment of aesthetic admiration and soft-focus eroticism:

> Was I therefore able to rip out her artful curls?
>   And yet, those disturbed locks did not detract from her attraction:
> She was beautiful that way; just like Atalanta, I'd say,
>   When she harassed the Arcadian beasts.   (1.7.11–14)

What began, at least on the literal level, as a cause of shame here becomes the locus of sexual attraction: Corinna looks good when slapped around a bit.

There follows a brief mythologically embellished narrative of the assault and its aftermath, in which the poet once more adopts a contrite attitude. He then ironically compares his "victory" to a Roman general's triumphal procession. The image recalls 1.2, in which the poet recounts Cupid's triumph. It also reminds the reader of another actual triumph, Augustus's over Cleopatra, which had been celebrated in 29 BCE. The intertextual echo, in turn, reinforces the political subtext. Poem 1.2 ends with a joking allusion to the fact that, according to the official genealogies, Augustus, as the descendant of Aeneas, was Cupid's cousin. It would thus be difficult for the reader of *Amores* not to think of Augustus when the triumph motif returns five poems later, and more specifically of the emperor's own triumph over a "girl":

> Come now, victor, celebrate a magnificent triumph,
>   Ring your hair in laurel, and give thanks to Jove,
> Let the crowd of your comrades, which follows your chariot,
>   Cry out, "Hail! The strong man conquers the girl!"
> And let the sad captive march before you, hair hanging loose,
>   If her scratched cheeks permitted, she would shine like a goddess.
> It would have been more fitting to bruise her neck with my lips
>   And to leave the bite mark of a caressing tooth.   (1.7.35–42)

This is a passage of rhetorical brilliance. It begins by calling into question the manhood of the speaker by ironically comparing him to a triumphing general, the emblem of Roman domination. It then deflates this comparison by noting that the poet has triumphed not over a mighty adversary but over a mere girl. At the same time, the political resonances of the passage create a distancing effect whereby the irony directed against the speaker can be reread as directed against Augustus, the self-styled moral reformer, restorer of republican virtue, and the last person to celebrate a triumph over a female foe.

In the third couplet, the image of the triumph modulates from self-deprecation and subtle political irony to a recollection of lines 11–14, where Ovid had described the heightened desire he experienced at observing the damage done to Corinna's hair ("She was beautiful that way"). In our present passage, Corinna is described as walking before the poet's triumphal car as a captive. Her hair is, as before, undone and hanging loose. This was the traditional attitude of mourning and would have been that struck by female captives marching in a triumphal procession. Her cheeks are scratched from what in the case of an actual triumph would have been the self-inflicted wounds that accompanied ritual mourning, but which, in this case, as the following couplet makes clear, are the result of Ovid's own eroticized "furor." Nonetheless, Corinna would be "utterly radiant" ("candida tota") if her cheeks allowed. The term "candida" in the context of erotic poetry recalls its use by Catullus, describing his beloved's entrance into the house where they were to consummate their adulterous love as the entrance of a "candida diva" 'a shining goddess' (poem 68, line 70). Ovid's final couplet completes the transition from the figurative violence of the imagined triumph to the erotics of violence in the combat of love. Far better it would have been for the poet to have covered her neck with bruises from his lips and to have left bite marks on it from his passion than to have scratched her face and ripped her hair. The ease with which the traces of a physical assault become transformed into the marks of love, as mediated through the figure of the triumph, is both breathtaking in its genius and utterly disturbing as it points to a deeper level on which there is a fundamental commutability between the gestures of love and those of assault.

This passage, in short, shows precisely how the enjoyment we receive from the admiration of Ovid's pyrotechnic skill makes us willing participants in the eroticization and naturalization of sexual violence. Its sheer rhetorical virtuosity, as in 2.7 and 2.8, as well as 1.4, makes it impossible not to admire these well-wrought poems, even as a sober consideration of their content cannot help leaving us appalled—if not at Ovid, then at the entire sex and gender system of which he is a part and we its heirs. Moreover, there is a real paradox here: the very rhetorical structures that serve to naturalize violence, to make it appear as a sexual norm and not a transgression, also serve to highlight those very processes of naturalization.

This leads to a difficult question concerning whether the purpose of this poetry is in fact the maintenance of ideological hegemony or the beginning of critique. To pose such a question, however, may be to fall into anachronism. Ovid would never have conceptualized his poetic purpose in such terms. The realistic answer for the modern reader, however, is that both are the case. By pushing the structures of belief and the accepted sexual norms of the period to the extreme, Ovid at once provokes our enjoyment of them, and hence our at-least-momentary libidinal investment in those norms, and at the same time reveals them as constructs that can be manipulated.

What Ovid never does, however, is posit an alternative, a form of sexual relations not based on implicit violence and the consequent illusion of consent, outside those norms (P. Miller 160–83). He momentarily inverts the normative relations of power for comic and rhetorical effect as at the end of 1.7, where he stretches forth his arms as a suppliant and demands that Corinna take vengeance on him, that she beat him and tear his hair—all of which, as he has already made clear, can be easily reread as a form of erotic play. Nonetheless, he does not let this momentary inversion stand. With the last couplet he returns to the normative model, and Corinna is asked to rearrange her hair to hide the signs of her abuse:

> Then again just hide the sad signs of my misdeed:
> Rearrange your hair and put it back in its place.
> (1.7.67–68)

We chuckle at the audacity but only too painfully recognize the behavior.

NOTES

[1] This is, of course, not the actual, autobiographical Ovid, but a literary character that the poems consistently invite us to confuse with the poet himself.

[2] The term is ambiguous and much debated (P. Davis 445–46). On the one hand, it suggests that he is Corinna's husband and hence that the relationship portrayed in *Amores* is an adulterous one. The most prominent advocate of this reading has been Gordon Williams, who argues that all the elegiac *dominae*, with the exception of Gallus's Lycoris, were adulterous *matronae* (528–29, 539, 542). At the same time, *vir* may refer merely to Corinna's man of the moment and reflect her status as a *meretrix*. Stroh is the most forceful advocate of this position (331–34). There is, then, a division of scholarly opinion. What does seem clear, however, is that the ambiguity inherent in the term provides Ovid with plausible deniability, allowing him to appear both subversive and submissive at the same time (P. Green, *Ovid: The Erotic Poems* 272).

[3] All translations are my own.

Ovid's Thisbe and a Roman Woman Love Poet
Judith P. Hallett

Ovid's *Metamorphoses* depicts several of its mythic female characters as skillful communicators, particularly in their erotic interactions. One such character is of particular interest to my students: the Babylonian maiden Thisbe in book 4, lines 55–166, whose tragic romance with the youth Pyramus is immortalized by Shakespeare in *A Midsummer Night's Dream*.

In this essay I would like to illuminate, as I do for my students, Ovid's portrayal of the fictional Thisbe by examining its affinities with a series of eleven amatory poems by and about Sulpicia, a historical woman writer contemporary with and well known to Ovid. Through his evocations of these Sulpicia poems, not only their language and themes but also their dramatic scenario, Ovid compares his own artistic creation Thisbe to Sulpicia, a real-life literary model. Through this comparison Ovid represents Thisbe—who speaks and is spoken of in dactylic hexameter verse—as a more admirable love poet than Sulpicia, and as a more admirable lover too.

Both Sulpicia and Thisbe are self-assertive women of many words. In this regard they differ from the women customarily depicted as the lovers of Roman elegiac poets, such as Corinna in Ovid's own *Amores*, who are assigned few if any words of their own. Yet Ovid also emphasizes major differences between Sulpicia and Thisbe. He represents Thisbe as facing more serious amatory obstacles than Sulpicia encounters and as being in a mutual and reciprocal love relationship.

In using Sulpicia's poetry to furnish a literary context for Ovid's portrayal of Thisbe, I assume that Sulpicia is the author of all eleven poems and that Ovid's evocations of them can in fact be used to demonstrate her authorship.[1] These poems are found, as elegies 8 through 18, in the third book of elegies credited to Tibullus, another love poet contemporary with Ovid. (Ovid himself laments Tibullus's untimely death in one of his own elegies, *Amores* 3.9.) Like both Ovid and Sulpicia, Tibullus enjoyed the literary patronage of Sulpicia's maternal uncle, Marcus Valerius Messalla Corvinus (Hallett 45–46).[2]

The eleven Sulpicia elegies, which portray Sulpicia's illicit love affair with a young man identified by the pseudonym Cerinthus, may be read as a series of dramatic moments in their developing amatory relationship, arranged in chronological order. The scenes in the first five elegies, 3.8–12, are set before she and Cerinthus have consummated their affair physically; elegies 3.13–18, the second six, treat episodes that occur thereafter. Elegy 3.8 launches the first segment of the narrative sequence by celebrating Sulpicia's dazzling physical appearance and apparel as well as her talents as a love poet; 3.13 inaugurates the second segment by testifying how her love poems have transformed her desires into physical reality.

Several of the eleven Sulpicia elegies depict obstacles posed to the couple's mutual amatory fulfillment—physical distance, illness, rivals for Cerinthus's affections, and family members. Yet they portray Sulpicia and Cerinthus as ultimately achieving the amatory success for which she has hoped and prayed. Sulpicia even encourages her audience to partake, vicariously, of this success. At 3.13.5–6, when proclaiming that her passion has been physically consummated at last, she offers to share her joys with readers who lack amatory pleasures of their own: "Venus has fulfilled her promises. If anyone will be said not to have had joys of his or her own, let that individual tell of mine."[3]

Ovid's Thisbe, in contrast, achieves amatory success only to the extent that she and her beloved Pyramus, prevented by their hostile families from fulfilling their reciprocated passions, are, in response to her prayers, united in and after death. At *Metamorphoses* 4.164–66, Ovid's narrator, a daughter of Minyas, concludes the story by emphasizing the lovers' union in death: "nevertheless her prayers touched the gods, touched their parents: for there is a dark color in the fruit, when it has fully ripened, and what remains from their funeral pyres lies at rest in the same cinerary urn."

The fruit is that of the mulberry tree, darkened by the blood of Pyramus's self-inflicted wounds. Its transformation from white to dark is the metamorphosis of this particular story. Before ending her own life by plunging a sword into her breast, Thisbe first prays that her own and Pyramus's parents will allow them to be buried together. She then prays to the tree that now covers "the body of one and will soon cover those of two" ("miserabile corpus / nunc tegis unius, mox es tectura duorum" [158–59]), asking that the tree "retain signs of [our] death, and always have dark offspring fit for expressions of grief, reminders of twofold blood" (160–61).[4] Rather than have this couple share—as Sulpicia does—joys mutually experienced, with each other and with his readers, Ovid accords them a common burial place and his audience a sorrowful and perennial memento of their suicides. By evoking Sulpicia's poems throughout the entire episode, he contrasts their ill-fated love affair with hers in other ways as well.

From its very start, Ovid's narrative about Pyramus and Thisbe prominently uses words, metaphors, and themes that play an important role in the eleven Sulpicia elegies. The characterization of Thisbe at 4.56 as "ranked above the girls whom the East has claimed" recalls the first of the Sulpicia elegies. In 3.8, Sulpicia is depicted not only as supremely beautiful and as more worthy of affirmation as a poet by Apollo and the Muses than any other girl but also as uniquely suited for finery from the east. At 3.8.15–20, she is said to be the "only one of the girls worthy" of wearing the sort of wools given by Tyre and of possessing "whatever the rich Arab reaps" and the pearls that the "dark Indian, nearest to Eastern waters, collects." At 3.8.11 Sulpicia is said to inspire fiery passion whether she wears a dress of Tyrian color or a "snow-white garment" ("nivea . . . veste"). Ovid uses the adjective for the white fruits that originally grew on the mulberry tree (4.89). "Vestis" appears twice in Ovid's descriptions of Thisbe's veil (4.107, 147), which Thisbe drops—on seeing and fleeing a lioness with blood-stained jaws—at the couple's secret meeting place outside the city, by the tomb of the Babylonian king Ninus, near the aforementioned mulberry tree.

Ovid's account of the couple's tragic encounters with the lioness has striking affinities with the second Sulpicia elegy, 3.9. Here Sulpicia worries about the dangers posed to Cerinthus by a hunting expedition he has planned. She begins, somewhat incongruously, by addressing a wild boar, ordering him to "spare my young man" ("parce meo iuveni") and asking why it is pleasing to enter, secretly, the "hiding places of wild beasts" ("latebras intrare ferarum" [3.9.9]). She speaks of the boar yet again when expressing her hopes that the boar himself will depart unharmed if he should come across her and Cerinthus making love before the hunting nets. She also threatens any female rival who sneaks up on their secret lovemaking with being torn to pieces by ferocious wild beasts ("in saevas diripienda feras" [3.9.22]).

By using the verb *lateant* ("that they hide" [88]; from the same root as *latebras*) when summarizing the plans made by Pyramus and Thisbe to meet secretly at night outside the city and by situating the lioness at their meeting place, Ovid recalls Sulpicia's description of Cerinthus's preferred hunting haunt. The final words of Ovid's Pyramus, who wrongly assumes, from the blood staining Thisbe's veil, that a lion has killed her, recall Sulpicia's similar address to a fearsome wild animal. Pyramus, however, addresses not the single lioness who has dyed Thisbe's veil with blood but "whoever you savage lions are that dwell beneath this rock" (4.114). Pyramus uses the imperative mood with these beasts much as Sulpicia does with the wild boar, ordering them to "tear apart my body, and devour my criminal entrails with your wild bestial bite" (4.112–13). Sulpicia, as we have seen, refers to wild beasts as *ferae* twice in 3.9, at 11 and 22, in the second instance calling them "saevas." Much as his character Pyramus describes the lion's bite as "ferus" (4.113), Ovid uses "saevus" and "ferus" to describe the lioness (4.102, 106).

Ovid portrays Pyramus as lacking the intellectual wherewithal for amatory success and survival: he wrongly ascribes the bloodying of Thisbe's veil to plural male lions instead of to a singular lioness and, more seriously, fails to comprehend that Thisbe herself has not been hurt by wild beasts. By recalling the scenario and language of Sulpicia 3.9, Ovid underscores that his lovers—unlike Sulpicia and Cerinthus—actually do encounter a wild beast and end their lives as a result of this encounter. Sulpicia, who merely imagines such encounters, may well be justified in fearing the damage that wild beasts might do to the beautiful body of her beloved. But she also wishes, in hyperbolic but mean-spirited words, for them to destroy her potential erotic competition and foolishly fantasizes about making love in the presence of a savage boar.

In 3.10 Sulpicia seeks the aid of Apollo, in his role as healer-god, to cure her from an illness. Like Ovid's Thisbe, she offers vows and prayers. She asks the god not to torture the youth, who offers "prayers" ("vota") "beyond counting" for his beloved, and notes that he sometimes prays ("vovet" [13]), and sometimes utters harsh words against the gods. Later, when asking Apollo to fulfill her own vows, she predicts, "Great glory will be granted to you for having restored two ["duos"] with the saving of one body ["in uno corpore"]," cleverly playing on the Latin words for "one" and "two" (3.10.19–20). As we have seen,

Thisbe's prayer to the mulberry tree (*Met.* 4.159) also plays on these two words, as does Pyramus's dying speech: "Una duos . . . nox perdet amantes," 'one night will destroy two lovers' (4.108). Sulpicia's and Cerinthus's vows are eventually fulfilled by the restoration of her health, and so the physical viability of Cerinthus and her as a couple is ensured. Thisbe's vows merely result in having the tree cover her dead body as well as that of Pyramus. With Thisbe's suicide, Pyramus's dying words, based on the false assumption that Thisbe has already died, prove ironically prophetic.

When Sulpicia claims, at 3.10.20, that Cerinthus will have more need to weep at the prospect of her ill temper when she has recovered than to cry over her death, she juxtaposes the words "fletu" 'weeping' and "lacrimis" 'tears.' Ovid too juxtaposes these words to describe how Thisbe "filled Pyramus's wounds with tears, and mixed her weeping with blood" ("vulnera supplevit lacrimis, fletumque cruori / miscuit" [*Met.* 4.140–41]). While Sulpicia uses this language in the context of her eventual recovery and the continuation of her love affair, Ovid's Thisbe does so in lamenting Pyramus's impending death. By recalling Sulpicia's vows and by depicting the lovers' happy outcome, Ovid underscores the sorrowful circumstances in which this couple is ultimately united.

In 3.11, celebrating Cerinthus's birthday, Sulpicia portrays her own passion figuratively, as fire, and expresses the hope that his feelings for her might be similarly characterized. After asserting that "I burn" ("uror") twice in 3.11.5, she says that her passion will please her if Cerinthus in turn harbors a "mutual flame" ("mutuus ignis"), and she prays that they may achieve a "mutual love" ("mutuus adsit amor"). She elaborates on the mutual passion that she seeks at 3.11.13–18 by voicing a desire that she and Cerinthus may be equally ("aeque") bound in love's slavery and by claiming that they both wish for the same thing. Although recognizing that Cerinthus is embarrassed to speak words of love openly, she explains that he wishes for the same things she does, but in a "more covered way" ("tectius optat" [3.11.17]). Ovid's initial description of Pyramus and Thisbe characterizes the couple's passion as both firelike and mutual, as blazing desire reciprocated: "both burned, equally, with minds taken captive" ("ex aequo captis ardebant mentibus ambo" [4.62]). The imagery reappears in Ovid's observation that the couple was forced to express their love through nods and gestures: "the more that their flame is covered, the more it, covered, burns" ("quoque magis tegitur, tectus magis aestuat ignis" [4.64]). By using Sulpicia's language to recall a very different affair, Ovid likens the love affair of Pyramus and Thisbe to that of Sulpicia and Cerinthus, or at least to the love affair that Sulpicia hopes to experience in 3.11. Simultaneously, Ovid calls attention to major differences between the two love affairs, in particular to differences between the erotic communications of Sulpicia and Thisbe. In 3.11 Sulpicia is portrayed as merely wishing for, not enjoying, the reciprocation of her passions. Representing Cerinthus's less than ardent conduct as "more covered" desire is noteworthy too: unlike Pyramus and Thisbe, Cerinthus is not forced to cover up his feelings.

More significantly, Thisbe's first words in Ovid's narrative, at 4.73–77, are an expression of mutual love with Pyramus: the same words, in fact. These verses, addressed to the wall shared by their adjoining houses and the crack through which they send their loving messages, simultaneously express frustration at the obstacle to their loving that the wall imposes, desire to join their bodies (or at least their lips), and appreciation for the opportunity the crack in the wall allows for their words to reach "loving ears." In contrast, Sulpicia's poems never assign any words to Cerinthus. We must take her word, and her word alone, that their passion is mutual and eventually achieved.

The language of 3.12, celebrating Sulpicia's own birthday, also represents her passion, figuratively, as "burning" ("uritur" [3.12.17]), likening Sulpicia to the swift flames on the hearth where sacrifices are offered to Juno. The theme of 3.12 also returns to mutual love, and Sulpicia asks Juno to "prepare reciprocal chains for the youth" ("iuveni quaeso mutua vincla para" [8]). Other themes and words, too, feature here and in Ovid's Pyramus and Thisbe narrative. Sulpicia wishes that "a watchful guard may not be able to catch the desirous lovers in the act, and that Love may supply them with a thousand ways of deceiving" ("nec possit cupidos vigilans deprendere custos / fallendique vias mille ministret Amor" [3.12.11–12]). At *Metamorphoses* 4.84–85, Pyramus and Thisbe decide to try "to deceive the guards" watching over them ("fallere custodes"); Ovid later describes Thisbe (4.94–96) as "deceiving her guards" ("fallit suos"), emboldened by Love ("audacem faciebat Amor"). The verb that Sulpicia uses at 3.9.12 to beg Juno that no one cause the lovers to part ("neu quis divellat amantes") is the same word that Pyramus uses when ordering the lions (*Met.* 4.112), literally, to tear his body apart (Glare 562). While Love helps Pyramus and Thisbe deceive their guards much as Sulpicia hopes Love will assist her and Cerinthus, this help is ultimately to no avail; and while lions do not actually dismember Ovid's lovers, their encounter with the lioness prevents their physical union.

Proclaiming in 3.13 that her love has been physically consummated, Sulpicia again uses a form of the verb *tegere* ("to cover") to assert that keeping her affair "under wraps" would be more shameful than exposing it. Sulpicia has been free to decide whether or not to "cover" her erotic conduct; Pyramus and Thisbe, on the other hand, do so under compulsion. Sulpicia's final line, voicing her wish to be called "a worthy woman having coupled with a worthy man" ("cum digno digna fuisse ferar" [3.13.10]), celebrates the lovers' new erotic bond. We have already seen the adjective "digna" ("worthy") at 3.8.15 and 24 describing Sulpicia's worthiness for oriental apparel and poetic approbation; here it is applied to her worthiness as Cerinthus's lover. Ovid's Pyramus, conversely, uses the superlative "dignissima" when he finds Thisbe's veil and believes her dead: "she was most worthy of a long life" ("illa fuit longa dignissima vita" [*Met.* 4.109]). Although Thisbe is not in fact dead at this point, Pyramus's suicide will soon provoke hers and so render his words accurate. If Ovid is recalling Sulpicia's repeated use of this word to describe what makes her own life worthwhile, he is also emphasizing the tragedy of Thisbe's untimely loss. Finally, Sulpicia uses the verb *componere* ("to put together, arrange" [3.13.9]) when maintaining that she refuses to arrange her public behavior for the sake of what people say. Thisbe chooses the same verb at *Metamorphoses* 4.157, when she asks her parents not to begrudge Pyramus and her a shared tomb. The contrast between Thisbe's hopes for a final resting place and Sulpicia's plans for positioning her "image" is powerful and painful.

Evocations of the other elegies depicting Sulpicia's affair after its physical consummation resound in Ovid's Pyramus and Thisbe narrative as well. In 3.14 Sulpicia beseeches her guardian Messalla to let her spend her birthday in Rome with Cerinthus instead of in the country. Messalla's opposition to her desires resembles the conduct Ovid attributes to Pyramus's and Thisbe's parents, who forbade their relationship. The opposition that Sulpicia constructs between urban and rural locales for their erotic suitability resembles Ovid's scenario too: after all, his narrative contrasts the city of Babylon where the couple dwell to the place outside the city to which they flee. In her final elegy, 3.18, Sulpicia tells her lover that she regrets having abandoned him the night before out of a desire to hide her "burning passion" ("ardor"); Ovid's Thisbe, of course, flees from the spot where she and Pyramus have arranged to meet and never gets the opportunity to express her passion for him physically.

Major differences remain between Sulpicia's circumstances and those of Ovid's Thisbe. Sulpicia's desire to spend her birthday in the city with Cerinthus (3.14) is but a momentary impulse, as is Messalla's opposition to it. Indeed, in 3.15 Sulpicia portrays herself as having persuaded Messalla to change his mind. Ovid, on the other hand, represents the passion of Pyramus and Thisbe as strong and enduring and the opposition of their families as no less so. Their parents are not easily cajoled, much less disregarded. While Sulpicia deems the city superior to the country because she and Cerinthus can be together there, Pyramus and Thisbe must flee the city to be together at all. And while Sulpicia faults her nocturnal conduct in 3.18 as foolish, the most regrettable error she has committed in her entire youth, Thisbe's nocturnal behavior in Ovid's narrative constitutes the last action Thisbe performs in her entire, young life.

Ovid does not allude to two of the other elegies among Sulpicia's final six, in both of which Sulpicia complains about Cerinthus's behavior: 3.16, where she speaks dismissively about a rival she regards as her social inferior, a paid sexual partner trying to pass as a respectable woman, and 3.17, where she claims that Cerinthus has neglected her during an illness. And it is clear why he does not make such allusions. Ovid's Pyramus and Thisbe never have the opportunity to experience such moments in their relationship. The opposition that they face from their parents is far more serious than the obstacles to amatory success experienced by Sulpicia. Thisbe's difficulties in communicating with Pyramus result in his well-intentioned but erroneous assumption that Thisbe has been slain by the lioness; far less consequential are Sulpicia's problems with Cerinthus, which stem from his apparent lack of attention.

As noted earlier, Ovid portrays Thisbe and Pyramus as not only mutually enamored but also engaged in mutual erotic communication. The beginning of his narrative foregrounds first their gestures and then their words. At *Metamorphoses* 4.68–70, the lovers are themselves directly addressed, congratulated for finding the crack in the wall and creating a "path for the voice" ("vocis iter") that enables "their sweet utterances to cross through, safe, with the slightest murmur." Lines 73–77 represent the exact words that both say to the wall, 83–90 the conversation in which they plan to flee the city.

Ovid also portrays Thisbe as by far the more verbally talented of the two at expressing her feelings and working her will—and as more serious about erotic communication. At *Metamorphoses* 4.129–30 he relates that when she returns to the spot where she and Pyramus had planned to meet, still frightened after her encounter with the lioness there, Thisbe not only "searches for her young man with her eyes and in her mind" but also "desires to tell what great dangers she has avoided" ("quantaque vitarit narrare pericula gestit"), in other words, to put her experiences in words and share them. While Pyramus misinterprets the significance of the bloodied veil, Thisbe quickly comprehends that and why he has taken his life. At *Metamorphoses* 4.137, by describing the moment when she recognizes her lover with the phrase "suos cognovit amores," Ovid plays on two meanings of "amores," "loved one" and "poems about love"; he thereby indicates that her communications with and about her passion for Pyramus are all important to Thisbe's identity as a lover.[5] Not only does Ovid portray Thisbe as more perceptive—and more committed to mutual erotic communication—than Pyramus. The speech that he crafts for her at *Metamorphoses* 4.148–61, when she discovers Pyramus's body and resolves to end her life, is longer and more artfully composed than the corresponding suicidal soliloquy delivered by Pyramus at lines 108–18. It is more rhetorically effective as well, since the gods and their parents grant her dying wishes.

By representing Thisbe as more skillful and successful than Pyramus in erotic communications and by repeatedly recalling several of the Sulpicia elegies in his narrative, Ovid signals that Thisbe is more skillful and successful than her historical Roman literary model in this regard as well. Of course, Thisbe and Pyramus never enjoy the kind of erotic success that Sulpicia claims that she has experienced with her lover and that she self-confidently enjoins her readers to relish as a substitute for their own lack of amatory gratifications. Nonetheless, Ovid portrays the emotional bond of the two young lovers as truly reciprocal and gives both lovers a voice. He also portrays the difficulties that they confront as far more serious than those faced by Sulpicia and Cerinthus. Ovid's Thisbe is more responsive and accommodating to her beloved than Sulpicia, whose elegies represent her as demanding and controlling. With Thisbe, Ovid has exerted his authorial control to create a fictive woman whose amatory experiences and communications his readers can readily admire, if not share.

NOTES

[1] For both the assumption that Sulpicia did not herself write the first five poems (3.8–12) in the sequence and various arguments challenging this assumption, see Hallett. One argument in support of single authorship by Sulpicia relies on intertextual evidence:

echoes of two earlier Latin literary works—Catullus's poems and Vergil's *Aeneid*—in both the first five and the final six Sulpicia elegies. By maintaining that Ovid's later narrative about Pyramus and Thisbe evokes elegies 3.8–12 as well as several of the final six elegies, this essay furnishes a different kind of intertextual evidence for authorial unity, inasmuch as these echoes suggest that Ovid knew most of the eleven Sulpicia poems and viewed them as her work.

[2] For Ovid's patronage by Messalla, see his *Epistulae ex Ponto* 1.7 and 2.3.

[3] All translations in this essay are my own; translations of Sulpicia are from Hallett.

[4] Both LaFleur 33 and Keith, "Etymological Wordplay" 310–12, make excellent observations about the language used to describe the transformation of the tree.

[5] For an earlier, comic consideration of Thisbe's merits relative to those of Pyramus, see the remarks of Demetrius in *A Midsummer Night's Dream*: "A mote will turn the balance, which Pyramus, which Thisby, is the better: he for a man, God warr'nt us; she for a woman, God bless us" (5.1.318–20).

The Lay of the Land:
The Rhetoric of Gender in Ovid's "Perseid"

Alison Keith

I have taught Ovid's *Metamorphoses* for over twenty years in the courses Women in Epic and Women in Classical Literature, which draw students primarily from two distinct undergraduate programs—classical civilization (i.e., classics in translation) and women's/gender studies, with some admixture of participants from literature and history departments. Every group of students has diverse, not to say divergent, interests, but all have contributed significantly to my understanding of the gender dynamics of Ovid's protean poem. Over the years, I have found that the Greek mythological hero Perseus offers a particularly rich focus for discussion of the rhetoric of gender in *Metamorphoses*.

In the last quarter of book 4, Ovid moves from a sequence of Theban tales into a "Perseid" that relates the adventures of the hero Perseus. Flying around the Mediterranean on the winged sandals given to him by the god Mercury, Perseus finds his heroic mettle tested in a series of epic trials ("labor" 'toil' [739]; "factum" 'deed' [757]; "pericula" 'dangers' [787]). In the course of his travels he masters not only the monstrous Medusa and a sea monster sent to devour the Ethiopian princess Andromeda but also, more abstractly, women and the features of the natural landscape associated with them. Perseus (like the paradigmatic Greek heroes Odysseus and Hercules) is a solitary voyager who travels through a series of feminized landscapes: the well-fortified dwelling of the Graeae, the twin daughters of Phorcys and Ceto (772–75); the house of the Gorgons (777–86); Libya, a figuratively maternal landscape that bears snakes after being fertilized by the blood that drips from the head of the Medusa (617–20); the garden of the Hesperides over which Atlas presides (627–29, 631–33, 637–38, 646–48); and the rocky crag on which a "marble" Andromeda, whom Perseus almost mistakes for a statue, is exposed to a sea monster (669–77). The chains that bind Andromeda's arms to the hard rocks (672) exemplify the figurative immobility of the female characters in this narrative sequence, who represent the fixed positions to and from which the mobile male hero travels.

My discussion of Perseus's relations with women and landscapes in *Metamorphoses*, book 4, begins from the observation of the feminist semiotician Teresa de Lauretis that the Perseus myth "rests on a specific assumption about sexual difference" (113):

> The hero, the mythical subject, is constructed as human being and as male; he is the active principle of culture, the establisher of distinction, the creator of differences. Female is what is not susceptible to transformation, to life or death; she (it) is an element of plot-space, a topos, a resistance, matrix and matter. (119)

Close study of the representation of nature and gender in Ovid's "Perseid" confirms this analysis. Indeed, Ovid's narrative dramatizes not only woman's natural function as plot space but also the ease with which woman is assimilated to the topography of heroic action. Occasionally, however, Ovid's "Perseid" reverses the gendered association of woman with landscape to fix male characters in the natural landscape as a result of contact with Medusa's gaze. I therefore also consider the gendered dynamics of control of the gaze in the "Perseid" as an important corollary to the association of woman with nature.

Ovid's Perseus narrative establishes a correlation between the male gaze and masculine subjectivity, both of which come together in the visual objectification of women (Medusa, Andromeda) and landscape (Libya, Ethiopia) to confirm the superiority of male (ruler) over female (landscape).[1] The literary critic Patricia Parker has noted "the impulse . . . to bring something under the control of the eye or gaze" in Vergil's *Aeneid*, and she astutely connects "its cartographic impulse and its repeated topos of taking command from a high place" to its imperial project, suggesting "why imperial gaze and male gaze come together so readily in . . . texts, where the impulse to master or dominate a feminized landscape is at the same time a matter for the eye" (151). Her suggestive reading of the co-implication of male gaze with imperial gaze in *Aeneid* furnishes a provocative parallel for Ovid's "Perseid."

Perseus ascribes the success of his assault on Medusa to his theft of the single eye shared by the Phorcides, the Gorgons' guardians:

> Then Perseus told them how, beneath cold Atlas,
> there was a shelter ringed by sturdy walls;
> two sisters lived just at the entranceway;
> those Graeae, Phorcys' daughters, shared one eye ["unius luminis"].
> Through subtle wiles and guile, the son of Danae—
> while one was passing that eye to the other—
> stretched out his hand and intercepted it.
> He held it fast as he advanced across
> uncharted, lonely tracts, across rough rocks
> and horrid gullies, till he reached the house
> of fierce Medusa and her sister Gorgons
> (another set of daughters born of Phorcys).
> Along the fields and paths where he had trekked,
> he saw ["vidisse"] the forms of men and animals
> who had been changed to stone because their gaze
> had dared to spy upon Medusa's face ["visa . . . Medusa"].
> (140–41; 772–81)

Perseus's success in winning Medusa's head is thus preceded by, and apparently predicated on, his theft of the Phorcides' eye. The hero's narrative lays bare the dependence of his heroic masculinity on his mastery of the gaze, first in his theft of their single shared eye (775–77) and then in his visual command (780) of the panorama of metamorphosed men and beasts in the landscape in which the Gorgons dwell.

By contrast, Medusa's affinity with wild nature is implied to be such that the mere sight of Medusa reduces men and beasts to topographic features of a fearsome and unnatural landscape as monstrous as she is (780–81). Perseus's control of the (Phorcides') gaze allows him to dispatch Medusa easily, though it is striking that he can only kill her by avoiding looking at her directly (141; 782–83): "But Perseus himself had found a way / to see ["aspexisse"] the dread Medusa yet escape / the fate of others, for his left hand held / a shield of bronze reflecting ["repercussae"] her dread form." Paradoxically, Perseus beheads the Gorgon by looking not at her but at her reflection in his shield. However, Ovid's treatment of Perseus's two earliest exploits—the theft of the Phorcides' single eye and the killing of Medusa (772–86)—fully confirms De Lauretis's analysis of gender dynamics in the mythic plot. Perseus actively masters women and landscapes with which they are associated, while, by contrast, the female characters embody immobile fixity on the level of both plot space and geographic place (topos).

Ovid structures his "Perseid" nonchronologically, so that Perseus's first exploits are the last Ovid recounts. Yet, from the start of the "Perseid," the Roman poet assumes Perseus's mastery of the gaze, for he introduces the hero flying over Libya in the aftermath of his most notable deed, the killing of Medusa:

> . . . Perseus . . . was already cleaving
> the soft air with his whirring wings, returning
> triumphant, bearing Gorgon's head; and as
> the son of Danae flew above the desert sands
> of Libya, from the memorable spoils
> of serpent-haired Medusa, drops of blood
> fell to the earth; and these the ground absorbed,
> and then gave life to snakes of varied sorts.
> (134; 614–19)

The blood that drips from Medusa's decapitated head, held aloft by Perseus, is conceived as watering and thereby fertilizing the dry sands of Libya, which animate the gore and thence bring forth different kinds of serpents. The shifting roles of Perseus, Medea, and the Libyan earth in this episode repay close attention. At the most basic level the rain of Medusa's blood, brought by Perseus, makes the Libyan earth fertile. In this regard, Ovid complicates the simple contrast between active masculine mobility and passive feminized landscape proposed by De Lauretis.

We may compare an earlier passage in the first book of the poem, in which the floodwaters Jupiter sends to destroy the human race (sparing only

Deucalion and Pyrrha) fertilize the earth, which regenerates the animal kingdom (1.416–37). Ovid represents Mother Earth metaphorically engaged in the process of childbearing:

> The other animals—arrayed in forms
> of such variety—were born of earth ["peperit"]
> spontaneously . . .
> . . . .
> And when, still muddy from the flood, the earth
> had dried beneath the sunlight's clement warmth,
> she brought forth countless living forms . . .
> (19, 20; 1.416–17, 434–36)

The poet explicitly likens this metaphoric childbearing to the gestation of the child in the mother's womb (19; 1.419–20): "The fertile seeds were nourished by the soil that gave them life / as in a mother's womb" ("vivaci nutrita solo ceu matris in alvo"). The Latin verbs Ovid uses throughout this passage ("peperit," "edidit," "genuit" [417, 436, 439]) are technical terms for childbearing appearing in the third-person singular with Mother Earth as subject; in this way he insistently documents the generative fertility of the earth. Culminating in the birth of the monstrous serpent-child, Python, the sequence in book 1 thus anticipates the more compressed narrative in *Metamorphoses*, book 4, where Perseus fertilizes the Libyan sands with Medusa's blood and thereby engenders her serpentine offspring. In book 4, however, the gender dynamics are interestingly complicated as the female monster's blood plays the generative male role of fertilizing the Libyan sands. Nevertheless, the intervention of the mobile male hero is required to bring it into contact with the fertile Libyan landscape, which reprises the role of Mother Earth from book 1.

Driven on by the winds, Perseus continues to focalize the landscapes over which he flies:

> From Libya, Danae's son was driven by
> the warring wind—now here, now there, much like
> a rain cloud; he surveyed ["despectat"] the lands that lay
> below; three times he saw ["vidit"] the northern Bears;
> three times he saw the pincers of the Crab.
> Winds bore him east, and then they bore him west.
> (134; 621–26)

Ovid emphasizes, on the one hand, the winds' mastery of Perseus's course as he flies, at the same time as he repeatedly draws attention, on the other hand, to Perseus's visual mastery of the landscape over which he flies. Eventually, tiring from the buffeting of the winds, Perseus seeks respite in the garden of the

Hesperides: "The day was fading now; he was afraid / to fly by night; descending from the sky, / he reached Hesperia, the land of Atlas" (134; 627–28). In his arrival at Hesperia, then, it seems that Perseus exerts control over his course. Yet in contextualizing Perseus's encounter with Atlas, Ovid consistently depicts the landscape in which the hero alights as a territory already under the rule ("regnis Atlantis" [628]; "tellus / rege sub hoc" [632–33]) of another figure, whose preeminent size (631) guarantees his heroic stature and potential rivalry to Perseus:

> This Atlas, son of Iapetus, was massive;
> no man could match his stature. And no land
> lay farther west than his domain—earth's edge
> and sea span that received the panting steeds
> and weary chariot of the Sun that set.
> He had a thousand flocks, and he could claim
> as many herds; they grazed on his green plain
> at will: no neighbors bordered his domain.
> (134; 631–36)

As in Perseus's relation to the landscape of Libya, a gendered dynamic animates Atlas's relation to the garden of the Hesperides, the daughters of Night according to Hesiod (215). While they make no appearance in Ovid's narrative, the poet may allude to their generation from Night in the juxtaposition "nocti ... Hesperio" ("iamque cadente die veritus se credere nocti / constitit Hesperio, regnis Atlantis, in orbe" [627–28], though in strict grammar "Hesperio" modifies "orbe" at the end of line 628); the appositional phrase "regnis Atlantis," moreover, embedded within the larger locative phrase "Hesperio ... in orbe" (628), gestures toward the description of the setting of the Hesperides' garden as "Atlas's land" in the earlier Greek *Argonautica* of Apollonius of Rhodes (χώρωι ἐν Ἄτλαντος [4.1398]). Ovid, however, expands Apollonius's attribution of the territory to Atlas (and the snake Ladon) in his elaborate description of the garden:

> And he had trees with gleaming golden leaves
> that covered golden boughs and golden fruit—
> the apples of the three Hesperides. . . .
> . . . .
> For fear of [an oracle], he had enclosed ["clauserat"] his orchards
>   ["pomaria"]
> with sturdy walls ["solidis moenibus"]; and as his guardian,
> Atlas had chosen an enormous dragon ["vasto draconi"]—
> and banned all strangers from his boundaries.
> (134–35; 637–38, 646–48)

Atlas's walled orchard is recognizable to the learned reader as the garden of the (unnamed) Hesperides by its location in the Westland ("Hesperio . . . in orbe" [628]).

The thick walls with which Atlas surrounds the garden are of particular interest in this context, since they anticipate the walled garden of Pomona (whose name is related to the Latin word for orchard used here, "pomaria" [646]). Ovid sketches Pomona's garden in book 14 as a feminized landscape that symbolizes her rejection of men and marriage (499–500; 14.635–36): "Pomona feared the peasants' brutish ways, / fenced off her orchards, and avoided men—/ she never let them in" ("vim tamen agrestum metuens *pomaria claudit* / intus et accessus prohibet refugitque viriles").[2] Unlike Pomona's orchard, however, the garden of the Hesperides, while also a figuratively feminine space, is already under the domination of a male ruler, Atlas, who epitomizes epic masculinity, both in his size (4.631–32) and in his delegation of his duty of care for the orchard to a huge phallic snake (647).[3]

The scene is thus set for a contest between Perseus and Atlas over possession of the Hesperides' orchard:

> "My lord," said Perseus, "if you prize high birth,
> I'd have you know that I am born of Jove;
> or if you would applaud amazing feats,
> you surely will esteem what I've achieved!
> Please let me be your guest—I need to rest."
> But Atlas was not ready to forget
> an ancient prophecy that he had heard
> from Themis of Parnassus. She had said:
> "The day will come, o Atlas, when your trees
> will be despoiled of all their gold; and he
> who gains that prize will be a son of Jove."
> . . . .
> To Perseus, too, he said: "Be off: you boast
> of mighty deeds and say you're born of Jove—
> all lies; and fables cannot help you now."
> And adding force to menace, Atlas tried
> to thrust back Perseus—who held his ground,
> while mingling heated words with words of calm.
> (135; 639–45, 649–52)

As in Libya, control of the gaze (in this case, again, Medusa's) enhances Perseus's heroic potency against the giant Atlas:

> But when, at length, he found he could not match
> the strength of Atlas (how could any man?),

> the son of Danae cried: "For you, I seem
> to be a thing so trivial, so mean—
> for that I shall requite you with this gift!"
> At that, he turned his back to Atlas—and
> held up Medusa's head with his left hand.
>
> (135; 653–56)

Just as Medusa herself had once transformed all those on whom she gazed into features of the natural landscape, so here Perseus reduces Atlas to inert ground:

> Great Atlas now became a mountain-mass
> as huge as he had been; his beard, his hair
> were changed to woods; his shoulders and his arms,
> to ridges; what had been his head was now
> a mountaintop; his bones were changed to stones.
>
> (135; 657–60)

Despite his transformation into what we might characterize (in De Lauretis's words) as "an element of plot-space, a topos, a resistance, matrix and matter," Atlas nonetheless retains an essentially masculine identity predicated on the superhuman physical strength for which he is celebrated in the episode both at the outset (631, qtd. above) and at the end, when his transformed body supports the heavens: "That done, in all his parts his form grew still / more huge—such was your will, o gods; his head / supported all of heaven and its stars" (135; 660–62).

After besting Atlas, Perseus quits the Hesperides' garden, flying to Ethiopia and the realm of Cepheus (668–69), where he sees the king's daughter Andromeda exposed to a sea monster on a crag, as penalty for her mother's impious disdain for the beauty of the Nereids (670–71). In his description of the hero's first sight of Andromeda, Ovid anatomizes the close relation between the male gaze and male desire:

> Andromeda was tied to a rough rock;
> and when he saw ["vidit"] her, Perseus would have thought
> she was a marble statue, were it not
> for a light breeze that stirred her hair, and warm
> tears trickling down her cheeks. He was struck dumb;
> a flame—its force was strange—swept through his limbs;
> her beauty gripped him ["visae correptus imagine formae"]—he almost forgot
> to beat his wings, to keep his airborne course.
>
> (136; 672–77)

Perseus here enacts the erotic cliché articulated by Ovid's friend and contemporary, the elegiac poet Propertius: "the eyes are the leaders in love" ("oculi sunt in amore duces" [2.15.12]). Andromeda's beauty attracts the hero's prolonged gaze (672–77) much as the petrifying sight of Medusa's snaky head compels the eternal gaze of those who look directly on her (780–81). Both Medusa and Andromeda, as mesmerizing objects of the gaze, endanger the men who look at them. Indeed, the episode has been interpreted as an exploration of the risks entailed by the male in his control of the gaze.[4] Perseus's stupefaction at the sight of the chained Andromeda, for example, is almost his undoing. The hero's reaction to his first sight of the beautiful Andromeda anticipates the permanent immobilization of those who view Medusa.

Yet we can also see Perseus responding to the sight of Andromeda through the lens of his earlier dealings with Medusa, for the Ethiopian princess is fixed in a rocky landscape just like the beasts and men transformed into "statues" of themselves and fixed in the landscape by Medusa. Unlike those figures fixed permanently in nature by Medusa's uncanny gaze, however, Andromeda is a living woman merely chained to her crag and therefore available to serve not only as the object of Perseus's sexual desire (which, manifested as it is at the sight of one whom he takes to be a statue, we might compare with Pygmalion's desire for his "ivory maiden" in book 10) but also as the object ("matrix and matter" in De Lauretis's words) of his heroic labors.[5] She thus constitutes both "the cause of and the reward for" the epic hero's duel ("pretiumque et causa laboris" [739]) with the sea monster sent by Jupiter Ammon to kill her in punishment for her mother's boasting tongue.

In combat with the sea monster, Perseus displays a distinct preference for "taking command from a high place," as Parker puts it (151), to secure mastery of the gaze. As soon as the sea monster appears on the scene, the hero flies aloft: "Then, springing upward from the ground ["tellure repulsa"], where he / had dug his heels, young Perseus suddenly / leaped high ["arduus"] into the clouds" (138; 711–12). From this vantage point the hero dominates the sea monster, who apprehends only his foe's shadow. By contrast, Perseus effectively counters the monster through his visual mastery of the battleground, which the poet compares to that of a bird soaring through the air, to deal the monster a mortal blow from above:

> And even as the sacred bird of Jove,
> when it has sighted in an open field
> a snake that stretches out its dappled back
> beneath the sun, will swoop in swift attack—
> but from behind, not frontally, so that
> the snake cannot twist back its savage fangs—
> the eagle grips its victim's scaly neck

> with eager claws: just so did Perseus plunge;
> down, through the empty air he swooped headlong ["praeceps per inane volatu"]
> assailing from above the roaring beast,
> he dug his curving blade unto the hilt
> into the snake's right shoulder. . . .
> (138; 714–20)

Perseus continues to elude the beast's attack by flying out of its reach ("with his swift wings Perseus leaps / above, aside" [138; 724–25]) until in its death throes, the monster soaks Perseus's winged sandals, thereby making flight difficult for him to sustain. Even then, however, Perseus continues his successful strategy of domination through visual mastery by taking up a stand on an outcrop above the sea:

> But Perseus' wings are soaked with sea spray now;
> his sandals are too water-logged to trust;
> and when he sights ["conspexit"] a shoal whose top juts out ["vertice summo"]
> in calm seas ["stantibus exstat aquis"], and is hidden when it's rough,
> it's there he takes his stand; from there he thrusts;
> he grips the outer edges of the rock;
> and with his right, again, again he strikes;
> he drives his blade three times and then a fourth:
> he sinks his sword into the monster's guts.
> (139; 729–34)

In his deliverance of the helpless stone maiden from her rocky crag, Perseus can truly be said to have mastered both woman and landscape.

The hero's visual mastery of both the Ethiopian landscape (668–69, qtd. above) and the Ethiopian princess (672–77) prefigures his marital conquest of her. Perseus explicitly demands her in marriage from her parents in exchange for saving her from the sea monster. In response to his demand for their daughter as his bride (695–703), Andromeda's parents offer to Perseus in addition their kingdom as their daughter's dowry:

> Both Cepheus and Cassiope accept
> that pact (who could refuse it?), and they plead
> with Perseus to be quick: they promise him
> their daughter and a kingdom in addition ["regnum dotale"].
> (137–38; 704–05)

In the double motivation recorded in Perseus's compact with Andromeda's parents, we can apprehend what Annette Kolodny has called "the lay of the land."

The Greek mythological association of the marriageable woman with the fertile field[6] is extended in Roman thought to the association of marriageable (foreign) women with (Roman) territorial conquest.[7]

Ovid's narrative thus documents Perseus's acquisition not only of a wife but also of a kingdom in Ethiopia. The solemnity of the occasion is matched by the solemnity of the language with which the marriage negotiations are conducted between Perseus ("paciscor" [703]) and Andromeda's parents—"they take his terms" ("accipiunt legem" [704])—and with which he duly secures Cepheus's kingdom as his daughter's dowry ("regnum dotale" [705]). In addition to characterizing Perseus's acquisition of a kingdom by means of this dynastic marriage as a peaceful and productive union of Greek and Ethiopian, the classical association of women with land *tout court*, along with the role that agriculture plays in both Greco-Roman theories of marriage and in the Roman practice of colonization, underpins the metaphorical system at play in the Ovidian passage; Perseus's marriage to the daughter of Cepheus necessarily entails Perseus's acquisition of Ethiopia. In this way the episode also articulates not only "the impulse . . . to bring something under the control of the eye or gaze" ("conspicit," "vidit," "visae" [669, 673, 676]) but also, indeed especially, why "the impulse to master or dominate a feminized landscape is at the same time a matter for the eye."

Each episode in Ovid's abbreviated "Perseid" can thus be seen to propose the gendered association of woman with natural landscape and man with its mastery, from Atlas's rule over the garden of the Hesperides to Perseus's conquest of a sea monster and attendant capture of a bride and kingdom. Throughout the sequence, women remain fixed in nature while the mobile Greek hero moves through this feminized landscape mastering both women and territory. This simple opposition, however, is complicated throughout in Ovid's rehearsal of Perseus's adventures. While the Phorcidae, the Hesperides, and Andromeda are all associated with a single geographic location—Phorcys's daughters' fortified home "under cold Atlas" ("gelido sub Atlante iacentem . . . locum" [772–73]), Hesperia or the Westland, and Ethiopia—Atlas himself is permanently fixed in the landscape through his transformation into a mountain range by Medusa's gaze and at Perseus's hands (655–60, qtd. above; cf. 772–73). Moreover, Medusa herself defies easy assimilation to the gendered dynamic of feminized landscape, for her gaze not only has the uncanny power to fix men in nature (780–81, qtd. above) but even travels, albeit after death and in the hands of Perseus, who appropriates it to his own heroic ends. Her blood even fertilizes the sands of Libya, which reprise the role of book 1's fertile Mother Earth and bring forth snakes. Ovid thereby shows that the male gaze is predicated, in this sequence at any rate, on that of the female, as Perseus's mastery of the gaze rests quite literally on his cunning theft of the gaze not only from the Phorcidae but also from Medusa.

NOTES

[1] On the male gaze, see Mulvey, "Visual Pleasure," "Afterthoughts," and *Visual and Other Pleasures*. On the gaze in Roman culture, see the essays collected in Fredrick, especially that by Sharrock, "Looking."

[2] See the articles by Gentilcore and Myers.

[3] Another suggestive lexical parallel between the two episodes is the repetition of the phrase "rege sub hoc" in the introduction of the two passages (4.633, 14.623).

[4] On the heroic masculinity of Ovid's Perseus, see the fuller discussion in Keith, "Versions of Epic Masculinity."

[5] On Pygmalian's desire, see Sharrock, "Womanufacture" and "Looking at Looking"; Liveley, "Reading Resistance."

[6] On the association, see in particular DuBois, *Sowing the Body*, and Dougherty 61–80.

[7] Cf. Keith, *Engendering Rome* 36–64, on the feminized "ground of representation" in Latin epic.

Teaching Ovidian Sexualities in English Renaissance Literature

Goran V. Stanivukovic

I begin my class on Ovid and Ovidianism in English Renaissance literature by looking at Michael Longley's contemporary poem "A Flowering," inspired by Ovid's account of Adonis's transformation into a flower. The speaker in Longley's poem imagines the effect of age as a hermaphroditic fantasy ("Now that my body grows woman-like") and depicts his own son's youthful beauty, paradoxically both blown away and preserved through the transformation into the "flower named after the wind, anemone" (Longley, lines 1, 11). When I use this poem to focus class discussion on Ovid and ideas about sexuality in the Renaissance, most of my students are confused by the sexual ambiguities of the speaker's body and the mysterious metamorphosis of the speaker's son. They are also puzzled by my mentioning that the subtext to this poem is the transformation of Adonis's dead body into a flower in Ovid's version of the myth of Venus and Adonis in *Metamorphoses*. Most of my undergraduate students have not heard of Ovid until then, and even those few who have heard of him do not know what his connection to English Renaissance texts may be or why I devote one entire class to Renaissance allusions to and adaptations and rewritings of Ovid's tales of sexual passion. Yet I begin with Longley's poem to illustrate that Ovid's poetry is a repository of curious and strange ideas about the body and desire that we resort to even today for imagining changing ideas about sexuality.

One pleasure of teaching English Renaissance literature for me has been teaching Ovid, particularly his influence on the shaping of literariness in the English Renaissance and the formative role his poetry played in the emergence of the literary fictions of sexuality. This pleasure comes from my understanding that some of the imaginatively most compelling and aesthetically accomplished representations of love and desire in English Renaissance literature are inspired by Ovid. Mindful of the responsibilities of the following statement, I tell my students that most of the Renaissance literary ideas about desire and sexuality came first and most strongly not from anatomical, medical, and humoral writing or from theories of the instability of gender as an effect of cross-dressing (especially in the public theater) but from responses to and dialogue with Ovid. I point out to them that the theme of the body's mutability derives from a systematic and continuous engagement in the English Renaissance with Ovid's *Metamorphoses*.[1]

Arthur Golding's 1567 translation of *Metamorphoses*, the first complete translation of Ovid's magnum opus in English, not only plays a crucial part in "the Englishing process" of bringing Ovid to England (Forey xiii) but also stands alongside such important books as the 1560 Geneva Bible and the 1568 Bishop's Bible. Thus, in my teaching of Ovid's impact on the new ideas about the body and sexuality in the English Renaissance, I illustrate to my students that the narratives of licentious sexuality in Golding's *Metamorphoses* stand in contrast to religious strictures of continence and chastity; its imagery "defies Christian concepts of sin" (Warner 107). It is through Golding's translation that premodern ideas about desire and corporeality, ideas that resist the Puritan doctrine of temperance, emerged and started to change ways of knowing and representing sexuality in early modern English literature. Because of the cultural importance of Golding's translation and because of his liberal adaptation of Ovid's text, I regard Golding's translation not merely as a source of literature but as a work of creative imagination in its own right. This is masterfully explored in Raphael Lyne's examination of the English translations of *Metamorphoses* within the larger cultural and political contexts of the sixteenth and seventeenth centuries (*Ovid's Changing Worlds*). In this essay I analyze an example from my teaching practice that suggests Ovid was central to the emergence of a language of transgressive sexuality in the English Renaissance.

I introduce the motif of Adonis's death in Shakespeare's *Venus and Adonis* with Longley's poem, because the erotic charge that accompanies his death is different in these two poems. *Venus and Adonis* is one of the most famous of Renaissance adaptations of Ovid and one of the most erotic Renaissance poems. I use Shakespeare as a model of creative adaptation to illustrate the continuity of ideas about sexuality from Ovid's original, through a translator, to the English poet-imitator. Ovid's account of Adonis's accidental death—"trux aper insequitur totosque sub inguine dentes / abdidit et fulva moribundum stravit harena" (10.715–16)—is rendered by Golding as, "his [the boar's] tusks as far as he could thrust, / He laid him all along for dead upon the yellow dust" (839–40), and Shakespeare adapts Golding as, "If he [the boar] did see his face, why then I know / He thought to kiss him, and hath killed him so" (1109–10).[2] Comparing the two English versions of this famous literary death scene—Golding's of Ovid and Shakespeare's of Golding—my students immediately notice that Shakespeare (perhaps with Ovid's original at his side, too) adds a kiss in his account, suggesting that the boar's intention was only to kiss, not kill, Adonis. In Shakespeare's version Adonis's death is an accident charged with erotic symbolism. When my students come to this moment in the poem, they either hesitate or rush to point out that the boar's kiss implies homoerotic encounter, which is clear from Shakespeare's description of the boar's intention to kiss Adonis, presumably only once. Some wish Shakespeare did not stop there; others wonder whether Adonis's death in the context of a homoerotic union was not meant as a warning about the destructive effect of male same-sex attraction.

This comparison is a good starting point for talking about how English Renaissance literature imagines homoeroticism and for drawing attention to the fact that the Ovidian minor epic became the poetic form that most enabled homoeroticism in literature of the 1590s. Obvious in its sodomitic charge, where the boar's tusk signifies the penis that penetrates a man's body,[3] the motif of

Adonis's death suggests that Shakespeare only teases out and makes explicit the homoeroticism already implied in Ovid's original, in the charge of the boar and the boy, in Adonis's boyish androgyny, and in the larger context of the story of Orpheus, "the patron saint of homosexuality" (Bate, *Shakespeare* 51), of which the tale of Venus and Adonis is a part. The story of Venus and Adonis is told by Orpheus in his dirge to the trees for the loss of Eurydice. Jonathan Bate points out that "[t]he Orphic section of the *Metamorphoses* begins with a series of tales of homosexual love" and reminds us that when Orpheus lost Eurydice, he "shunned all love of women and turned to boys instead" (51). The homoerotic signification of the deadly encounter between the boar and Adonis is therefore emphasized through the larger narrative context within which it occurs: Orpheus's story. Orpheus laments the loss of Eurydice, but his sad poetry resonates throughout his story of Venus and Adonis and could be said to extend to the death of Adonis as well. Orpheus's lament is about the loss of the young, the beautiful, and the desirous: it is about Eurydice, but it provides the background for Adonis's death as well.

The same context of the boar's encounter with Adonis is present in Golding as well, but his suppression of the kiss, the signifier of a homoerotic union, suggests that he felt compelled to intervene with his moralizing pen at this point (but not others) to make Ovid's poem permissible to his Christian readers, precisely because the *homoerotic* kiss resonates ominously with forbidden desire.[4] This triangular relationship—Ovid-Golding-Shakespeare—shows, on the one hand, the circuitous yet firm route homoerotic poetry traveled in Renaissance literature. On the other, it suggests the dangers of the transgressing power of Ovid's poetry about pagan gods and their riotous desires. Both Golding and Shakespeare reflect the humanist belief that one can use antiquity selectively for a specific purpose. In this instance, both writers recast the climax of the boar-Adonis clash in Ovid in such a way that the outcome of their critical engagements with Ovid creates two different effects: Shakespeare's version of the death scene is invested with sodomy, whereas Golding's erases any trace of that carnal sin.

At a time when both civic and religious laws condemned sodomy, to want to put it back into poetry was not merely an act of aesthetic subversion of cultural laws but also an appeal to the educated and upwardly mobile young men of the Inns of Court.[5] If, as Bate argues, "Cyparissus homoeroticizes the audience of Orpheus" (*Shakespeare* 52), *Venus and Adonis* homoeroticizes the readers of Shakespeare's version of the story of Venus and Adonis and, more important, Adonis's lack of interest in Venus's rapacious love and his wish to be with his friends hunting the boar. At this point I draw my students' attention to that part of the story in which the boar episode lures Adonis away both from the homosocial narrative of hunting with his friends (a typical masculine pursuit) and from the heteroerotic narrative of seductive chase, instigated by Venus, that he is already trying to escape. The sodomitic anticlimax of the boar's chase of Adonis, therefore, eliminates both the socially promoted masculine alliance and the culturally privileged heterosexual pursuit. Thus, sodomy is constructed as a socially destructive charge and a warning to noble youth to beware the tragic consequences of succumbing to a grave sin. The connection between Cyparissus and Adonis is established through Orpheus's lament, because, as Bate reminds us, "[a]mong the trees to which he sings is the cypress, etiologized as the metamorphosed form of a boy loved by Apollo, Cyparissus, who erroneously killed a tame stag whom he loved." Coming from Orpheus's mouth and his harp, the symbolic echo of Apollo's illicit love of Cyparissus, the erroneous killing of the loved stag, and Cyparissus's death all resonate with different aspects of the myth of homosexuality in the subtext of the boar-Adonis encounter. The homoerotics of this layer of the myth of Adonis are then further established by the fact that Orpheus is singing to trees about the boys to whom he has turned his love, making him a god not just of homosexuality but "of pederasty," as Bate points out (*Shakespeare* 51). Thus, to comprehend how the process of imitation is made to signify homoeroticism, I tie together all these layers of the myth of Venus and Adonis and suggest that, while they may not be apparent in Shakespeare's version of the story, they constitute part of the myth of Venus and Adonis. I also point out to my students that the select readers (presumably learned noblemen) to whom Shakespeare alludes in the Latin motto borrowed from Ovid's *Amores* (1.15.35–36) would likely have grasped the extent and complexity of the various levels of the myth of Adonis and would likely have picked up on the homoerotic resonance of this myth.[6] The reference to Apollo—one of the lovers of boys in Orpheus's complex narrative that contextualizes the myth of Adonis—in the epigraph from *Amores* provides one of the clues to the homoerotic reading of the poem. This interpretation of Adonis's death sparks a class discussion about Ovid and Ovidianism as cultural agents (and Golding and Shakespeare as cultural mediators) in the formation of literary ideas about masculinity in the new humanist culture. In this new humanism, the male subject, educated in the humanist practice of reading the classics with some moral or pedagogical purpose in mind, achieves power and status in the exchange of knowledge and desire with other men.

Shakespeare's adaptation of Adonis's death ("queer death," as one student called it) also usefully illustrates different textual strategies for imagining sexuality, especially male same-sex eroticism, in Renaissance literature. In contemporary Renaissance scholarship, homoerotic literature is treated alongside nonliterary texts as producing homoerotic discourses in Renaissance culture. Often in such criticism, literature is denied an autonomous status that sets it apart from other types of socially produced discourses of homoeroticism, such as historical, religious, travel, or legal writing. Sexual union between men, for example, is called a "detestable vice of buggery" (Borris 90) in An Act for the Parliament of the Vice of Buggery (1563) during Queen Elizabeth I's reign, and the condemnatory tone in which this carnal sin is described is witness to the period's horror over such a transgression. Cultural context provides a foundation for an argument about sodomy because literature itself can be ambiguous on the subject. One could, for example, interpret Iago's account of his dream as an instance, as Stanley Wells argues, "of one man making love to another . . . anaesthetized by its presentation as a heterosexual dream" (85):

> I lay with Cassio lately;
> And, being troubled with a raging tooth,
> I could not sleep. There are a kind of men
> So loose of soul that in their sleeps will mutter
> Their affairs—of this kind is Cassio:
> In sleep I heard him say 'Sweet Desdemona,
> Let us be wary, let us hide our loves';
> And then, sir, would he gripe and wring my hand,
> Cry, 'O, sweet creature!', and then kiss me hard,
> As if he plucked up kisses by the roots
> That grew upon my lips, then laid his leg
> Over my thigh, and sighed, and kissed.
> (*Othello* 3.3.415–26)

This passage raises a host of provocative speculations about who is really imagined to make love to whom: Is Iago imagining himself to be a voyeur in the scene of Desdemona's clandestine sexual lovemaking with Cassio? Is Iago imagining Cassio making love to Desdemona while imagining himself in her place? Is Iago, or Cassio in Iago's fantasy, one of that "kind of men" who sleep with other men? What kind of love anyway is wished to be hidden here? And why? The horrifying and titillating love in Iago's erotic fantasy might be sodomy, referred to as "detestable and abominable sin, among Christians not to be named, committed by carnal knowledge against the ordinance of the Creator and order of nature," as stated in the section "Of Buggery; or Sodomy" in the third part of the Institutes of the Laws of England (Borris 97).[7]

The difference, however, between reading sodomy in Iago's dream and finding it in the scene of Adonis's death depends on how we interpret the relation between the texts we juxtapose. What differentiates *Venus and Adonis* from *Othello* in this regard is that the status of the minor epic as a creative imitation grants legitimacy to a specific literary form of imagined sexuality, especially homoeroticism. The homoeroticism of the death scene is already present in the Ovidian source and is only made more prominent in the death scene. But in *Othello* the homoerotic ambiguity of Iago's dream is Shakespeare's invention, not the result of a creative adaptation of a specific source. If read as a homoerotic gesture, Iago's dreamed kiss is not too different from the kiss Shakespeare adds to Adonis's death scene. Yet what complicates the interpretation of Iago's erotic dream is its immediate thematic context, which confuses the meaning of that kiss and obscures the fantasy's real sexual players.

When I compared the passage quoted above from *Othello* with the end of *Venus and Adonis* in class, suggesting that in both cases sodomy may be an issue, my students rightly asked me whether Shakespeare would have known any of the legal statutes against buggery that I used to prop up my reading of Iago's dream. But they took for granted the creative relation between Ovid and Shakespeare, assuming that a literary imitation is legitimized by its source and that Shakespeare just wrote Ovid in Modern English. They grasped that English Renaissance discourses of homoeroticism imagined in literature exist apart from other kinds of cultural productions of homoeroticism and that the creative relation between Ovid, Golding, and Shakespeare, with its attendant suppressions and reinscriptions of homoerotic charges, already tells a cultural story about condemnation and affirmation of sodomy in the English Renaissance. Seen as an exercise in creative imagination, the representation of sodomy at the end of *Venus and Adonis* is an example of imitation that accomplishes its own kind of cultural evaluation. The metamorphosis into a flower at the end of the poem can be read as either undercutting sodomy or shrouding it in mystery without any attendant horror. Homoerotic charges at the end of *Venus and Adonis* thus belong as much to an Ovidian etiology of sexuality as to the native culture that uses *Metamorphoses* as a resource for its own erotic verses.

The attentiveness with which Shakespeare reacts to Golding's rendering of Ovid and with which Golding rewrites Ovidian desires in his own versions of Ovid's myths suggests that Golding's translation was crucial to the emergence of the rhetoric of desire and sexuality in English erotic literature and that it therefore lies at the heart of a new, Ovidian conception of sexuality in the English Renaissance. The seductive ambiguity of desires in Golding's Ovid (and Shakespeare's, by means of Golding) and the sexual ambivalence of the bodies mobilized by such desires often remind my students of some of the recent theories of "undoing gender" (Butler), of subsuming gender to sexuality, and of redefining possible meanings of sexual identifications within gendered bodies. The questions they ask about sexualized bodies in Golding and Shakespeare—What is sexuality in these texts? What does gender mean in these verses? What does it mean to love and to desire?—are questions that have animated much of queer theory's writing about the discursive and cultural constructions of gender and sexuality. The varied and different uses of Ovid we study provide students with some answers to those questions, because Ovid and his Renaissance imitators imagine the body as fragile and subject to change and sexuality outside marriage as a flexible and uncontrollable category. I approach these texts as examples of how ideas, if not defined concepts, of homoerotic desire and homosexuality (as well as heterosexuality) emerged and were represented in Renaissance literature. Since most of my students do not expect to find homosexuality in literary texts read in class, they are surprised when we discuss it. They tend to think of homoeroticism as a contemporary concept, and when they recognize it in early modern literature, they use it as a tool for bringing a literature removed in time closer to their own understanding of the world. I often return to Golding and *Venus and Adonis* not only to point out the varied ways in which the Renaissance practice of imitation worked but also to start a discussion about ambiguous sexualities in Shakespeare's sonnets and plays; Christopher Marlowe's narrative poem, "Hero and Leander"; Philip Sidney's prose romance, *Arcadia*; or Edmund Spenser's epic, *The Faerie Queene*. By linking *Venus and Adonis* and Golding to these writers and texts, I not only maintain a thematic coherence in class, but, more important, I highlight the continuing presence of "the wicked pleasures of Ovidianism" (Burrow 304) in erotic discourses in English Renaissance literature.

The return to Golding and *Venus and Adonis* also helps me remind my students that Renaissance literature does not emerge in isolation from its classical predecessors. I emphasize that Ovid is important not only as a source but also as the originator "of a worldview and an aesthetic" (Barkan, *Gods* xv). In that worldview, fascination with transformation of the body in literature, however exciting it is, points to other changes that occurred in the larger world of the English Renaissance, in which change was considered at once fascinating and disturbing. Those larger changes included a shift in religion, a move from a feudal to protocapitalist urban economy, overseas discoveries and expansions of mercantile possibilities, and the emergence of science. I show my students that the last one hundred or so lines of *Metamorphoses* are not only about mutability of the body or about desire, they are also an apotheosis of Caesar, a celebration of his militant and imperial powers. This seems to them like a shift from our discussion of the homoerotics of Adonis's death in *Venus and Adonis*, but just as the ending of *Metamorphoses* is a reminder that the mutability of the body, the central theme of Ovid's poem, is part of the story about a change in the ruling order in Rome, so is the ending of *Venus and Adonis* a reminder that the social and the sexual are never far apart. Adonis's death involves the horror the Renaissance associated with sodomy, seen as undermining the symbolic order and as running counter to procreative discourses promoted by Protestantism. At the same, however, by alluding to sodomy in Adonis's death, the poem's ending makes homoeroticism part of the narrative about a heterosexual love chase. Sodomy, therefore, interrupts a normative pursuit; the one does not allow the other to succeed. The links between the social and the sexual and between the titillation and horror attributed to aberrant and, from the period's point of view, nonnormative sexual pursuits are among the lessons my students take from a class on Ovidian eroticism in English Renaissance literature to other courses in which they study gender and sexuality in different cultural contexts and in which they are likely to hear that the social discomfort with, and proscription of, homosexuality did not end with the Renaissance.

NOTES

[1] On the Ovidian subtext to Renaissance literature of the body and desire see Bate, *Shakespeare*; Enterline; Lyne, *Ovid's Changing Worlds*; Rimell; Stanivukovic; and Taylor.

[2] Citations to Golding are to Forey's edition. The Loeb translation of these lines reads, "deep in the groin he [the boar] sank his long tusks, and stretched the dying boy upon the yellow sand" (Ovid, Metamorphoses [ed. Goold (1984)] 115).

[3] I draw my students' attention to the fact that in Renaissance literature a groin wound is often an erotic, in this instance, a homoerotic wound. Coppélia Kahn (77–143) has made a similar argument about the (heterosexual) eroticism of the groin wound that emasculates heroic men in Shakespeare's Roman plays.

[4] Lyne also argues (*Ovid's Changing Worlds* 32–36) that while Golding's translation does not completely follow the medieval tradition of the moralized Ovid, Golding selectively moralizes in some parts of his translation.

[5] See Ellis on the cultural context within which the minor epic originated, especially with respect to the convergence of sexuality and nationhood.

[6] The motto reads, "Vilia miretur vulgus: mihi flavus Apollo / pocula Castalia plena ministret aqua." Burrow translates, "Let the common herd be amazed by worthless things; but for me let golden Apollo provide cups full of the water of the Muses" (Shakespeare, *Complete Sonnets* 173).

[7] Borris says that this tract is dated 1644 but was probably written earlier (97).

Teaching Marlowe's Translation of *Amores*
Patrick Cheney

Instructors can profitably include Christopher Marlowe's translation of *Amores* in undergraduate courses in the English Renaissance. Marlowe's translation, known as *Ovid's Elegies*, is particularly helpful for introducing students to the relation between two concepts often fused by male authors in this period yet typically kept separate in recent criticism: the idea of a literary career and the masculine representation of the female. Following Ovid's lead, Marlowe recurrently links the sexual with the literary, gender with genre, female object with male subject. By highlighting these links, instructors can help students learn how Marlowe uses Ovid to enter into dialogue with such contemporary authors as Philip Sidney, Edmund Spenser, and William Shakespeare.

Typically, I teach *Ovid's Elegies* in an upper-division course in the English Renaissance at Penn State, but the work is well suited to other types of courses, such as the early British literature survey. My course has thirty to forty students, half of them English majors and the other half from education, comparative literature, and liberal arts (occasionally, engineers and scientists). I cannot depend, therefore, on their having had much prior experience with the English Renaissance, although some have taken our early British survey and thus have read selections of Sidney, Spenser, and Shakespeare, perhaps even Marlowe himself (usually "The Passionate Shepherd to His Love," *Hero and Leander*, or *Doctor Faustus*). Very few will have heard of *Ovid's Elegies*, although some recent anthologies do include sample elegies, notably 1.5 and 1.13.[1]

In my course, I usually include *Ovid's Elegies* in a unit titled "Erotic Poetry: Sonnet and Elegy," which I precede with the unit "Pastoral: Eclogue, Lyric, Drama" and follow with the units "Epic, Counter-epic, Minor Epic," "Tragedy," and "Narrative Poetry: Marriage, Separation, Betrayal." My opening unit on pastoral foregrounds Spenser's *Shepheardes Calender*, Marlowe's "Passionate Shepherd," and Shakespeare's *As You Like It*, while the second unit on erotic poetry includes excerpts from Petrarch's *Rime Sparse*, Sidney's *Astrophil and Stella*, Spenser's *Amoretti*, and Shakespeare's *Sonnets*; other Petrarchan sequences can work well too, such as those by Samuel Daniel, Michael Drayton, Fulke Greville, or Mary Wroth. I mention this structure because it provides the specific context in which my students encounter the Elizabethan dialogue surrounding Marlowe's translation of Ovid.

Usually, I have time for only a single class on *Ovid's Elegies*, or perhaps two, with a week being a real treat. Here are three options for assigning individual elegies:

> *One-Day Unit:* Elegies 1.1,° 1.5,° 1.7,° 1.13,° 1.14, 1.15, 2.1,° 2.13–14,° 2.18,° 3.1,° 3.2, 3.6, 3.14°
> (° indicates the most important elegies for the discussion I suggest, if instructors need to cut back the reading further)

Two-Day Unit: Elegies 1.1, 1.4, 1.5, 1.6, 1.7, 1.8, 1.10, 1.13, 1.14, 1.15, 2.1, 2.2, 2.6, 2.12, 2.13, 2.14, 2.18, 3.1, 3.2, 3.6, 3.7, 3.8, 3.11, 3.14

Three-Day Unit: All forty-eight elegies[2]

The goal of all three units can remain the same: to help students see how the Renaissance poet uses the Roman poet to illuminate a historic representation, at once original and important: the feminine origin to Ovidian art (see Sharrock, "Gender" and "Ovid"). Nowhere is this representation more historic than in elegy 3.1, where Ovid narrates how one day, as he is walking in the woods, he arrives at a sacred fountain and encounters two ladies engaged in debate: Dame Elegy and Dame Tragedy. In this elegy, Ovid imagines literary form in the shape of two female figures, with his description of their dress, body, and temperament representing individual features of generic form:

> Elegia came with hairs perfumed sweet,
> And one, I think, was longer of her feet;
> A decent form, thin robe, a lover's look,
> By her foot's blemish greater grace she took.
> Then with huge steps came violent Tragedy:
> Stern was her front, her cloak on ground did lie;
> Her left hand held abroad a regal sceptre,
> The Lydian buskin in fit paces kept her.
> (Marlowe, *Ovid's Elegies* 3.1.7–14)

In addition, in the urban fiction of the elegies, Ovid presents his Roman mistress with a name that he borrows from the sixth-century BCE Greek poetess traditionally thought to be Pindar's teacher, Corinna. In this way, Ovid inflects his primary female figure with *poesis*. In fact, Ovid elsewhere suggests that, in part because of her name, his contemporaries wondered whether Corinna was real or merely a figment of his imagination (*Ars amatoria* 3.538; Sharrock, "Ovid" 151). The device draws attention to a hallmark of Ovidian poetics and its reception in the English Renaissance: the absolute fusion of authorship and the feminine.

The Author and His Literary Career

To encourage students to talk about "authorship" in *Ovid's Elegies*, instructors may well begin with the bibliographic problem underlying Marlowe's translation. We do not know when Marlowe produced *Ovid's Elegies* or even when it was published or where. We also lack information on what his intentions might have been, how he proceeded, or by which principles. We know only that three editions exist: two of them print ten poems, titled *Certain of Ovid's Elegies*, while the third prints "all" forty-eight, titled *All Ovid's Elegies*; the known copies of the three editions are curiously said to be "By C. M." Conventionally, Elizabethan translations print the phrase "translated by" on the title page, as does the 1600 edition of *Lucan's First Book*: "Translated Line for Line, By Chr. Marlowe." In contrast, the early editions of *Ovid's Elegies* present a paradox that instructors can discuss to advantage: the elegies of Ovid are "by" Christopher Marlowe. Such an advertisement happily speaks to the conclusion of modern scholarship: although a line-by-line translation of a Latin work, *Ovid's Elegies* becomes an Elizabethan poem, an original Ovidian work "by" Christopher Marlowe.

Although we do not know in which order the three editions appeared, all were printed with John Davies's *Epigrams*, another collection of forty-eight poems. To complicate matters, all three editions are printed in Middleborough, Holland, even though recent scholarship argues that this place is spurious—a cover for a press in England (Nicholl). Finally, we know that in 1599 the bishops of the Church of England ordered *Ovid's Elegies* to be publicly banned and burned, along with other books thought seditious (McCabe; Moulton). While we do not know when Marlowe composed his translation, when it was printed, or where, most scholars assign an early date of composition, when Marlowe was still a student at Cambridge University (around 1585), with publication likely occurring during the mid-1590s (around 1595).[3]

Scholars may lack certainty about much of the bibliographic information of Marlowe's translation, but they agree that it is a historic achievement, and students can benefit from learning just how. For starters, it is the very first full translation of *Amores* into *any* European vernacular (Striar 187). *Amores* is also notable as this author's inaugural volume, the foundation of his literary career; furthermore, it alone among his works became taboo during the Renaissance, making its way into the British school curriculum only in the seventeenth century (Cheney, *Marlowe's Counterfeit Profession* 49). Finally, Marlowe's translation is important because it is the first English Renaissance poem published in sustained heroic couplets, anticipating his more famous *Hero and Leander* and of course Alexander Pope (G. Brown, "Marlowe's Poems"). Until recently, criticism has focused almost exclusively on the nature and accuracy of Marlowe's translation (e.g., Gill, "Marlowe"); but critics are becoming increasingly interested now in *Ovid's Elegies* as a literary work in its own right (Stapleton). Instructors can profitably discuss both aspects of the erotic volume, to emphasize just how Marlowe's technique of translation produces an original composition.

Particular elegies useful for teaching the author and his literary career include elegies 1.1, 1.15, 2.1, 2.18, 3.1, 3.14 (the "programmatic poems") and elegies 1.3, 1.10, 2.17, 3.7, 3.8 (other poems that voice poetic fame). In his translation, Marlowe follows Ovid in using the six programmatic poems to frame his volume of love elegies. By providing this frame to students, instructors have an unusual opportunity to introduce (or advance) the topic of classical and Renaissance authorship and the allied topic of literary careers (see Farrell, "Greek Lives").

Most students find the career frame of Ovidian and Marlovian authorship new and intriguing. Some of them are themselves "writers," but most are students of literature, naturally interested in the art and career of the author. I start by showing students our first important "career document," the verses prefacing Roman, medieval, and Renaissance editions of Vergil's *Aeneid* (Vergil may or may not have composed the verses):

> I am the poet who once tuned his song
> On a slender reed and then leaving the woods
> Compelled the fields to obey the hungry farmer,
> A pleasing work. But now War's grim and savage
> Arms I sing . . .   (xiv)

Here "Vergil" presents himself as an author with a tripartite literary career, progressing from the low genre of pastoral *otium* (*Eclogues*) to the middle genre of georgic *labor* (*Georgics*) to the high genre of national epic duty (*Aeneid*; see Cheney, Introduction). I emphasize that the Vergilian progression operates typologically (Coolidge): pastoral predicts georgic and epic; georgic enfolds pastoral and predicts epic; epic enfolds both pastoral and georgic (cf. Neuse).

I next look at the opening eight lines of Marlowe's translation (1.1–8), which are well known to respond to the Vergilian career document, and I encourage students to discover the details of Ovid's response. Not simply does Ovid present his work as being in motion, having shrunk from "five books" to "three" when the first edition turned into a second (Cameron), but he began the work as a Vergilian-type national epic only to be interrupted by "Love," who changed his epic meter from dactylic hexameter to that of love elegy (a dactylic hexameter line followed by a line of dactylic pentameter). Ovid responds to Vergil by self-consciously veering from the career path of the national poet. Then I show students elegy 2.1, which extends the Ovidian narrative of the poet's turn from Vergilian-type national epic to love elegy.

Once students grasp Ovid's historic career shift, I introduce them to perhaps the most significant turn in the Ovidian *cursus*: the inclusion of tragedy. The first elegy to make this second turn explicit is 2.18, which illustrates a three-part pattern that begins with the lower genre of love elegy and turns to the higher genres prized by Aristotle in the *Poetics*: tragedy and epic (Cheney, *Marlowe's Counterfeit Profession* 29–67; cf. Hardie, Introduction; Harrison). Elegy 2.18 introduces yet another complication, which becomes (I argue) Ovid's career signature: rather than progress typologically from pastoral to georgic to epic the way Vergil does, Ovid presents himself oscillating through his three preferred genres. He starts with epic but veers into elegy; he plans to write tragedy and epic but pens a tragedy before completing his elegy. Lines 13–14 of 2.18 foreground this contradiction, for they refer to Ovid's one known tragedy, *Medea*, extant in two lines and known in antiquity as the mark of his genius (Seneca the Elder, *Suasoriae* 3.7; Quintilian 7.5.6, 10.1.98; Tacitus, *Dialogus* 12.6). In other words, Ovid refers to a tragedy already started that he is supposed to write only after he completes the very elegy we are reading. We know that he plans to turn from elegy to tragedy because he tells us so in the volume's concluding elegy (3.14). We have to take the plan seriously because of contemporary evidence for his *Medea*.

Ovid's elegiac writing of tragedy is more formally the topic of elegy 3.1, when Ovid encounters Dame Elegy and Dame Tragedy beside the *fons sacer*. Students tend to find this mininarrative intriguing, since the poet is forced to negotiate with stern Tragedy by promising to write in her genre if she will let him write first in the genre of Lady Elegy. The details by which Ovid presents literary genre in the garb of the feminine create a segue to Ovid's representation of his mistress Corinna.

The Masculine Perception of the Female

Elegies useful for teaching the masculine representation of the female include elegies 1.4, 1.5, 1.6, 1.7, 1.8, 1.13, 1.14, 2.2, 2.8, 2.12, 2.13, 2.14, 2.15, 3.2, 3.3, 3.6 (some Corinna poems) and elegies 2.4, 2.8, 2.10, 3.10 (poems on promiscuity more generally). Instructors will know or discover which poems work best, but the most famous is elegy 1.5, Corinna's noontime visit to Ovid's bedroom. Because this poem is so sexually explicit, and the narrative of seduction so captivating, students attend to it eagerly.

The details are again exquisite, for we learn a lot about this young woman. I always begin by asking students to sift through the details of the elegy to characterize Corinna: when making love, she likes the room dark; although striving against her lover, she seeks to be won by him; physically stunning, head to toe, she does not tire easily; and so forth.

Elegy 1.5 is the quintessence of Ovidian love poetry, not simply for its witty and urbane narrative of male-female lovemaking but also for its masculine representation of the female. Here, teachers can (re-)introduce the blazon (lines 17–22; see Vickers), for the poet carefully inventories the parts of Corinna's body: her arms and shoulders, her breasts, her belly and waist, her leg, and her "lusty thigh" (line 22). While students will quickly see the beauty of Corinna's body, some will notice the violence that Ovid showcases, not only when the rapt lover snatches off her gown and throws her on the bed but also when she encourages his roughhousing and even her own betrayal (line 16).

Since we will already have read Spenser's *Aprill* eclogue, I encourage students to think, talk, and even write about Marlowe's elegy 1.5 in intertextual dialogue with Spenser's masculine representation of "fayre Eliza, Queene of shepheardes all" (*Shepheardes Calender*, line 34). They quickly see that Spenser and Marlowe present the female very differently; Colin Clout and "Ovid" perceive women in radically different terms. The key word is "terms," and here students can benefit from the help of Louis Montrose, who shows that in Colin's song "Elisa becomes a personification of pastoral poetry; she embodies the literary mode of the poem in which she appears" (321). In other words, not simply does Colin see Eliza as a purified figure of grace and redemption important to his career as England's budding laureate or national poet (Helgerson), but he imagines the queen in the very terms of his own authorship. Significantly for subsequent English literature, I point out, Spenser's representation of the female is written through with the discourse of masculine art and career. Paired analysis of Colin's "song of Eliza" and Marlowe's elegy 1.5 pays off for the rest of the course, no matter which authors are read, from John Donne to John Milton, because now students have a hermeneutic for reading the masculine representation of the female: such a representation introduces the way men perceive women but leaves a record of the literary nature of the representation. By studying such a representation, students can learn a good deal about the ways in which male authors use feminine form to depict the form of their own authorship.

I also use this intertextual moment to say something about the tradition underlying it. Teachers might introduce their own genealogy (to my knowledge, the topic has never been studied); but my version begins with Ovid, in *Amores*, and progresses to Petrarch's Laura (both cited by E. K. in his glosses on the *Calender* ["Januarye" lines 120–22, "Aprill" 190–91]). By studying this tradition and specific representations of the blazon within it, students can learn something not only about the way men perceive women in the Western literary tradition but also about the way male poets invent a feminine-based art form.

We see the details of this art form played out in other Corinna poems, but not before students compile a composite biography of this out-front young woman. (Instructors can have students compose their own biographies through a written assignment or construct one collectively in class discussion.) Students are surprised (and sometimes shocked) to see that Corinna anticipates the desires and lives of many modern women—more viscerally perhaps than Sidney's Stella or Spenser's Elizabeth Boyle, with Shakespeare's Dark Lady from the *Sonnets* surely Corinna's younger sister. Students find it meaningful to compare Corinna with such early modern representations of the female, especially if I share with them Stephen Orgel's remark locating *Ovid's Elegies* within the field of English Petrarchism: "In a sense, this is Marlowe's sonnet sequence, the psychomachia of a poet-lover whose love is both his creation and his ultimate monomania, frustration and despair" (*Christopher Marlowe* 233).

Through analysis, students see that Corinna, who at one point even attempts to surmount Ovid's impotence (3.6), does not merely like to make love in his bedroom; she has an attractively robust character, of considerably potent agency. She enjoys going to the horse races (3.2); she values nice things, including rings (2.15); she dyes her hair, even if it falls out (1.14); she commits adultery, not simply with the poet, and even has the gall to sleep with her husband (1.4; see 2.12); she is a guilt-free liar (3.3); when the poet impregnates her, she has an abortion (2.13 and 14); and when she suffers physical abuse by her lover, she strikes back (1.7). In Ovid's memorable portrait, Corinna's body changes; her desires transform; her actions alter: she becomes an icon for Ovidian metamorphosis itself, always in motion, in touch, yet exquisitely out of reach.

Students have fun reading about Corinna, but in the process they also learn about the nature of Marlowe's Ovidian poetics. For Marlowe, as for Ovid, and indeed as for other authors like Petrarch, Spenser, Sidney, and Shakespeare, female desire and sexuality are deeply implicated in the creation of masculine authorship. This Ovidian fusion of the sexual and the literary remains open to feminist critique, or open to interpretation by other models. Whichever methodologies instructors bring to the Ovidian classroom of Marlowe, students find a genuine opportunity to learn something fresh and valuable about the gender-based invention of poetry, Roman and English.

NOTES

[1] Norbrook and Woudhuysen include elegy 1.13. Payne and Hunter include elegies 1.1, 1.4, 1.5, 1.7, 1.8, 2.6, 2.9, 3.7, and 3.11. Braden includes elegies 1.5 and 1.13.

[2] The edition of *Amores* that Marlowe used does not include the dream-vision poem that the Loeb edition (Heroides *and* Amores) prints as elegy 3.5 but that virtually all modern editions set off in brackets as not in fact Ovid's work. This affects the numbering of the remaining poems, so that, for instance, Marlowe's elegy 3.14 is the Loeb's 3.15. Marlowe also read elegies 2.9A and 2.9B as a single poem, although these are now generally agreed to be two separate poems.

[3] For details on the complex publication history, see the major scholarly editions: Brooke; L. C. Martin; MacLure; Bowers, *Complete Works*; Gill, *Poems*. See also Gill and Krueger; Bowers, "Early Editions"; Nosworthy, "Publication" and "Marlowe's Ovid."

Teaching Tiresias: Issues of Gender and Sexuality in Ovid and Beyond

Phyllis Katz

Ovid's story of Tiresias's transsexual changes from male to female to male (*Met.* 3.316–78) provides a paradigm for exploration of issues of sexual and gender identity.[1] Indeed, Tiresias's significance as a "transsexual" in ancient culture makes his story appropriate as a literary trope for modern depictions of transsexual and androgynous persons and of those born with ambiguous genitalia. Such complex identities occur in a number of works that I have introduced in my classes as a complement to Ovid's Tiresias episode, including T. S. Eliot's *Waste Land* (1922), Virginia Woolf's *Orlando* (1928), John Colapinto's *As Nature Made Him* (2001), Jennifer Boylan's *She's Not There* (2002), and Jeffrey Eugenides's *Middlesex* (2000). Ovid's version of Tiresias's changes from male to female to male provides a point of departure for discussions about these later authors and their own explorations of gender and sexual identity, of "masculine and feminine, male and female." Together with these works, I have used the Tiresias passage to explore traditional and nontraditional sex and gender issues—heterosexual dominance, gender hierarchy, androgyny, bisexuality, and transsexuality among them.

In Ovid's *Metamorphoses*, Tiresias's transformations occur because Tiresias seemingly haphazardly strikes a pair of copulating snakes he encounters in the forest. When he hits the snakes he becomes a female; seven years later, again in the forest, he meets another pair of snakes having intercourse, strikes them, and becomes a male once again.[2] Because Tiresias has been both male and female, the poet claims that "he / knew love both as a woman and a man" (90; 3.323 "Venus huic erat utraque nota"). Thus Tiresias is consulted as arbiter of a seemingly humorous quarrel between Jupiter and Juno about whether males or females derive more pleasure from sex. Jupiter argues that females have more pleasure; Juno disagrees. The humor is one-sided. Jupiter alone is described as in jest; Juno is given no humor and no real voice. She disagrees—"illa negat" (3.322)—but otherwise takes no active part in the debate.

Tiresias decides in favor of Jupiter's view, whereupon Juno blinds him, and Jupiter, in recompense, endows Tiresias with the gift of prophecy. The poet does not explain Juno's rage about the judgment; however, her anger must surely be rooted in her resentment over the assessment of women's greater sexual pleasure when there is no evidence to indicate that Juno herself has ever found any pleasure in sex. Moreover, Juno's fury at Jupiter's numerous infidelities, Callisto, Semele, and Io among them, is manifest in her unmitigated cruelty toward her mate's lovers.

Although the text asserts that Tiresias had known love and sex as both a man and a woman, Ovid provides no examples of his experiences. The poet does, however, suggest that Tiresias has not truly changed identity and that even when he is a woman he behaves as a man, walking alone in the woods, carrying a staff, and using it to strike a blow: "... His stout staff dealt a blow; / and he regained the shape he had before, / the shape the Theban had when he was born" (90; 3.325, 330–31). The persistence of Tiresias's masculinity leads Genevieve Liveley to claim that "[in Ovid's Tiresias episode], masculine and feminine, male and female, are shown to be open positions that either sex may occupy, rather than mutually exclusive poles" ("Tiresias" 161). This aspect of the story has persisted beyond Ovid into the modern era.

Tiresias's sexual transformations, the first in the poem, echo the general fluidity of bodily form that concerns Ovid throughout *Metamorphoses*. For women, such fluidity is often, though not always, precipitated by male sexual aggression and leads to female victimization, often with bodily change. Students will have read in books 1 and 2 some notable examples of male sexual aggression against women: Daphne pursued by Apollo is only saved by transformation into a laurel tree; Io, changed to a cow by Jupiter to evade Juno's notice, is driven to Egypt, where she regains her female shape and is impregnated by Jupiter; Europa is tricked, carried off, and raped by a disguised Jupiter. Often, such male aggression results in gender transformation as well: Mestra, daughter of Erysichthon, at her request is changed to a male by Neptune after he rapes her and so will no longer be vulnerable to male sexual violence (281–83; 8.843–78); Thetis changes her female shape many times before yielding to the sexual demands of Peleus (369–70; 11.229–65); Caenis too is transformed from female to male by her ravager Neptune to protect her from further sexual assault (404–05; 12.168–209). In her new male identity, Caeneus is also impenetrable; as Sharrock comments:

> historians of sexuality express something of the defining characteristic of Roman sexuality through the distinction between the active penetrator and the passive penetrated. Real men are not penetrated; "women" are, as the notorious phrase *muliebria pati* ("to suffer female things") eloquently proclaims. ("Gender" 97)

Caenis becomes a mighty warrior and is only defeated and killed by suffocation. On another occasion, a girl, Iphis, is raised as a boy, lest, not being male, she be put to death by her father. Iphis acquires her male identity through nurture; she is ultimately changed into a man by the goddess Isis so that she may marry Ianthe (316–21; 9.666–797).

Bodily change into the opposite sex can also be the result of punishment of a male by an aggressive female: the abbreviated Ovidian story of Sithon, first a man, then a woman (120; 4.286–88), complements the non-Ovidian tale told of Siproites, whose sex was changed from male to female for having seen Artemis bathing (Antoninus Liberalis 17).[3] Both stories offer opportunities for discussions about gender and sexuality in the ancient world and suggest that for Ovid, sexual fluidity most often serves as a means of asserting gender superiority or escaping gender aggression.

Of course, myth has many functions in the works of Ovid; one, however, is its pliancy, for the poet can examine a variety of gendered behaviors, ranging from adolescent sexual immaturity to rape to incest to adultery to fidelity in marriage, without linking them directly to any historical reality. Luc Brisson's 2002 book on the topic of sexual fluidity in the ancient world looks at the disparity between what is acceptable in myth versus what is unacceptable in society. Brisson discusses the "rejection" in antiquity of persons with dual sexuality, characters who were viewed as monsters in "real life." In the ancient world children with ambiguous genitalia were either killed or exhibited as "strange phenomena" (*Sexual Ambivalence* 7–40), and expiatory rites of purification were performed to protect the community from pollution.[4] Brisson argues that in myth, however, stories of androgynes or hermaphrodites appear paradoxically to represent a fundamental desire for fusion, a return to an archetypal wholeness, a desire in antiquity that reaches back to Aristophanes's definition of love in Plato's *Symposium* (72–114).[5] If, as Ovid suggests, the division between masculine and feminine was permeable in antiquity, scientific studies today confirm how very unstable this binary pair really is but how little we still know about this complex topic. As Anne Fausto-Sterling comments:

> For some time, experts on gender development have distinguished between sex at the genetic level and at the cellular level (sex-specific gene expression, X and Y chromosomes); at the hormonal level (in the fetus, during childhood and after puberty); and at the anatomical level (genitals and secondary sexual characteristics). Gender identity presumably emerges from all of those corporeal aspects via some poorly understood interaction with environment and experience. (16)

Recognizing chromosomal differences provides only a partial explanation for gender and sex identity, although we are beginning to perceive that the explanations for genital ambiguities and gender identifications may be found in increased understanding of the brain.[6]

After having examined sex and gender fluidity in *Metamorphoses*, I apply the issues raised in the poem to modern works.[7] My choice of readings is based on what can be accomplished in an academic term. After Ovid, I generally choose T. S. Eliot because he centers his *Waste Land* on Ovid's Tiresias, and I assign Sigmund Freud's "Some Psychological Consequences of the Anatomical Distinction between the Sexes" to ground the students in what was then newly emerging work on psychosexuality. In *The Waste Land*, Eliot describes Tiresias as if he were androgynous, writing in a footnote to the Tiresias passage (part 3, "The Fire Sermon") that

> Tiresias, although a mere spectator and not indeed a "character," is yet the most important personage in the poem, uniting all the rest. Just as the one-eyed merchant, seller of currants, melts into the Phoenician Sailor,

and the latter is not wholly distinct from Ferdinand Prince of Naples, so all the women are one woman, and the two sexes meet in Tiresias. What Tiresias *sees*, in fact, is the substance of the poem. (84n218)

To emphasize Ovid's importance, Eliot then cites the Latin passage in its entirety. Eliot's note requires us to read the characters in *The Waste Land*, both male and female, as a kind of androgynous composite of all the males and females in the poem, a composite epitomized by Tiresias. The image is a dark and negative one. Indeed, as Georgia Nugent says of Ovid's tale of Salmacis and Hermaphroditus (4.285–388), "the androgynous being [is] not self-sufficient or excessive but . . . ambiguous and deficient" (177).

Ambiguity and deficiency typify the male and female characters in Eliot's *Waste Land*. They are fused into a complicated and problematic androgynous whole that wreaks havoc with the notion of individual identity as well as with the sexual binary long taken for granted in Western society. The men and women who inhabit the world of the poem are sexually dysfunctional, as much so as are some of the characters in *Metamorphoses*.[8]

Disappointment in love in *The Waste Land* begins with the hyacinth girl in part 1. The women of the poem are objects of mystery or failed or violent eroticism: Madame Sosostris the fortune teller; the mysterious wealthy woman in part 2; Philomel in part 2, whose tongue was cut out by Tereus lest she reveal that he had raped her; the nervous wife Lil, with her hatred of sex; the bored typist in part 3 who engages in mechanical sex and thinks, "Well now that's done: and I'm glad it's over" (252); the lustful Elizabeth I, "supine on the floor of a narrow canoe" (295); the adulterous Francesca da Rimini in part 5.

Similarly, the men in *The Waste Land* are connected with death and sterility: Stetson in part 1 has planted a corpse in his garden; the woman's companion in part 2 thinks "we are in rats' alley / Where the dead men lost their bones" (115–16); also in part 2, Albert "wants a good time" (147); the speaker fishes in "the dull canal" while rats creep about him (189); there is Mr. Eugenides the probable homosexual in part 3; the clerk "makes a welcome" of the sexual indifference of the typist (242); Saint Augustine is "burning burning burning burning" with lust in part 3 (308); and there is drowned Phlebas in part 4. Tiresias, who has "walked among the lowest of the dead" (246), a man "though blind, throbbing between two lives / Old man with wrinkled female breasts" (218–19), incorporates them all, his androgyny corrupted by his physical deformity, his seeming hermaphroditism. Like the other males and females in the poem, Tiresias inhabits a world of drought and sterility that appears to reflect Eliot's view of post–World War I Europe.[9]

Virginia Woolf's *Orlando* was also published in the uncertain years after World War I (1928). Woolf's concerns, however, are far different from Eliot's. Among other themes in this novel/biography, Woolf investigates the fluidity of gender and sexual identity in a fantasy work, where Orlando changes from male to female, lives through a period of three hundred years, and retains a fundamental identity the entire time. This seriocomic work, based in part on the life and family history of Vita Sackville-West, provides students with Woolf's unique perspective on gender fluidity. Though Woolf never mentions Ovid or Tiresias directly, J. H. Stape comments on Woolf's interest in androgyny, or the need to be "woman-manly or man-womanly" (Woolf, *Room* 157), that

> [*Orlando*] was stimulated by her fascination and emotional involvement with Vita Sackville-West, and also influenced by contemporary sexual politics and debates about psychosexual theory, particularly Freud. *The emblematic Tiresias of Greek legend and drama, who simultaneously perceives and experiences life as a man and as a woman, provides one of the novel's most obvious sources.* (xx; my emphasis)

Woolf's Orlando begins life as a male of noble birth living in the late fifteenth to early sixteenth centuries and growing up during the Great Frost in London. He has a disastrous love affair, and to escape from his depression when his lover disappears, he travels to Turkey as an ambassador. There he awakes after a trance to find that he has been transformed into a woman.[10] Woolf writes:

> Orlando had become a woman—there is no denying it. But in every other respect, Orlando remained precisely as he had been. The change of sex, though it altered their future, did nothing whatever to alter their identity.... The change seems to have been accomplished painlessly and completely and in such a way that Orlando herself showed no surprise at it. Many people, taking this into account, and holding that such a change of sex is against nature, have been at great pains to prove (1) that Orlando had always been a woman, (2) that Orlando is at this moment a man. Let biologists and psychologists determine. It is enough for us to state the simple fact; Orlando was a man till the age of thirty; when he became a woman and has remained so ever since. (102–03)

Woolf depicts Orlando's fundamental nature as unchanged; however, both the tone and subject matter introduce a significant element of doubt, as does the author's lack of faith in biologists and psychologists. The tone and language, moreover, are very Ovidian.[11] By oblique reference to Ovid, Woolf signals to her readers that her exploration of sexual transformation is both serious and fanciful. Male-female relationships based on pursuit and flight are typical and expected, although since gender hierarchy is basic to them, they are also frequently tragic.

The novel posits a fanciful androgyny, a state where a person's identity partakes of both male and female qualities because of what Pamela Caughie calls Woolf's "refusal to choose" (44). Hence Woolf playfully suggests that one can enact the role of male or female but actually be male and female simultaneously. In contrast to Eliot, for whom the blending of sexual identities is a sign of sterility, for Woolf gender and sexual identity are as fluid as they are in Ovid; yet Woolf's concept of fluidity is much more positive, providing, in the end, a source of creative strength for Orlando.

In Ovid, Tiresias's sexual transformation is not based on sexual preference, biological nature, or familial or social nurture. These modern—in other words, newly recognized—causes for gender ambiguity and transformation are explored in several recent works. *As Nature Made Him*, by John Colapinto, is a nonfiction account of the tragic life of David Reimer, born a male identical twin but raised as a female after a botched circumcision. The narrative of the terrible accident and of the disastrous advice the boy's parents received from Dr. John Money to castrate the child further, redesign his genitalia, and raise him as a girl is a harrowing account of the assumptions about nurture and gender that persist today.[12]

She's Not There, by Jennifer Boylan, is a memoir of the author's change as an adult from male to female through sex-reassignment surgery. Just as Reimer innately knew that he was not a girl, Boylan was convinced from the time she was three years old that she was female, despite her male sex. She struggled with her sexual identity through childhood, adolescence, and young adulthood, marrying in the hope that this commitment would settle her identity confusion. Finally, after years of increasing stress, Boylan, with the agreement of his wife, had sex-reassignment surgery and became a woman.[13] After her recovery from her surgery, the question asked of Tiresias by Jupiter and Juno is answered by Boylan. She describes her first orgasm as a woman:

> The sensation (which I'd cautiously, curiously, produced all on my own) was like nothing I'd experienced, and yet, sure, it was familiar. The Greek prophet Tiresias, who was said to have lived as both a man and a woman, claimed that "the pleasure for a woman is ten times that of the man." To this, all I can add is that what it reminds me of, more than anything else, is the difference between Spanish and Italian. (241)

Jeffrey Eugenides's *Middlesex* is a fictional story based on a syndrome called 5-Alpha Reductase Deficiency. In this novel, a baby with ambiguous genitalia is raised as Calliope, a girl, until, at puberty, her dominant male genes begin to assert themselves. Sexual ambiguity is a biological reality for Calliope, who has been raised as a girl but has a "crocus-like" penis that begins to grow as she matures. The novel explores her external transformation from female to male during puberty, when she is diagnosed with 5-Alpha Reductase Deficiency, a condition unrecognized by her doctor or parents and a consequence of repeated incest in earlier generations of her family, incest that occasionally produced children with ambiguous genitalia. When Calliope's condition is discovered in a hospital emergency room after an accident, she is taken to a specialist who recommends that she be treated surgically and hormonally to maintain her female gender. Calliope decides in the end not to have gender-reconstruction surgery and chooses to present herself as a male named Cal and to come to terms with her condition. Cal begins the novel thus:

> I was born twice: first, as a baby girl, on a remarkably smogless Detroit day in January of 1960; then again, as a teenage boy . . . in August of 1974. . . . My birth certificate lists my name as Calliope Helen Stephanides. . . . Like Tiresias, I was first one thing and then the other. . . . (1)

Teaching gender and sexual identity through Ovid's *Metamorphoses* offers rich opportunities to students to explore how different cultures envision gender and sexuality. They learn that in hierarchies where heterosexuality is the norm, there are always persons who are not unequivocally male or female. Ovid's Tiresias has come to symbolize both the positive and the negative in the lives of these people: Juno blinds him because of his judgment about sexual pleasure, but Jupiter, in recompense, gives him the gift of prophecy. The characters who people *The Waste Land* play gendered but lonely and sterile sexual roles. Their androgyny is negative, providing no pleasure. Eliot's Tiresias has seen it all but gained nothing. Woolf's Orlando, on the other hand, slips fluidly from one sex to another, remaining fundamentally the same person and discovering that her identity as a writer transcends both sex and gender. Colapinto's David Reimer is too damaged by years of forced false identity to live comfortably with who he really is. Boylan, after many painful years of feeling that he has the wrong body, chooses gender-reconstruction surgery; his sexual body becomes female, but she is still the funny, clever, loving person that he was. At fourteen, Calliope discovers that she is biologically mixed but hormonally male. She chooses to become Cal, and the novel closes with Cal in exile, unsure of his ability to have a satisfactory sexual relationship. As it is retold across the ages, Ovid's story of Tiresias provides a way to think about identity, sexuality, and acceptance of biological difference. At the same time, stories of sexual changes and of gender fluidity reveal how problematic sexual identity is and always has been.

NOTES

[1] Ovid's version of Tiresias's changes is the most well known; see also Brisson, *Mythe*, and the very fine discussion of the myth and its variations in O'Hara. In the fragmentary work O'Hara discusses, Tiresias changes shape six times. He is a young girl, man, mother, ugly man, young woman, and old man and finally becomes a mouse.

[2] Of course, Tiresias's action is not random at all, for copulating snakes were considered sacred in many cultures, among them the cultures of ancient Greece and Rome (Apollodorus 364–65n1). To injure them would of necessity result in disaster, in Tiresias's case causing both his sexual transformations and his loss of sight.

[3] Brisson appears to believe that Siproites and Sithon are the same (*Sexual Ambivalence* 165–66n6); he offers no evidence for this, however.

[4] The perception of children with ambiguous genitalia as monsters is not, sadly, confined to the ancient world. In Jeffrey Eugenides's *Middlesex*, the fourteen-year-old protagonist Calliope, having discovered that she is physically a hermaphrodite, finds to her horror that the synonym for the term *hermaphrodite* in the dictionary she consults is *monster* (430).

[5] I begin my graduate course Gender and Sexuality: The Construction of Identities with *The Symposium*. This dialogue, like *Metamorphoses*, provides an ongoing reference point for the course.

[6] To clarify these points, I often assign a chapter on "sex determination" in Gilbert.

[7] As preparation for other writers, I sometimes include passages from Christine de Pisan's *Le livre de la mutacion de Fortune*, where Christine describes her own "transformation" from female to male and compares herself to Tiresias (see fuller details in Katz). For *Metamorphoses*, I typically assign all of books 1–12 over three or four class meetings, often omitting the last three books because of time limitations.

[8] Byblis (book 9) lusts after her brother; Myrrha (book 10) commits incest with her father; and Tereus, Philomela, and Procne (book 6) are linked in a horrifying story of rape, infanticide, and cannibalism. Jupiter commits countless adulteries; Juno is perpetually jealous and vindictive; few heterosexual unions are long-lasting and happy (Deucalion and Pyrrha in book 1 and Baucis and Philemon in book 8 are notable exceptions). Teaching these passages adds to students' understanding of the complexity of gender issues in *Metamorphoses*.

[9] On Judith Butler's theories of gender performativity vis-à-vis Eliot, see Pondrom.

[10] This and other scenes from the novel are wonderfully portrayed in the film *Orlando*.

[11] To underscore Woolf's connection to Ovid, I often compare Orlando's description—as a woman—of male pursuit and female flight (90) with Ovid's depiction of Apollo's pursuit of the terrified Daphne (23; *Met.* 1.528–32).

[12] I also assign a recent *New York Times* article by Elizabeth Weil that reviews David's story and the growing awareness of the need to recognize and accept as they are children whose sex is ambiguous. Students also enjoy viewing "Sex: Unknown," a *Nova* documentary about Reimer's life.

[13] Boylan's memoir demonstrates her achievement of a satisfactory new identity as a woman; at times, as she moves into her new body, her new identity, she even overcompensates in her efforts to look and act female. She still lives with her wife, and their two sons appear to have accepted Jennifer's new identity and their restructured family. There are a number of good recent medical studies of transsexuals and the success rates of sex-reassignment surgery. Gooren gives a brief account of the inconclusive scientific research being done on transsexuals.

METATEXTUAL OVID

Metamorphoses Metamorphosed: Teaching the Ovidian Tradition

Jamie C. Fumo

Courses on the classical backgrounds of European literature, especially the Ovidian tradition, are of enormous value and interest to English and comparative literature majors. At universities with understaffed or institutionally beleaguered classics programs, faculty members based in literature departments who teach the classical tradition perform an important service to classics majors filling program requirements, even as they broaden the classical literacy of students majoring in modern literatures. A course I have developed titled The Literature of Metamorphosis provides one effective model, informed by an interdisciplinary methodology, for teaching the Ovidian tradition in translation in an English or comparative literature department. This course, which is centered on metamorphosis and its bearing on identity in a variety of imaginative discourses (i.e., cultural, artistic, and philosophical), applies a broadly historical approach to how notions of change themselves change over time and across cultures, using Ovid and his influence as a kind of nerve center for conceptions of metamorphosis in later periods. The central rationale of the course is that an appreciation of change as an artistic principle is vital to an understanding of both Ovid's *Metamorphoses* and its appeal to a broad range of writers and artists influenced by Ovid from late antiquity to the present. By studying direct and indirect adaptations of (and challenges to) *Metamorphoses*, students achieve a richer understanding of Ovid's poetry as well as of the workings of literary transmission.

That the notion of radical transformation fascinates students is no surprise: not only is twenty-first-century popular culture as spellbound by shape-shifters and hybrids as was the culture of Ovid's Rome (one needs only to visit the nearest checkout lane, with its homages to the marvels of plastic surgery and its motivational guides to self-transformation), but most undergraduates find themselves in the midst of the most intense and confusing period of change—personal, social, intellectual—thus far in their lives. The suppleness and universality of flux as an essential feature of the human condition provide excellent leverage with which to encourage students to connect intellectually with otherwise unfamiliar and historically distant material, as well as to recognize how metamorphosis functions as an artistic and interpretive principle. The conceptual challenges of teaching such a course, in my experience, are twofold. First, students must be pushed beyond the assumption that Ovidian metamorphosis (girl into tree, man into bug, etc.) is merely fantastic, that its meaning ends with its shock value. It takes effort for students to recognize what for scholars of Ovid is largely intuitive: that Ovid's metamorphoses are a goad to hermeneutical and epistemological debate and that we as readers, just like Ovid's creative adapters, are agents in the process of transformation, compelled with each metamorphic spectacle to "refigure [our] relationship to the text, [our] understanding of the narratives it contains, and ultimately how it functions as a literary representation" (Feldherr 165). Second, the instructor must expose the fallacy of the assumption (often brought to the class by mythological enthusiasts through their young-adult reading in popular guides to classical mythology) that Ovid and later Ovidian authors are simply "transmitters" of archetypal myths that can be removed unproblematically from context. Students must learn early on that writers working within the classical tradition, even one as ancient (from the point of view of a contemporary twenty-year-old) as Ovid, render traditional materials in individual, even idiosyncratic ways, emphasizing certain details and reshaping or challenging others, with a wide range of ulterior motives (narrative, thematic, political, satirical, etc.). Once students recognize the diverse artistic texture of these materials, the course runs no risk of monotony. Moreover, a course in the literature of metamorphosis is sufficiently flexible to be adapted with relative ease to different levels: with some adjustments to the number and intensity of readings and writing assignments, I have taught it both as a writing-intensive freshman seminar composed of undeclared majors at a small American liberal arts college and as an upper-level course for junior and senior English majors at a large Canadian university. What follows is a broad outline of the dimensions of the course with a focus on my approach to some of the less commonly taught modern examples of "metamorphosis literature."[1]

Ovid lays indisputable claim to the heart of this course because, after him, it becomes virtually impossible for Western writers and artists to conceive of metamorphosis—whether in its physical or metaphorical dimensions—without responding to Ovid's precedent. Even if all the course's texts do not articulate their influence by Ovid in equal measure, the master of change, like Narcissus's flirtatious image, is never far from the surface. Beginning with a close analysis of about three-quarters of Ovid's *Metamorphoses* (to which I devote approximately three weeks, focusing on the narrative and thematic function of the metamorphoses), the course investigates the ways in which metamorphosis functions as an aesthetic, epistemological, hermeneutical, and—in postclassical literature—moral issue that dramatizes an ever-changing set of cultural preoccupations. From Ovid's triumphant *vivam* we turn directly to three strategically selected modern adaptations of parts of *Metamorphoses*: Rainer Maria Rilke's "Orpheus. Eurydice. Hermes," Denise Levertov's "A Tree Telling of Orpheus" (both available in Kossman's anthology), and Roger Moss's short story "Hick, Hack, Hock" from Philip Terry's *Ovid Metamorphosed*.[2] This exercise gives students the gratifying opportunity to apply their newly honed expertise in Ovid right away: finding that they are well equipped to identify and evaluate classical allusions in modern literature (of which these are engaging examples, if less than Joycean in complexity) is a sure confidence booster. Appreciation both of the narration of Ovidian myth from alternative perspectives and of the invention of new myths by means of free combination of disparate Ovidian motifs, which are well illustrated by these three modern adaptations, is essential intellectual equipment for the course. Students give this equipment a test run in a five-to-seven-page essay assignment in which they are asked to analyze the creative friction between one episode from *Metamorphoses* and a postclassical adaptation of the story. Ovidian adaptations are to be selected from a packet of a half dozen adaptations that I provide—the contents of which are not discussed in class—including provocative, self-contained material from a range of poets and playwrights from the Renaissance, eighteenth century, and late twentieth century (culled from the anthologies of Christopher Martin, *Ovid in English*; Hofmann and Lasdun; and Miles). The packet includes Thomas Heywood's comic dramatization of the story of Mercury and Argus in his *Pleasant Dialogues and Dramma's*, Jonathan Swift's satirical rendition of Baucis and Philemon as country parson and wife, and Craig Raine's postmodern evocation of the last thoughts of a geriatric Cadmus.

Having gained practical experience in the analysis of direct adaptation of Ovid, students are ready for immersion in the Ovidian tradition writ large, which is more amorphous and therefore more challenging. At this point, the course rewinds to the classical period and thenceforth proceeds diachronically, beginning with two weeks on Apuleius's reimagination of Ovidian metamorphosis as romance autobiography in the *Golden Ass*. Nearly four weeks on medieval conceptions of metamorphosis follow, for which I set the stage with a lecture on the Christianization of metamorphosis and the metamorphic language of Christianity in medieval culture (for which Dimmick; Hexter, "Ovid in the Middle Ages"; and esp. Barkan, *Gods*, 94–136 are essential guides). Readings for this segment are eclectic but cohere in responding to Ovidian metamorphosis as a venue for articulating changing cultural notions of selfhood. Materials include an excerpt from book 4 of Boethius's *Consolation of Philosophy*, in which Circe's magic acts as a counterpoint to inner deformation, read alongside cantos 24 and 25 of Dante's *Inferno*, in which sin is equated with the metamorphic loss of self;[3] selections from Petrarch's *Canzoniere* delineating the tension between the Ovidian notion of the changeable erotic self and the Christian ideal of metamorphosis as conversion; and medieval lore concerning the intersection of faerie and Ovidian ideas of shape-shifting, particularly in the form of werewolf legends (ultimately descended from Ovid's story of Lycaon) such as Marie de France's *Bisclavret* and the anonymous *Arthur and Gorlagon* (for context, see Salisbury 159–66; Bynum 77–111; and Otten). The Renaissance debate over the influence of demons and the reality of metamorphosis (e.g., Heinrich Kramer and Jacob Sprenger's *Malleus Maleficarum* and Reginald Scot's *Discoverie of Witchcraft*, both of which I supply in excerpted form) provides a natural point of transition from medieval conceptions of lycanthropy to Shakespeare's *A Midsummer Night's Dream*, in which Ovidian and Apuleian traditions of metamorphosis comically interpenetrate.

The final segment of the course brings us back full circle to the modern period, though our concern is now with a peculiarly modern vocabulary of transformation: Darwinian evolution. Reading excerpts from Darwin's *Descent of Man*, students are asked to consider to what extent the theory of evolution responds to, extends, or reorients premodern ideas of metamorphosis. They are often struck, for example, by the similarity between Darwin's and Ovid's views of the world as a place of constant, necessary, and to a large extent nonteleological change. We then read Franz Kafka's *Metamorphosis* within this context as a psychological study in alienation as devolution and conclude the course with a postmodern work, Italo Calvino's *Cosmicomics*, which, in essence, maps Ovidian metamorphosis onto a universe shaped by Darwinian evolution. It is useful at this point to assign Calvino's influential essay "Ovid and Universal Contiguity" so that students are able to compare Calvino's critical commentary on Ovid with his creative absorption of his work in *Cosmicomics*. Like Ovid's stories of Phaethon and Callisto, *Cosmicomics* mythologizes complex cosmological processes in human terms, by rendering those processes as family drama or thwarted romance and associating them with sudden metamorphosis. As a story collection, its narrative structure invites sustained comparison with *Metamorphoses*, while its narrator and protagonist, Qfwfq, emerges as a deeply Ovidian presence who embodies all the change and potential for change in the universe ("in the midst of the world's transformations, being transformed myself" [Calvino 81]). As in *Metamorphoses*, the *Canzoniere*, and *A Midsummer Night's Dream*, a central concern of *Cosmicomics* is the capacity of love to produce and embody change, as well as to function as a creative force. Calvino engages directly with Ovidian myth, notably in two stories from *Cosmicomics*: his reimagination of Orpheus and Eurydice as star-crossed lovers in a preatmospheric Earth in "Without Colors" and in his presentation of a mollusk's creation of his own shell as an unlikely corrective to Ovid's Narcissus in "The Spiral."

A final long essay assignment gives students the opportunity to investigate in depth a topic of their choosing from the semester's readings, provided that it focus on some aspect of metamorphosis and treat at least two of the course texts, drawn from at least two different literary periods. Most students have little opportunity to write comparative, transhistorical essays in English courses, so this assignment has the potential to bring out the best in them. Successful student-designed essay topics in my classes have included fragmentation and reunification of the self in *Canzoniere* and in Ovid's Hermaphroditus and Narcissus episodes, metamorphosis as disguise (i.e., through play-acting) in *A Midsummer Night's Dream* in relation to Ovid's narrative "disguises" within his fiction (e.g., through self-identification with Arachne and Orpheus), and the acceptance or refusal of food as a form of communication in *Arthur and Gorlagon* and Kafka's *Metamorphosis* (in which characters' relation to food defines their proximity to animality and their capacity for intact selfhood).

In the space that remains, I discuss one specific cluster of readings, the twentieth-century adaptations of *Metamorphoses* by Rilke, Levertov, and Moss, to illustrate more closely the kinds of interpretive skills that such an arrangement of texts can elicit. Moss's "Hick, Hack, Hock" invites treatment as a modern epilogue to Ovid's *Metamorphoses*; centering on the loss inherent in change (here, the loss of cultural memory over time as a corrosive force on Ovid's text and the vulnerability of books themselves as material objects), it offers a useful point of entry to a discussion of the implicit ambivalence in Ovid's projection of imperial and poetic permanence at the end of *Metamorphoses*. (For this reason, it is wise to have acquainted students with brief selections from *Tristia*, such as 1.1 and 1.7, as supplementary reading to book 15 of *Metamorphoses*.) For Moss, the myth of Orpheus is a locus of these anxieties about textual impermanence. One of the characters in his story is a modern reader of Ovid, who is impaired by a fear of Latin despite his training in school and who tries repeatedly to read a translation of *Metamorphoses* "but . . . never gets much beyond Orpheus. Something in him has stayed unchanged, as if a part of him was long ago turned to stone by the nightmares of school" (R. Moss 26). Why is Orpheus the stopping point? Perceptive students will make a connection with the idea of looking back (i.e., of the character's looking back to his past experience of Ovid) and *losing* something. Ovid himself is what gets lost for Moss's character, what is not (for him) successfully brought back to life.

From this metatextual deployment of Orpheus to limn the ambivalence of Ovid's own poetic position as agent of *carmen perpetuum*, a natural transition can be made to Rilke's and Levertov's Orpheus poems, in which alternative perspectives and free conflation unsettle Ovid's text. There is much to discuss in Rilke's rich poem: of first importance is the surprising characterization of Orpheus as aggressive, even serpentlike, in his love for Eurydice ("In great bites his stride devoured the path" [97]) and the dead Eurydice's perspective on the events (she is oblivious to Orpheus's love; he is "someone or other whose face / was not to be recognized" [99]). Students will look more closely at *how* Rilke presents Eurydice if they are asked to locate the metamorphosis in Ovid's version of the story (a trick question, but one that reminds them that Ovid's deployment of metamorphosis can never be taken for granted) and in Rilke's, in which the metamorphosis is simply, inscrutably, death (for Eurydice, a paradoxical fulfillment and rebirth). The imagery of Eurydice's metamorphosis amalgamates various Ovidian motifs, and students should be encouraged to enter freely into Rilke's play of associations: for instance, the recollection of Proserpina's pomegranate, fruit of death, in the simile of Eurydice as a "fruit of sweetness and of darkness, / . . . so full of her great death" and the startling association with Daphne elicited by the climactic assertion that, even before Orpheus turns back, Eurydice "was already root" (98–99). Discussion of the function of these associations will lead students to a valuable appreciation of what happens when Ovid's *Metamorphoses* itself is metamorphosed into new forms. Rilke's pomegranate allusion is not merely decorative: it deepens, through association of Orpheus's bride with Pluto's, the extent of Eurydice's repossession by death. The echo of Daphne's experience in Eurydice's rootedness, furthermore, both gives substance to the earlier description of Eurydice as "a virgin, again / untouchable; her sex, closed" and also evokes Apollo's chase of Daphne, which one could argue Rilke imagines here in reverse: Orpheus, as "pursuer," must hasten ahead, while the unwilling Eurydice trails behind (98).

Levertov's "A Tree Telling of Orpheus," taking more than one cue from the Old English *Dream of the Rood*, imagines Orpheus's story not through Eurydice's eyes but from the perspective of one of the trees drawn out of the soil to shade the harp-playing Orpheus in the grove. A lively discussion is certain to result from focused comparison of Levertov's poem with Rilke's as responses to Ovid's Orpheus. The first point to emphasize is that, whereas Rilke figuratively metamorphoses Eurydice into a virginal, Daphne-like tree who retains her integral selfhood in resistance to her poet-suitor, Levertov imagines the tree who follows Orpheus as a *lover* of the musician, metamorphosed (in implicitly Christian terms) from a state of death, or unconsciousness, to "new life," to the extent that the tree feels the potential to become "man or a god" (Levertov 113–14). Alert students will point out that the tree's emotionally charged psychology and rhythms of speech, expressing the paradoxes of passion, recall those of Ovid's Myrrha (who is said to fall like a great tree, even before she becomes one). Others will note that, in its awakening to language and love, the tree is a positive version of Eurydice, successfully vivified by music and thus ready to *follow* Orpheus wherever he goes. Sexual fluorescence, then, supplants chaste rigidity: unlike Ovid's Daphne and Rilke's Eurydice, this tree *desires* a man, wants to join with him. If the archetypal poet-musician Apollo appropriates Daphne, as laurel, as an image of his own art, Levertov's tree affirms and legitimizes the art of Apollo's son Orpheus by celebrating the generative moment of desire out of which such art originated.

From these three short Ovidian pieces, a mere fifteen pages altogether, students gain considerable experience in the art of close reading, the dynamics of literary transmission and intertextuality, and the creative malleability of Ovidian tradition. Quite painlessly, they find themselves possessed of a more sophisticated handle on literary allusion and the interpretive significance of metamorphosis both as spectacle and as venue of literary exchange across cultural and historical divides.

NOTES

[1] It is easy to imagine a variety of other readings working successfully within this framework; the course I describe reflects my own literary tastes and, no doubt, my biases as a medievalist. It would also be quite possible to narrow the historical scope of the course by exploring the relationship between *Metamorphoses* and notions of change, say, in eighteenth-century literature and culture.

[2] If time allows, Mary Zimmerman's play, although lacking the full impact in print that it has on stage, works well at this point in the course, enabling discussion of framing techniques and the effect of principles of selection on interpretation of *Metamorphoses*. See Farrell, "*Metamorphoses*: A Play," for a sensitive discussion of Zimmerman's play as an adaptation of Ovid.

[3] Skulsky 114–28 and Warner 35–43 usefully situate these cantos within the context of Ovidian metamorphosis.

Metamorphoses, Its Tradition, and the Work of Art
Sean Keilen

> For this is the beginning of all poetry, to cancel the progression and laws of rationally thinking reason, and to transplant us once again into the beautiful confusion of imagination, into the original chaos of human nature, for which I know as yet no more beautiful symbol that the motley throng of the ancient gods.
> —Friedrich Schlegel

For several years at the University of Pennsylvania, I and a colleague in classical studies collaboratively taught a course about Ovid's *Metamorphoses* and its influence on the development not only of Western literature but also of Western painting, sculpture, music, decorative art, architecture, landscape design, and film. At its inception, the course was offered as part of an experimental interdisciplinary curriculum for first- and second-year undergraduates. Later it took shape as an upper-level seminar for advanced English, classical studies, and comparative literature majors and as part of the honors curriculum at Penn, which is open to all undergraduates but normally attracts the brightest and most unusual students in the School of Arts and Sciences, the Engineering School, and the Wharton School. Along the way, the course bore many different names, including Metamorphoses and Ovid and the Consequences.[1] Had my colleague and I not left the university for other appointments, likely we would have changed the course's name again—perhaps to Ovid's Afterlife. This title comes a little closer than the others to describing what we hoped to study during the course: the peculiar kind of life that Ovid announces that he shall have long after his biological life has ended ("vivam," the last word of *Metamorphoses*). That is to say, we wanted to investigate the life of the work of art and of the tradition that continues to issue from it.

In this brief description of our course, methods, and goals, I can speak only about my own perceptions. When we first proposed to teach Ovid's *Metamorphoses* together, it seemed to me that both of us had grown skeptical of certain ways of reading and teaching literature and also of justifications for those activities that are orthodox in the American university today. For me, the course was an opportunity to discover whether it was possible to dislodge Ovid's poem from the social, political, and ideological contexts in which a generation of scholarship had embedded it and still to speak about the relation between the past and the present in a meaningful way. *Metamorphoses* also extended an invitation to ponder several related questions about the nature of the human imagination, the processes according to which it transforms experience into art, and the purpose of studying literary and other traditions in a historically sensitive academic context. Whatever paths our discussions happened to take during class, and however far we traveled along them, I believe that mainly we retraced our steps to the insoluble problems from which the humanities spring and in which they seek renewal: Do literature and other forms of art merely reflect real human experiences, or do they constitute a reality all their own? Is this imaginary reality different from the history on which it impinges and, if so, how? What is a context for understanding a work of art, historical or otherwise, and are some contexts "better" than others? Is the "historical" context of a work of art the period in which it was first created and received, or does its "historical context" include the full range of its different receptions, ending only when the work of art and all its progeny are themselves forgotten? Is the meaning of a work of art exhausted by its original context (however we might define it), and, if not, how might its meaning be imagined in different terms and with what consequences?

Let me be more specific. The subject of our course was the agency of artists in relation to their raw materials, and we asked why Ovid's particular relation to his materials in *Metamorphoses* should have attained paradigmatic status for countless artists, literary and otherwise, who came after him. Attuned in this way to the stories that Ovid's poem tells about its own creation, we focused on those episodes that evidently represent artists at work at their craft (Arachne and Minerva, Philomela and Tereus, Orpheus and Eurydice, Daedalus and Icarus), as well as episodes in which it is not immediately apparent that art itself is Ovid's subject (Apollo and Daphne, Diana and Actaeon, Phaethon and Apollo, Echo and Narcissus). In each class meeting we compared different episodes in Ovid's text while weighing the poem with many works of art that imitate it. I hoped that one day we would challenge ourselves to spend the entire course on *Metamorphoses* alone, devoting one week of the semester to each of the poem's fifteen books and nothing else. However, it was our custom to spend a month to six weeks at the beginning of the semester reading the poem slowly in translation (we used Mandelbaum's version), shifting our emphasis during the rest of the course to post-Ovidian (or should I say to Ovidian?) works of art. These included selections from Lucius Apuleius's ancient novel *Metamorphoses* (or as it has come to be known in Robert Graves's English translation, *The Golden Ass*); Giovanni Boccaccio's prose fiction *Caccia di Diana*; Renaissance majolica plates depicting the myths of Narcissus, Marsyas, Pan and Apollo, and Venus and Adonis; Parmigianino's frescoes of Diana and Actaeon at Rocca Sanvitale in Fontanellato; Luigi Vanvitelli's ambitious program of gardens, sculptures, and fountains at Palazzo Reale La Reggia in Caserta, which are based on the Actaeon myth; Diego Velázquez's painting *The Spinners*, a retelling of the weaving contest between Arachne and Minerva; Caravaggio's portrait of Narcissus gazing on his reflection and Benvenuto Cellini's sculpture of the same subject; numerous illustrated editions of Ovid's *Metamorphoses* from the sixteenth and seventeenth centuries; William Shakespeare's *Venus and Adonis* and *Titus Andronicus*; Ben Jonson's *Poetaster*; John Milton's *Mask Presented at Ludlow Castle*; Poliziano's *Orfeo* as well as Claudio Monteverdi's; several surrealist responses to Ovid, including Pablo Picasso's illustrations for an edition of *Metamorphoses*, Salvador Dali's *Metamorphosis of Narcissus*, Guillaume Apollinaire's *Le bestiaire ou le cortège d'Orphée*, Jean Cocteau's films inspired by the myths of Narcissus and Orpheus (*Orphée* and *Le sang d'un poete*) and Jacques Lacan's theory of the mirror stage; Pieter Brueghel the Elder's painting *Landscape with the Fall of Icarus* and W. H. Auden's companion poem, "Musée des Beaux Arts"; Franz Kafka's *Metamorphosis*; Mary Zimmerman's *Metamorphoses: A Play*; and the poems anthologized in *After Ovid: New Metamorphoses* (ed. Hofmann and Lasdun).

Generally speaking, we arranged these materials chronologically, in order to move from ancient to modern during the course of a semester. Often, however, thematic affinity took precedence in the way that the course unfolded, and we did not hesitate to move back and forth across the span that the syllabus described to focus on the consequences of a particular episode in Ovid's poem. At different points, Gian Biagio Conte's *Latin Literature* and Gilbert Highet's *The Classical Tradition* provided light background reading, and to these texts I would now add the indispensable survey of Renaissance mythophilia, *The Mirror of the Gods*, by Malcolm Bull (published in 2005 and now available in an affordable soft-cover format for student use). At the beginning of each class meeting, we would select a few details from the material under discussion and, from that starting point, work toward questions of greater consequence, using an approach that combined close reading, close looking, and close listening and an eagerness to compare one artistic medium with another through Socratic interrogation of our students and each other.

We had grown frustrated with conventional methods of assessment and wanted to devise assignments that we and participants in the course would enjoy in equal measure—methods that would extend to our students the kinds of invitations that *Metamorphoses* makes to the tradition that follows it. Since we recognized that none of our students could be expected to have read *Metamorphoses* before enrolling in the course, it was an article of faith with us that they could not read Ovid's poem too often or too closely. Therefore we kept the written work to an absolute minimum, exhorting them to read and reread the whole text throughout the semester to increase their facility in recognizing similarities and differences between the poem's episodes and between the poem and its imitations. Reading, looking, listening, and communicating with us and with other students about Ovid were the most important assignments in the course.

To make this clear, we allowed class participation in this expanded sense to count for thirty percent of the final grade. Following the initial four- to six-week period during which the course devoted its attention to *Metamorphoses*, we gave a simple exam to determine how well the students had read and remembered the poem. This exam counted for twenty percent of the final grade. At the end of the semester, we asked our students either to write a fifteen- to twenty-page essay considering the development of an episode from Ovid's poem in two subsequent elaborations (one could be drawn from the course materials, the other had to be discovered independently) or to take a three-hour exam, in which we introduced post-Ovidian materials that they had not seen before and directed them to write essays about the concepts of authority, tradition, imitation, and individual talent that arose between those materials and *Metamorphoses*. This last assignment counted for fifty percent of the final grade.

We were concerned with the quality, not the quantity, of our students' written work, and as we decreased the amount of formal writing assignments in the course, our students increased their investments in the material and creatively embraced more responsibility for making sense of a subject matter and a discourse of questions that grew ever more complex, surprising, and diverse as the semester wore on. Of course, not every student took it upon herself or himself to keep a reading journal; correspond at length with other students about the course; compose musical scores, short stories, and play texts based on Ovid's poem; sketch and paint scenes from *Metamorphoses* or take photographs that were inspired by them; or write essays that had not been assigned and ask us to respond to them. But quite a few did, each semester, inspiring us to urge other students to do the same. Those remarkable voluntary efforts are the clearest evidence I have that we succeeded in doing one thing we had set out to do: transform the nature of our authority as teachers as well as our students' perception of themselves as thinkers and writers in a tradition that stretches back to Ovid.

In the process, we changed the dynamic between the teachers and students. In an environment relatively free of grading, every assignment will count for more in a student's eyes. Inevitably for some, this feature of the course was a source of panic and consternation, but for other students (most, I would say) our authority—in the sense of our more extensive knowledge of Ovid and Ovidian art—came to be understood as a resource for the development of their own ideas instead of a form of coercion or inhibition; and in this sense, it was the source of strange and wonderful things. Or to put it another way: we aspired, through our pedagogy, to enact theories about the Ovidian tradition that lay at the heart of the course. When we placed ourselves in the same relation to our students that we had placed Ovid in relation to the artists who followed him, we discovered that many members of the course were able to attribute more importance to, and to derive more pleasure from, the work that we asked of them and that they asked of themselves.

Since authority and pedagogy were such important themes for us, it is not surprising that we concluded each semester with Cees Nooteboom's *The Following Story*, a novella in which a teacher of Ovid's *Metamorphoses* tells the story of his life to a cherished student at the moment of his death (the student is dead already, as the story gradually makes clear)—an interval that lasts as long as it takes for the story itself to change the narrator from a teller into a tale. Through the act of narration, the teacher becomes both the subject and the object of his tale, just as his spectral interlocutor does (and as we do). Having begun our course months earlier with Ovid's account of the creation of the world, in which an unnamed god differentiates subjects and objects for the first time from an "undigested mass / of crude, confused, and scumbled elements," we made a point of concluding with a text in which the most elementary distinctions—between author and reader, teacher and student—finally give way (Mandelbaum 3). (The final allusion in Nooteboom's novella is not to Ovid's *Metamorphoses* but to Cicero's *De amicitia*, a text that posits likeness and equality as the basis of all friendship and friendship as the ideal form of human relationship, including the relationship between the living and the dead.)

The mention of subject and object in the previous paragraph, and of distinction and indistinction in relation to the act of creation, brings me to a final point about the course. When I reduce it to its essence, I find that there is one idea that holds the course's disparate materials together and provides some insight into the question that I posed earlier: Why has Ovid's *Metamorphoses* been so conspicuously influential not only for writers but also for other kinds of artists? The idea is this: the influence of *Metamorphoses* stems from the way that Ovid represents artistic composition in virtually every episode of his poem. If we agree to understand the event of metamorphosis as an allegory for the artist's transformation of raw materials into works of art, it is not difficult to see that Ovid distills the process of making art to a dynamic relation of subjects and objects, in which both participants are active and acted on.

This relation is conspicuous in episodes that explicitly tell stories about artwork: the myth of Arachne and Minerva, for example, in which girl and goddess are both weavers and woven art (in the sense that they are figures in each other's tapestries and characters in Ovid's *textus*). However, it also emerges from other episodes in which the nature of artwork does not appear to be at issue. In the myth of Diana and Actaeon, for example, vision (instead of language, stone, paint, or thread) is the medium in which Ovid establishes the dynamic relation between subject and object that is fundamental to his conception of poetic art. For it is not only Actaeon who undergoes a change as the result of being seen by Diana in the sacred grove. Actaeon's gaze changes the goddess too, and though she turns the hunter into prey to prevent this subtler transformation from taking effect ("Now go," she says, "feel free to say that you have seen / the goddess without veils—if you can speak"), Diana cannot alter the fact that from this moment forward, she is as much Actaeon's object as he is hers (Mandelbaum 84). As the object of Diana's wrath, Actaeon may be mute and murdered, but evidently his story survived his death—thus its "retelling" in *Metamorphoses*. In a poem where the experience of objectification is always tantamount to dying, it would appear that Actaeon's survival as a subject (someone who sees) is inseparable from his status as an object (something that is seen). Or to put it another way, Ovid would have us understand that without Actaeon to see her, Diana would be invisible; and without Diana to silence him, Actaeon would have no voice.

In the context of these ideas, our class often found itself in the curious position of having to ask of Ovid's poem what it means to be an artist, in the sense of composing new objects from existing materials or of simply looking at things (or at people) as though they were works of art. In one of its most exhilarating gestures, however, *Metamorphoses* also invited us to ask what it means to be a work of art, as it were, from the inside of objectivity, and from this different perspective—the perspective of Narcissus's reflection in the pool or of Ovid's representation of himself at the end of the poem ("vivam")—to look back on the artist or beholder whose attention is limited and limiting but finally transformative. The paradoxical suggestion that lies behind these questions is that *Metamorphoses* may have taught generations of artists how to perform their craft by showing them not only what it is like to be a subject/artist but also what it is like to be an object / work of art: by showing them how to be open to being changed, sometimes violently, by the very things that are constituted by our own imaginations and desires. On this threshold, we began to understand some of the strangest passages in the tradition that issues from *Metamorphoses*: why Philomela, in her aspect as a raped and mutilated girl, should emerge as a figure for the writer in Shakespeare's *Titus Andronicus* or why Rainer Maria Rilke, referring to an archaic torso of Apollo, observes that "there is no place on this stone / that does not see you. You must change your life" (qtd. in Barkan, *Satyr* 78). At the same moment, we recognized that we no longer stood apart from the Ovidian tradition as from an object of study but stood within it; and from this perspective there was no limit to the discoveries that we could make about Ovid's text, its progeny, and one another.

NOTE

[1] The first version of this course was a collaboration between Emily Steiner, Shane Butler, and me. Subsequently, Shane Butler and I taught the course alone. It is to the later versions of the course that this essay refers.

Island Hopping: Ovid's Ariadne and Her Texts
Barbara Weiden Boyd

I regularly teach the works of Ovid in a variety of different contexts, from advanced seminars for undergraduate Latin students (on *Metamorphoses*, *Fasti*, Roman elegy, or didactic poetry) to courses addressed to nonclassicist (and, by and large, Latinless) audiences. Regardless of course level, audience background, and size and regardless of the particular work(s) of Ovid under discussion, one challenge remains constant: how can I best demonstrate and explain to my students the ubiquitous interplay between Ovid's poetry and its models, or intertexts, without leaving my students with the impression that Ovid is either an inveterate plagiarist, a hack imitator, or a relentless parodist? All three characterizations, after all, informed—indeed, dominated—classical scholarship about Ovid during much of the twentieth century, when most of the modern authoritative studies in English about Ovid's poetry—still regularly cited by scholars for their many virtues and still available to our (generally undiscriminating) students on the shelves of their college library—were published. Indeed, many scholars and students alike have been troubled (and rightly so, in my opinion) by the combination of humor and aestheticism that pervades so much of Ovid's poetry, and so they have (unfortunately, in my opinion) resorted to explanations that effectively strip Ovid of both responsibility and brilliance by casting his work as derivative, enervated, even inane. The welcome theoretical shift of the past twenty-five years or so has transformed the way scholars look at Ovid's poetry and has resulted in an embarrassment of critical riches for specialists in the field—from new critical editions and commentaries to scores of articles and numerous books and dissertations every year. I still face the challenge, however, of translating this new appreciation for Ovid's poetry into a language undergraduates will understand and appreciate, without either invalidating their reader response or overstating the level of theoretical sophistication required to read and to appreciate Ovid.

A second and related concern involves literary (and intellectual) traditions writ large. I think it is crucial for my students to have a sense not only of the social and political contexts within which Ovid worked but also of the history of ideas that made his work possible. This is of course a grandiose (and all too often failed) aspiration. Yet it is worth trying to sensitize my students to the idea that Ovid (together with his poetry) is not on a deserted island, so to speak, inaccessible and immune, and trapped unmoving in a place we call "classical antiquity"; rather, he (together with his poetry) is engaged in an unending conversation with texts and ideas, and he includes us in that conversation when he revisits the old stories of which his and our literary histories are composed. The challenge, again, is to present this to undergraduates, many of whom have little idea about what a literary tradition is or might be and even fewer of whom have any idea why it might, or could, or should, matter.

In this essay I demonstrate, by focusing on one set of related narratives in the Ovidian corpus, how to begin opening up the ideas of tradition and intertextuality to students. To do so, I point to a character who enters Latin poetry trapped and at least apparently inaccessible, abandoned on a deserted island of her own: Ariadne. Students of Latin literature know well that Ariadne's career in the Latin poetic tradition begins spectacularly with Catullus, who in poem 64 describes in highly self-conscious and stylistically precious detail the events surrounding the last great conjoining of gods and heroes, at the wedding of the mortal Peleus to the divine Thetis (an occasion that results in the birth of Achilles and so makes the *Iliad* possible). At this wedding, guests entering the palace of Peleus walk past the *pulvinar* ("wedding couch") displayed in the central hall (a Roman anachronism at this wedding); as they pass, their eyes are inevitably drawn to the marvelous coverlet draping the couch, on which is depicted a trompe-l'oeil embroidered narrative detailing the abandonment of Ariadne by Theseus in the wake of her escape with him from Crete, where he had, with her help, defeated the Minotaur and so ended the requirement that Athens send as annual tribute to Crete a living sacrifice of Athenian youths and girls. In poem 64, a combination of flashbacks, reported direct speech, and disconcerting shifts of scene encompass Ariadne's state of abandonment as well as the events leading up to and following it, culminating in the arrival of Bacchus and his entourage, apparently intent on carrying Ariadne off to her own divine marriage.[1]

Catullus's Ariadne (along with the remainder of the poem in which she is featured) enacts a decisive moment in Latin literary history, as Catullus demonstrates the ability of the Latin language to transform Greek subjects and styles and in the process to articulate a new and distinctively Roman sensibility about the narrative potential of myth.[2] Students new to Catullus, poem 64, who have already read the *Aeneid* are struck by the similarity between Catullus's Ariadne and Vergil's Dido; I have repeatedly had to convince such readers that Catullus actually wrote first and was read by Vergil, instead of the other way around. In fact, both Catullus and his Ariadne display an already sophisticated awareness of themselves in relation to their literary predecessors: his virtuoso evocation of earlier literary heroines, especially Medea (not coincidentally Ariadne's cousin), gives Ariadne a pedigree ranging from Euripides, Callimachus, and Apollonius to the Roman tragedians Ennius and Accius (Thomas, "Catullus," gives details). In addition to providing the proximate role model for Vergil's Dido, Ariadne appears (or is at least alluded to)—again in the context of an ekphrasis—at the opening of *Aeneid*, book 6, when Aeneas and his companions study the elaborately crafted doors on the temple of Apollo at Cumae, on which are depicted the events surrounding the Minotaur and his labyrinth.[3]

The repetition of a familiar story presents both risks and rewards for any writer; it is all the more remarkable, therefore, to consider the challenge Ovid sets for himself in returning repeatedly to Ariadne—not one, not two, not three, but four times. On four occasions, in four poems, Ovid features the story of Ariadne's abandonment by Theseus, along with the events preceding and following it. I propose to look briefly at each of these treatments of her story, in what is arguably a chronological sequence based on the likely date of their composition and/or publication (White). In the process, I follow Ovid in revisiting Ariadne's island repeatedly (and so paradoxically redeeming her from the isolation that makes her Ariadne in the first place). Ovid's repetition functions as an investigation into the cognitive processes that allow readers to recognize a character they have "met" elsewhere in a text and to appreciate the play of similarities and differences that enables the invention of tradition.[4]

Heroides, *Poem 10*

At 150 verses (in elegiac couplets), Ovid's first Ariadne is both the most expansive and the most static. The very nature of the poem, a love letter written by Ariadne to the absent Theseus and essentially "read" *in propria persona*, reflects the perspective of its narrator, Ariadne, at a precise moment in time. At least initially, then, *Heroides*, poem 10, comes closest to its Catullan intertext, in which Ariadne is depicted as delivering a lengthy monologue (64.132–201). One glaring difference, however, undermines the tragic demeanor of Ovid's Ariadne even as it highlights a puzzling feature of Catullus's poem. To his lengthy description of Ariadne, her prehistory, and her lament Catullus had added a coda of fourteen hexameters, describing the arrival of Bacchus and his retinue as a separate scene on the coverlet (64.251–64). Other sources (including Ovid, but going back at least to Hesiod) inform us that Bacchus's arrival heralds the sacred marriage of the god to Ariadne, but Catullus's description of the scene is oddly pregnant, mentioning as it does Bacchus's love for Ariadne but never alluding to their eventual union; the ekphrasis imposes from without a kind of closure not inscribed in the scene itself.

Other features of Ariadne's letter present Ariadne as a competent reader of Catullus—in other words, she demonstrates that she knows Catullus, poem 64. Near the opening of the letter, she locates herself by saying that the letter Theseus is (if only!) reading comes to him "from that shore from which sails carried your ship away without me" ("ex illo . . . litore . . . / unde tuam sine me vela tulere ratem" [3–4]).[5] The first three words I have quoted are unqualified in the hexameter, so that the reader may at first take Ariadne's "illo" not simply as a means of specification but as an example of the demonstrative used in the sense "that famous [one]," in other words, as a way of saying "from that famous shore—you know! The one I was on in Catullus, poem 64!" The very first line of Catullus's ekphrasis (64.52) locates Ariadne on the shore, and Catullus's Ariadne emphasizes the location when she speaks within the ekphrasis, opening by asking Theseus how he—treacherous one!—could have left her like this on the deserted shore (64.132–33). Again, Ovid's Ariadne later compares herself to a woman aroused by Bacchic frenzy: "like a bacchant excited by the Ogygian god" ("qualis ab Ogygio concita Baccha deo" [10.48]), displaying a sort of pre-Freudian recognition of her Catullan destiny in a poem that otherwise omits reference to Bacchus.[6] Immediately after comparing herself to a bacchant, Ovid's Ariadne uses a second simile, saying that while sitting on a stone looking out to the sea, she became as rocklike as her seat itself: "as much as my seat was a stone, so much was I myself a stone" ("quamque lapis sedes, tam lapis ipsa fui" [10.50]). Ariadne thus separates into its constituent parts the simile Catullus had used to capture her appearance on the shore at 64.61: "like a stone statue of a bacchant" ("saxea ut effigies bacchantis"). Finally, we may note the continuing preoccupation of Ovid's Ariadne with her bed ("torum" [10.12, 51]; "toro" [10.55]; "lectule" [10.58]); her fixation not only suggests that she has transformed her own story from that of a woman whose abandonment decorates a marriage bed (cf. Catullus's "pulvinar"; Barchiesi, "Future Reflexive" 346–47) to that of a woman betrayed by the bed in which she sleeps ("perfide . . . lectule" 'treacherous bed' [10.58]) but also glances in passing at the model provided by Vergil's Dido, who lies in her bed at night sleepless, thinking about Aeneas (*Aen.* 4.82–83), and who, after he abandons her, builds a pyre in the palace on which she will burn their bed (*Aen.* 4.494–98, 648). Dido, as I have mentioned, is a literary "daughter" of Catullus's Ariadne; Ovid's Ariadne thus both acknowledges the complex tradition and makes it her own in reclaiming the bed for herself.

Ars amatoria *1.525–64*

In book 1 of *Ars amatoria*, Ovid uses several extended mythological exempla to illustrate his recommendations about how best to find and seduce women. The story of Ariadne's abandonment by Theseus and rescue by Bacchus is a prelude to Ovid's argument that wine is a useful tool in the business of seduction, at least when used in moderation: it stirs physical warmth and, when spilled on a table at a banquet, can be used as a sort of ink for writing surreptitious messages to one's lover. But this rationale for the story comes only after its narration; Ovid takes an unusual perspective to create an artificial sense of suspense around an extremely familiar story. In this version of the Ariadne story, Ovid emphasizes what was missing before: the rescue of Ariadne by Bacchus and their divine marriage, both unanticipated in *Heroides*, poem 10. Here the rescue and marriage provide the frame for the Ariadne episode and dominate the scene. Ovid begins, "Lo, Bacchus Liber is summoning his poet" ("ecce suum vatem Liber vocat" [*Ars* 1.525]), gesturing to the arrival of Bacchus that concludes the description of Ariadne's dire curse in Catullus but now explicitly "closing" the story with marriage. After announcing the story, Ovid briefly summarizes the familiar details, confident that his readers already know them: the deserted shore, the clothing slipping from Ariadne's shoulders, her tearful address to the absent Theseus (1.527–34). Then, combining verbal echo with editorial comment, Ovid compresses her lengthy Catullan lament—and its extensive reworking in *Heroides*, poem 10—into a few brief lines (*Ars* 1.535–38):

> iamque iterum tundens mollissima pectora palmis
>   "perfidus ille abiit: quid mihi fiet?" ait;
> "quid mihi fiet?" ait; sonuerunt cymbala toto
>   litore et attonita tympana pulsa manu.

> And now, striking with her hands yet again her tender bosom, "That traitor has left; what will become of me?" she says; "What will become of me?" she says; cymbals and drums beaten by astonished hand sounded along the entire shore.

This Ariadne says all of nine words, three of which are simply repeated; and these nine words amount to three clauses, each of three words, in place of the high-voltage rhetoric of Catullus, poem 64 (where Ariadne uses the vocative "perfide" 'betrayer,' 'traitor,' twice in quick succession at the opening of her monologue to address the absent Theseus [132–33]), or even the wordy exercise in futility that is *Heroides*, poem 10. Her tendency to repeat herself is illustrated in action as well as words: in striking her breast she repeats a behavior already seen at *Heroides* 10.15, "my breast resounded as I struck it with the palms of my hands" ("adductis sonuerunt pectora palmis")—a repetition that Ovid effectively annotates with the adverb "iterum" 'again.' The interruption that occurs midline with the arrival of Bacchus's retinue comes presumably not a moment too soon, saving us the tedium of hearing Ariadne repeat herself yet again.

The remainder of this scene instead focuses on the companions of the god and the epiphany of the god himself (1.541–62), who swiftly announces to Ariadne his intent to marry her—"Set aside your fear; you will be the Cretan bride of Bacchus" ("pone metum, Bacchi Cnosias uxor eris" [556])—and to make her divine (557–58). His followers close the scene with a combination of ecstatic cries and wedding hymns (563), and the concluding words—"so the god and his bride are joined in the sacred bed" ("sic coeunt sacro nupta deusque toro")—unite Bacchus and Ariadne definitively. Ovid's final word, "bed," of course echoes Ariadne's own preoccupation from *Heroides*, poem 10 (see esp. 10.51, "saepe torum repeto" 'I often revisit the bed'), and sends his readers back to Catullus, poem 64, where the story of Ariadne decorated a marriage couch; but whereas the coverlet ekphrasis of Catullus is incomplete, Ovid's narrative gives us a reassuring "and they lived happily ever after" conclusion (and presumably a guarantee that Ariadne's complaints have been silenced for good).

Fasti 3.459–516

Throughout his calendar poem, Ovid uses the appearance of constellations and the rising and setting of stars to mark the change in seasons and the passing of time. Many aetiological myths concerning the existence of various stars and constellations and their presence in the sky were available to Ovid; in *Fasti*, book 3, he uses them to elaborate on his mention of the constellation Corona, seen in the sky during the night of March 8. Mythical tradition explained this constellation as the catasterism ("placement among the stars") of Ariadne's crown, given to her by either Theseus or Bacchus (the variant versions appear to be quite early [Gantz 1: 264–65]).

When my students reach this passage in *Fasti*, I generally ask them to think about why Ovid included it. After all, he mentions many constellations and stars in the poem, but only a select few receive such lengthy treatment. If we were to posit an Ovidian economy of myth, we might well feel that Ariadne has already been "done," so to speak—after all, the episodes discussed earlier would seem to have said all there was to be said, and then some. In fact, Ovid himself, along with Ariadne, seems to have anticipated this question, because now when Ariadne speaks she is explicit about the repetitiousness of our reading (and her whining) experience: with the words "poor me! How often shall I say these words?" ("me miseram, quotiens haec ego verba loquar?" [*Fasti* 3.486]) she preempts our expected reaction by suggesting that she too is growing weary of being hauled out by Ovid to reprise the same role again and again.

Ironically, however, the story she tells here is actually *not* the same as the one we heard before. *Fasti*, book 3, offers what is essentially a sequel to the familiar story of abandonment by Theseus followed by rescue by Bacchus followed by marriage to Bacchus: in other words, it tells the very story that the structure of the narrative in *Ars amatoria*, book 1, had excluded by so tidily putting the happily married Bacchus and Ariadne to bed. In book 3 of *Fasti*, Ariadne has an entirely new and unanticipated problem: it seems that, in his eastern campaigns, her new husband took for himself some beautiful captive women, and among them there is one—like Ariadne herself, daughter of a king (3.468)—whom Bacchus appears to be a bit too fond of. Thus Ariadne's problem is not now abandonment per se but the aftereffects of temporary separation from her husband: he has found a replacement for her. The play between novelty and repetition here is a brilliant move on Ovid's part, as he foregrounds the metatextual dilemma of the poet writing within a tradition: if it's been done before, how can it possibly also be new?

Ariadne's awareness of her literary history includes not only her previous appearances in Ovid but also her "classic" performance in Catullus, poem 64. As her speech continues, she repeatedly draws attention to the earlier poem (3.471–76):

> en iterum, fluctus, similes audite querellas,
>   en iterum lacrimas accipe, harena, meas.
> dicebam, memini, "periure et perfide Theseu!"
>   ille abiit, eadem crimina Bacchus habet.
> nunc quoque "nulla viro" clamabo "femina credat":
>   nomine mutato causa relata mea est.

Now, waves, hear my similar laments again; now again, sand, receive my tears. I used to say, I recall, "You lying, treacherous Theseus!" He left, and now Bacchus is open to the same charge. Now too I shall shout, "let no woman trust in a man": with the name changed, my situation has been produced again.

The repetition of "en iterum" establishes the idea that the entire passage is an echo of something similar in the past; the adjectives "similes" and "eadem" and the temporal expression "nunc quoque" reinforce this idea. The most obvious indication of the past's implication in this scene, however, is Ariadne's use of the vocabulary of memory, which functions here like a sort of footnote announcing the role of literary history in shaping this episode (J. F. Miller, "Ovidian Allusion"). And Ariadne's memory is good: the epithets she recalls using to accuse Theseus of treachery ("periure et perfide" [473]) echo the language she had used at Catullus 64.132–35, and the words she promises to shout ("nulla viro . . . femina credat" [475]) are a precise quotation of 64.143, with the same metrical shape and place in the line (Conte, *Rhetoric* 60–63).

Unlike Theseus, however, Bacchus finally reappears and ends her lament, showing his sympathy for Ariadne's audience in the process: "he had been listening for some time to the complaining woman's words" ("audibat iamdudum verba querentis" [3.507]). He assuages her sorrows as quickly as possible and promises her a transformation—her name will be changed to Libera to match his epithet, Liber (3.511–12). In addition, her crown will become a constellation—and with a circular movement that parallels the shape of Ariadne's crown, this episode comes to an end with the stars of Corona now shining in heaven. Ovid thus replicates the closural gesture that had seemed so certain at the end of the Ariadne episode in book 1 of *Ars*; and with this act of repetition he acknowledges the potential for subversion that is embedded in any narrative that claims definitive status.

Metamorphoses 8.169–82

Given the frustration Ariadne expresses about her own repetitious predicament in *Fasti*, book 3, she can join her readers in breathing a sigh of relief when she reaches her story in book 8 of *Metamorphoses*: not only does Ovid give her nothing at all to say, but most of "her" story now becomes the story instead of Scylla—whose doomed love for Minos precedes Ariadne both in the organization of *Metamorphoses* (i.e., Scylla's story begins book 8, while Ariadne's follows) and in the mythical "history" of Minos and his adventures on Crete. Scylla's story in turn comes after the Medea story in book 7 and so is itself already a repetition of the plotline we might summarize as "enamored princess betrays her father for her lover and is betrayed in turn." The entire Ariadne story from start to finish, therefore, is given a scant fourteen verses in the entire poem, from the imprisonment of the Minotaur in the labyrinth and his gruesome sacrificial repast to the catasterism of Ariadne's crown—and more than five of these fourteen verses are given entirely to the crown and its fate. Ariadne's presence is acknowledged first with the words "with a maiden's help" ("ope virginea" [8.172]), qualifying Theseus's successful negotiation of the labyrinth; Ariadne next appears as "having been carried away" ("rapta Minoide" [8.174]) by him; and her abandonment itself is reduced to a mere two verses, in which Ariadne's predicament is efficiently summarized in the half line "abandoned and lamenting a great deal" ("desertae et multa querenti" [8.176]).[7]

In addition to relief, this episode is likely to provoke a variety of reactions from students. Some wonder whether Ovid finally realized he had "done" Ariadne (more than) enough already; some suppose Ovid simply has nothing novel left to say and that he thus in effect acknowledges his own poetic inadequacy; some simply attribute the brevity of this scene to Ovid's famous sense of humor and leave it at that. I suspect such responses parallel those of at least some of the members of his ancient audience. While gently reminding readers, however, that no one other than Ovid himself chose to write these fourteen lines as we have them and to locate them where he did, I encourage them to think about where Ovid has taken them before and to consider another possibility: that, in incorporating into *Metamorphoses*, book 8, a version of the Ariadne story that emphasizes the catasterism of her crown while simultaneously including in *Fasti*, book 3, a version of her story that is much more elaborate and grander in its narrative aspirations than we might expect of an elegiac poem on the calendar,[8] Ovid uses poetry as a vehicle not only to interrogate the boundaries of genre (is Ariadne an epic figure, as Catullus styles her and Vergil reads her, or is she an elegiac paradigm?) but also to explore the very nature of reading and memory, since we read what is new "through" everything we have read before. No text, after all, is a solitary island that lacks subterranean connections to all other texts;[9] and with every text we read, we bring along the map of memories that allow us—as they allow Ariadne—to remain ourselves while continuing as works in progress. As an indication of this, I invite my students to observe that on not a single occasion in any of the four versions of her story that we have read does Ovid ever name her—Ariadne is always identified by a periphrasis, like "Cretan woman" ("Cnosis" [*Ars* 1.527]) or "daughter of Minos" ("Minoide" [*Met.* 8.174]). Yet we recognize her always, because we remember her—indeed, we'd know her anywhere.

NOTES

[1] Catullus's ekphrasis, along with the narrative frame into which it is set, has long intrigued classical scholars and has recently been the subject of a number of valuable critical studies: see, for example, those by Gaisser and Laird.

[2] Indeed, so remarkable is Catullus's achievement that scholars have long debated whether poem 64 represents a translation or adaptation of a lost Greek original. In its earlier incarnations, this theory was premised on the belief that such a remarkable poem could hardly be an entirely new invention on the part of a young Roman poet working in a previously not very refined literary language; while that approach has long since

faded from the critical repertoire, Knox ("Ariadne") has demonstrated the likelihood that there was an earlier Greek treatment of the story, known to both Catullus and Nonnus, an Egyptian Greek poet of the fifth century CE. While this argument has important implications for scholars working on the relation of Hellenistic Greek to Roman poetry and vice versa, I do not pursue it further here for reasons of space and focus. I note the strong probability that Ovid knew well not only Catullus's poetry but also everything that Catullus had read and that his treatment of Ariadne is likely to have been informed and deepened by that reading.

[3] Vergil's mention of a *regina* out of pity for whom Daedalus finds a way out of the labyrinth (*Aen.* 6.28–30) is studiedly opaque—the absence of a name to identify her makes the allusion ambiguous and so embraces both Ariadne and her mother, Pasiphae, the wife of Minos (Putnam 179–80).

[4] Conte, *Rhetoric* 57–69, is foundational; see also Hinds, *Allusion* 3–4, and Barchiesi, *Speaking Volumes* 18–25. Tarrant ("Roads" 69–72) suggests that the Ariadne episode in book 8 of *Metamorphoses* can be understood as an invitation from Ovid to see the poem's composition as both arbitrary and inevitable and that the drastic foreshortening seen here of a story made famous earlier "could be a form of modesty, a gesture of deference to a canonical predecessor . . . with the amusing corollary that the masters thus honored include Ovid himself" (70).

[5] All translations in this essay are my own.

[6] See especially Barchiesi, "Future Reflexive."

[7] I develop the structural and narratological implications of this episode more fully in Boyd, "Two Rivers."

[8] I believe that this is in fact exactly what Ovid was doing—writing both poems at the same time—and that at least occasionally he incorporates into one or the other or both a clue to their interconnectedness. Scenes like those under discussion here are an important part of the process.

[9] Except of course Delos—a mythical "fact" exploited for its rich metatextual potential by Callimachus in his *Hymn to Delos*.

The Case of Ovid in Dante
Madison U. Sowell

This essay illustrates the value of teaching undergraduates a specific type of intertextuality—that of a devoutly Christian author, Dante Alighieri, who intentionally weaves into his compositions the unmistakable threads of a pagan *poeta*, Publius Ovidius Naso. Intertextuality presumes an intertwining or an interweaving of texts that may be viewed metaphorically as woven objects or seamless tapestries.[1] At its simplest, this literary phenomenon involves allusions in one text (e.g., Dante's medieval corpus) to characters, plots, settings, words, images, ideas, or structures in an earlier (con)text (e.g., Ovid's classical poetry). Sometimes this new contextualization occurs blatantly through direct translations or citations of authors or their texts, as when Dante cites by name and title Ovid's *Remedia amoris* (*Cures for Love*) in chapter 25 of the *Vita nova* (*New Life*) and then proceeds to quote verbatim an excerpt in Latin. Two obvious and especially pertinent examples occur in *The Divine Comedy*. The first relates to the appearance of Ovid as a character in *Inferno* 4.90 ("Ovidio è 'l terzo..." 'Ovid comes third [after Homer and Horace] ...'), when Dante-pilgrim encounters the classical poets in limbo and is invited to join their ranks.[2] The second refers to the silencing of Ovid in *Inferno*, when Dante-poet boasts that he surpasses the Latin *auctor* in the ability to present complex metamorphoses in verse:

> Taccia di Cadmo e d'Aretusa Ovidio,
> ché se quello in serpente e quella in fonte
> converte poetando, io non lo 'nvidio.

> Concerning Cadmus and Arethusa let Ovid be silent, for if he, poetizing, converts the one into a serpent and the other into a fountain, I envy him not.

> (*Inf.* 25.97–99)

Regarding Ovid in Dante, scholars have long recognized and stressed the widespread nature of such allusions.[3] After all, Dante himself in a key passage of his treatise on the vernacular tongue elevates Ovid to the same lofty company as Vergil, Statius, and Lucan in a discussion of exemplary models—whom he refers to as the "regulati poetae"—of literary art (*De vulgari eloquentia* 2.6.7):

> You should not be surprised, reader, at the number of authors I have recalled for you; for only through such examples could I indicate to you what I call the highest construction. And, to familiarize oneself with this construction, it would perhaps be most useful to look at the poets who follow the rules [of art], meaning Virgil, Ovid in the *Metamorphoses*, Statius, and Lucan.

(45)

In addition to the four instances cited above, Dante refers to Ovid by name (usually as "Ovidio") a dozen more times in a variety of works: *De vulgari eloquentia* 1.2.7; *Convivio* 2.1.3, 2.5.14, 2.14.5, 3.3.7 (where "Ovidio Maggiore" means *Metamorphoses*), 4.15.8, 4.23.14, 4.27.17 and 19; *Monarchia* 2.7.10 and 2.8.4; and *Epistolae* 3.4 (where the phrase "Auctoritatem vero Nasonis" refers to the authority of the Latin poet and proves that Dante knew Ovid's cognomen, Naso). In fact, over a century has passed since Paget Toynbee first outlined Dante's use of Ovidian sources for his accounts of Arethusa (*Met.* 5.572–641) and Cadmus (*Met.* 4.570–603) in *Inferno* 25.97; Orpheus (*Met.* 11.1–84) in *Convivio* 2.1; Cupid and Venus (*Met.* 5.365-84) in *Convivio* 2.6; Prometheus, son of Iapetus (*Met.* 1.78–83), in *Convivio* 4.15; the horses of the sun (*Met.* 2.153–234) in *Convivio* 4.23; Aeacus and Cephalus (*Met.* 7.474–865) in *Convivio* 4.27 (Toynbee 399–400). Also at the turn of the nineteenth century, Edward Moore discussed in cursory fashion over thirty instances of Dante's incorporation of Ovidian personages, myths, and motifs, including those of Niobe and Arachne, Aglauros, Procne, Erysichthon, Polydorus and Polymestor, Athamas, Hermaphrodite, Nessus, Phalaris and Perillus, Antaeus and Ninus and Semiramis, Typhoeus, Ulysses and Circe, dreams at daybreak, the golden age, the Naiads, Calliope and the magpies, Argus, and Jason and the Argonauts (206–28).

While such lists suggest the long afterlife of a variety of mythological figures and offer a quantitative measure of Ovid's impact on Dante, the listing or tracing of Ovidian allusions in Dante does not in and of itself teach students how to grasp the import of the Florentine poet's medieval intertextuality. A more promising approach to the presence of Ovid in Dante emphasizes not only where and which Ovidian allusions are found but also how and why they are used. To understand what the practice of Dantean intertextuality really signifies, we must ponder a series of much harder, and more intriguing, questions: How would Dante have viewed and read Ovid in the context of medieval Italy or Europe? How does Dante's use of the pagan Ovid's Latin writings intersect or mesh with the Christian author's vernacular and allegorical agenda? What thematic and historical parallels exist between the two authors, and how does Dante exploit those parallels? I treat these three larger questions in the remainder of this essay.

How would Dante have viewed and read Ovid in the context of medieval Italy?

The best introduction to Dante's *Divine Comedy* remains the *Vita nova*, the pseudo-autobiographical account of the poet's meeting and falling in love with Beatrice, the story of her death, and the setting forth of Dante's decision to write of her that which had never been written of any woman. The great novelty is that the *libello* (literally, a "little book") is actually a *prosimetro*—that is, a marvelous blend of prose (forty-two chapters) and poetry (thirty-one lyrics). Seeking to find models for Dante's inspiration, scholars have invariably turned to one of two late classical or early medieval works, Martianus Capella's fifth-century *De nuptiis Philologiae et Mercurii* ("On the Marriage of Philology and Mercury") or, more often, Boethius's sixth-century *De consolatione Philosophiae* ("On the Consolation of Philosophy"). Both of these works notably combine prose and lyrics. What is much less often acknowledged is that a plenitude of other models existed. Where? Dante could easily have found examples of such a *prosimetrum* in medieval manuscripts of such classics as *Aeneid* and, more to our point, *Metamorphoses*.[4] While today's students of Latin poets are most likely to encounter a classical text presented more or less in isolation and filling an entire page (e.g., the Loeb Classical Library text or the even more solitary Oxford Classical Text edition), the medieval reader of Ovid invariably would have encountered the poetic text surrounded on all sides by prose marginalia and interlinear commentary.

The renowned medievalist Michelangelo Picone makes this point perhaps more succinctly and certainly more emphatically than anyone else:

> Dante read Ovid, therefore, not in the modern way, having in front of himself only the poetic text, but in the one way in which a man of the Middle Ages could read it: that is, in a manuscript that displayed in the center of the page the poetic text, the expression of ancient wisdom, and that amassed in the four margins, not to mention between the lines, the prose gloss, the revelation of the Christian sense only intuited by the author. (my trans.)[5]

Medieval readers of Ovid, in other words, studied the Latin poet through a typological filter of Christian commentaries that had accreted gradually over the centuries (Sowell, "Ovid in the Middle Ages"). Long before the lifetime of Dante (1265–1321), apologists and allegorists produced any number of positive, Christianized readings of Ovid, dating from at least the early fifth century, when Prudentius, dubbed the "Christian Ovid" by later commentators, wrote descriptive Ovidian verses in his antiheathen tract *Contra Symmachum*. To cite two widely known examples closer to Dante's period, we have Arnulf of Orléans's *Allegoriae super Ovidii Metamorphosin* from the mid–twelfth century and, from the following century, the grammarian John of Garland's *Integumenta super Ovidium Memamorphoseos*, in elegiac distichs. During the lifetime of our Florentine exile, Giovanni del Virgilio, one of Dante's correspondents, produced *Allegoriae librorum Ovidii Metamorphoseos*. At more or less the same time (most likely between 1316 and 1328), an anonymous French moralizer composed the most famous medieval reading of Ovid, the *Ovide moralisé* (see Cormier, in this volume). The composer, occasionally identified as Chrétien Legouais, wrote this popular work in octosyllabic couplets that paraphrase and moralize the entire *Metamorphoses*. For example, Ovid's giants who attack heaven's throne (*Met*. 1.151–62) stand for the haughty of the earth. Thus they prefigure Dante's portrayal of giants (*Inf*. 31), the guardians of hell's ninth circle who also represent pride. The god Apollo symbolizes Christ, and knowing this interpretation makes Dante-poet's invocation of the sun god by name in *Paradiso* 1.13 much more comprehensible to the modern reader. It clarifies for the student Christ's role as a guiding light for the Christian pilgrim, it anticipates the extraordinary light imagery that characterizes Dante's third and final canticle, and it invites the reader to review and rethink in allegorical terms all previous Dantean allusions to the pagan gods.[6]

How does Dante's use of the pagan Ovid's Latin writings intersect or mesh with the Christian author's vernacular and allegorical agenda?

The answer to this question reveals itself generally in the religious nature of much of the marginalia and commentary in the medieval manuscripts of Ovid's verse and explicitly in moralizations such as those alluded to above. Simply put, Dante invariably viewed Ovidian characters as symbols or types of biblical figures. A straightforward but elegant example of this occurs in Dante's allusion to the tragic tale of the star-crossed lovers Pyramus and Thisbe (*Met.* 4.55–166) in an extended simile found in *Purgatorio* 27.37–42. In the Italian text, Dante-pilgrim finds himself on the seventh terrace of purgatory standing before a wall of fire. He must pass through the flames to reach Beatrice, but he is understandably fearful of being burned to death. Vergil entices him to enter the fire by explaining that "between Beatrice and you is this wall" (*Purg.* 27.35–36). The mention of his beloved's name wins over Dante-pilgrim, and in the ensuing simile Beatrice is compared to Thisbe and the pilgrim to Pyramus:

> Come al nome di Tisbe aperse il ciglio
>   Piramo in su la morte, e riguardolla,
>   allor che 'l gelso diventò vermiglio;
> così, la mia durezza fatta solla,
>   mi volsi al savio duca, udendo il nome
>   che ne la mente sempre mi rampolla.

> As at the name of Thisbe, Pyramus, at the point of death, opened his eyelids and looked at her, when the mulberry turned red, so, my stubbornness being softened, I [Dante-pilgrim] turned to the wise leader [Vergil] when I heard the name [Beatrice] which ever springs up in my mind.
> (*Purg.* 27.37–42)

Medieval Ovidian allegories, such as Pierre Bersuire's *Ovidius moralizatus*, interpreted Pyramus as a *figura Christi* and the bloodstained mulberry as a type of the cross that dripped with Christ's blood (Sowell, "Pyramus"). Beatrice as Thisbe comes, then, to signify the church, for which Dante-pilgrim as Pyramus-Christ dies. While the pilgrim does not shed his blood, as did Pyramus and Christ, he nevertheless enters the purifying flames to kill the "old man" of sin (see Rom. 6.6). On the other side of the refiner's fire he will be reunited with Beatrice, who soon arrives to take her place in the chariot representing the church. In this case Dante's intention to write of Beatrice that which has never been written of any woman is greatly furthered when we understand that his Ovidian allusions are best interpreted allegorically and in a decidedly Christian light.

What thematic and historical parallels exist between the two authors, and how does Dante exploit those parallels?

When examined in general terms, the historical and thematic parallels between Dante and Ovid prove so striking that they may account in no small part for the Italian poet's fascination with the pagan author. First, throughout the Middle Ages Ovid appears as the classical poet of love par excellence, since his early works treat little else. His erotic poems include *Amores*, *Heroides*, *Ars amatoria*, *Remedia amoris*, and *Medicamina faciei femineae*. But Ovid also represents the classical poet of exile, for at the end of his life he composed *Tristia*, *Ibis*, and *Epistulae ex Ponto*. Finally, the theme of metamorphosis preoccupied him, as the subject of his greatest work testifies.

The Florentine poet and his contemporaries could not have failed to see the striking comparisons between the lives of Ovid and Dante, for the latter stands in many ways as the most exemplary medieval poet of love and exile. Similarly, the concept of metamorphosis, as famously revealed in the episode of transmogrifying thieves in canto 25 of the *Inferno*, stands out as one of Dante's most virtuoso poetic performances—at once a tribute to Ovid and a challenge to the Latin poet's supremacy.[7] In the most Ovidian of Dante's cantos, Dante-pilgrim silences his guide Vergil by placing a finger from (the pilgrim's own) chin to nose: "mi puosi 'l dito su dal mento al *naso*" 'I placed my finger upwards from my chin to my *nose*' (*Inf.* 25.45; my emphasis). This act of silencing almost certainly involves wordplay, since "naso" can also signify Publius Ovidius *Naso*. In essence, when Dante-pilgrim points to *naso/Naso*, Dante-poet is hinting visually at what is shortly to come to pass textually: Naso's *Metamorphoses* will replace Vergil's *Aeneid* as the primary subtext for the remainder of the canto, and the Christian poet will present a series of metamorphoses inspired by and modeled on Ovid's writings. To this end, compare *Inferno* 25.58–60 (the image of ivy clinging to a tree) and *Metamorphoses* 4.365 (the identical image); *Inferno* 25.69–72 (Cianfa the serpent and Agnello the man) and *Metamorphoses* 4.373–79 (Salmacis and Hermaphroditus); *Inferno* 25.97 (Cadmus and Arethusa) and 25.103–08 (a series of infernal metamorphoses) and *Metamorphoses* 4.576–80, 4.586–89 (Cadmus), and 5.572–641 (Arethusa). In an episode dealing with dramatic transformations (i.e., thieves who are punished by continually being metamorphosed), it is apt that "naso" be both itself and something else. But just as Dante calls attention to Vergil only to silence him, so our Florentine poet does with Ovid in the "taccia" passage quoted near the beginning of our essay (*Inf.* 25.97–99). Such silencing highlights the difference between classical poetry of transmutation, which focuses on the inevitability of change, and Christian poetry of conversion and transfiguration, which underscores the didactic and thus serves God's higher purposes.

The love theme also offers a fertile parallel. The *Vita nova* collects many, though not all, of Dante's early love poems, and it strings them together within an invented narrative that highlights love's dramatic effects on the poet. The love Dante experienced as a young man comes across as primarily Ovidian: physical, carnal, and erotic. In chapter 3 of the *Vita nova* the poet records a dream of Love appearing to him holding a naked woman wrapped in a blood-red cloth and eating Dante's burning heart. But as the story of the poet's infatuation with Beatrice unfolds and continues even after her death, it is clear that the poet's love evolves into something far different from Ovid's. It transmogrifies into a purer, nonphysical love that centers on and embraces the Christian notion of *agape* or *caritas*. Beatrice affects not just Dante but all with whom she comes into contact, and her influence improves everyone. Interestingly, while the language of love, whether erotic or ecstatic, remains remarkably similar, the context Dante creates determines how we interpret the meaning of that love. The fire of love still persists in Dante's imagination, but it becomes, as seen in the purgatorial example cited above, a fire of purgation and purification, something quite foreign to Ovid's focus on *amor*.

As for the theme of exile, the Black Guelph government in Florence exiled Dante, a White Guelph, in late January 1302. Ironically he was then serving in an official political mission at the papal court of Boniface VIII in Rome. Fewer than two months later, the initial two-year exile became permanent, a lifetime banishment from the city. Dante writes of his dismay and despair, pain and alienation, in *Convivio* 1.3.4, where he describes himself as a pilgrim who is now a "piagato" ("wounded one"). Such bitterness echoes Ovid's own disappointment, frustration, and anger at being banned from Rome. The marked difference between the two poets, one a pagan and the other a Christian, once again emerges in how Dante eventually transforms his exile into a type that parallels Adam's exile from Eden (see *Par.* 26.116, where Adam refers to his own banishment from the garden as an "essilio") and the exodus of the Jews from Egypt to Jerusalem (see *Par.* 25.55–56, where Beatrice speaks of Dante's leaving Egyptian exile for the promised land).

Ultimately, the theme of Dante's own exile is best read against the pilgrim's own journey—a true pilgrimage—from the "selva oscura" 'dark wood' (*Inf.* 1.2) of error to the "somma luce" 'Light Supreme' (*Par.* 33.67) of the beatific vision. Dante is, above all, a Christian poet, and for the faithful follower of Christ no tragedy exists if one assumes a long-term view of things—a vision, in other words, sub specie aeternitatis. For this reason Dante's magnum opus, a Christian allegory, is entitled a "comedy" (see *Inf.* 21.2), while Vergil's pagan epic is pointedly referred to as a "tragedy" (see *Inf.* 20.113), and both Vergil and Ovid, when all is said and done, are condemned for eternity to limbo, the first circle of hell. Dante-pilgrim, on the other hand, experiences a vision of the Trinity and an assurance that his ultimate destiny, despite his earthly exile, is to return, following his death, to paradise. The ostensible parallels, therefore, between the lives of Ovid and Dante dissipate when their belief systems are compared. Ovid, like Dante's guide Vergil, lived "nel tempo de li dèi falsi e bugiardi" 'in the time of the false and lying gods' (*Inf.* 1.72). Our Florentine poet, by contrast, lived after the "[v]erbo di Dio discender piacque" ("it pleased the word of God to descend" [*Par.* 7.30]). In fine, Dante's intertextuality vis-à-vis Ovid ironically pays homage to the learning and artistry of antiquity even as it dramatizes the shortcomings of paganism.

NOTES

[1] The Italian word for *woof* is *trama*, which doubles as the term for a (literary) plot; therefore, in Italian studies it is natural to connect cloth making and plot making. Ludovico Ariosto, for example, uses the image of poet as weaver or tapestry maker to justify the complex, interwoven plots of the *Orlando furioso* (see canto 2, st. 30, lines 5–6; canto 13, st. 81, lines 1–2). The reverse notion of tapestry as text is at least as old as Homer's image of Penelope weaving while she awaits the return of Odysseus. For a fascinating exploration of the classical meanings—political, sexual, and literary—of the union of warp and woof in weaving, see Scheid and Svenbro.

[2] All quotations from *The Divine Comedy*, both in Italian and in English translation, come from Singleton.

[3] For a lengthy bibliography that treats Ovid in the Middle Ages and also the specific relation of Dante to Ovid, see Sowell, *Dante and Ovid* 153–72. For succinct synopses of Ovid's life and medieval *Nachleben*, see Sowell, "Ovid" and "Ovid in the Middle Ages."

[4] A recent monograph even argues that the conclusion of the *Vita nova*, in which Dante promises not to write again of Beatrice until he is capable of writing that which has never been written of any woman, is modeled on the first elegy of the third book of Ovid's *Amores*. See Carrai 39–41.

[5] "Dante leggeva quindi Ovidio non in modo moderno, avendo davanti il solo testo poetico, ma nell'unico modo in cui poteva leggerlo un uomo del Medioevo: in un manoscritto cioè che disponeva al centro della pagina il testo poetico, l'espressione della sapienza antica, e che ammassava ai quattro margini, oltre che nell'interlinea, il testo prosastico, l'inveramento del senso cristiano solo intuito dall'*auctor*" (112).

[6] Other fourteenth-century allegories of Ovid include Pierre Bersuire's *Ovidius moralizatus*, Robert Holkot's *Moralia super Ovidii Metamorphoses*, and Giovanni dei Bonsogni's *Allegorie ed esposizioni delle Metamorphosi*.

[7] For a bibliography devoted to interpretations of *Inferno*, canto 25, Dante's most Ovidian, see Sowell, *Dante and Ovid* 155–56.

Captured in Ekphrasis: Cervantes and Ovid

Frederick A. De Armas

In my courses on early modern Spain, I often turn to Ovid, since his versions of classical myths pervaded the literature of the period. A look at the reception of Ovid's poetry during the sixteenth and seventeenth centuries, however, shows him to be contaminated by medieval interpretations or by moralizing translations. His metamorphoses and his gods have been clothed in allegory, be it historical, physical, or moral.[1] In the Renaissance, such interpretations were often countered by a recovery of the classics. Gods and goddesses were asked to shed their medieval garb to take on a more authentic appearance. This is the view of Ovid I emphasize, one that may be less common but is more alluring—and one that was often featured in the art of the period. Of course, the immense historical and cultural gap that separated Renaissance Italy from classical Greece and Rome created a sense of anxiety.[2] At the same time, the desire for a conversation with the ancients was also a journey toward the recovery of the human form in its most beautiful and erotic aspects. Contributing to a revival of the "authentic" ancient, humanists aided painters in creating programs for their mythological works, programs that in turn were affected by the patrons who ordered these works. Many of these works were based on Ovid. We need only think of Raphael's *Triumph of Galatea* or the many "mythologies" that Titian sent to the kings of Spain, including *Danae*, *Rape of Europa*, and *Venus and Adonis* (see Redford, in this volume).[3]

In early modern Spain, Italy was seen as the repository of pictorial myth. If Spanish patrons wished to obtain religious paintings, there were many esteemed local artists to enlist.[4] If these patrons wanted to display the brilliance of an art that bordered on the risqué and foregrounded the pagan, the erotic, and even the cosmological, however, they almost invariably turned to Italy. Thus, through imported images and the proliferation of engravings and copies of Italian art, Spanish courtiers effectively canonized these works by displaying them and discussing them to demonstrate their knowledge, passion, and culture. Writers of the period, well aware of the cultural primacy of Italian art, incorporated these images into their work in the form of ekphrases (sing. *ekphrasis*, the pause in a narrative to describe an art object). Sometimes—and oxymoronically—ekphrasis took on a dramatic function, propelling narrative through images from art. The inclusion of ekphrasis in narrative would allow the reader to "see" and recall memorable and seductively dangerous images. Thus, when I deal in class with imitations of Ovid, I always begin with the classical text, pointing to some medieval and Renaissance permutations of his myths, and then turn to works of art that impinge on the textual allusion or imitation under consideration.

Ovid was widely read in early modern Spain—although side by side with countless allegorizing treatments, opposition to his more erotic episodes was still to be encountered. In addition to many Latin editions and commentaries, some eight translations of *Metamorphoses* were available. *Ars amatoria, Ibis, Heroides, Epistulae ex Ponto, Remedia amoris,* and *Tristia* were also available (at least in part) in the vernacular (Beardsley 154).[5] Ovid's works were profusely cited and his tales reworked by the leading Spanish writers of the period: Miguel de Cervantes, Luis de Góngora, Lope de Vega, and Francisco Quevedo. In this brief essay, I focus on Ovid's calendar poem, *Fasti*; it was not translated into Spanish during the early modern period, even though it was much prized by Renaissance readers and used by Italian artists. Although *Fasti* is not the only model for Botticelli's *Primavera*, for the sake of simplicity I ask my class to look briefly at Lucretius, Poliziano, and Apuleius (all of whom feature a very similar set of figures and topics to those found in Botticelli) but to concentrate on *Fasti*, which is less familiar but equally important for understanding Botticelli's painting.[6]

Two works by Cervantes conjoin the Renaissance canvas and the classical text: his pastoral romance *La Galatea* (1585) and the second part of his masterpiece *Don Quixote* (1615). That Cervantes would turn to *Fasti* for inspiration should come as no surprise, since Ovid incorporates many mythological tales into this work in discussing the festivals held throughout the Roman year. While Cervantes may poke fun at those who imitate a well-known work like *Metamorphoses*,[7] he takes it upon himself to bring out many aspects of the less familiar *Fasti*. Cervantes is also likely to have been attracted to the *Fasti* because of its ideological dimension: as Carole Newlands suggests, "The *Fasti* advertises its concern with the conditions for lawful (*fas*) speech . . . it provocatively foregrounds the ideological management of 'truth'" (*Playing* 200). Written at a time when, under Augustus, freedoms were beginning to erode, the poem would have resonated with a period in the history of the Spanish empire when imperial glory was giving way to disillusionment. In the *Quixote*, the knight himself warns against those who would make "malicious comments," for they "put themselves at risk of being banished to the Isles of Pontus" (589). This is a direct reference to Ovid, who, having displeased Augustus, was banished to Pontus on the Black Sea, where he spent the last nine years of his life in exile. Cervantes thus demonstrates his awareness of the dangers of displeasing a superior. By recalling Ovid's *Fasti* even as his main character warns of the dangers of saying too much, Cervantes may be exercising a kind of self-censorship, emulating Ovid but stopping short of danger. Instead of voicing explicit criticism, Cervantes invites his reader to look at beautiful images. I ask the class: what may Cervantes be hiding?

The episode from *Fasti* to which I turn my students' attention at first seems hardly controversial. In book 5, Ovid describes the feast of the Floralia, which begins on 28 April and concludes in early May (5.183–378). Bringing to class an image of Botticelli's painting (either in printed form or in a *PowerPoint* presentation), I engage students in a discussion of the role of imitation and the impact of visual culture in the Renaissance. Although I make it clear that neither Ovid nor Botticelli is the only important influence on Cervantes, I encourage them to see how the Spanish writer foregrounds the brilliance of Renaissance Italian art and counts on the knowledge of classical literature and Renaissance art possessed by his most learned and courtly readers. Cervantes takes as a point of departure a moment in the history of the Renaissance. For Frederick Hartt,

> [t]he entanglements of Botticelli's mythologies typify the learning and social graces of a society bent on reviving antiquity on a new scale, less for the moral lessons that interested Alberti than for private delight. Botticelli's painting has given this rarefied ideal its perfect embodiment, and at the same time raised it to the level of poetry. (335)

Cervantes in turn seeks to imbue his text with a capaciousness that words often struggle to acquire. He wishes not only to make the text compete with visual culture but also to bring to the minds of his readers the beauty, mystery, and allure of art. Thus Ovid is captured in ekphrasis. By this I mean that the appeal of the visual seems to restrain the power of the original words. Cervantes turns to the image to re-create Ovid through ekphrasis, while the Ovidian text is held hostage to art. Paradoxically, this interpretative move may capture the vividness of Ovid's original description, while dispelling some of Cervantes's anxieties concerning the process of imitation. The Renaissance image assuages the confrontation between ancient text and modern readings.

La Galatea offers a clear example of how the Ovidian Floralia can be transformed into a mysterious feast resembling Botticelli's canvas. This would argue in favor of the notion that Cervantes is captured by the image rather than by the text. George Camamis argues that there are three key passages in *La Galatea* that derive from Botticelli and that could also point to Ovid. The first one occurs in the first book; the narrator describes "[a] thick dark wood, Zephyr blowing his wind and the green ground covered with sweet smelling flowers" (Camamis 189; Cervantes, *Galatea* 182). As we examine this Cervantine passage in class, students usually agree there is little here of Ovid's Floralia and much from Botticelli. Although the "dark wood" does seem to come from the painter and not from the classical author, I ask the class to look more carefully at Ovid. In *Fasti*, the poetic voice asks the goddess to reveal herself since "the opinion of men is fallacious" (5.191).[8] This statement reflects Renaissance attitudes, as writers sought to recapture an ancient culture while knowing the impossibility of the task. Just as Ovid asks the goddess to speak, Cervantes calls forth the past in his writings, knowing that to make it come alive again, the text must somehow make the classics speak with an ancient yet paradoxically modern voice.

Ovid's deity confesses that originally she was the nymph Chloris and was pursued by the wind god Zephyr: "However, he made amends for violence by giving me the name of bride, and in my marriage-bed I have naught to complain of. I enjoy perpetual spring" (5.205–07). Indeed, Zephyr commanded, "Goddess, be queen of flowers" (5.212). Cervantes uses Renaissance images as a bridge between the classics and the sixteenth century. To the viewer's right in

Botticelli's painting, we witness Zephyr pursuing Chloris. To their left emerges a woman dressed in a flower-covered dress, which accentuates the green field filled with flowers. The juxtaposition indicates that an Ovidian metamorphosis has occurred and that Chloris is now Flora, the goddess of spring.[9] The students then are asked to decide if the interaction between the west wind and Flora is equally important in Cervantes's text.

I also invite the class to think about other scenes in Cervantes's *Galatea* besides that under consideration here. They repeatedly recall that Elicio, who arrives at the springlike locale, has just heard the story of Lisandro, who killed two evil villagers responsible for the death of his beloved. Cervantes, the students come to realize, shows that this moment in time and space that seems to denote spring is not as peaceful as it may appear. Although it signifies a revival of life, it is surrounded by death. In Ovid's *Fasti*, the goddess tells how she can turn violent death into the flowers of spring. The purple iris or grape hyacinth derives from Hyacinthus's blood (5.223) and the eponymous Narcissus, the violets of Attis, and the anemone of Adonis all spring from blood, violence, and death (5.225, 227).[10] Thus Cervantes's scene places classical text and painting in conflict as it foregrounds the opposition of life and death in the erotic violence that hides among the flowers. Finally, as we continue to focus on Cervantes and Ovid, the class begins to understand that there is much more violence in Cervantes and in Ovid than in Botticelli. In Cervantes, Zephyr softly "wounds" ("hería" [182]) Elicio. This may be a partial recollection of the wind's erotic violence as described by Ovid. Hinting at the rape of Chloris, Cervantes tells how the sweet smell is actually robbed by the wind as it passes the flowers (182). Once again, no matter how "softly" ("mansamente") this is done, thieving violence is involved.

The second important moment in this fragmented ekphrasis occurs immediately thereafter, when Elicio, aided by the wind, hears a lament. Lisardo is bemoaning the death of his beloved Leonida and desires to be free of his body to be reunited with her. As Elicio approaches, Lisardo adopts a pose: "he had his right foot forward and his left one behind, and the right arm raised as if he were expecting to throw something" ("estaba con el pie derecho delante y el izquierdo atrás, y el diestro brazo levantado a guisa como de quien esperaba hacer algún recio tiro"). Viewing this stance from the perspective of ekphrasis, Camamis asserts, "Cervantes has actually reproduced exactly the figure of Mercury in Botticelli's *Primavera*" (190); that is, he appears in contrapposto. I suggest, however, that Cervantes may have had in mind both Botticelli's painting and Ovid's text. I ask students to search for clues of Mercury's presence in Ovid's *Fasti*. They soon discover that, although not mentioned in the description of the Floralia, the god appears in the introduction to the month of May. Son of Jove and Maia (the most beautiful of the Pleiades), he evinced his filial devotion by naming the month of May after her. Thus there is an Ovidian precedent for Botticelli's introduction of Mercury into his painting. Student discussion often ensues concerning other possible explanations for Mercury's presence such as his role as *psychopompos*, as guide of souls back to the heavens, or as revealer of secret or hermetic knowledge (Wind 121–22).[11] But Ovid, unlike Botticelli, emphasizes that this god is the patron of thieves (5.104). I then ask the class which aspects of the god are more evident in Cervantes's pastoral. Some believe that the mystery of Botticelli's painting permeates the scene, while others come to agree that the whole tale of Lisardo, like the scene of Zephyr and the flowers, has been about thieving. While Zephyr has stolen the fragrance of flowers and the body of Chloris to create Primavera, Lisardo has been the target of thievery: his beloved has been stolen from him. Thus he is the victim of Mercury instead of his embodiment. Cervantes plays with text and painting to come up with new and striking meanings. He imitates words and images, giving them an unexpected turn that requires the reader to enjoy both his thieving art and his originality.

The third and last ekphrastic episode takes place in the sixth and last book of the pastoral. As the shepherds move toward the valley of the cypresses they discover a place akin to the Elysian fields. Its description includes four major elements (two of which have appeared before) from Botticelli's *Primavera*: the figures of Primavera, Venus, Zephyr, and Flora.[12] Camamis adds (186) that this Venus is Galatea herself and that we ought to recall that elsewhere in the novel she is accompanied by the three Graces (Cervantes, *La Galatea* 209). It is quite possible that the Ovidian model is here discarded.[13] I then ask the students to write a brief paper for the next class, attempting to unravel the tangled web of imitation. I remind them that, while the Graces accompany Venus in Botticelli, they are with Flora in *Fasti*. I also remind them that Galatea's beloved companion in the novel is named Florisa.[14] Is she a manifestation of the Ovidian Flora or has the Floralia been discarded for a more obvious imitation of Botticelli? Perhaps while Cervantes looks to Ovid for the revelations of Flora, who produces flowers from the violence of men and nature, he turns to Botticelli for the mysteries she conceals.[15] We end our discussion of the pastoral by delving into the management of "truth" and Cervantes's strategies for concealment. Returning to the Pontus reference and to the Flora-Florisa equation, we discuss questions of gender and genre, violence, epic, and empire. Is the hidden violence within pastoral a pointer to the dangers and fallacies of empire? Does peace always require a previous war? To deal with these questions, we look at Cervantes's evocation of Vergil's *Eclogues* and Augustus's empire in his preface.

Thirty years after writing his pastoral, Cervantes published the second part of *Don Quixote* (1615). In chapter 10, the knight has gone to El Toboso to find Dulcinea and her palace. Not happening upon it at night, he retires to the forest and asks Sancho to bring his princess to him the following day. Sancho, aware that there is no Dulcinea and not knowing what to do, sits under a tree and tries to determine his future course. Reasoning that his master believes that windmills are giants, he figures it would not be too difficult to persuade him that any woman is Dulcinea. Returning late in the afternoon to where Don Quixote waits, Sancho sees three peasant women riding on donkeys. He tells his master to emerge from the woods where he had been waiting so that he can see his beloved Dulcinea and two of her ladies. As Erich Auerbach has succinctly explained, what happens here is truly surprising:

> [F]or the first time roles are exchanged. Until now it had been Don Quixote who, encountering everyday phenomena, spontaneously saw and transformed them in terms of the romances of chivalry, while Sancho was generally in doubt and often tried to contradict and prevent his master's absurdities. Now it is the other way around. Sancho improvises a scene after the fashion of the romances of chivalry, while Don Quixote's ability to transform events to harmonize with his illusion breaks down before the crude vulgarity of the sight of the peasant women. (339)

I suggest that this passage includes, albeit in a grotesque manner, the major elements of Botticelli's *Primavera*. In a double vision in which narrative recalls and redraws a painting on a rustic landscape, Sancho appears as Mercury the messenger,[16] Dulcinea as Primavera/Venus herself, the three peasant women as the three Graces,[17] the wind as Zephyr seeking Chloris, the flowers of springtime as Flora, and the backdrop of the wood as the dark woods on the canvas. Even Don Quixote's negative response to Sancho can be traced to Ovid. If Sancho is Mercury, then he stands for eloquence (and also for thievery, since he has taken a rustic scene and attempted to transform it into a canonical and mysterious painting). But the imaginative knight cannot see this canvas and decides that a malicious enchanter "has placed clouds and cataracts over my eyes" (Cervantes, *Don Quixote* 548–49). In Botticelli's painting, we see Mercury holding his wand ("caduceus") upward toward some clouds. This recalls his role in *Aeneid* 4.245–46, where he "gains control over the clouds and winds" (Wind 122). The text suggests that Sancho's rustic picture and his lesser powers of eloquence have made him into a lesser god, unable to communicate the beauty and mysteries of Botticelli to Don Quixote.

Not only is the painting poorly described, but the text also seems to play down features that *Fasti* foregrounds and that are seen in Botticelli. Zephyr can only be gleaned from the ladies' hair as it is tossed by the wind, "like sunbeams playing with the wind" (Cervantes, *Don Quixote* 547); Flora meanwhile is blatantly erased when Don Quixote confesses that the "sweet smell that they [Dulcinea and her ladies] derive from living among ambergris and flowers" has actually turned into the "odor of raw garlic" (Cervantes, *Don Quixote* 550). It appears that Sancho is not only unable to capture Botticelli but also that he and his master are even worse at "viewing" Ovid. And yet a second look at the scene may make us wonder if Ovid does not in fact provide an alternative model for Sancho. In Ovid, Flora's festival is marked by "greater wantonness and broader jests" (5.331–32). With his trickery, Sancho likewise has turned a mysterious vision into a comic scene. As for wantonness, the way the would-be lady rides her beast, "vaulting, as swift as a falcon, on the pack-saddle, where she sat stride as if she were a man" (Cervantes, *Don Quixote* 549), is enough to suggest the bawdiness of the situation. But Don Quixote cannot see it. He will not laugh with Ovid's and Sancho's jests but rejects the "rakish stage" (5.347). Ovid knows that the Floralia is for the common people and that Flora is not a "high-flown" goddess. I invite students, then, to join Cervantes's Floralia, and turning away from the high mysteries to revel in the comic.

This scene in *Don Quixote*, although seemingly caught in Botticelli's ekphrasis, fails to deliver the great mysteries of the painting. Instead, it looks to the ambience of Ovid's Floralia and to Flora's rakish stage as means to recapture the ancient through a double vision that brings a divine mystery into harmony with the Floralia. It is no wonder, then, that Don Quixote cannot see his Dulcinea. She belongs to Botticelli, while Cervantes's scene is nothing more than a pagan feast where Flora can indeed commune with her beloved peasants. If this is so, I ask my students, why did Cervantes look to this painting and this text? Why is this pagan feast so important to the development of Cervantes's novel?[18]

Although Ovid appears to be captured in ekphrasis and to have been erased from Cervantes's work through the allure of Botticelli's *Primavera*, my students come to realize that Ovid is actually enlivened through a reading of Cervantes that resists Botticelli's mysteries to reveal Ovid's designs. In Cervantes's pastoral romance, we see the metamorphic and Ovidian violence and death that underlie the coming of spring and the thieving nature of Mercury that takes away its beauties. In Cervantes's comic masterpiece, the lesser power of the god's eloquence, along with the god's thieving aspect, emerges in the person of Sancho—Sancho, after all, "steals" the *Primavera* to deceive his master. But Botticelli is certainly not ignored. While Don Quixote searches for the spring-like beauty of Dulcinea—in other words, for Botticelli's canvas—Sancho can only give him a rakish and rustic Floralia. In the end, Ovid loosens the bonds of ekphrasis through a playful, erotic, violent, and free spirit that counters the management of truth with laughter, rebellion, and licentiousness.

NOTES

[1] On the different ways that the pagan gods "survived" the Middle Ages (historical, physical, moral, and encyclopedic traditions), see Seznec. As Barnard observes, Ovid's *Metamorphoses* was viewed "as an allegory of theological and moral wisdom. The Bible of the Gentiles—as Ovid's collection of mythological tales was dubbed by the Alfonsine compilers of the *General Estoria*, where Ovid was allegorized at length—was believed to have veiled truth beneath the guise of fable" (44).

[2] As Greene asserts, "The humanist text reaches a cultural gap and takes the risk of anachronism. The reader then has the right to ask whether this initiative is completed and authenticated, whether the conflict of cultures and the potential conflict of attitude are put to use, whether something occurs within the imitation which truly renews" (37).

[3] Of the many "mythologies" or paintings that narrate through art a particular myth, the first four painted by Titian for the Spanish Hapsburgs dealt with four "sinners" being

punished in Hades. These canvases were commissioned by Mary of Hungary (regent of the Netherlands) for her palace at Binche and were later sent to Spain. Charles V and Philip II were the recipients of the more erotic paintings (Panofsky 144–71).

[4] Jonathan Brown believes that the "home market was confined mainly to an ecclesiastical clientele" (4).

[5] Although Beardsley begins his volume with 1482, decades earlier Ovid had already become fashionable. As Schevill points out, the *Epístolas de Ovidio* (or *Bursuario*) "represents one of the first steps of the process by which the works of Ovid, notably the *Metamorphoses* and the *Heroides*, assumed a modern garb and so became a part of Spanish fiction of the Renaissance" (115–16). Brownlee shows how the *Bursuario* author points to the Spanish sentimental romances by using *Heroides* in unexpected ways, even creating a "literary counterfeit" by attributing three of his own letters to Ovid (39).

[6] Comparing the passage in *Fasti* with the *Primavera*, Wiseman asserts, "Without prejudice to the more arcane, neo-Platonic interpretations of the iconography, we can read the surface meaning clearly enough as an illustration of Ovid's text" (6). This is very much to the point of what I try to do in my class. At the same time, the notion of recapturing the imitative process of the passage is fraught with difficulties, since it was used as part of the program for Botticelli's painting, where it competed with other classical texts. Indeed, we could ask, as Dempsey has done, "What could Lucretius's didactic poem *De rerum natura*, Ovid's *Fasti*, a didactic poem of the Roman calendar, a lyric invocation by Horace, Seneca's philosophical essay *De beneficiis* and Hesiod's *Georgics* [i.e., his *Works and Days*] have, after all, in common?" (37). Hartt has also stressed the complexity of imitation in Botticelli's painting: "A treasury of classical sources has been amassed for most of the elements in the painting, drawn from the ancient writers Horace, Ovid, Lucretius and Columella" (335). He could have added the tenth book of Apuleius's *Metamorphoses*, which is central to Gombrich's interpretation of the painting.

[7] In *Don Quixote*, Cervantes also parodies imitations of *Metamorphoses* when a "humanist" in the text tells us the ridiculous ways in which he is going to continue Ovid's work: "I've written another book which I'm going to call Metamorfoseos, or the *Spanish Ovid*, and its contents are most novel and unusual, because I imitate Ovid in a burlesque style and describe the Giralda in Seville and the Angel Weather-Vane . . . complete with allegories, metaphors and similes to delight, amaze and instruct all at once" (633).

[8] Throughout this essay I quote from the translation of *Fasti* that appears in the Loeb Classical Library edition (ed. Goold).

[9] Baldini shows that the restoration of the painting has clarified Zephyr's role as bringer of spring: "Removal of varnish has revealed that Zephyr 'breathes' on Chloris in faint lines of color . . . for Zephyr appears no longer as a ghostly shadow clutching at the nymph but rather as the deity of spring engages in the act of generating life" (51).

[10] Botticelli's painting also depicts many varieties of flowers: "Of the 190 flowering plants [in the painting], about 138 real individual plants have been identified, 33 others are either stylized or entirely imaginary . . . the daisy and sweet violet occur most frequently in the picture" (Baldini 106). Some critics stress the theme of marriage in the painting, noting that "[t]he pinks and cornflowers symbolize marriage and conjugal love," and compare the marriage of Lorenzo de' Medici to Semiramide Appiani (Baldini 56); others, like Levi D'Ancona, have emphasized that, in addition to marriage flowers, the painting depicts plants associated with grief and death such as the buttercup, the fern, and the ragwort, as allusions to the assassination of Giuliano de' Medici.

Frederick A. De Armas   249

¹¹ Actually, Lisardo would like to find a guide to the heavens to be reunited with his beloved.

¹² The Cervantine text states, "Aquí se ve en cualquiera sazón del año andar la risueña Primavera con la Hermosa Venus en hábito sucinto y amoroso, y Céfiro que la acompaña con la madre Flora delante, esparciendo a manos llenas varias y odoríferas flores" 'Here you see throughout the year dreamlike Spring accompanied by amorous Venus, and Zephyr who is preceded by Flora, spreading with her hands full many flowers of delightful odor' (*Galatea* 542; my trans.). This passage is very similar to one in Lucretius: "On come Spring and Venus, and Venus' winged harbinger marching before, with Zephyr and mother Flora a pace behind him strewing the whole path in front and filling it with brilliant colours and scents" (5.737–40).

¹³ The description of spring in the sixth book of *La Galatea* could be more easily explained as an imitation of Lucretius, Apuleius, and even the Renaissance writer Angelo Poliziano. I am particularly struck by a passage in "The Countryman," a poem in the *Silvae*: "Bounteous Venus accompanies her sister and the little cupids accompany Venus, and Flora lavishes welcome kisses on her lusty husband. Between them, her hair loosened, her breasts bare, a Grace dances with alternating step" (45).

¹⁴ For the role of Florisa in the pastoral see De Armas, "Ekphrasis and Eros." In my response to Dudley, I was also caught in ekphrasis, neglecting the importance of Ovid ("Goddess on the Edge").

¹⁵ For Barkan (*Gods*), Botticelli's work must be studied as an event that takes place before the Ovidian Renaissance: "The *Primavera* is certainly cosmological in the sense that it is concerned with the great motions of time in the universe. . . . [It] requires the viewer to look beyond the veil . . . at a world in which the pagan gods represent some natural essence" (175). Thus, he argues, it is easier to discover Christian mysticism here than sensual paganism. For the latter, and its erotic violence, Cervantes looks to Ovid.

¹⁶ Sancho is thrice described as messenger. Don Quixote commands, "you deliver my message" (543); the knight describes what Sancho is to see when talking to Dulcinea: "actions and movements made by lovers while the conversation concerns their love are messengers" (544); and Sancho tells himself, "You're but a messenger, my friend" (545).

¹⁷ Sancho's description of the Graces coincides with Botticelli's painting: "one blaze of flaming gold, all spindlefuls of pearls, they're all diamonds, all rubies, all brocade . . . " (547).

¹⁸ By linking Flora to Dulcinea, Cervantes may be underlining the powers of invention. As Boyd asserts, "Ovid's Flora seems to be entirely his own creation, assembled from allusions to what were probably among Ovid's favorite poems." Dulcinea, then, belongs neither to Ovid nor to Botticelli. Like a new Minerva, she is born from the knight's mind, and, like Flora, she revels in her own "novelty and lack of authority" (Boyd, "'*Celabitur Auctor*'" 76, 77).

Ovid and Ransmayr:
Translating across Cultures and Times

Susan C. Anderson and Mary Jaeger

One of the exciting things about teaching language and literature is to watch students expand their cultural outlook by engaging with modern works that draw their inspiration and subject matter from ancient classics and in turn transform our understanding of the old. Thus the approach we outline integrates the teaching of Ovid's *Metamorphoses* and Christoph Ransmayr's 1988 postmodern novel *Die letzte Welt* (*The Last World*), which draws its material and inspiration from *Metamorphoses*.

We teach at a large public university, where, generally speaking, students of Latin have not studied much German, and students of German have not studied much Latin. Because of the size of our departments (classics and Germanics) and the level of language proficiency required, upper-division courses are generally open to graduate students as well as undergraduates. The main challenge we face is how to convey to students unfamiliar with Latin some of the important features of *Metamorphoses* and how to convey to students unfamiliar with German what is most important about Ransmayr's rereading of Ovid. In addition, we want to give students a sense of the traditions in which both authors work, those of Augustan poetry on the one hand and those of the postmodern European novel on the other. Accordingly, we offer some ideas, strategies, and questions for exploration based on our experience with both of these works and our plans to team teach a course on them.

All the students will read *Metamorphoses* first, in Allen Mandelbaum's English translation, and then Ransmayr's novel, either in German or in the English translation by John E. Woods. Students of Latin will also use the 2004 edition of *Metamorphoses* (ed. Tarrant). Although there is little secondary literature in English on Ransmayr's use of Ovid, we recommend Duncan Kennedy's fairly recent essay in the *Cambridge Companion to Ovid* and articles by Peter G. Christensen and by Anita McChesney. For readers of German, there is Uwe Wittstock's collection of reviews and essays on *Die letzte Welt* as well as Helmuth Kiesel and Georg Wöhrle's volume, Thomas Epple's study and Esther Felicitas Gehlhoff's interpretation. Also important is Ransmayr's own anticipatory discussion of his proposed novel, "Entwurf zu einem Roman" ("Draft of a Novel"), in which he claims of his novel that "its theme is the disappearance and reconstruction of literature, of poetry; its materials are the M/metamorphoses of Publius Ovidius Naso" ("sein Thema ist das Verschwinden und die Rekonstruktion von Literatur, von Poesie; sein Stoff sind die Metamorphosen des Publius Ovidius Naso" [196; our trans.]). Not only does Ransmayr's book turn Latin hexameter verse into German prose, but Ransmayr first conceived of it after having been asked to translate *Metamorphoses* into German. Accordingly, at the introductory meeting, students should brainstorm about what is involved in translating literary texts and discuss how translation is itself a form of metamorphosis.

One of the joint sessions, led by the students of Latin, can begin by comparing two passages: a scene from early in *The Last World* and the closing lines of *Metamorphoses*. In *The Last World*, the protagonist, Cotta, who has traveled from Rome to Tomis, or Tomi, as Ransmayr calls it, in search of the exiled Ovid, has traced the poet (called simply Naso) as far as his house in Trachila but has found only his elderly servant, Pythagoras, hiding under the stairs. In chapter 3 Pythagoras leads Cotta into the garden, where he begins to pour vinegar on mats of slugs that cover a group of large stones. On the stones Cotta discovers inscribed words and phrases. The text lists some individually: "FEUER" 'FIRE,' "ZORN" 'WRATH,' "GEWALT" 'POWER,' "STERNE" 'STARS,' and "EISEN" 'IRON'; Cotta arranges and rearranges these fragments of text, "[beginning] the game anew" (50, 38; our trans.), until he comes up with the following fifteen lines (one for each menhir or for each chapter of the novel or for each book of *Metamorphoses*):

> ICH HABE EIN WERK VOLLENDET
> DAS DEM FEUER STANDHALTEN WIRD
> UND DEM EISEN
> SELBST DEM ZORN GOTTES UND
> DER ALLESVERNICHTENDEN ZEIT
>
> WANN IMMER ER WILL
> MAG NUN DER TOD
> DER NUR ÜBER MEINEN LEIB
> GEWALT HAT
> MEIN LEBEN BEENDEN
>
> ABER DURCH DIESES WERK
> WERDE ICH FORTDAUERN UND MICH
> HOCH ÜBER DIE STERNE EMPORSCHWINGEN
> UND MEIN NAME
> WIRD UNZERSTÖRBAR SEIN   (50–51)
>
> I HAVE COMPLETED A WORK
> THAT WILL WITHSTAND FIRE
> AND IRON
> EVEN THE WRATH OF GOD AND
> ALL-CONSUMING TIME
>
> WHENEVER IT WILL
> LET DEATH NOW COME
> HAVING ONLY MY BODY
> WITHIN ITS POWER
> AND END MY LIFE

> BUT THROUGH THIS WORK
> I WILL LIVE ON AND
> LIFT MYSELF HIGH ABOVE THE STARS
> AND MY NAME
> WILL BE INDESTRUCTIBLE.
> (Ransmayr, *Last World* 38)

This "inscription" loosely rewrites the narrator's words at the end of *Metamorphoses*:

> Iamque opus exegi, quod nec Iovis ira nec ignis
> nec poterit ferrum nec edax abolere vetustas
> cum volet, illa dies, quae nil nisi corporis huius
> ius habet, incerti spatium mihi finiat aevi;
> parte tamen meliore mei super alta perennis
> astra ferar, nomenque erit indelebile nostrum;
> quaque patet domitis Romana potentia terris
> ore legar populi, perque omnia saecula fama
> (si quid habent veri vatum praesagia) vivam.
> (bk. 15. 871–79)

> And now my work is done: no wrath of Jove
> nor fire nor sword nor time, which would erode
> all things, has power to blot out this poem.
> Now, when it wills, the fatal day (which has
> only the body in its grasp) can end
> my years however long or short their span.
> But, with the better part of me, I'll gain
> a place that's higher than the stars: my name
> indelible, eternal, will remain.
> And everywhere that Roman power has sway,
> in all domains the Latins gain, my lines
> will be on peoples' lips; and through all time—
> if poets' prophecies are ever right—
> my name and fame are sure: I shall have life.
> (Mandelbaum 549)

A close reading of Ovid's Latin will bring to light the epilogue's famous intertextuality, for this passage alludes to some of Ovid's own poetry (most notably the concluding poem of his first book of love elegies, *Amores* 1.15), to Horace's ode 3.30, and more distantly to the Greek poet Pindar (*Pythian* 6.10–14) and a fragment of Simonides (lines 4–5). Students of Latin will prepare and present a close reading, tracing these allusions and discussing their effects. (For lists of allusions, they can consult Bömer as well as Nisbet and Rudd's commentary on Horace's *Odes*, book 3; for discussions of allusivity and intertexuality, see Hinds, *Allusion and Intertext*; Conte, *Rhetoric of Imitation*; and Edmunds.) Discussion then will move to the dynamic relation between Ovid's texts and those to which they allude. How, for example, do the allusions to Horace, ode 3.30, which begins, "Exegi monumentum aere perennius" 'I have built a monument more lasting than bronze,' affect our reading of both Ovid and Horace? Next our discussion will turn to comparing Ovid's poetics of allusion and intertextuality and those of postmodernism. A more general discussion about the novel's impact on the epic will offer a chance for students of Latin to take a particularly active role by comparing what Ransmayr does to the text of the *Metamorphoses* and what Ovid does to the texts of his predecessors. They can go on to evaluate the effects of the ways Ovid and Ransmayr link past and present. Ovid, for example, compares the neighborhood of the Olympian gods to the Augustan Palatine in *Metamorphoses*, book 1; Ransmayr disconcertingly blends images of a decaying Augustan Rome with those of a rusting modern world.

Ransmayr's "inscription" in the third chapter of the novel and Ovid's epilogue show how the structure of each work varies: Ovid disposes his material among fifteen books of hexameter lines, running from primordial chaos to the reign of Augustus, whereas Ransmayr arranges his work in fifteen chapters that cover two years in Tomis, with flashbacks to Cotta's—and Naso's—life in Rome. The story of Lycaon, for example, the first metamorphosis of human into animal in Ovid, is a discrete episode, yet it also introduces the idea of the "wrath of Jove," which brings about the great flood. Ovid also returns to it in the epilogue, when he claims that "no wrath of Jove . . . has power to blot out this poem" (549). In *The Last World*, Lycaon's story follows a different narrative path: he is the first person to take notice of the newly arrived Cotta, to whom he rents a room; but that he is a werewolf emerges only obliquely over the course of the book through clues and signs perceived by Cotta. Yet here too the story illustrates one of the novel's pervasive themes, that "der Mensch ist dem Menschen ein Wolf" 'man is a wolf to man' (266; 203).[1] Likewise, the story of Tereus, Procne, and Philomela, another discrete episode in Ovid, runs through the novel as a town mystery that is introduced in chapter 1 and finally exposed in chapter 14, when the mutilated Philomela, long thought dead, staggers into Tomis. Students of German might chime in here with Ransmayr's claim in his essay "Entwurf zu einem Roman" that his main figure, or "researcher" ("Forscher"), will gather testimony from fifteen "witnesses" of the various metamorphoses and strange figures created by the exiled author (197). Are these "witnesses" the fifteen books of *Metamorphoses*, the menhirs, or members of Tomis's enigmatic and shape-shifting population?

A close reading of the "inscription" and its immediate context in Ransmayr, led by the students of German, will move discussion in other directions. Here too, we will begin with allusion, this time the connections evoked by the name of Ransmayr's protagonist, Cotta. While this name denotes Ovid's friend Cotta Maximus Messalinus, at the same time it brings to mind the most powerful German publisher in the early nineteenth century: Johann Friedrich Freiherr Cotta von Cottendorf. J. F. Cotta became the head of the Cotta'sche Buchhandlung (Cotta Book Company, founded in 1659) in 1787 and remained in charge until his death in 1832, the year in which Johann Wolfgang von Goethe died. Indeed, Cotta was the publisher of Goethe and Friedrich Schiller, arguably the two most influential writers in German literary history. Cotta also published the works of other major German writers, such as Johann Gottfried von Herder, Friedrich Hölderlin, and Heinrich von Kleist. The Cotta'sche Buchhandlung remained in business until it was purchased in 1977 by Klett Publishers and transformed into the Klett-Cotta Verlag, a prominent German publisher of literary and scholarly books. Thus, Cotta calls to the mind of the German speaker German classical literature and the major figures of German Romanticism. What signals about the discovery and preservation of literature does Ransmayr give by assigning his protagonist such an evocative name?

Other details of the scene raise questions that can guide this discussion further. For example, the description of the dying slugs foregrounds the German Romantic notion of the suffering one must endure in order to experience beauty:

> ... und Cotta begriff, dass dies der Lärm des Sterbens war, das Entsetzen und der Schmerz der Schnecken ... und sah, wie in dieses zähe, feuchte Strickwerk aus Fühlern und Leibern die Bewegung des Todes kam, ein jähes, zuckendes Leben. (49)

> ... and Cotta realized that this was the noise of dying, the terror and the pain of the slugs ... and saw how the motion of death entered into the tough, moist webwork of feelers and bodies—hasty, twitching life. (37)

In the midst of such pain "auf einer solchen, vom Leben befreiten Stelle" 'on one of the spots now freed of life' [49, 37]), the last words of Ovid's text appear, beginning with "FEUER" ("FIRE"), a reference to the illuminating clarity that Cotta seeks. Our discussion considers this brief description of art emerging from death in the context of the whole novel's emphasis both on Cotta's finding and reconstructing Ovid's text while coming to terms with Ovid's demise and on the sense of suffering. (Kiel connects a struggle for survival with new ways to pose old questions [186].) It also considers whether Ransmayr is hinting at how a certain way of reading can bring to life a "dead" text.

Together, the ideas of the fifteen "witnesses" and of the dead past brought to life will lead to a discussion of the Ovidian "repertoire," the key to mythological figures at the end of Ransmayr's novel. Duncan Kennedy, who points out that the "repertoire" parodies the keys often found at the end of historical novels, suggests that the juxtaposition of the myths in Ovid and in the novel undermines the authority of the Ovidian version. But the juxtaposition also suggests that Ovid's versions of the myths have petrified simply by becoming European civilization's canonical versions. Perhaps, we suggest, Ovid's *Metamorphoses* has in Ransmayr's eyes been turned to stone, like some of the figures in his novel, to be brought back to life by his own work.

After more words appear from beneath the tortured slugs, Cotta runs from one stone to another, "gierig nach dem Zusammenhang und Sinn der Sätze" 'eager to discover the meaning and syntax of the sentences' (50, 38), reading much as a translator would. Indeed, the paragraph before the presentation of the poet's last words hints at Cotta's, and the novel's, rehabilitation of the Latin work:

> Cotta entzifferte und flüsterte die Worte wie einer, der lesen lernt, zerriß nun mit seinen eigenen Händen die Schneckenmäntel dort, wo er neue Worte vermutete und fügte, was zum Vorschein kam, aneinander, prüfte und verwarf den Sinn und Zusammenhang einmal und wieder, begann das Spiel irgendwo anders und neu, bis ihm schließlich schien, als seien alle Möglichkeiten der Zusammensetzung und Verbindung der Bruchstücke in einer einzigen Nachricht erschöpft. (50)

> Cotta unriddled and whispered the words like someone learning to read, tearing a blanket of slugs away with his bare hands wherever he suspected new words. He patched together what was revealed, checked it for sense and syntax, discarded it once, twice, began the game anew elsewhere, until at last it seemed to him that he had exhausted all the possibilities for combining and connecting the fragments into a single message. (38)

It is to Cotta, then, that the "inscription" we read appears to make sense. After quoting the inscription, the passage goes on to implicate Cotta's judgment once again by pointing out that Cotta knew only one man, "der zu einer solchen Vision fähig war" 'who was capable of such a vision' (50, 38). If, as these details suggest, it is Cotta who determines the final arrangement of words and Cotta who judges one man only to be capable of such vision, the question arises, Whose reality are we talking about? To what degree is Naso's text Cotta's creation or translation? To what degree is Naso's story the creation of others and his work the creation of readers? From here discussion can explore more deeply how Ransmayr's restructuring of Ovid questions the authority of any one narrative structure and how the work exemplifies one of the central traits of postmodernism: that reality is a construct (Kennedy points out several other passages in the novel that lend themselves well to such a discussion).

Other questions to discuss include the following: What does Ransmayr's novel imply by connecting pain, beauty, and attempts at understanding? How does Cotta's mediating function hinder or help in comprehending Ovid's ancient words? How can one gain direct access to art, according to the novel? To whom does the pronoun *Ich* refer, which Pythagoras uncovers on the stone, just after Cotta asks him who engraved the words?

Finally, students can explore how Cotta's reality completes its transformation into Naso's fiction in the final chapter and how Cotta overcomes the distance between understanding and direct experience. The students who know German should first work together to discuss Ransmayr's use of the term "verrückt" 'crazy' (286, 218) and its relation to the verb "rücken" 'to move over' to describe Cotta as he walks through Tomis, talking to himself. Cotta's move away from reason, from his efforts to grasp Naso (and his literary work) by understanding the inscriptions, is accompanied by descriptions of transformed nature (a new mountain appears; the sun is shining) and of a "klares Licht" 'clear light' (284, 217) bathing the mountains and chasing away the fog. At the same time, Cotta no longer perceives human beings, only the creatures into which they have metamorphosed. How do these references to clarity and madness demonstrate Ransmayr's notion of what it means to read (or translate) literature?

When Cotta climbs the path to Trachila, with giggly high spirits (286, 219), two sentences from the first chapter—"Hier war Naso gegangen. Das war Nasos Weg" 'Here Naso had walked. This was Naso's path' (14, 8)—have changed slightly to become one sentence: "Hier war Naso gegangen; *dies* war Nasos Weg" 'Here Naso had walked. *This* was Naso's path' (286, 219). Students should discuss how substituting "dies" for "das" shows Cotta's identification with Naso and how this hints at the two-syllable name that he recognizes as his own in its echo. Which name is this: Cotta, Naso, Ovid, Christoph (Ransmayr as reader/translator of Ovid)? What is Ransmayr getting at when he writes shortly before this about Naso's freeing his world "von den Menschen und ihren Ordnungen" 'of human beings, of their rules and regulations' (287, 219) through his narrating of every story to its end and through his subsequent disappearance into this world? (Neukirchen and Theisen also address this question.) The final question for discussion circles back to the first close reading: how does this "last world," the one that appears when a story has been narrated to its end, respond to Ovid's concluding remarks about art and the name of the artist in *Metamorphoses*?

This approach can be used on the small scale, as we have done so far, through reciprocal guest lectures in independent German and Latin classes. It can also be expanded into a team-taught course to fit the quarter or even the semester, depending on the number of contemporary novels included (see Kennedy for other possibilities). Students can meet separately according to primary language interest to explore selections from the Latin or the German closely, or they can meet jointly on occasion to discuss broader issues raised by their close readings, with students of German and Latin alternating the responsibility for presenting material. Their own dialogue will show students how each text rewrites the other, thus translating Ovid and Ransmayr across cultures and time.

NOTE

[1] Citations to Ransmayr in German are to *Letzte Welt*; translations are from *Last World*.

NOTES ON CONTRIBUTORS

Susan C. Anderson, professor of German at the University of Oregon, works on German and Austrian literature from the late nineteenth century to the present. Her current research focuses on ideas of difference and identity and on modern reworkings of epic traditions. Recent publications have addressed metaphors of seeing, the figure of the outsider, storytelling and desire, and translation. She is completing a book on notions of the foreign in contemporary German narrative and film.

William S. Anderson is professor of Latin emeritus at the University of California, Berkeley. His publications on Ovid span a scholarly career dedicated to Latin poetry and include the Teubner edition of Ovid's *Metamorphoses* and commentaries on books 1–5 and books 6–10 of *Metamorphoses*. He edited (with Lorina Quartarone) *Approaches to Teaching Vergil's Aeneid* and has completed a student reader of select plays of Terence.

Barbara Weiden Boyd is Henry Winkley Professor of Latin and Greek at Bowdoin College. She specializes in the literature of the late Roman Republic and early principate, especially the poetry of Vergil and Ovid. Her publications include a monograph on Ovid's *Amores* and *Brill's Companion to Ovid* as well as a textbook on selections from Vergil's *Aeneid* for use in high schools and colleges. Her projects include a commentary on Ovid's *Remedia amoris*.

Patrick Cheney is Distinguished Professor of English and Comparative Literature at Pennsylvania State University. His publications include *The Cambridge Companion to Marlowe* and (with Brian J. Striar) the Oxford edition of *The Collected Poems of Christopher Marlowe*. He is coediting (with Philip Hardie) the Renaissance volume in the forthcoming "Oxford History of Classical Reception in English Literature."

Raymond Cormier is visiting professor of French in the Department of English and Modern Languages at Longwood University. His publications on medieval romance include *Three Ovidian Tales of Love: Piramus et Tisbé, Narcisus et Dané, and Philomela et Procné*.

Frederick A. De Armas is Andrew W. Mellon Professor in Humanities and chair of the Department of Romance Languages and Literatures at the University of Chicago. His publications include *Writing for the Eyes in the Spanish Golden Age, Ekphrasis in the Age of Cervantes*, and *Quixotic Frescoes: Cervantes and Italian Renaissance Art*. His collection of essays, "Ovid in the Age of Cervantes," will be published in the summer of 2010.

Jim Ellis is associate professor of English at the University of Calgary. His publications include *Sexuality and Citizenship: Metamorphosis in Elizabethan Erotic Verse* and *Derek Jarman's Angelic Conversations*. His projects include a study of the connections between Renaissance pleasure gardens and the construction of space in epic poetry.

Nikolai Endres is associate professor of world literature at Western Kentucky University. He has published articles on Plato, Petronius, Gustave Flaubert, Walter Pater, Oscar Wilde, John Addington Symonds, Edward Carpenter, André Gide, E. M. Forster,

F. Scott Fitzgerald, Mary Renault, Gore Vidal, Patricia Nell Warren, and others. His next project is a study of platonic love as a homoerotic signifier in gay novels.

Cora Fox is assistant professor of English at Arizona State University. She is the author of *Ovid and the Politics of Emotion in Elizabethan England* (2009) and has published on how Ovidianism shapes late Elizabethan English literature and culture. Her current projects include a study of how classicism accomplishes cultural work in Renaissance popular culture.

Jamie C. Fumo is associate professor of English at McGill University. She has published articles on Chaucer, fifteenth-century Scottish and English poetry, and medieval Ovidianism in *Chaucer Review*, *Studies in Philology*, *Neophilologus*, *Viator*, *Mediaevalia* and various anthologies. Her book on the figure of Apollo in medieval culture, "The Legacy of Apollo: Antiquity, Authority, and Chaucerian Poetics," is forthcoming with the University of Toronto Press.

Judith P. Hallett is professor of classics in the College of Arts and Humanities at the University of Maryland, College Park. Her publications include *Fathers and Daughters in Roman Society: Women and the Elite Family*; *Compromising Traditions: The Personal Voice in Classical Scholarship* (with Thomas van Nortwick); and *Roman Sexualities* (with Marilyn B. Skinner). Her projects include a biography of Fulvia and a college-level Latin textbook of writings by and about Roman women.

R. W. Hanning is professor of English and comparative literature emeritus at Columbia University. He has published widely on medieval and Renaissance literature. He was invited to deliver the thirteenth Leonard Hastings Schoff Memorial Lectures at Columbia University in 2005; the lectures will be published in 2010 as *Serious Play: Desire and Authority in the Poetry of Ovid, Chaucer, and Ariosto*. He is a fellow of the Medieval Academy of America.

Ronald W. Harris is a member of the English department at the University of Wisconsin, Madison. He teaches classes on Ovid, the relations between classical and modern literature, Renaissance drama, technical writing, and composition. He is writing a book on the intersections of kinship and language in Livy and other Augustan writers.

Ralph Hexter is president of Hampshire College and professor of classics and comparative literature emeritus from the University of California, Berkeley. He is the author of *Ovid and Medieval Schooling: Studies in Medieval School Commentaries on Ovid's* Ars Amatoria, Epistulae ex Ponto, *and* Epistulae heroidum. He edited (with Daniel Selden) *Innovations of Antiquity*. His interests in the reception of classical literature span the medieval and modern periods.

Samuel Huskey is chair of the Department of Classics and Letters and Joseph Paxton Presidential Professor of Classics and Letters at the University of Oklahoma. He has published articles on Ovid's *Tristia* in *Arethusa*, *Classical Journal*, *Vergilius*, and *Philologus*. His projects include a critical edition of Ovid's *Ibis*, an edition of previously unpublished scholia to books 1–3 of Lucan's *Bellum civile*, and a translation of Boccaccio's Latin poetry.

Mary Jaeger is professor of classics at the University of Oregon. Her books include *Livy's Written Rome* and *Archimedes and the Roman Imagination*. She is working on a textbook of selections from Livy and a study of literary representations of food.

Phyllis Katz is senior lecturer in classics at Dartmouth College. She is the coauthor (with Charbra Adams Jestin) of *Ovid:* Amores, Metamorphoses *Selections*. Her other publications focus on Ovid, medieval literature, and Ovid's reception in later periods. She is working (with Cecilia Gaposhkin) on the translation of Latin manuscripts of two lives of Louis IX of France.

Sean Keilen is associate professor of English at the College of William and Mary. He is the author of *Vulgar Eloquence: On the Renaissance Invention of English Literature* and editor (with Leonard Barkan and Bradin Cormack) of *The Forms of Renaissance Thought: New Essays on Literature and Culture*. He was awarded a Guggenheim Fellowship for 2008–09.

Alison Keith is professor of classics and women's studies at the University of Toronto. Her publications include *The Play of Fictions: Studies in Ovid's* Metamorphoses, *Book II*; *Engendering Rome: Women in Latin Epic*; and (with Stephen Rupp) *Metamorphosis: The Changing Face of Ovid in Medieval and Early Modern Europe*. Her projects include a commentary on book 4 of Ovid's *Metamorphoses*.

Peter E. Knox is professor of classics at the University of Colorado. He is the author of *Ovid's* Metamorphoses *and the Traditions of Augustan Poetry* as well as a commentary on selected *Heroides*. He edited *Oxford Readings in Ovid* and *A Companion to Ovid*.

Scott Maisano is assistant professor in the English department at the University of Massachusetts, Boston. His projects include a monograph on Shakespearean romance in the context of the scientific revolution and a minigraph on Shakespeare and primatology. He also recently spoke about Shakespeare after 9/11 on the MLA radio program *What's the Word*?

Christopher M. McDonough is associate professor of classics at Sewanee: The University of the South. His publications include studies of Roman religious rituals and essays on classical influence and reception in works by Shakespeare and Fitzgerald and in contemporary films. His projects include a book on religion in the Roman republic.

Matthew McGowan is assistant professor of classics at Fordham University. He is the author of *Ovid in Exile: Power and Poetic Redress in the* Tristia *and* Epistulae ex Ponto. He has been a fellow at the *Thesaurus Linguae Latinae* and is working on a history of Latin lexicography.

Paul Allen Miller is the Carolina Distinguished Professor of Classics and Comparative Literature at the University of South Carolina. His publications include *Subjecting Verses: Latin Love Elegy and the Emergence of the Real* and *Postmodern Spiritual Practices: The Reception of Plato and the Construction of the Subject in Lacan, Derrida, and Foucault*. He is working on a study of Roman irony.

Frank Palmeri is professor of English at the University of Miami. He is the author of *Satire in Narrative* and *Satire, History, Novel: Narrative Forms, 1665–1815*, as well as the editor of *Humans and Other Animals in Eighteenth-Century British Culture*. He is working on the influence of eighteenth-century conjectural history on the constitution of the social sciences in the nineteenth century.

Wendy Chapman Peek is associate professor of English at Stonehill College. Her publications include articles on masculinity in Western films and on reality television. She is completing a study of Chaucer's *Troilus and Criseyde* and a monograph on masculinity in 1950s Westerns.

Lorina N. Quartarone is the coeditor of the MLA's *Approaches to Teaching Vergil's Aeneid* and the author of "Roman Forests, Vergilian Trees: Our Ambiguous Relationship with Nature," which appears in *Thinking about the Environment: Our Debt to the Classical and Medieval Past*, and "Teaching the *Aeneid* through Ecofeminism." She is working on a book on Margaret Atwood's *Penelopiad*.

Bruce Redford is University Professor and professor of art history and English at Boston University. He is the editor of *The Letters of Samuel Johnson* and the author of *Dilettanti: The Antic and the Antique in Eighteenth-Century England*. His projects include a cultural history of the swagger portrait and an essay on the reception of the classical epistolary tradition.

Madison U. Sowell is professor emeritus of Italian and comparative literature at Brigham Young University and an adjunct professor and member of the Board of Trustees at Southern Virginia University. His publications include *Dante and Ovid: Essays in Intertextuality* and a translation (with Sidney Sondergard) of *The Cabala of Pegasus* by Giordano Bruno. He is working on a study of nineteenth-century Italian ballet libretti.

Goran V. Stanivukovic teaches English Renaissance literature at Saint Mary's University in Halifax, Canada. He has edited *Ovid and the Renaissance Body*, *Prose Fiction and Early Modern Sexualities in England, 1570–1640* (with Constance C. Relihan), *Remapping the Mediterranean World in Early Modern English Writings*, and a critical edition of Emanuel Ford's *Ornatus and Artesia*. He has completed a monograph, *Knights in Arms: Travels in the Eastern Mediterranean and Romances in Early Modern England*.

M. L. Stapleton is Chapman Distinguished Professor of English at Indiana University–Purdue University, Fort Wayne. He is the author of *Thomas Heywood's* Art of Love: *The First Complete English Translation of Ovid's* Ars amatoria; *Fated Sky: The Femina Furens in Shakespeare*; *Admired and Understood: The Poetry of Aphra Behn*; and *Spenser's Ovidian Poetics*. He is the editor of the New Variorum edition of *Julius Caesar* (with Sarah K. Scott).

CONTRIBUTORS AND SURVEY PARTICIPANTS

Susan C. Anderson, *University of Oregon*
William S. Anderson, *University of California, Berkeley*
Beau Boudreaux, *Tulane University*
Betsy Bowden, *Rutgers University*
Patrick Cheney, *Pennsylvania State University*
Raymond Cormier, *Longwood University*
Frederick De Armas, *University of Chicago*
Megan Drinkwater, *Agnes Scott College*
Jim Ellis, *University of Calgary*
Nikolai Endres, *Western Kentucky University*
Owen Ewald, *Seattle Pacific University*
Raymond-Jean Frontain, *University of Central Arkansas*
Jamie C. Fumo, *McGill University*
Evelyn Haller, *Doane College*
Judith P. Hallett, *University of Maryland, College Park*
R. W. Hanning, *Columbia University*
Ronald W. Harris, *University of Wisconsin, Madison*
Martin Helzle, *Case Western Reserve University*
Stephen Hinds, *University of Washington*
Samuel J. Huskey, *University of Oklahoma*
Mary Jaeger, *University of Washington*
Patricia Johnson, *Boston University*
Phyllis Katz, *Dartmouth College*
Sean Keilen, *The College of William and Mary*
Alison Keith, *University of Toronto*
Peter E. Knox, *University of Colorado*
Scott Maisano, *University of Massachusetts, Boston*
Christopher McDonough, *Sewanee: University of the South*
Matthew McGowan, *Fordham University*
Paul Allen Miller, *University of South Carolina*
Ian Moulton, *Arizona State University*
Frank Palmeri, *University of Miami*
Wendy Chapman Peek, *Stonehill College*
Lorina N. Quartarone, *University of Saint Thomas*
Bruce Redford, *Boston University*
Roy Rosenstein, *American University of Paris*
Elizabeth Sauer, *Brock University*
Ruth Scodel, *University of Michigan*
Joseph Solodow, *Southern Connecticut State University*
Madison U. Sowell, *Brigham Young University*
Goran V. Stanivukovic, *Saint Mary's University*
M. L. Stapleton, *Indiana University–Purdue University*
James Tatum, *Dartmouth College*

WORKS CITED

Adams, J. N. *The Latin Sexual Vocabulary*. London: Duckworth, 1982. Print.
Agee, James. *Film Writing and Selected Journalism*. Ed. Michael Sragow. New York: Literary Classics of the United States, 2005. Print.
Allen, Graham. *Intertextuality*. London: Routledge, 2000. Print. New Central Idiom.
Althusser, Louis. *Lenin and Philosophy*. New York: Monthly Review, 1971. Print.
Ambrose, Z. Philip, trans. *Ovid:* Metamorphoses. Newburyport: Focus, 2004. Print.
Amielle, Ghislaine. *Recherches sur des traductions françaises des* Métamorphoses *d'Ovide, illustrées et publiées en France à la fin du XVe siècle et au XVIe siècle*. Paris: Touzot, 1989. Print. Caesarodunum, Textes et Images de L'antiquité.
Anderson, William S., ed. *Ovid's* Metamorphoses, *Books 1–5*. Norman: U of Oklahoma P, 1997. Print.
———, ed. *Ovid's* Metamorphoses, *Books 6–10*. Norman: U of Oklahoma P, 1972. Print.
———, ed. *P. Ovidii Nasonis Metamorphoses*. Stuttgart: Teubner, 1977. Print.
Antoninus Liberalis. *The Metamorphoses of Antoninus Liberalis*. Trans. F. Celoria. London: Routledge, 1992. Print.
Apollodorus. *The Library*. Ed. and trans. James G. Frazer. Vol. 1. Cambridge: Harvard UP, 1921. Print. Loeb Classical Lib.
Apollonius. *Apollonii Rhodii Argonautica*. Ed. H. Fränkel. Oxford: Oxford UP, 1961. Print.
Ariosto, Ludovico. *Orlando furioso*. Ed. Emilo Bigi. 2 vols. Milano: Rusconi, 1982. Print.
Aristotle. *Politica*. Ed. W. D. Ross. Oxford: Clarendon, 1957. Print.
Armstrong, Rebecca. *Ovid and His Love Poetry*. London: Duckworth, 2005. Print.
Auerbach, Erich. *Mimesis*. Trans. Willard R. Trask. Princeton: Princeton UP, 1968. Print.
Augustine. *The City of God*. Trans. Marcus Dodds. Grand Rapids: Eerdmans, 1956. Print. Vol. 2 of *The Nicene and Post-Nicene Fathers*. Philip Schaff, gen. ed.
Baldini, Umberto. Primavera: *The Restoration of Botticelli's Masterpiece*. New York: Abrams, 1986. Print.
Barchiesi, Alessandro. "Future Reflexive: Two Modes of Allusion and Ovid's *Heroides*." *Harvard Studies in Classical Philology* 95 (1993): 333–65. Print.
———. *The Poet and the Prince: Ovid and Augustan Discourse*. Berkeley: U of California P, 1997. Print. Trans. of *Il poeta e il principe: Ovidio e il discorso Augusteo*. Rome: Laterza, 1994.
———. *Speaking Volumes: Narrative and Intertext in Ovid and Other Latin Poets*. London: Duckworth, 2001. Print.
Barkan, Leonard. *The Gods Made Flesh: Metamorphosis and the Pursuit of Paganism*. New Haven: Yale UP, 1986. Print.

WORKS CITED

———. *Satyr Square: A Year, A Life in Rome*. New York: Farrar, 2006. Print.
Barnard, Mary E. *The Myth of Apollo and Daphne from Ovid to Quevedo: Love, Agon, and the Grotesque*. Durham: Duke UP, 1987. Print.
Barolsky, Paul. "As in Ovid, So in Renaissance Art." *Renaissance Quarterly* 51.2 (1998): 451–74. Print.
Barsby, John, ed. *Ovid: Amores, Book 1*. Oxford: Oxford UP, 1973. Print.
Barthes, Roland. *Mythologies*. Comp. and trans. Annette Lavers. New York: Hill, 1972. Print.
Bassnett, Susan. *Comparative Literature: A Critical Introduction*. Oxford: Blackwell, 1993. Print.
Bate, Jonathan. Introduction. Bate, *Shakespeare* 1–121.
———. *Shakespeare and Ovid*. Oxford: Clarendon, 1993. Print.
Bean, John C. *Engaging Ideas: The Professor's Guide to Integrating Writing, Critical Thinking, and Active Learning in the Classroom*. San Francisco: Jossey-Bass, 2001. Print.
Beardsley, Theodore S. *Hispano-Classical Translations Printed between 1482 and 1699*. Pittsburgh: Duquesne UP, 1970. Print.
Benoît de Sainte-Maure. *Le roman de Troie*. Ed. and trans. Emmanuèle Baumgartner and Françoise Vielliard. Paris: Livre de Poche, 1998. Print. Lettres Gothiques.
Bernini, Gian Lorenzo. *Apollo and Daphne*. 1622–25. Marble. Borghese Gallery, Rome.
Bickerman, Elias J. *Chronology of the Ancient World*. 2nd ed. Ithaca: Cornell UP, 1980. Print.
Binns, J. W., ed. *Ovid*. London: Routledge, 1973. Print.
Blumenfeld-Kosinski, Renate. *Reading Myth: Classical Mythology and Its Interpretations in Medieval French Literature*. Stanford: Stanford UP, 1997. Print.
Boedeker, Deborah. "Becoming Medea: Assimilation in Euripides." Clauss and Johnston 127–48.
Boer, Cornelis de. Introduction. *Ovide moralisé* [1966] 3: 3–7.
Bömer, Franz, ed. *P. Ovidius Naso: Metamorphosen*. 7 vols. Heidelberg: Winter, 1969–86. Print.
Booth, J., ed. *Ovid: Amores II*. Warminster: Aris, 1991. Print.
Borris, Kenneth, ed. *Same-Sex Desire in the English Renaissance: A Sourcebook of Texts, 1470–1650*. New York: Routledge, 2004. Print.
Boswell, Jeanetta. *Past Ruined Ilion—: A Bibliography of English and American Literature Based on Greco-Roman Mythology*. Metuchen: Scarecrow, 1982. Print.
Bowers, Fredson, ed. *The Complete Works of Christopher Marlowe*. 2nd ed. 2 vols. Cambridge: Cambridge UP, 1981. Print.
———. "The Early Editions of Marlowe's *Ovid's Elegies*." *Studies in Bibliography* 25 (1972): 149–72. Print.
Boyd, Barbara Weiden. "The *Amores*: The Invention of Ovid." Boyd, *Brill's Companion* 91–116.
———, ed. *Brill's Companion to Ovid*. Leiden: Brill, 2002. Print.

———. "'*Celabitur Auctor*': The Crisis of Authority and Narrative Patterning in Ovid, *Fasti* 5." *Phoenix* 54. 1-2 (2000): 64–98. Print.

———. Rev. of *Ovid's* Fasti: *Historical Readings at Its Bimillennium,* ed. G. Herbert-Brown. *Bryn Mawr Classical Review*. Web. 12 Feb. 2009. 2003.09.34.

———. *Ovid's Literary Loves: Influence and Innovation in the* Amores. Ann Arbor: U of Michigan P, 1997. Print.

———. "Two Rivers and the Reader in Ovid, *Metamorphoses* 8." *Transactions of the American Philological Association* 136.1 (2006): 171–206. Print.

Boylan, Jennifer. *She's Not There*. New York: Broadway, 2002. Print.

Boyle, A. J., and R. D. Woodard, trans. *Ovid:* Fasti. 2002. London: Penguin, 2004. Print.

Braden, Gordon, ed. *Sixteenth-Century Poetry: An Annotated Anthology*. Oxford: Blackwell, 2005. Print.

Brantley, Ben. "Theater Review: How Ovid Helps Deal with Loss and Suffering." *New York Times* 10 Oct. 2001. Web. 22 July 2008.

Bray, Alan. "Homosexuality and the Signs of Male Friendship in Elizabethan England." *Queering the Renaissance*. Ed. Jonathan Goldberg. Durham: Duke UP, 1994. 40–61. Print.

Brisson, Luc. *Le mythe de Tirésias: Essai d'analyse structurale*. Leiden: Brill, 1976. Print. Études Préliminaires aux Religions Orientales dans L'empire Romain 55.

———. *Sexual Ambivalence: Androgyny and Hermaphroditism in Graeco-Roman Antiquity*. Berkeley: U of California P, 2002. Print.

Brooke, C. F. Tucker, ed. *The Works of Christopher Marlowe*. Oxford: Clarendon, 1910. Print.

Brown, Georgia. "Marlowe's Poems and Classicism." Cheney, *Cambridge Companion* 106–26.

———. *Redefining Elizabethan Literature*. Cambridge: Cambridge UP, 2004. Print.

Brown, Jonathan. *The Golden Age of Painting in Spain*. New Haven: Yale UP, 1991. Print.

Brown, Sarah Annes. *The Metamorphosis of Ovid: From Chaucer to Ted Hughes*. New York: St. Martin's, 1999. Print.

———. *Ovid: Myth and Metamorphosis*. London: Duckworth, 2005. Print.

Brownlee, Marina Scordilis. *The Severed Word: Ovid's* Heroides *and the Novela Sentimental*. Princeton: Princeton UP, 1990. Print.

Bull, Malcolm. *The Mirror of the Gods: How Renaissance Artists Rediscovered the Pagan Gods*. Oxford: Oxford UP, 2005. Print.

Burke, Edmund. *A Philosophical Enquiry into the Origin of Our Ideas of the Sublime and Beautiful*. Ed. J. T. Boulton. London: Routledge; New York: Columbia UP, 1958. Print.

Burkert, Walter. *Greek Religion*. Trans. John Raffan. Cambridge: Harvard UP, 1985. Print.

Burrow, Colin. "Re-embodying Ovid: Renaissance Afterlives." Hardie, *Cambridge Companion* 301–19.

Bush, Douglas. *Mythology and the Renaissance Tradition in English Poetry*. New York: Norton, 1963. Print.

Butler, Judith. *Undoing Gender*. New York: Routledge, 2004. Print.

Bynum, Caroline Walker. *Metamorphosis and Identity*. New York: Zone, 2001. Print.

Calabrese, Michael. *Chaucer's Ovidian Arts of Love*. Gainesville: UP of Florida, 1994. Print.

Callimachus. *Hymns, Epigrams, Select Fragments*. Trans. Stanley Lombardo and Diane Rayor. Baltimore: Johns Hopkins UP, 1988. Print.

Calvino, Italo. *Cosmicomics*. Trans. William Weaver. San Diego: Harcourt, 1968. Print.

———. "Ovid and Universal Contiguity." *The Uses of Literature: Essays*. Trans. Patrick Creagh. San Diego: Harvest, 1986. 146–61. Print.

Camamis, George. "The Concept of Venus-*Humanitas* in Cervantes and Botticelli." *Cervantes* 8.2 (1988): 183–223. Print.

Cameron, Alan. "The First Edition of Ovid's *Amores*." *Classical Quarterly* 18.2 (1968): 320–33. Print.

Carrai, Stefano. *Dante elegiaco: Una chiave di lettura per la* Vita nova. Firenze: Olschki, 2006. Print.

Carson, Anne. "On Ovid." *Plainwater: Selected Prose and Poetry*. New York: Knopf, 1995. 32. Print.

Carter, Angela. *Nights at the Circus*. New York: Penguin, 1993. Print.

Casali, Sergio. "*Quaerenti Plura Legendum*: On the Necessity of 'Reading More' in Ovid's Exile Poetry." *Ramus* 26 (1997): 80–112. Print.

Catullus. *C. Valerii Catulli Carmina*. Ed. R. A. B. Mynors. Oxford: Clarendon, 1958. Print.

Caughie, Pamela. "Virginia Woolf's Double Discourse." *Discontented Discourses: Feminism / Textual Intervention / Psychoanalysis*. Ed. Marleen S. Barr and Richard Feldstein. Urbana: U of Illinois P, 1989. 41–53. Print.

Caxton, William, trans. *The* Methamorphoses *of Ovid Translated by William Caxton, 1480*. Ed. Douglas Bush. Facsim. ed. New York: Braziller, 1968. Print.

Cervantes, Miguel de. *Don Quixote*. Trans. John Rutherford. New York: Penguin, 2000. Print.

———. *La Galatea*. Ed. Francisco López Estrada and María Teresa López García-Berdoy. Madrid: Cátedra, 1995. Print.

———. *El ingenioso hidalgo don Quijote de la Mancha*. Ed. Luis Murillo. 2 vols. Madrid: Castalia, 1978. Print.

Chaucer, Geoffrey. *The Canterbury Tales*. Trans. Neville Coghill. 1951. Rev. ed. London: Penguin, 2003. Print.

———. *Love Visions*. Trans. Brian Stone. London: Penguin, 1983. Print.

Cheney, Patrick, ed. *The Cambridge Companion to Christopher Marlowe*. Cambridge: Cambridge UP, 2004. Print.

———. Introduction. Cheney and De Armas 1–23.

———. *Marlowe's Counterfeit Profession: Ovid, Spenser, Counter-nationhood*. Toronto: U of Toronto P, 1997. Print.

Cheney, Patrick, and Frederick A. De Armas, eds. *European Literary Careers: The Author from Antiquity to the Renaissance*. Toronto: U of Toronto P, 2002. Print.

Christensen, Peter G. "The Metamorphosis of Ovid in Christoph Ransmayr's *The Last World.*" *Classical and Modern Literature: A Quarterly* 12.2 (1992): 139–51. Print.

Christine de Pisan. *Le livre de la mutacion de fortune*. Ed. S. Solente. Paris: Picard, 1959. Print.

Churchyard, Thomas, trans. *The Thre First Bookes of Ouid De Tristibus, Translated into Englishe*. London: Marshe, 1572. Print.

Chwalek, Burkard. *Die Verwandlung des Exils in die elegische Welt. Studien zu den Tristia und Epistulae ex Ponto Ovids*. Frankfurt: Lang, 1996. Print.

Cicero. *De natura deorum [On the Nature of the Gods]; Academica*. Trans. H. Rackham. Cambridge: Harvard UP, 1933. Print. Loeb Classical Lib.

Claassen, Jo-Marie. *Displaced Persons: Literature of Exile from Cicero to Boethius*. Madison: U of Wisconsin P, 1999. Print.

———. "Meter and Emotion in Ovid's Exilic Poetry." *Classical World* 82.5 (1989): 351–65. Print.

———. "Ovid's Poetic Pontus." *Papers of the Leeds International Latin Seminar* 6 (1990): 65–94. Print.

Clausen, Wendell, ed. *Virgil*: Eclogues. Oxford: Oxford UP, 1994. Print.

Clauss, James J., and Sarah Iles Johnston, eds. *Medea: Essays on Medea in Myth, Literature, Philosophy, and Art*. Princeton: Princeton UP, 1997. Print.

Colapinto, John. *As Nature Made Him: The Boy Who Was Raised as a Girl*. New York: Harper, 2001. Print.

Conte, Gian Biagio. *Latin Literature: A History*. Trans. J. B. Solodow. Rev. ed. D. Fowler and G. W. Most. Baltimore: Johns Hopkins UP, 1994. Print.

———. *The Rhetoric of Imitation: Genre and Poetic Memory in Virgil and Other Latin Poets*. Ed. and trans. Charles Segal. Ithaca: Cornell UP, 1986. Print.

Coolidge, John S. "Great Things and Small: The Virgilian Progression." *Comparative Literature* 17.1 (1965): 1–23. Print.

Copeland, Rita. *Rhetoric, Hermeneutics, and Translation in the Middle Ages*. Cambridge: Cambridge UP, 1991. Print.

Cormier, Raymond J. "Tisbé, Dané, and Procné: Three Old French/Ovidian Heroines in Quest of Personal Freedom." *Susquehanna University Studies (Sexuality, the Female Gaze, and the Arts Conference)*. Ed. R. Dotterer and S. Bowers. Selinsgrove: Susquehanna UP, 1992. 102–14. Print.

Correggio. *Jupiter and Io*. 1530. Oil on canvas. Kunsthistorisches Museum, Vienna.

Dante Alighieri. *Il convivio*. Ed. Maria Simonelli. Bologna: Pàtron, 1966. Print.

———. *The Divine Comedy*. Trans. Charles S. Singleton. 3 vols. Princeton: Princeton UP, 1970–75. Print.

———. "Epistola III." *Tutte le opere*. Ed. L. Blasucci. Florence: Le Monnier, 1989. *Bibliotheca Augustana*. Web. 28 July 2008.

———. *Vulgari. Literary Criticism of Dante Alighieri*. Trans. Robert S. Haller. Lincoln: U of Nebraska P, 1973. 3–60. Print.

Darwin, Charles. *The Descent of Man* and *Selection in Relation to Sex*. 1871. Princeton: Princeton UP, 1981. Print.

———. *The Expression of the Emotions in Man and Animals.* 1872. Oxford: Oxford UP, 1998. Print.

———. *The Origin of Species.* 1859. Cambridge: Harvard UP, 2001. Print.

Daube, David. "No Kissing, or Else. . . ." *The Classical Tradition: Literary and Historical Studies in Honor of Harry Caplan.* Ed. Luitpold Wallach. Ithaca: Cornell UP, 1966. 222–31. Print.

Davis, Gregson. *The Death of Procris: "Amor" and the Hunt in Ovid's* Metamorphoses. Roma: Edizioni dell'Ateneo, 1983. Print.

Davis, P. J. "Ovid's *Amores*: A Political Reading." *Classical Philology* 94.4 (1999): 431–49. Print.

De Armas, Frederick A. "Ekphrasis and Eros in *La Galatea*: The Case of the Blushing Nymphs." *Cervantes for the Twenty-First Century: Studies in Honor of Edward Dudley.* Ed. Francisco La Rubia Prado. Newark: Cuesta, 2000. 33–48. Print.

De Lauretis, Teresa. *Alice Doesn't: Feminism, Semiotics, Cinema.* Bloomington: Indiana UP, 1984. Print.

De Luce, Judith. " 'O for a Thousand Tongues to Sing': A Footnote on Metamorphoses, Silence, and Power." *Woman's Power, Man's Game: Essays on Classical Antiquity in Honor of Joy K. King.* Ed. Mary De Forest. Wauconda: Bolchazy-Carducci, 1993. 305–21. Print.

Demats, Paule. *Fabula: Trois études de mythographie antique et médiévale.* Geneva: Droz, 1973. Print.

Dempsey, Charles. *The Portrayal of Love: Botticelli's "Primavera" and Humanist Culture at the Time of Lorenzo the Magnificent.* Princeton: Princeton UP, 1992. Print.

Desmond, Marilynn. *Ovid's Art and the Wife of Bath: The Ethics of Erotic Violence.* Ithaca: Cornell UP, 2006. Print.

Dewar, M. "*Siquid habent veri vatum praesagia*: Ovid in the 1st–5th Centuries A.D." Boyd, *Brill's Companion* 383–412.

Dickinson, R. J. "The *Tristia*: Poetry in Exile." *Ovid.* Ed. J. W. Binns. London: Routledge, 1973. 154–90. Print.

Dimmick, Jeremy. "Ovid in the Middle Ages: Authority and Poetry." Hardie, *Cambridge Companion* 264–87.

Dinesen, Isak. *Last Tales.* New York: Random, 1957. Print.

Donno, Elizabeth Story. Preface. *Elizabethan Minor Epics.* Ed. Donno. New York: Columbia UP, 1963. 1–20. Print.

Dougherty, Carol. *The Poetics of Colonization: From City to Text in Archaic Greece.* Oxford: Oxford UP, 1988. Print.

Douglas, Mary. *Purity and Danger: An Analysis of the Concepts of Pollution and Taboo.* New York: Routledge, 2005. Print.

Dryden, John. "The Preface to *Ovid's Epistles, Translated by Several Hands.*" *"Of Dramatic Poesy" and Other Critical Essays.* Ed. George Watson. London: Dent, 1962. 262–73. Print.

DuBois, Page. *Sowing the Body: Psychoanalysis and Ancient Representations of Women.* Chicago: U of Chicago P, 1988. Print.

———. *Trojan Horses: Saving the Classics from Conservatives*. New York: New York UP, 2001. Print.

Dudley, Edward. "Goddess on the Edge: The Galatea Agenda in Raphael, Garcilaso and Cervantes." *Calíope* 1.1-2 (1995): 27–45. Print.

Duffy, Eamon. *The Stripping of the Altars: Traditional Religion in England, 1400–1580*. 2nd ed. New Haven: Yale UP, 2005. Print.

DuRocher, Richard. *Milton and Ovid*. Ithaca: Cornell UP, 1985. Print.

Edmunds, Lowell. *Intertextuality and the Reading of Roman Poetry*. Baltimore: Johns Hopkins UP, 2001. Print.

Edwards, Thomas. *"Cephalus and Procris" and "Narcissus."* Ed. W. E. Buckley. London: Roxburghe Club, 1882. Print.

Elbow, Peter. *Writing without Teachers*. New York: Oxford UP, 1973. Print.

Eliot, T. S. *The Waste Land*. Ed. Michael North. New York: Norton, 2001. Print.

———. "What Is a Classic?" *On Poetry and Poets*. London: Faber, 1957. 53–71. Print.

Ellis, Jim. *Sexuality and Citizenship: Metamorphosis in Elizabethan Erotic Verse*. Toronto: U of Toronto P, 2003. Print.

Enterline, Lynn. *The Rhetoric of the Body from Ovid to Shakespeare*. Cambridge: Cambridge UP, 2000. Print.

Epple, Thomas. *Christoph Ransmayr,* Die letzte Welt*: Interpretation*. Munich: Oldenbourg, 1992. Print.

Eugenides, Jeffrey. *Middlesex*. New York: Farrar, 2002. Print.

Evans, Harry B. *Publica Carmina: Ovid's Books from Exile*. Lincoln: U of Nebraska P, 1983. Print.

Ewans, Michael. *Wagner and Aeschylus:* The Ring *and* The Oresteia. New York: Cambridge UP, 1983. Print.

Fantham, Elaine, ed. *Ovid*: Fasti, *Book IV*. Cambridge: Cambridge UP, 1998. Print.

———. "Ovid's *Fasti*: Politics, History, and Religion." Boyd, *Brill's Companion* 197–233.

———. *Ovid's* Metamorphoses. New York: Oxford UP, 2004. Print.

———. "Recent Readings in Ovid's *Fasti*." *Classical Philology* 90.4 (1995): 367–78. Print.

Farrell, Joseph. "Greek Lives and Roman Careers in the Classical *Vita* Tradition." Cheney and De Armas 24–46.

———. "*Metamorphoses*: A Play by Mary Zimmerman." *American Journal of Philology* 123 (2002): 623–27. Print.

Fausto-Sterling, Anne. "The Five Sexes Revisited." *Gender through the Prism of Difference*. Ed. Maxine Baca Zinn, Pierrette Hondagneu-Sotelo, and Michael A. Messner. New York: Oxford UP, 2005. 13–18. Print.

Feeney, Denis. *The Gods in Epic: Poets and Critics of the Classical Tradition*. Oxford: Clarendon, 1991. Print.

———. *Literature and Religion at Rome: Cultures, Contexts, and Beliefs*. Cambridge: Cambridge UP, 1998. Print.

Feimer, Joel N. "Medea in Ovid's *Metamorphoses* and the *Ovide moralisé*: Translation as Transmission." *Florilegium* 8 (1986): 40–55. Print.

Feldherr, Andrew. "Metamorphosis in the *Metamorphoses*." Hardie, *Cambridge Companion* 163–79.

The flores of Ouide de arte amandi with theyr englysshe afore them: and two alphabete tablys. London: Wynkyn de Worde, 1513. Print.

Forbis, Elizabeth Peyton. "Voice and Voicelessness in Ovid's *Metamorphoses, Tristia* and *Epistulae ex Ponto*." MA thesis. U of North Carolina, Chapel Hill, 1985. Print.

Forey, Madeleine. Introduction. Golding, *Ovid's* Metamorphoses [ed. Forey] xi–xxxv.

Fowler, William Warde. *The Roman Festivals of the Period of the Republic*. London: Macmillan, 1899. Print.

Fraenkel, Hermann. *Ovid: A Poet between Two Worlds*. Berkeley: U of California P, 1945. Print.

Frazer, James G., ed. and trans. *Publii Ovidii Nasonis Fastorum Libri Sex*. 5 vols. London: Macmillan, 1929. Print.

Fredrick, David, ed. *The Roman Gaze*. Baltimore: Johns Hopkins UP, 2002. Print.

Frenzel, Elisabeth. *Stoffe der Weltliteratur: Ein Lexikon dichtungsgeschichtlicher Längsschnitte*. 8th ed. Stuttgart: Kröner, 1992. Print.

Freud, Sigmund. "Some Psychological Consequences of the Anatomical Distinction between the Sexes." 1925. *Sexuality and the Psychology of Love*. Ed. Philip Reiff. New York: Collier, 1963. 183–93. Print.

Fyler, John. *Chaucer and Ovid*. New Haven: Yale UP, 1979. Print.

Gaisser, J. "Threads in the Labyrinth: Competing Views and Voices in Catullus 64." *American Journal of Philology* 116.4 (1995): 579–616. Print.

Gaius. *The Institutes of Gaius*. Trans. W. M. Gordon and O. F. Robinson. Ithaca: Cornell UP, 1988. Print.

Galasso, Luigi, Guido Paduano, and Alessandro Perutelli, eds. *Le metamorfosi*. Turin: Einaudi, 2000. Print. Ovidio Opere 2.

Galinsky, Karl. *Augustan Culture*. Princeton: Princeton UP, 1995. Print.

———. *Ovid's* Metamorphoses: *An Introduction to the Basic Aspects*. Berkeley: U of California P, 1975. Print.

Gantz, T. *Early Greek Myth*. 2 vols. Baltimore: Johns Hopkins UP, 1993. Print.

Gehlhoff, Esther Felicitas. *Wirklichkeit hat ihren eigenen Ort: Lesarten und Aspekte zum Verständnis des Romans* Die letzte Welt *von Christoph Ransmayr*. Paderborn: Schöningh, 1999. Print.

Gentilcore, Roxanne. "The Landscape of Desire: The Tale of Pomona and Vertumnus in Ovid's *Metamorphoses*." *Phoenix* 49.2 (1995): 110–20. Print.

Gibson, Roy K., ed. *Ovid:* Ars amatoria, *Book 3*. Cambridge: Cambridge UP, 2003. Print.

Gibson, Roy, Steven Green, and Alison Sharrock, eds. *The Art of Love: Bimillennial Essays on Ovid's* Ars amatoria *and* Remedia amoris. Oxford: Oxford UP, 2006. Print.

Gibson, Roy K., and C. S. Kraus, eds. *The Classical Commentary: History, Practices, Theory*. Leiden: Brill, 2002. Print.

Gilbert, Scott. *Developmental Biology*. Sunderland: Sinauer, 2003. Print.

Gilde, Helen C. "Spenser's Hellenore and Some Ovidian Associations." *Comparative Literature* 23.3 (1971): 233–39. Print.

Gill, Roma. "Marlowe and the Art of Translation." *"A Poet and a Filthy Play-Maker": New Essays on Christopher Marlowe*. Ed. Kenneth Friedenreich, Gill, and Constance B. Kuriyama. New York: AMS, 1988. 327–41. Print.

———, ed. *Poems, Translations, and "Dido, Queen of Carthage."* Oxford: Clarendon, 1987. Print. Vol. 1 of *The Complete Works of Christopher Marlowe*. Ed. Gill. 5 vols. 1987–98.

Gill, Roma, and Robert Krueger. "The Early Editions of Marlowe's Elegies and Davies's Epigrams: Sequence and Authority." *Library* 5th ser. 26 (1971): 243–49. Print.

Glare, P. G. W. *Oxford Latin Dictionary*. Oxford: Clarendon, 1982. Print.

Glauche, Günter. *Schullektüre im Mittelalter. Entstehung und Wandlungen des Lektürekanons bis 1200 nach den Quellen dargestellt*. Munich: Arbeo-Gesellschaft, 1970. Print.

Golding, Arthur. "Epistle of 1567." Golding, *Ovid's* Metamorphoses [ed. Nims] 405–22.

———. "Epistle to Leicester." Golding, *Ovid's* Metamorphoses [ed. Forey] 5–22.

———, trans. *The .xv. Bookes of P. Ovidius Naso, entytuled, Metamorphosis*. 1567. *"Shakespeare's Ovid": Arthur Golding's Translation of the* Metamorphoses. Ed. W. H. D. Rouse. Carbondale: Southern Illinois UP, 1961. Print.

———. "Preface to the Reader." Golding, *Ovid's* Metamorphoses [ed. Forey] 23–29.

———. "Preface to the Reader." Golding, *Ovid's* Metamorphoses [ed. Nims] 423–29.

———, trans. *Ovid's* Metamorphoses. Ed. John Frederick Nims. Philadelphia: Dry, 2000. Print.

———, trans. *Ovid's* Metamorphoses. Ed. Madeleine Forey. Baltimore: Johns Hopkins UP, 2002. Print.

Gombrich, E. H. *Symbolic Images: Studies in the Art of the Renaissance II*. Chicago: U of Chicago P, 1972. Print.

Goold, G. P. "The Causes of Ovid's Exile." *Illinois Classical Studies* 8 (1983): 94–105. Print.

Gooren, Louis. "The Biology of Human Psychosexual Determination." *Hormones and Behavior* 50.4 (2006): 589–601. Print.

Graf, Fritz. "Medea, the Enchantress from Afar: Remarks on a Well-Known Myth." Clauss and Johnston 21–43.

Grafton, Anthony. *Defenders of the Text*. Cambridge: Harvard UP, 1991. Print.

Grasmück, Ernst Ludwig. *Exilium. Untersuchungen zur Verbannung in der Antike*. Paderborn: Görres-Gesellschaft, 1978. Print.

Green, C. M. C. "Varro's Three Theologies and Their Influence on the *Fasti*." Herbert-Brown 74–99.

Green, Peter. "*Carmen et error*: πρόφασις and αἰτία in the Matter of Ovid's Exile." *Classical Antiquity* 1.2 (1982): 202–20. Print.

———, trans. *Ovid: The Erotic Poems*. London: Penguin, 1983. Print.

———, trans. *Ovid: The Poems of Exile:* Tristia *and* Black Sea Letters. Berkeley: U of California P, 2005. Print.

———, trans. *The Poems of Catullus: A Bilingual Edition*. Berkeley: U of California P, 2005. Print.

Greene, Thomas M. *The Light in Troy: Imitation and Discovery in Renaissance Poetry*. New Haven: Yale UP, 1982. Print.

Gregory, Horace, trans. *Ovid: The Metamorphoses*. New York: Viking, 1958; New American Lib., 2001. Print. Signet Classic.

Griffiths, Emma. *Medea*. London: Routledge, 2006. Print.

Guido delle Colonne. *Historia destructionis Troiae*. Trans. Mary Elizabeth Meek. Bloomington: Indiana UP, 1974. Print.

Guthmüller, Bodo. "Lateinische und Volkssprachliche Kommentare zu Ovids *Metamorphosen*." *Der Kommentar in der Renaissance*. Ed. A. Buck and O. Herding. Boppard: Boldt, 1975. 119–39. Print.

Hagstrum, Jean H. *The Sister Arts: The Tradition of Literary Pictorialism and English Poetry from Dryden to Gray*. Chicago: U of Chicago P, 1958. Print.

Hall, Edith, and Fiona Macintosh. *Greek Tragedy and the British Theatre, 1660–1914*. Oxford: Oxford UP, 2005. Print.

Hallett, Judith P. "The Eleven Elegies of the Augustan Poet Sulpicia." *Women Writing Latin in Roman Antiquity, Late Antiquity, and the Early Christian Era*. New York: Routledge, 2002. 45–65. Print. Vol. 1 of *Women Writing Latin: From Roman Antiquity to Early Modern Europe*. Ed. Laurie J. Churchill, Phyllis R. Brown, and Jane E. Jeffrey.

Hamilton, Edith. *Mythology*. New York: New American Lib., 1942. Print.

Hardie, Philip, ed. *The Cambridge Companion to Ovid*. Cambridge: Cambridge UP, 2002. Print.

———. *The Epic Successors of Virgil: A Study in the Dynamics of a Tradition*. Cambridge: Cambridge UP, 1993. Print.

———. Introduction. Hardie, *Cambridge Companion* 1–10.

Hardie, Philip, Alessandro Barchiesi, and Stephen Hinds, eds. *Ovidian Transformations: Essays on Ovid's* Metamorphoses *and Its Reception*. Cambridge: Cambridge Philological Soc., 1999. Print.

Harris, Stephen L., and Gloria Platzner. *Classical Mythology: Images and Insights*. 4th ed. New York: McGraw, 2003. Print.

Harrison, Stephen. "Ovid and Genre: Evolutions of an Elegist." Hardie, *Cambridge Companion* 79–94.

Hartigan, Karelisa V. *Muse on Madison Avenue: Classical Mythology in Contemporary Advertising*. Frankfurt: Lang, 2002. Print.

Hartt, Frederick. *History of Italian Renaissance Art*. Rev. David G. Wilkins. 4th ed. New York: Abrams, 1994. Print.

Haughton, Hugh. "'The Importance of Elsewhere': Mahon and Translation." *The Poetry of Derek Mahon*. Ed. Elmer Kennedy-Andrews. Buckinghamshire: Smythe, 2002. 145–83. Print.

Hawthorne, Nathaniel. A Wonder Book *and* Tanglewood Tales. Ed. Fredson Bowers. Columbus: Ohio State UP, 1972. Print. Vol. 7 of *The Centenary Edition of the Works of Nathaniel Hawthorne*. Ed. William Charvat et al.

Heaney, Seamus. *Crediting Poetry: The Nobel Lecture*. New York: Farrar, 1996. Print.

———. "Exposure." *North*. London: Faber, 1975. 72–73. Print.

———. "The Language of Exile (Derek Walcott)." *Parnassus: Poetry in Review* 8.1 (1979): 5–11. Print.

———. "The Redress of Poetry: An Inaugural Lecture Delivered before the University of Oxford on 24 October 1989." *The Redress of Poetry*. New York: Farrar, 1995. 1–16. Print.

Helgerson, Richard. *Self-Crowned Laureates: Spenser, Milton, Jonson, and the Literary System*. Berkeley: U of California P, 1983. Print.

Herbert-Brown, Geraldine, ed. *Ovid's* Fasti: *Historical Readings at Its Bimillennium*. Oxford: Oxford UP, 2002. Print.

Herescu, N. I., ed. *Ovidiana: Recherches sur Ovid: Publiée à l'occasion du bimillénaire du poète*. Paris: Les Belles Lettres, 1958. Print.

Herodotus. *Herodotus' History*. Ed. H. B. Rosén. Vol. 1. Leipzig: Teubner, 1987. Print.

Hesiod. *Theogony*. Trans. Richard S. Caldwell. Newburyport: Focus, 1987. Print.

Hexter, Ralph J. *Ovid and Medieval Schooling: Studies in Medieval School Commentaries on Ovid's* Ars amatoria, Epistulae ex Ponto, *and* Epistulae heroidum. Munich: Arbeo-Gesellschaft, 1986. Print.

———. "Ovid in the Middle Ages: Exile, Mythographer, and Lover." Boyd, *Brill's Companion* 413–42.

Highet, Gilbert. *The Classical Tradition*. New York: Oxford UP, 1949. Print.

Hill, D. E., ed. and trans. *Ovid:* Metamorphoses. 4 vols. Warminster: Aris, 1985–2000. Print.

Hinds, Stephen. *Allusion and Intertext: Dynamics of Appropriation in Roman Poetry*. Cambridge: Cambridge UP, 1998. Print.

———. "Booking the Return Trip: Ovid and *Tristia* 1." *Proceedings of the Cambridge Philological Society* 31 (1985): 13–32. Print.

———. "Medea in Ovid: Scenes from the Life of an Intertextual Heroine." *Materiali e discussioni per l'analisi dei testi classici* 30 (1993): 9–47. Print.

———. *The Metamorphosis of Persephone: Ovid and the Self-Conscious Muse*. Cambridge: Cambridge UP, 1987. Print.

———. "Ovid." *Oxford Classical Dictionary*. Ed. Simon Hornblower and Anthony Spawforth. 3rd ed. Oxford: Oxford UP, 1996. 1084–87. Print.

Hoffman, Richard. *Ovid and the* Canterbury Tales. Philadelphia: U of Pennsylvania P, 1966. Print.

Hofmann, Michael, and James Lasdun, eds. *After Ovid: New Metamorphoses*. New York: Farrar, 1994. Print.

Hollis, A. S., ed. *Ovid,* Ars amatoria *Book I*. Oxford: Clarendon, 1977. Print.

———, ed. *Ovid,* Metamorphoses: *Book VIII*. Oxford: Clarendon, 1970. Print.

Hopkinson, N., ed. *Ovid,* Metamorphoses: *Book XIII*. Cambridge: Cambridge UP, 2000. Print.

Horace. *Q. Horati Flacci opera*. Ed. E. C. Wickham. Oxford: Clarendon, 1959. Print.

Hughes, Ted. *Tales from Ovid*. New York: Farrar, 1997. Print.

Humphries, Rolfe, trans. *Metamorphoses*. Bloomington: Indiana UP, 1955. Print.

Huskey, Samuel J. "Ovid at the Fall of Troy in *Tristia* 1.3." *Vergilius* 48 (2002): 88–104. Print.

———. "Ovid's Metamorphoses in *Tristia* I, 1." *Studies in Latin Literature and Roman History* 13 (2006): 335–57. Print.

———. "*Quaerenti plura legendum*: Ovid on the Necessity of Reading in *Tristia* 1.1.21–22." *Studies in Latin Literature and Roman History* 12 (2004): 234–49. Print.

Innes, Mary M., trans. *The* Metamorphoses *of Ovid*. London: Penguin, 1955. Print.

Ionesco, Eugène. Rhinoceros *and Other Plays*. Trans. Derek Prouse. New York: Grove, 1960. Print.

Isbell, Harold, trans. *Ovid:* Heroides. London: Penguin, 1990. Print.

Jacobson, Howard. *Ovid's* Heroides. Princeton: Princeton UP, 1974. Print.

Jacoff, Rachel, and Jeffrey Schnapp, eds. *The Poetry of Allusion: Virgil and Ovid in Dante's* Commedia. Stanford: Stanford UP, 1991. Print.

James, Heather. "Ovid and the Question of Politics in Early Modern England." *ELH* 70.2 (2003): 343–73. Print.

———. *Shakespeare's Troy: Drama, Politics, and the Translation of Empire*. Cambridge: Cambridge UP, 1997. Print.

Jestin, Charbra Adams, and Phyllis B. Katz. *Ovid:* Amores, Metamorphoses: *Selections*. 2nd ed. Wauconda: Bolchazy-Carducci, 2000. Print.

Johnson, Barbara. "Apostrophe, Animation, and Abortion." *A World of Difference*. Baltimore: Johns Hopkins UP, 1987. 184–99. Print.

Johnson, W. R. "The Counter-classical Sensibility and Its Critics." *California Studies in Classical Antiquity* 3 (1970): 123–51. Print.

Jonson, Ben. "Masque of Blackness." *Norton Anthology* 1294–1303.

Jung, Marc-René. "*L'Ovide moralisé*: De l'expérience de mes lectures à quelques propositions de lecture actuelle." *Ovide Métamorphosé: Les lecteurs médiévaux d'Ovide*. Ed. Laurence Harf-Lancer. Paris: Presse Sorbonne Nouvelle, 2009. 107–22. Print.

Kafka, Franz. *The Metamorphosis*. Trans. Joachim Neugroschel. *The Norton Anthology of World Masterpieces: The Western Tradition*. 7th ed. Vol. 2. Ed. Sarah Lawall et al. New York: Norton, 1999. 1640–72. Print.

Kahn, Coppélia. *Roman Shakespeare: Warriors, Wounds, and Women*. London: Routledge, 1997. Print.

Katz, Phyllis B. "Shifting Ground: The Metamorphoses of Ovid's Tiresias in Christine de Pisan's *Le Livre de la Mutacion de Fortune* and T. S. Eliot's *The Waste Land*." *Classical and Modern Literature* 26.2 (2006): 161–77. Print.

Kay, Sarah. "Sex and the Sacred: Metamorphosis and Anamorphosis in the *Ovide Moralisé*." Conference on Sex and the Sacred. Dept. of French Studies, U of Manchester. 25 Mar. 2002. Address.

Keith, Alison. *Engendering Rome: Women in Latin Epic*. Cambridge: Cambridge UP, 2000. Print.

———. "Etymological Wordplay in Ovid's 'Pyramus and Thisbe' (*Met*. 4.55–166)." *Classical Quarterly* 51.1 (2001): 309–12. Print.

———. "Ovidian Personae in Statius' *Thebaid*." *Arethusa* 35 (2002): 381–402. Print.

———. "Ovid's Theban Narrative in Statius' *Thebaid*." *Hermathena* 177-78 (2004–05): 181–207. Print.

———. "Versions of Epic Masculinity in Ovid's *Metamorphoses*." *Ovidian Transformations: Essays on Ovid's* Metamorphoses *and Its Reception*. Hardie, Barchiesi, Hinds 214–39.

Keith, Alison, and Stephen Rupp, eds. *Metamorphosis: The Changing Face of Ovid in Medieval and Early Modern Europe*. Toronto: Centre for Reformation and Renaissance Studies, 2007. Print. Essays and Studies 13.

Kennedy, Duncan F. "Recent Receptions of Ovid." Hardie, *Cambridge Companion* 320–35.

Kenney, E. J. "Ovid and the Law." *Yale Classical Studies* 21 (1969): 241–63. Print.

———, ed. *Ovid:* Heroides *XVI–XXI*. Cambridge: Cambridge UP, 1996. Print.

———. Rev. of *Ovid's* Metamorphoses, *Books 6–10*, by W. S. Anderson. *Classical Review* 25 (1975): 33–35. Print.

———. "Ovid." *The Age of Augustus*. Vol. 2, pt. 3 of *The Cambridge History of Classical Literature*. Ed. Kenney and W. V. Clausen. Cambridge: Cambridge UP, 1982. 124–61. Print.

Kiel, Martin. *NEXUS: Postmoderne Mythenbilder—Vexierbilder zwischen Spiel und Erkenntnis: Mit einem Kommentar zu Christoph Ransmayrs* Die letzte Welt. Frankfurt am Main: Lang, 1996. Print.

Kiesel, Helmuth, and Georg Wöhrle, eds. *"Keinen bleibt seine Gestalt":* Ovids Metamorphoses *und Christoph Ransmayrs* Letzte Welt: *Essays zu einem inderdisziplinären Kolloquium*. Bamberg: Otto-Friedrich-Universität, Arbeitsbereich der Neueren Deutschen Literaturwissenschaft, 1990. Print. Fußnoten zur neueren deutschen Literatur 20.

Kleinhenz, Christopher, ed. *Medieval Italy: An Encyclopedia*. 2 vols. New York: Routledge, 2004. Print.

Knox, Peter E. "Ariadne on the Rocks: Influences on Ovid, *Her*. 10." *Style and Tradition: Studies in Honor of Wendell Clausen*. Ed. Knox and C. Foss. Stuttgart: Teubner, 1998. 72–83. Print.

———, ed. *Companion to Ovid*. Malden: Wiley-Blackwell, 2009. Print.

———, ed. *Ovid:* Heroides. *Select Epistles*. Cambridge: Cambridge UP, 1995. Print.

———. *Ovid's* Metamorphoses *and the Traditions of Augustan Poetry*. Cambridge: Cambridge Philological Soc., 1986. Print. Proceedings of the Cambridge Philological Society Supplementary Volume 11.

———, ed. *Oxford Readings in Ovid*. Oxford: Oxford UP, 2006. Print.

———. "The Poet and the Second Prince: Ovid in the Age of Tiberius." *Memoirs of the American Academy in Rome* 49 (2004): 1–20. Print.

———. "Savagery in the *Aeneid* and Virgil's Ancient Commentators." *Classical Journal* 92.3 (1996–97): 225–33. Print.

Kolodny, Annette. *The Lay of the Land: Metaphor as Experience and History in American Life and Letters*. Chapel Hill: U of North Carolina P, 1975. Print.

Kossman, Nina, ed. *Gods and Mortals: Modern Poems on Classical Myths*. Oxford: Oxford UP, 2001. Print.

Kuskin, William. *Symbolic Caxton: Literary Culture and Print Capitalism*. Notre Dame: U of Notre Dame P, 2007. Print.

Lafaye, Georges. *Les Métamorphoses d'Ovide et leurs modèles grecs*. 1904. Hildesheim: Olms, 1971. Print.

LaFleur, Richard A. *Love and Transformation: An Ovid Reader*. 2nd ed. Upper Saddle River: Prentice, 1999. Print.

Laird, Andrew. "Sounding Out Ecphrasis: Art and Text in Catullus 64." *Journal of Roman Studies* 83 (1993): 18–30. Print.

La Mettrie, Julien Offray de. *Man a Machine*. 1747. Trans. Richard A. Watson and Maya Rybalka. Indianapolis: Hackett, 1994. Print.

Leach, Eleanor Winsor. "Ekphrasis and the Theme of Artistic Failure in Ovid's *Metamorphoses*." *Ramus* 3 (1974): 102–42. Print.

Lee, A. G., ed. Metamorphoses *Book I*. 1953. Bristol: Bristol Classical P, 1984. Print.

Lee, Guy, trans. *Ovid:* Amores. New York: Viking, 1968. Print.

Levertov, Denise. "A Tree Telling of Orpheus." Kossman 111–15.

Levi d'Ancona, Mirella. *Botticelli's "Primavera": A Botanical Interpretation Including Astrology, Alchemy and the Medici*. Florence: Olschki, 1983. Print.

Levine, Robert. "Exploiting Ovid: Medieval Allegorizations of the *Metamorphoses* Source." *Medioevo Romanzo* 14.2 (1989): 197–213. Print.

Linderski, Jerzy. "Roman Religion and Livy." *Roman Questions: Selected Papers*. Stuttgart: Steiner, 1995. 608–19. Print. Rpt. of *Livius: Aspekte seines Werke*. Ed. Wolfgang Schuller. Konstanz: Universitätsverlag Konstanz, 1993. 53–64.

Liveley, Genevieve. *Ovid: Love Songs*. London: Duckworth, 2005. Print.

———. "Reading Resistance in Ovid's *Metamorphoses*." Hardie, Barchiesi, and Hinds 197–213.

———. "Tiresias/Teresa: A 'Man-Made-Woman' in Ovid's *Metamorphoses* 3.318–38." *Helios* 30.2 (2003): 147–62. Print.

Llewellyn, Nigel. "Illustrating Ovid." Martindale, *Ovid Renewed* 151–66.

Lodge, Thomas. "Scillaes Metamorphosis: Enterlaced with the Unfortunate Love of Glaucus." Donno, *Elizabethan Minor Epics* 21–47.

Longley, Michael. "A Flowering." *After Ovid: New Metamorphoses*. Hofmann and Lasdun 59.

Lord, Carla. "Three Manuscripts of the *Ovide moralisé*." *Art Bulletin* 57 (1975): 161–75. Print.

Luck, Georg, ed. *Ovid:* Tristia. 2 vol. Heidelberg: Winter, 1967–68. Print.

Lucretius. *De rerum natura*. Trans. W. H. D. Rouse. 2nd rev. ed. Martin F. Smith. Cambridge: Harvard UP, 1982. Print. Loeb Classical Lib.

Lyne, Raphael. "Ovid in English Translation." Hardie, *Cambridge Companion* 249–63.

———. *Ovid's Changing Worlds: English Metamorphoses, 1567–1632*. Oxford: Oxford UP, 2001. Print.

Mack, Sara. *Ovid*. New Haven: Yale UP, 1988. Print.

MacLure, Millar, ed. *The Poems: Christopher Marlowe*. London: Methuen, 1968. Print. The Revels Plays.

Mahon, Derek. "Ovid in Tomis." *The Hunt by Night*. Winston-Salem: Wake Forest UP, 1983. 37–42. Print.

Malouf, David. *An Imaginary Life*. New York: Braziller, 1978. Print.

Mandelbaum, Allen, trans. *The Metamorphoses of Ovid: A New Verse Translation*. San Diego: Harcourt, 1993. Print.

Mandelstam, Osip Emilevich. "Tristia." *Complete Poetry of Osip Emilevich Mandelstam*. Trans. Burton Raffel and Alla Burago. Albany: State U of New York P, 1973. 102–03. Print.

Mansion, Colard, trans. *Metamorphoses d'Ovide moralisées*. Paris: Le Noir, 1523. Print. Rpt. of *La bible des poètes*. 1484. Paris: Vérard, 1507.

Marlowe, Christopher. "Hero and Leander." Donno 48–69.

———. "Hero and Leander." *The Oxford Book of Sixteenth Century Verse*. Ed. Emrys Jones. Oxford: Oxford UP, 1992. 488–506. Print.

———. *Ovid's Elegies*. *The Collected Poems of Christopher Marlowe*. Ed. Patrick Cheney and Brian J. Striar. New York: Oxford UP, 2006. 33–136. Print.

Marston, John. "The Metamorphosis of Pigmalions Image." Donno 244–52.

Martin, Charles, trans. *Ovid: Metamorphoses*. New York: Norton, 2004. Print.

Martin, Christopher, ed. *Ovid in English*. London: Penguin, 1998. Print.

———. *Policy in Love: Lyric and Public in Ovid, Petrarch, and Shakespeare*. Pittsburgh: Duquesne UP, 1994. Print.

Martin, L. C., ed. *Marlowe's Poems*. London: Methuen, 1931. Print. Vol. 4 of *The Works and Life of Christopher Marlowe*. Ed. R. H. Case. 6 vols. London: Methuen, 1930–33.

Martindale, Charles, ed. *The Cambridge Companion to Virgil*. Cambridge: Cambridge UP, 1997. Print.

———, ed. *Ovid Renewed: Ovidian Influences on Literature and Art from the Middle Ages to the Twentieth Century*. Cambridge: Cambridge UP, 1988. Print.

McCabe, Richard. "Elizabethan Satire and the Bishops' Ban of 1599." *Yearbook of English Studies* 11 (1981): 188–93. Print.

McChesney, Anita. "On the Repeating History of Destruction: Media and the Index in Sebald and Ransmayr." *Modern Language Notes* 121.3 (2006): 699–719. Print.

McGinn, T. A. J. *Prostitution, Sexuality, and the Law in Ancient Rome*. Oxford: Clarendon, 1998. Print.

McKeown, J. C., ed. *Ovid. Amores. Text, Prolegomena and Commentary*. 3 vols. to date. Liverpool; Leeds: Cairns, 1987– . Print.

McLaughlin, Martin. *Italo Calvino*. Edinburgh: Edinburgh UP, 1998. Print.

Melville, A. D., trans. *Ovid: Metamorphoses*. Oxford: Oxford UP, 1986. Print.

———, trans. *Ovid: Sorrows of an Exile*. Oxford: Oxford UP, 1995. Print.

———, trans. *Ovid: The Love Poems*. Oxford: Oxford UP, 1990. Print.

Melville, Herman. *Bartleby the Scrivener*. 1853. London: Hesperus, 2007. Print.

Michels, Agnes Kirsopp Lake. *The Calendar of the Roman Republic*. Princeton: Princeton UP, 1967. Print.

Miles, Geoffrey, ed. *Classical Mythology in English Literature: A Critical Anthology*. London: Routledge, 1999. Print.

Miller, John F. "Callimachus and the Augustan Aetiological Elegy." *Literatur der augusteischen Zeit: Allgemeines, einzelne Autoren (Sprache und Literatur)*. Ed. Wolfgang Haase. Berlin: de Gruyter, 1982. 371–414. Print. Vol. 30.1 of *Aufstieg und Niedergang der römischen Welt* pt. 2.

———. "The *Fasti*: Style, Structure, and Time." Boyd, *Brill's Companion* 167–96.

———, ed. *Ovid: Fasti II*. Bryn Mawr: Bryn Mawr Coll., 1985. Print.

———. "Ovidian Allusion and the Vocabulary of Memory." *Materiali e discussioni per l'analisi dei testi classici* 30 (1993): 153–64. Print.

———. *Ovid's Elegiac Festivals: Studies in the* Fasti. Frankfurt: Lang, 1991. Print.

Miller, Paul Allen. *Subjecting Verses: Latin Love Elegy and the Emergence of the Real*. Princeton: Princeton UP, 2004. Print.

Momigliano, Arnaldo. "The Theological Efforts of the Roman Upper Classes in the First Century B.C." *Classical Philology* 79.3 (1984): 199–211. Print.

Montaigne, Michel de. *An Apology for Raymond Sebond*. 1580. Trans. M. A. Screech. New York: Penguin, 1993. Print.

Montrose, Louis Adrian. "The Elizabethan Subject and the Spenserian Text." *Literary Theory / Renaissance Texts*. Ed. Patricia Parker and David Quint. Baltimore: Johns Hopkins UP, 1986. 303–40. Print.

Moore, Edward. *Studies in Dante: First Series, Scripture and Classical Authors in Dante*. Oxford: Clarendon, 1896. Print.

Morford, Mark P. O., and Robert J. Lenardon. *Classical Mythology*. 8th ed. New York: Oxford UP, 2007. Print.

Morrison, Toni. *Beloved: A Novel*. New York: New American Lib., 1987. Print.

Morse, Ruth. *The Medieval Medea*. Cambridge: Brewer, 1996. Print.

Moss, Ann. *Latin Commentaries on Ovid from the Renaissance*. Signal Mountain: Lib. of Renaissance Humanism, 1998. Print.

Moss, Roger. "Hick, Hack, Hock." Terry 19–27.

Most, G. W., ed. *Commentaries—Kommentare*. Göttingen: Vandenhoeck, 1999. Print.

Moulton, Ian Frederick. " 'Printed Abroad and Uncastrated': Marlowe's *Elegies* and Davies' *Epigrams*." *Marlowe, History, and Sexuality: New Critical Essays on Christopher Marlowe*. Ed. Paul Whitfield White. New York: AMS, 1998. 77–90. Print.

Mourning Becomes Electra. By Eugene O'Neill. Adapt. and dir. Dudley Nichols. Perf. Rosalind Russell, Michael Redgrave, Raymond Massey. RKO, 1947. Film.

Mulvey, Laura. "Afterthoughts on 'Visual Pleasure and Narrative Cinema' Inspired by *Duel in the Sun*." *Framework* 15-16-17 (1981): 12–15. Print.

———. *Visual and Other Pleasures*. Bloomington: Indiana UP, 1989. Print.

———. "Visual Pleasure and Narrative Cinema." *Screen* 16.3 (1975): 6–18. Print.

Myers, K. Sara. "*Ultimus Ardor*: Pomona and Vertumnus in Ovid's *Met*. 14.623–771." *Classical Journal* 89.3 (1994): 225–50. Print.

Nagle, Betty Rose, trans. *Ovid's* Fasti: *Roman Holidays*. Bloomington: Indiana UP, 1995. Print.

———. *The Poetics of Exile: Program and Polemic in the* Tristia *and* Epistulae ex Ponto *of Ovid*. Brussels: Latomus, 1980. Print.

Neukirchen, Thomas. " 'Aller Aufsicht entzogen': Nasos Selbstentleibung und Metamorphose: Bemerkungen zum (Frei)Tod des Autors in Christoph Ransmayrs Roman *Die letzte Welt*." *Germanisch-Romanische Monatsschrift* 52.1 (2002): 191–209. Print.

Neuse, Richard. "Milton and Spenser: The Virgilian Triad Revisited." *ELH* 45.4 (1978): 606–39. Print.

Newlands, Carole. "*Mandati memores*: Political and Poetic Authority in the *Fasti*." Hardie, *Cambridge Companion* 200–16.

———. "The Metamorphosis of Ovid's Medea." Clauss and Johnston 178–208.

———. *Playing with Time: Ovid and the* Fasti. Ithaca: Cornell UP, 1995. Print.

The Nibelungenlied. Trans. A. T. Hatto. London: Penguin, 1969. Print.

Nicholl, Charles. " 'At Middleborough': Some Reflections on Marlowe's Visit to the Low Countries in 1592." *Christopher Marlowe and English Renaissance Culture*. Ed. Darryll Grantley and Peter Roberts. Aldershot: Scolar; Brookfield: Ashgate, 1996. 38–50. Print.

Nicolson, Adam. *God's Secretaries: The Making of the King James Bible*. New York: Harper, 2003. Print.

Nims, John Frederick. Introduction. Golding, *Ovid's* Metamorphosis [ed. Nims] xiii–xxxv.

Nisbet, Robin George Murdoch, and Niall Rudd, eds. *A Commentary on Horace, Odes, Book III*. Oxford: Oxford UP, 2004. Print.

Nooteboom, Cees. *The Following Story*. Trans. I. Rilke. New York: Harcourt, 1993. Print.

Norbrook, David, and H. R. Woudhuysen, eds. *The Penguin Book of Renaissance Verse*. 1992. Harmondsworth: Penguin, 1993. Print.

Norton Anthology of English Literature. Ed. Stephen Greenblatt, Barbara Kiefer Lewalski, George M. Logan, and M. H. Abrams. 7th ed. Vol. 1B. New York: Norton, 1997. Print.

Nosworthy, J. M. "Marlowe's Ovid and Davies's Epigrams—A Postscript." *Review of English Studies* 15.60 (1964): 397–98. Print.

———. "The Publication of Marlowe's Elegies and Davies's Epigrams." *Review of English Studies* 4.15 (1953): 260–61. Print.

Nugent, Georgia. "This Sex Which Is Not One: De-constructing Ovid's Hermaphrodite." *Differences: A Journal of Feminist Cultural Studies* 2.1 (1990): 160–85. Print.

Oakley-Brown, Liz. *Ovid and the Cultural Politics of Translation in Early Modern England*. Aldershot: Ashgate, 2006. Print.

O'Hara, James J. "Sostratus Suppl. Hell. 733: A Lost, Possibly Catullan-Era Elegy on the Six Sex Changes of Tiresias." *Transactions and Proceedings of the American Philological Association* 126 (1996): 173–219. Print.

Orgel, Stephen, ed. *Christopher Marlowe: The Complete Poems and Translations*. Harmondsworth: Penguin, 1971. Print.

———. "Nobody's Perfect; or, Why Did the English Stage Take Boys for Men?" *South Atlantic Quarterly* 88.1 (1989): 7–29. Print.

Orlando. Written and dir. Sally Potter. 1993. Columbia TriStar, 1999. DVD.

Orwell, George. *1984*. New York: Signet, 1990. Print.

Osama. Dir. Siddiq Barmak. Perf. Marina Golbahari, Arif Herati, Zubaida Sahar. United Artists, 2003. Film.

Otis, Brooks. *Ovid as an Epic Poet*. 1966. 2nd ed. Cambridge: Cambridge UP, 1970. Print.

Otten, Charlotte F, ed. *A Lycanthropy Reader: Werewolves in Western Culture*. Syracuse: Syracuse UP, 1986. Print.

Ovid. Art of Love *and Other Poems*. Trans. J. H. Mozley. 1929. Ed. and trans. G. P. Goold. 2nd rev. ed. Cambridge: Harvard UP, 1979. Print. Loeb Classical Lib.

———. *Fasti*. Trans. James George Frazer. 1931. Ed. and trans. G. P. Goold. 2nd rev. ed. Cambridge: Harvard UP, 1989. Print. Loeb Classical Lib.

———. Heroides *and* Amores. Trans. Grant Showerman. 1914. Ed. and trans. G. P. Goold. 2nd rev. ed. Cambridge: Harvard UP, 1977. Print. Loeb Classical Lib.

———. *The Heroycall Epistles of the Learned Poet Publius Ouidius Naso*. Trans. George Turberville. London: Charlewoode, 1584. Print.

———. Metamorphoses, *Books I-VIII*. Trans. Frank Justus Miller. 1916. Ed. and trans. G. P. Goold. 3rd rev. ed. Cambridge: Harvard UP, 1977. Print. Loeb Classical Lib.

———. Metamorphoses, *Books IX-XV*. Trans. Frank Justus Miller. 1916. Ed. and trans. G. P. Goold. 2nd rev. ed. Cambridge: Harvard UP, 1984. Print. Loeb Classical Lib.

———. *Ovidii Nasonis Fastorum libri sex*. Ed. E. H. Alton, E. W. Wormell, and E. Courtney. Leipzeg: Teubner, 1978. Print.

———. *Ovidii Nasonis Tristium libri quinque, Ibis, Ex Ponto libri quattuor, Halieutica, fragmenta*. Ed. S. G. Owen. Oxford: Clarendon, 1915. Print.

———. *Ovidi Nasonis Metamorphoses*. Ed. R. J. Tarrant. Oxford: Clarendon, 2004. Print.

———. *P. Ovidi Nasonis Amores, Medicamina faciei femineae, Ars amatoria, Remedia amoris*. Ed. E. J. Kenney. Corrected 2nd ed. Oxford: Clarendon, 1995. Print.

———. Tristia *and* Ex Ponto. Trans. A. L. Wheeler. 1924. Ed. and trans. G. P. Goold. 2nd rev. ed. Cambridge: Harvard UP, 1988. Print. Loeb Classical Lib.

The Ovid Collection. U of Virginia. N.d. Web. 23 July 2008.

Ovide moralisé en prose (texte du quinzième siècle). Ed. Cornelis de Boer. Amsterdam: North-Holland, 1954. Print.

Ovide moralisé: Poème du commencement du quatorzième siècle publié d'après tous les manuscrits connus. Ed. Cornelis de Boer, Martina G. de Boer, and Jeannetter Th. M. van't Sant. Amsterdam: Müller, 1915–38. 5 vols. Wiesbaden: Sandig, 1966. Print.

Pairet, Ana. *Les mutacions des fables: Figures de la métamorphose dans la littérature française du Moyen Âge*. Paris: Champion, 2002. Print.

The Palm Beach Story. Dir. Preston Sturges. Perf. Claudette Colbert, Joel McCrea, Mary Astor, Rudy Vallee. Paramount, 1942. Film.

Palmeri, Frank. "The Autocritique of Fables." *Humans and Other Animals in Eighteenth-Century Culture: Representation, Hybridity, Ethics*. Ed. Palmeri. Aldershot: Ashgate, 2006. 83–100. Print.

"Paloma Picasso's 'Minotaure.'" *Sorcery of Scent: A Perfume Blog*. 10 July 2008. Web. 21 Dec. 2009.

Panofsky, Erwin. *Problems in Titian, Mostly Iconographic*. New York: New York UP, 1969. Print.

Parker, Patricia. *Literary Fat Ladies: Rhetoric, Gender, Property*. London: Methuen, 1987. Print.

Payne, Michael, and John Hunter, eds. *Renaissance Literature: An Anthology*. Oxford: Blackwell, 2003. Print.

Pease, A. S., ed. *M. Tulli Ciceronis De natura deorum*. 2 vols. Cambridge: Harvard UP, 1955. Print.

The Piano. Dir. Jane Campion. Perf. Holly Hunter, Harvey Keitel, Sam Neill. Miramax, 1992. Film.

Picone, Michelangelo. "L'Ovidio di Dante." *Dante e la "bella scola" della poesia: Autorità e sfida poetica*. Ed. Amilcare A. Iannucci. Ravenna: Longo Editore, 1993. 107–44. Print.

Pindar. "Pythian 6." *Pindar: Olympian Odes; Pythian Odes*. Ed. and trans. William H. Race. Cambridge: Harvard UP, 1997. 314–19. Print. Loeb Classical Lib.

Plutarch. "The Eating of Flesh." *Moralia*. Vol. 12. Trans. Harold Cherniss and William C. Helmbold. Cambridge: Harvard UP, 1957. 540–79. Print. Loeb Classical Lib.

———. "Julius Caesar." *Plutarch's Lives*. Trans. Bernadotte Perrin. 11 vols. London: Heinemann; New York: Putnam's, 1916. Print.

Podossinov, Alexander. "Die Exil-Muse Ovids in russischer Dichtung des XX. Jahrhunderts (Mandelstam und Brodsky)." *Ovid: Werk und Wirkung. Festgabe für Michael von Albrecht zum 65. Geburtstag*. Ed. Werner Schubert. Frankfurt am Main: Lang, 1999. 1061–77. Print.

Poduska, Donald M. "Classical Myth in Music: A Selective List." *Classical World* 92.3 (1999): 195–276. Print.

Poliziano, Angelo. *Silvae*. Ed. and trans. Charles Fantazzi. Cambridge: Harvard UP, 2004. Print. The I Tatti Renaissance Lib.

Pondrom, Cyrena. "T. S. Eliot: The Performativity of Gender in *The Waste Land*." *Modernism/Modernity* 12.3 (2005): 425–41. Print.

Possamaï-Pérez, Marylène. *L'Ovide moralisé: Essai d'interprétation*. Paris: Champion, 2006. Print. Nouvelle Bibliothèque du Moyen Âge 78.

Powell, Barry. *Classical Myth*. 5th ed. Upper Saddle River: Prentice, 2006. Print.

Prawer, Sigbert S. *Comparative Literary Studies: An Introduction*. New York: Harper, 1973. Print.

Pretty Woman. Dir. Garry Marshall. Perf. Richard Gere, Julia Roberts, Ralph Bellamy, and Jason Alexander. Buena Vista Pictures, 1990. Film.

Propertius. *Sexti Properti elegiarum. Libri IV*. Ed. P. Fedeli. Stuttgart: Teubner, 1984. Print.

Pugh, Syrithe. *Spenser and Ovid*. Aldershot: Ashgate, 2005. Print.

Putnam, M. C. J. "Daedalus, Virgil and the End of Art." *American Journal of Philology* 108 (1987): 173–98. Print.

Quintilian. *The* Institutio Oratoria *of Quintilian*. Trans. H. E. Butler. 4 vols. Cambridge: Harvard UP, 1969. Print. Loeb Classical Lib.

Raeburn, David, trans. *Metamorphoses*. London: Penguin, 2004. Print.

Rainolds, John. *Th'overthrow of Stage-Playes*. London, 1599. Print.

Ransmayr, Christoph. "Entwurf zu einem Roman." *Jahresring: Jahrbuch für Kunst und Literatur* 34 (1987–88): 96–98. Print.

———. "Die Erfindung der Welt." *Die Erfindung der Welt: Zum Werk von Christoph Ransmayr*. Ed. Uwe Wittstock. Frankfurt am Main: Fischer, 1997. 198–202. Print.

———. *The Last World: A Novel with an Ovidian Repertory*. Trans. John E. Woods. New York: Weidenfeld, 1990. Print.

———. *Die letzte Welt: Roman mit einem Ovidischen Repertoire*. Frankfurt am Main: Fischer Taschenbuch, 1991. Print.

Rawson, Elizabeth. *Intellectual Life in the Late Roman Republic*. Baltimore: Johns Hopkins UP, 1985. Print.

Regio, Raffaele, ed. *P. Ouidii Metamorphosis cum integris ac emendatissimis Raphaelis Regii enarrationibus*. Venice: Benalius, 1493. Print.

Reid, Jane Davidson, ed. *The Oxford Guide to Classical Mythology in the Arts, 1300–1990s*. 2 vols. New York: Oxford UP, 1993. Print.

Reynolds, L. D., and N. G. Wilson. *Scribes and Scholars: A Guide to the Transmission of Greek and Latin Literature*. 3rd ed. Oxford: Clarendon, 1991. Print.

Rich, Adrienne. *Of Woman Born: Motherhood as Experience and Institution*. 1976. New York: Norton, 1995. Print.

Rilke, Rainer Maria. "Orpheus. Eurydice. Hermes." Trans. Rika Lesser. Kossman 97–99.

Rimell, Victoria. *Ovid's Lovers: Desire, Difference and the Poetic Imagination*. Cambridge: Cambridge UP, 2006. Print.

Roller, Lynn E. "The Legend of Midas." *Classical Antiquity* 2.2 (1983): 299–313. Print.

Rosati, Gianpiero. "Form in Motion: Weaving the Text in the *Metamorphoses*." Hardie, Barchiesi, and Hinds 240–53.

Ross, David O. *Backgrounds to Augustan Poetry: Gallus, Elegy, and Rome*. Cambridge: Cambridge UP, 1975. Print.

Rubin, Gayle. "The Traffic in Women: Notes on the Political Economy of Sex." *Toward an Anthropology of Women*. Ed. Rayne R. Reiter. New York: Monthly Review, 1975. 157–210. Print.

Rudich, Vasily. *Dissidence and Literature under Nero: The Price of Rhetoricization*. London: Routledge, 1997. Print.

Russell, Anna. *The (First) Farewell Concert*. Baltimore Museum of Art. Rec. 7 Nov. 1984. Video Artists International, 2001. DVD.

Salisbury, Joyce E. *The Beast Within: Animals in the Middle Ages*. New York: Routledge, 1994. Print.

Sandys, George. *Ovid's* Metamorphoses *Englished, Mythologized, and Represented in Figures, by George Sandys*. Ed. Karl K. Hulley and Stanley T. Vandersall. Lincoln: U of Nebraska P, 1970. Print.

Scheid, John, and Jesper Svenbro. *The Craft of Zeus: Myths of Weaving and Fabric*. Trans. Carol Volk. Cambridge: Harvard UP, 1996. Print.

Schevill, Rudolph. *Ovid and the Renascence in Spain*. New York: Georg Olms Verlag, 1971. Print.

Schilling, Robert. *La religion romaine de Vénus*. Paris: Boccard, 1954. Print.

Schlegel, Friedrich. *Dialogue on Poetry and Literary Aphorisms*. Trans. Ernst Behler and Roman Struc. University Park: Pennsylvania State UP, 1968. Print.

Schmitzer, Ulrich, ed. *Tenerorum lusor amorum: Ovid im WWW—die Homepage*. 2007. Web. 23 July 2008.

Seneca the Elder. *Suasoriae*. *The Elder Seneca: Declamations*. Trans. Michael Winterbottom. Vol. 2. Cambridge: Harvard UP, 1974. 484–611. Print. Loeb Classical Lib.

Seneca the Younger. "Medea." *L. Annaei Senecae Tragoediae*. Ed. Rudolf Peiper and Gustavus Richter. Leipzig: Teubner, 1867. 117–54. Print.

Servius. *Servii grammatici qui feruntur in Vergilii carmina commentarii*. Ed. G. Thilo and H. Hagen. 3 vols. Leipzig: Teubner, 1878–1902. Print.

"Sex: Unknown." *Nova*. Prod. Andrew Cohen and Stephen Sweigart. PBS. WGBH, Boston, 30 Oct. 2001. Television.

Seznec, Jean. *The Survival of the Pagan Gods: The Mythological Tradition and Its Place in Renaissance Humanism and Art*. Princeton: Princeton UP, 1972. Print.

Shakespeare, William. *A Midsummer Night's Dream*. Shakespeare, *Riverside Shakespeare* 217–49.

———. *Othello*. Ed. Michael Neill. Oxford: Oxford UP, 2006. Print.

———. *The Riverside Shakespeare*. Ed. G. Blakemore Evans. Boston: Houghton, 1974. Print.

———. *Titus Andronicus*. Ed. Jonathan Bate. London: Thomson, 1995. Print. The Arden Shakespeare, 3rd ser.

———. *Twelfth Night*. Ed. Barbara A. Mowat and Paul Werstine. New York: Washington Square, 2005. Print.

———. *Venus and Adonis*. Shakespeare, *Riverside Shakespeare* 1703–19.

———. *Venus and Adonis*. *Complete Sonnets and Poems*. Ed. Colin Burrow. Oxford: Oxford UP, 2002. 171–236. Print.

Sharrock, Alison. "Gender and Sexuality." Hardie, *Cambridge Companion* 95–107.

———. "Looking at Looking: Can You Resist a Reading?" Fredrick 265–95.

———. "Ovid and the Discourses of Love: The Amatory Works." Hardie, *Cambridge Companion* 150–62.

———. *Seduction and Repetition in Ovid's* Ars amatoria II. Oxford: Clarendon, 1994. Print.

———. "Womanufacture." *Journal of Roman Studies* 81 (1991): 36-49. Print.

Shelley, Percy Bysshe. "A Vindication of Natural Diet." *The Prose Works of Percy Bysshe Shelley*. Ed. E. B. Murray. Vol. 1. Oxford: Clarendon, 1993. 77–91. Print.

Sidney, Philip. *An Apology for Poetry*. Ed. Geoffrey Shepherd. Manchester: Manchester UP, 1973. Print.

Simonides. Fragment 26. *Poetae melici Graeci*. Ed. Denys Page. Oxford: Clarendon, 1962. 276. Print.

Simpson, Michael, trans. *The Metamorphoses of Ovid*. Amherst: U of Massachusetts P, 2001. Print.

Singer, Peter. *Animal Liberation*. 1975. New York: Harper, 2002. Print.

Skulsky, Harold. *Metamorphosis: The Mind in Exile*. Cambridge: Harvard UP, 1981. Print.

Slavitt, David R., trans. *The Metamorphoses of Ovid*. Baltimore: Johns Hopkins UP, 1994. Print.

Smalley, Beryl. *English Friars and Antiquity in the Early Fourteenth Century*. Oxford: Blackwell, 1960. Print.

Solodow, Joseph B. *The World of Ovid's Metamorphoses*. Chapel Hill: U of North Carolina P, 1988. Print.

Sowell, Madison U. *Dante and Ovid: Essays in Intertextuality*. Binghamton: Medieval and Renaissance Texts and Studies, 1991. Print.

———. "Ovid." Kleinhenz 2: 812–13.

———. "Ovid in the Middle Ages." Kleinhenz 2: 813–14.

———. "Pyramus." *The Dante Encyclopedia*. Ed. Richard Lansing. New York: Garland, 2000. 732. Print.

Spenser, Edmund. *The Faerie Queene*. Ed. A. C. Hamilton. Text ed. Hiroshi Yamashita and Toshiyuki Suzuki. London: Longman, 2001. Print.

———. *The Shepheardes Calender*. *The Poetical Works of Edmund Spenser*. Ed. J. C. Smith and Ernest de Sélincourt. Oxford: Clarendon, 1909–10. 415–67. Print.

———. *The Yale Edition of the Shorter Poems of Edmund Spenser*. Ed. William A. Oram, Einer Bjorvand, Ronald Bond, Thomas H. Cain, Alexander Dunlop, and Richard Schell. New Haven: Yale UP, 1989. Print.

Stanivukovic, Goran, ed. *Ovid and the Renaissance Body*. Toronto: U of Toronto P, 2001. Print.

Stape, J. H. Introduction. *Orlando*. By Virginia Woolf. Oxford: Blackwell, 1998. xi–xxx. Print.

Stapleton, M. L. *Harmful Eloquence: Ovid's Amores from Antiquity to Shakespeare*. Ann Arbor: U of Michigan P, 1996. Print.

Statius. Thebaid *Books 8–12; Achilleid*. Trans. and ed. D. R. Shackleton Bailey. Cambridge: Harvard UP, 2003. Print. Loeb Classical Lib.

Striar, Brian J. "Theories and Practices of Renaissance Verse Translation." Diss. Claremont Graduate School, 1984. Print.

Stroh, Wilfried. "Ovids Liebkunst und die Ehegesetze des Augustus." *Gymnasium* 86 (1979): 323–52. Print.

Suetonius. "Deified Julius." *Suetonius*. Trans. J. C. Rolfe. Cambridge: Harvard UP, 1959. Print. Loeb Classical Lib.

Swift, Jonathan. *Gulliver's Travels*. 1726. New York: Penguin, 2003. Print.

Syme, Ronald. *History in Ovid*. Oxford: Clarendon, 1978. Print.

Tacitus. *Dialogus de oratibus. Tacitus: "Dialogus," "Agricola," "Germania."* Trans. William Peterson. Cambridge: Harvard UP, 1963. 18–129. Print. Loeb Classical Lib.

Tarrant, R. J. "Roads Not Taken: Untold Stories in Ovid's *Metamorphoses*." *Materiali e discussioni per l'analisi dei testi classici* 54 (2005): 65–89. Print.

Taylor, A. B., ed. *Shakespeare's Ovid: The* Metamorphoses *in the Plays and Poems*. Cambridge: Cambridge UP, 2000. Print.

Terry, Philip, ed. *Ovid Metamorphosed.* London: Chatto, 2000; New York: Vintage, 2001. Print.

Theisen, Bianca. "Metamorphosen der Literatur: Christoph Ransmayrs *Die letzte Welt.*" *Modern Language Notes* 121.3 (2006): 582–91. Print.

Thibault, John C. *The Mystery of Ovid's Exile.* Berkeley: U of California P, 1964. Print.

Thomas, Richard F. "Catullus and the Polemics of Poetic Reference (Poem 64.1–18)." *American Journal of Philology* 103.2 (1982): 144–64. Print.

———. *Virgil and the Augustan Reception.* Cambridge: Cambridge UP, 2001. Print.

Thompson, Ann. "Philomel in *Titus Andronicus* and *Cymbeline.*" *Shakespeare Survey* 19 (1978): 23–32. Print.

Thury, Eva M., and Margaret K. Devinney. *Introduction to Mythology: Contemporary Approaches to Classical and World Myths.* New York: Oxford UP, 2005. Print.

Tibullus. *Tibulli aliorumque carminum libri tres.* Ed. Johannes Percival Postgate. Oxford: Clarendon, 1915. Print.

Tissol, Garth. *The Face of Nature: Wit, Narrative, and Cosmic Origins in Ovid's* Metamorphoses. Princeton: Princeton UP, 1996. Print.

Titian. *Death of Actaeon.* 1559–75. Oil on canvas. Natl. Gallery, London.

———. *Diana and Actaeon.* 1556–59. Oil on canvas. Natl. Gallery, London / Natl. Gallery, Scotland.

———. *The Rape of Europa.* 1562. Oil on canvas. Isabella Stewart Gardner Museum, Boston.

Toynbee, Paget. *Concise Dictionary of Proper Names and Notable Matters in the Works of Dante.* 1914. New York: Phaeton, 1968.

Traub, Valerie. Afterword. Stanivukovic 260–68.

Traube, Ludwig. *Einleitung in die lateinischen Philologie des Mittelalters.* Ed. Paul Lehmann. 1910. Print. Vol. 2 of *Vorlesungen und Abhandlungen.* Ed. Franz Boll. 3 vols. 1911. Munich: Pera-Druck, 1965.

Tyrtaeus. Fragment 12. *Greek Elegiac Poetry.* Ed. and trans. Douglas E. Gerber. Cambridge: Harvard UP, 1999. 56–61. Print. Loeb Classical Lib.

Van Tress, Heather. *Poetic Memory: Allusion in the Poetry of Callimachus and the* Metamorphoses *of Ovid.* Leiden: Brill, 2004. Print.

Vasari, Giorgio. *Lives of the Painters, Sculptors and Architects.* Trans. Gaston du C. de Vere. 2 vols. New York: Knopf, 1996. Print.

Verdière, Raoul. *Le secret du voltigeur d'Amour ou le mystère de la relégation d'Ovide.* Brussels: Latomus, 1992. Print.

Vergil. *P. Vergili Maronis Opera Omnia.* Ed. R. A. B. Mynors. Oxford: Clarendon, 1969. Print.

———. *Virgil:* Aeneid. Trans. Stanley Lombardo. Indianapolis: Hackett, 2005. Print.
Veyne, Paul. *Did the Greeks Believe in Their Myths? An Essay on the Constitutive Imagination.* Trans. Paula Wissing. Chicago: U of Chicago P, 1988. Print.
Vickers, Nancy J. " 'The Blazon of Sweet Beauty's Best': Shakespeare's *Lucrece.*" *Shakespeare and the Question of Theory.* Ed. Patricia Parker and Geoffrey Hartman. New York: Methuen, 1985. 95–115. Print.
Videau-Delibes, Anne. *Les Tristes d'Ovide et l'élégie romaine: Une poétique de la rupture.* Paris: Klincksieck, 1991. Print.
Wagner, Richard. *Der Ring des Nibelungen.* Dir. Brian Large. Prod. Patrice Chéreau. Perf. Donald McIntyre, Gwyneth Jones, Matti Salminen, Fritz Hübner, Hanna Schwarz, Helmut Pampuch, Ilse Gramatzki, Jeannine Altmeyer. Bayreuth Festspielhaus. Cond. Pierre Boulez. 1976. Deutsche Grammophon, 2005. DVD.
———. *Der Ring des Nibelungen.* Dir. Peter Gelb and Otto Schenk. Perf. Hildegard Behrens, James Morris, Siegfried Jerusalem, Ekkehard Wlaschiha, Christa Ludwig, Matti Salminen. The Metropolitan Opera New York. Cond. James Levine. 1990. Deutsche Grammophon, 2002. DVD.
———. *The Ring of the Nibelung.* Trans. Andrew Porter. New York: Norton, 1976. Print.
Walcott, Derek. "The Hotel Normandie Pool." *Derek Walcott: Collected Poems, 1948–1984.* New York: Farrar, 1986. 439–45. Print.
Wallace-Hadrill, Andrew. "Time for Augustus: Ovid, Augustus and the *Fasti.*" *Homo Viator: Classical Essays for John Bramble.* Ed. M. Whitby et al. Bristol: Bristol, 1987. 221–30. Print.
Warner, Marina. *Fantastic Metamorphoses, Other Worlds: Ways of Telling the Self.* Oxford: Oxford UP, 2002. Print.
Weil, Elizabeth. "What If It's (Sort of) a Boy and (Sort of) a Girl?" *New York Times Magazine* 24 Sept. 2006: 48–53. Print.
Weisenberger, Steven. *Modern Medea: A Family Story of Slavery and Child-Murder from the Old South.* New York: Hill, 1998. Print.
Weisstein, Ulrich. *Comparative Literature and Literary Theory: Survey and Introduction.* Bloomington: Indiana UP, 1973. Print.
Wells, H. G. *The Island of Doctor Moreau.* 1896. New York: Bantam, 1994. Print.
Wells, Stanley. *Looking for Sex in Shakespeare.* Cambridge: Cambridge UP, 2004. Print.
White, P. "Ovid and the Augustan Milieu." Boyd, *Brill's Companion* 1–25.
W[hitney]., I[sabella]. "The admonition by the Auctor, to all young Gentlewomen: And to al other Maids being in Loue." *The copie of a letter, lately written in meeter, by a yonge gentilwoman To her vnconstant louer.* London: Richard Jones, 1567. A5v–A8v. Print.
Wilford, John Noble. "Statuette Is Traced to Midas; Alas, Not Golden, Just Ivory." *New York Times* 3 Jan. 2002. Web. 22 July 2008.
Wilkinson, L. P. *Ovid Recalled.* Cambridge: Cambridge UP, 1955. Print.
———. *Ovid Surveyed.* Cambridge: Cambridge UP, 1962. Print.

Williams, Gareth. *Banished Voices: Readings in Ovid's Exile Poetry*. Cambridge: Cambridge UP, 1994. Print.

———. *The Curse of Exile: A Study of Ovid's* Ibis. Cambridge: Cambridge Philological Soc., 1996. Print. Proceedings of the Cambridge Philological Soc. Supplementary Volume 19.

———. "Ovid's Exile Poetry: *Tristia, Epistulae ex Ponto* and *Ibis*." Hardie, *Cambridge Companion* 233–45.

———. "Ovid's Exilic Poetry: Worlds Apart." Boyd, *Brill's Companion* 337–81.

Williams, Gordon. *Tradition and Originality in Roman Poetry*. Oxford: Clarendon, 1968. Print.

Wind, Edgar. *Pagan Mysteries in the Renaissance*. New York: Barnes, 1968. Print.

Wiseman, T. P. *The Myths of Rome*. Exeter: U of Exeter P, 2004. Print.

Wishart, David. *Ovid*. London: Hodder, 1995.

Wittstock, Uwe, ed. *Die Erfindung der Welt: Zum Werk von Christoph Ransmayr*. Frankfurt: Fischer, 1997. Print.

Woolf, Virginia. *Orlando*. New York: Harcourt, 2006. Print.

———. *A Room of One's Own*. London: Hogarth, 1929. Print.

Zimmerman, Mary. *Metamorphoses: A Play*. Evanston: Northwestern UP, 2002. Print.

Ziolkowski, Theodore. *Ovid and the Moderns*. Ithaca: Cornell UP, 2005. Print.

Zyroff, Ellen S. "The Author's Apostrophe in Epic from Homer through Lucan." Diss. Johns Hopkins U, 1971. Print.

INDEX

Accius, 226
Adams, J. N., 110, 111, 113
Aeschylus, 80, 87n4
Aesop, 100n1
Agee, James, 63
Alberti, Leon Battista, 243
Allen, Graham, 134
Alfonso X (the Learned), king of Castile and León, 10
Althusser, Louis, 104
Ambrose, Z. Philip, 34, 37–38, 44
Amielle, Ghislaine, 19
Anaxarete, 83
Anderson, William S., 29, 42, 51, 52, 66
Antoninus Liberalis, 205
Antony, Mark, 8
Apollinaire, Guillaume, 221
Apollodorus, 210n2
Apollonius, 66, 70, 72n2, 103, 182, 226
Appiani, Semiramide, 248n10
Apuleius, Lucius, 43, 80, 160n4, 214, 220, 242, 248n6, 249n13
Ariosto, Ludovico, 132n1, 240n1
Aristophanes, 206
Aristotle, 152, 153, 155, 200
Armani, Giorgio, 85
Armstrong, Rebecca, 45
Arnulf of Orléans, 236
Arthur and Gorlagon, 215
Auden, W. H., 84, 221
Auerbach, Erich, 246
Augustine, 13, 207
Augustus, 7–8, 9, 11, 14–15, 16n8, 18, 40 50, 60, 69, 73, 77–79, 81, 90, 92, 100n2, 110–16, 117, 118, 122, 139, 167, 242, 245, 253

Bacon, Francis, 149
Baldini, Umberto, 248nn9–10
Barchiesi, Alessandro, 17n14, 51, 55, 228, 233 (nn 4, 6)
Barkan, Leonard, 45, 53, 134, 142, 150n1, 195, 214, 224, 249n15
Barnard, Mary E., 247n1
Barolsky, Paul, 24
Barsby, John, 45, 51
Barthes, Roland, 104
Bassnett, Susan, 102, 107n1
Bate, Jonathan, 45, 54, 134, 135, 141nn1–2, 149–50, 191–92, 195n1
Bean, John C., 105
Beardsley, Theodore S., 242, 248n5
Benoît de Sainte-Maure, 20–21
Bernini, Gian Lorenzo, 11, 26

Bersuire, Pierre, 10, 19, 145, 237, 240n6
Bible, 23, 80, 82, 86n3, 88, 143–45, 147, 189, 247n1
Bickerman, Elias J., 17n12
bin Laden, Osama, 85
Binns, J. W., 50
Blumenfeld-Kosinski, Renate, 19–20
Boccaccio, Giovanni, 220
Boedeker, Deborah, 105
Boer, Cornelis de, 19, 22n2
Boethius, 214, 236
Bömer, Franz, 29, 50, 158
Boniface VIII (pope), 253
Bonsogni, Giovanni de, 240n6
Booth, J., 29
Borghese, Scipione Caffarelli (cardinal), 26
Borris, Kenneth, 192–93, 196n7
Boswell, Jeanetta, 108n3
Botticelli, Sandro, 242–47, 248 (nn 6,10), 249 (nn 15, 17–18)
Bowers, Fredson, 203n3
Boyd, Barbara Weiden, 16 (nn 2,10), 44, 45, 51, 52, 63n3, 71, 109, 116n2, 233n7, 249n18
Boylan, Jennifer, 204, 209, 210, 211n13
Boyle, A. J., 44
Braden, Gordon, 203n1
Brantley, Ben, 139–40
Bray, Alan, 128
Brisson, Luc, 206, 210 (nn 1,3)
Brodsky, Josef, 43
Brooke, C. F. Tucker, 203n3
Brown, Georgia, 55, 199
Brown, Jonathan, 248n4
Brown, Sarah Annes, 45, 55, 123
Brownlee, Marina Scordilis, 248n5
Brueghel, Pieter, the Elder, 11, 221
Bull, Malcolm, 221
Burke, Edmund, 59
Burkert, Walter, 61
Burrow, Colin, 195, 196n6
Bursuario. See *Epístolas de Ovidio*
Bush, Douglas, 53
Butler, Judith, 194, 211n9
Butler, Shane, 224n1
Bynum, Caroline Walker, 215

Caesar Augustus. *See* Augustus
Caesar, Julius (Gaius Julius Caesar), 7, 15, 17n12, 70, 122, 195
Calabrese, Michael, 53
Callimachus, 8, 16n10, 51, 226, 233n9
Calvin, John, 145

Calvino, Italo, 85, 215
Calvus (Gaius Licinius Calvus), 78
Camamis, George, 243, 244, 245
Cameron, Alan, 200
Campion, Jane, 62
Capellanus, Andreas, 43
Caravaggio (Michelangelo Merisi), 220
Carew, Thomas, 93
Carrai, Stefano, 240n4
Carson, Anne, 117, 122, 124, 124n1
Carter, Angela, 100n3
Casali, Sergio, 75
Catullus (Gaius Valerius Catullus), 7, 40, 42, 74, 78, 168, 177n1, 226–32, 232nn1–2, 233n2
Caughie, Pamela, 208
Caxton, William, 19, 31
Cellini, Benvenuto, 220
Cervantes, Miguel de, 242–47, 248n7, 249 (nn 12, 15, 18)
Charlemagne, 10
Charles V (Holy Roman emperor), 248n3
Chaucer, Geoffrey, 19, 40, 52–53, 62–63, 90
Cheney, Patrick, 31, 54, 199, 200
Christensen, Peter G., 250
Christine de Pisan, 19, 211n7
Churchyard, Thomas, 90
Chwalek, Burkard, 125n4
Cicero, 13, 16n3, 27, 73, 78, 223
Claassen, Jo-Marie, 73, 78, 79, 125 (nn 2, 5)
Clausen, Wendell, 49
Clauss, James, 103
Cleopatra, 8, 167
Cocteau, Jean, 221
Colapinto, John, 204, 209, 210
Colbert, Claudette, 61
Columella, Lucius Junius Moderatus, 248n6
Conte, Gian Biagio, 221, 231, 233n4, 253
Coolidge, John S., 200
Copeland, Rita, 18
Cormier, Raymond, 1, 11, 16n5, 19, 28, 236
Correggio, 24
Corvinas, Marcus Valerius Messalla, 170
Cotta (Gaius Aurelius Cotta), 13–14
Cotta (Maximus Messalinus Cotta), 254
Cotta, Johann Friedrich, Freiherr von Cottendorf, 254
Cowley, Abraham, 23
Croesus, 152
Cyrus, 152

Dali, Salvador, 221
Daniel, Samuel, 131, 197
Dante Alighieri, 40, 43, 49, 52–53, 107, 214, 234–40
Darwin, Charles, 95, 100, 101n4, 215
Daube, David, 163
Davies, John, 199
Davis, Gregson, 67

Davis, P. J., 169n2
De Armas, Frederick A., 249n14
De Lauretis, Teresa, 178, 180, 184–85
De Luce, Judith, 68
Demats, Paule, 20
Dempsey, Charles, 248n6
Descartes, Rene, 95
Deschamps, Eustache, 19
Desmond, Marilynn, 53
Devinney, Margaret K., 82
Dewar, M., 28
Diana, Princess of Wales (née Spencer), 85
Dickinson, R. J., 77, 78
Dimmick, Jeremy, 53, 214
Dinesen, Isak, 62
Donne, John, 93, 143, 202
Donno, Elizabeth Story, 147
Dougherty, Carol, 188n6
Douglas, Mary, 95, 98, 100
Drayton, Michael, 147, 197
Dream of the Rood, 217
Dryden, John, 23
DuBois, Page, 106–07, 188n6
Dudley, Edward, 249n14
Duffy, Eamon, 147
DuRocher, Richard, 54

Edmunds, Lowell, 253
Edwards, Thomas, 126–32, 147
Elbow, Peter, 105
Eliot, T. S., 43, 49, 80, 204, 206–07, 210, 211n9
Elizabeth I (queen), 192
Ellis, Jim, 55, 196n5
Elyot, Thomas, 145
Ennius, 16n4, 78, 226
Enterline, Lynn, 45, 54, 55, 134, 195n1
Epic of Gilgamesh, 81
Epístolas de Ovidio, 248n5
Epple, Thomas, 250
Eugenides, Jeffrey, 204, 209, 211n4
Euripides, 80, 103, 105, 226
Evans, Harry B., 77
Ewans, Michael, 87n4

Fantham, Elaine, 16n10, 45, 51, 68, 81
Farrell, Joseph, 199, 218n2
Fausto-Sterling, Anne, 206
Feeney, Denis, 16 (nn 4, 7)
Feimer, Joel, 21
Feldherr, Andrew, 213
Forbis, Elizabeth Peyton, 68
Forey, Madeleine, 33n2, 142, 147, 150, 189, 195n2
Fowler, William Warde, 16n10
Fox, Cora, 34, 43, 44
Fraenkel, Hermann, 50
Francesca da Rimini, 207

INDEX

Frazer, James G., 16n10, 248n8
Fredrick, David, 187n1
Frenzel, Elisabeth, 108n3
Freud, Sigmund, 206, 208
Fyler, John, 53

Gaisser, J., 232n1
Gaius, 163
Galasso, Luigi, 29
Galinsky, Karl, 16n8, 45, 50
Gallus (Gaius Cornelius Gallus), 7, 169n2
Gantz, T., 45, 230
Garner, Margaret, 105
Gay, John, 100n1
Gehlhoff, Esther Felicitas, 250
General Estoria, 247
Gentilcore, Roxanne, 187n2
Gere, Richard, 85
Gibaldi, Joseph, 1
Gibson, R. K. *See* Gibson, Roy K.
Gibson, Roy K., 29, 52, 112
Gilbert, Scott, 211n6
Gilde, Helen C., 93
Gill, Roma, 199, 203n3
Glare, P. G. W., 174
Glauche, Günter, 28
Goethe, Johann Wolfgang von, 254
Golding, Arthur, 31–33, 33n2, 34, 43, 46, 127–28, 142–43, 145–47, 149–50, 189–95, 195n2
Gombrich, E. H., 248n6
Gonzaga, Federigo II, 24
Goold, G. P., 34, 44, 45, 75, 76, 125n4, 248n8
Gooren, Louis, 211n13
Gosson, Stephen, 147
Gower, John, 19
Graf, Fritz, 108n3
Grafton, Anthony, 28
Grasmück, Ernst Ludwig, 125n6
Graves, Robert, 220
Green, C. M. C., 16n2
Green, Peter, 44, 74, 76, 77, 78, 117, 118, 125n4, 169n2
Green, Steven, 52, 76
Greene, Thomas M., 247n2
Gregory, Horace, 34–36
Greville, Fulke, 197
Griffiths, Emma, 103, 108n3
Guido delle Colonne, 21
Guillaume de Machaut, 19
Gunn, Thomas, 84
Guthmüller, Bodo, 28

Hagstrum, Jean H., 26
Hall, Edith, 105
Hallett, Judith P., 170, 176n1, 177n3
Hamilton, Edith, 133
Handel, George Frideric, 11

Hardie, Philip, 45, 52, 55, 56n2, 87n6, 200
Harris, Stephen L., 45
Harrison, Stephen, 200
Hartigan, Karelisa V., 85
Hartt, Frederick, 243, 248n6
Haughton, Hugh, 123
Hawthorne, Nathaniel, 151, 154, 158–60, 160n6
Heaney, Seamus, 43, 117, 119–20, 122, 124
Helgerson, Richard, 202
Herbert-Brown, Geraldine, 52
Herder, Johann Gotfried von, 254
Herescu, N. I., 50
Herodotus, 151–52
Hesiod, 80, 85, 227, 248n6
Hesse, Hermann, 80
Hexter, Ralph, 1, 28, 53, 88, 214
Heywood, Thomas, 147, 214
Highet, Gilbert, 221
Hill, D. E., 29
Hinds, Stephen, 51, 52, 55, 67, 103, 108n3, 233n4, 253
Hoffman, Richard, 53
Hofmann, Michael, 44, 46, 214, 221
Hölderlin, Friedrich, 254
Holkot, Robert, 240n6
Hollis, A. S., 29, 51
Homer, 23, 26, 64, 70, 102, 120, 234, 240n1
Hopkinson, N., 30, 273
Horace, 10, 23, 27, 67, 234, 248n6, 252–53
Hughes, Ted, 44, 55, 59
Humphries, Rolfe, 34–36, 44
Hunter, John, 203n1
Huskey, Samuel, 74, 76, 77
Huston, John, 63
Hyginus (Gaius Julius Hyginus), 20

Innes, Mary M., 44
Ionesco, Eugène, 80–81, 83–84
Isbell, Harold, 44

Jackson, Michael, 85
Jacobson, Howard, 50
Jacoff, Rachel, 53
James I of England (James VI of Scotland), 143–44
James, Heather, 54, 55, 134, 145
Jean de Meun, 90, 100
Jeanne of Navarre, 18
Jestin, Charbra Adams, 42
John of Garland, 20, 236
John, Saint, 11
Johnson, Barbara, 104
Johnson, Magic, 85
Johnson, W. R., 53, 100n2
Johnston, Sarah Iles, 103
Jonson, Ben, 23, 143, 144, 148–49, 220
Jung, Carl, 86n1

292　INDEX

Jung, Marc-René, 21
Juvenal, 27

Kafka, Franz, 43, 80–81, 83–84, 215, 216, 221
Kahn, Coppélia, 196n3
Katz, Phyllis B., 42, 211n7
Kay, Sarah, 20
Keith, Alison, 55, 56, 177n4, 188 (nn 4, 7)
Kennedy, Duncan, 250, 254–55, 256
Kenney, E. J., 29, 51, 64, 163
Kiel, Martin, 254
Kiesel, Helmuth, 250
Kleist, Heinrich von, 254
Knox, Peter, 1, 27, 29, 34, 44, 45, 51, 52, 76, 125n4, 233n2
Kolodny, Annette, 186
Kossman, Nina, 84, 214
Kramer, Heinrich, 215
Kraus, C. S., 29
Krueger, Robert, 203n3
Kuskin, William, 33n1

Lacan, Jacques, 221
Laclos, Choderlos de, 11
Lafaye, Georges, 67
LaFleur, Richard, 42, 177n4
La Fontaine, Jean de, 100n1
Laird, Andrew, 232n1
La Mettrie, Julien Offray de, 95, 100
Lasdun, James, 44, 46, 214
Lavinius, Petrus, 150
Leach, Eleanor Winsor, 98
Lee, A. G. See Lee, Guy
Lee, Guy, 45, 51
Legouais, Chrétien, 236
Leicester, Earl of (Robert Dudley), 31, 145
Lenardon, Robert J., 45, 82, 86n1, 87n6
Levertov, Denise, 214, 216, 217
Levi d'Ancona, Mirella, 248n10
Levine, Robert, 18, 22n2
Lewis, C. S., 32
Linderski, Jerzy, 14
Liveley, Genevieve, 45, 188n5, 205
Livy, 258
Llewellyn, Nigel, 23
Lodge, Thomas, 147–48
Longley, Michael, 189–90
Lord, Carla, 24
Lucan (Marcus Annaeus Lucanus), 49, 199, 234
Luck, Georg, 74
Lucretius, 78, 242, 248n6, 249nn12–13
Luis de Góngora y Argote, 242
Lyne, Raphael, 28, 31, 33n1, 54, 146, 190, 195n1, 196n4

Macintosh, Fiona, 105
Mack, Sara, 45
MacLure, Millar, 203n3
Mahon, Derek, 117, 122–24
Malouf, David, 12

Mandelbaum, Allen, 34, 36, 38, 44, 63n1, 69, 71, 85, 134, 138, 141nn3–4, 220, 223, 250, 252
Mandelstam, Osip Emilevich, 117, 120–21, 122, 124
Mann, Thomas, 80
Mansion, Colard, 19
Marie de France, 215
Marlowe, Christopher, 31, 43–44, 54, 126, 127, 129, 131, 195, 197–203, 203n2
Marston, John, 126, 128, 130
Martianus Minneus Felix Capella, 236
Martin, Charles, 34, 38, 44
Martin, Christopher, 44, 54, 87n6, 214
Martin, L. C., 203n3
Martindale, Charles, 53, 56n1
Marvell, Andrew, 93
Mary of Hungary, 247n3
McCabe, Richard, 199
McChesney, Anita, 250
McDonough, Christopher, 1, 9
McGinn, T. A. J., 112
McKeown, J. C., 29, 110, 116nn3–4, 163
McLaughlin, Martin, 85
Medici, Guiliano de, 248n10
Medici, Lorenzo de, 248n10
Melville, A. D., 34–36, 44
Melville, Herman, 62
Messalla (Marcus Valerius Messalla Corvinus), 175, 177
Michels, Agnes Kirsopp Lake, 17n12
Miles, Geoffrey, 87n6, 214
Miller, John F., 16 (nn 10–11, 16), 17, 30, 44, 117, 168, 195n2, 231
Miller, Paul Allen, 117, 214
Milton, John, 54, 143, 149, 202, 220
Momigliano, Arnaldo, 16 (nn 1, 3)
Monroe, Marilyn, 86
Montaigne, Michel de, 95, 100, 100n3
Monteverdi, Claudio, 220
Montrose, Louis Adrian, 201
Moore, Edward, 235
More, Thomas, 149
Morford, Mark, 45, 82, 86n1, 87n6
Morrison, Toni, 105
Morse, Ruth, 18, 20–21
Moss, Ann, 145
Moss, Roger, 214, 216
Most, G. W., 29
Moulton, Ian Frederick, 199
Mozart, Wolfgang Amadeus, 11
Mulvey, Laura, 187n1
Myers, K. Sara, 187n2
Mynors, R. A. B., 38n1

Naevius, 16n4
Nagle, Betty Rose, 45, 77, 125 (nn 2, 5)
Neukirchen, Thomas, 256
Neuse, Richard, 200
Newlands, Carole, 17n14–15, 51, 104, 242

Nibelungenlied, The, 80, 83
Nicholl, Charles, 199
Nicholson, Adam, 143
Nims, John Frederick, 32, 33n2
Nisbet, Robin George Murdoch, 253
Nonnus, 233n2
Nooteboom, Cees, 222–23
Norbrook, David, 203n1
Nosworthy, J. M., 203n3
Nugent, Georgia, 207

Oakley-Brown, Liz, 54
O'Hara, Frank, 84
O'Hara, James J., 210n1
O'Neill, Eugene, 80
Orgel, Stephen, 129, 202
Orwell, George, 15
Otis, Brooks, 50, 67
Otten, Charlotte, 215
Ovide moralisé, 10, 16n5, 18–22, 22n1, 24, 31, 88, 145, 236

Paduano, Guido, 29
Page, Denys, 252
Pairet, Ana, 19
Palmeri, Frank, 100n1
Panofsky, Erwin, 25, 248n3
Parker, Patricia, 179, 185
Parmigianino (Girolamo Francesco Maria Mazzola), 220
Payne, Michael, 203n1
Pease, A. S., 16 (nn 3, 6)
Peri, Jacopo, 11
Perutelli, Alessandro, 29
Petrarch, 11, 43, 88, 127, 129–31, 197, 202, 203, 214
Philip II (king of Spain), 24, 248n3
Philip IV (king of France). *See* Philip the Fair
Philip the Fair, 18
Philo Judaeus, 145
Picasso, Pablo, 221
Picasso, Paloma, 85
Picone, Michelangelo, 236
Pindar, 23, 105, 198, 252
Plato, 16n3, 80, 102, 206
Platzner, Gloria, 45
Plutarch, 17n12, 99
Podossinov, Alexander, 120
Poduska, Donald, 108n3
Poliziano, Angelo, 220, 242, 249n13
Pondrom, Cyrena, 211n9
Pope, Alexander, 199
Possamaï-Pérez, Marylène, 21
Pound, Ezra, 32, 43, 80
Powell, Barry, 45
Prawer, Sigbert S., 103, 107n1
Propertius (Sextus Propertius), 7, 16n10, 78, 184
Prudentius (Aurelius Prudentius Clemens), 236

Pugh, Syrithe, 54
Putnam, M. C. J., 233n3

Quevedo, Francisco, 242
Quintilian (Marcus Fabius Quintilianus), 200

Racine, Jean, 80
Raeburn, David, 34, 37, 44
Raine, Craig, 214
Rainolds, John, 129
Ransmayr, Christoph, 12, 43, 250, 256n1
Raphael (Raffaelo Sanzio), 241
Rawson, Elizabeth, 16n1
Redford, Bruce, 1, 11, 241
Regio, Raffaele, 28, 30
Reid, Jane Davidson, 84, 108n3
Reimer, David, 209, 211
Rembrandt, 11
Reynolds, Henry, 147
Reynolds, L. D., 27
Rich, Adrienne, 104
Richardson, Samuel, 11
Rilke, Rainer Maria, 214, 216, 217, 224
Rimell, Victoria, 195n1
Roberts, Julia, 85
Roller, Lynn, 151
Rosati, Gianpiero, 100n2
Ross, David O., 76
Rubens, Peter Paul, 11
Rubin, Gayle, 103
Rudd, Niall, 253
Rudich, Vasily, 79
Rupp, Stephen, 55
Rushdie, Salman, 80
Russell, Anna, 86n2

Sabinus, 8
Sackville-West, Vita, 208
Sade, Marquis de, 161
Salisbury, Joyce, 215
Sandys, George, 31, 32–33, 34, 46, 143
Sappho, 40, 107
Sartre, Jean-Paul, 80
Scheid, John, 240n1
Schevill, Rudolf, 248n5
Schiller, Friedrich, 254
Schilling, Robert, 16n2
Schlegel, Friedrich, 219
Schmitzer, Ulrich, 46
Schnapp, Jeffrey, 53
Scot, Reginald, 215
Seneca the Elder, 200
Seneca the Younger, 103, 104, 105, 248n6
Servius (Maurus Servius Honoratus), 27–28, 30
Seznec, Jean, 53, 247n1
Shakespeare, William, 40, 43, 54–55, 62, 91, 126, 127, 129, 131, 133–39, 140–41, 143, 144, 148, 149–50, 170, 177, 190–95, 196n3, 197, 202, 203, 215, 220, 224

Sharrock, Alison, 51, 52, 187n1, 188n5, 198, 205
Shaw, George Bernard, 80
Shelley, Mary, 80
Shelley, Percy Bysshe, 99
Sidney, Philip, 131, 143, 195, 197, 202, 203
Simonides, 252
Simpson, Michael, 34, 37, 44
Singer, Peter, 95
Singleton, Charles S., 240n2
Skulsky, Harold, 218n3
Slavitt, David, 34, 36–37
Smalley, Beryl, 22n2
Solodow, Joseph, 51, 67, 69
Sosigenes, 17n12
Sowell, Madison, 53, 236, 237, 240 (nn 3, 7)
Spenser, Edmund, 40, 43, 54, 80, 90, 92, 93, 131, 143–44, 148, 195, 197, 201–02, 203
Sprenger, Jacob, 215
Stanivukovic, Goran, 45, 55, 195n1
Stape, J. H., 208
Stapleton, M. L., 54, 199
Statius (Publius Papinius Statius), 49, 234
Steiner, Emily, 224n1
Strauss, Richard, 11
Striar, Brian J., 199
Stroh, Wilfried, 169n2
Sturluson, Snorri, 81
Suetonius (Gaius Suetonius Tranquillus), 17n12
Sulpicia, 7, 170–76, 176n1
Svenbro, Jesper, 240n1
Swift, Jonathan, 95, 100n1, 214
Syme, Ronald, 16n10

Tacitus (Cornelius Tacitus), 200
Tarrant, Richard, 52, 233n4, 250
Taylor, A. B., 54, 195n1
Terry, Philip, 44, 46, 214
Theisen, Bianca, 256
Thibault, John C., 75, 125n4
Thomas, Richard F., 56, 226
Thompson, Ann, 141n2
Thury, Eva M., 82
Tiberius, 9, 276
Tibullus (Albius Tibullus), 7, 67, 170
Tissol, Garth, 45, 52, 146
Titian, 11, 24–26, 241, 247n3
Toynbee, Paget, 235
Traub, Valerie, 55
Traube, Ludwig, 10, 52
Tyrtaeus, 151–52

Updike, John, 80
Ustinov, Peter, 80

Valerius Flaccus, 103
Van Tress, Heather, 76
Vanvitelli, Luigi, 220

Varro (Marcus Terentius Varro), 13–14, 16
Vasari, Giorgio, 24
Vega, Lope de, 242
Velázquez, Diego, 220
Verdière, Raoul, 125n4
Vergil, 9–10, 13, 23, 26, 27, 28, 35, 38, 49–50, 52–53, 56 (nn 1–2), 64, 66, 70, 76, 77, 78, 102, 112, 127, 131, 143, 149, 177, 179, 200, 226, 228, 232, 233n3, 234, 238, 239, 245
Versace, Gianni, 85
Veyne, Paul, 16n7
Vickers, Nancy J., 201
Victoria (queen), 160
Videau-Delibes, Anne, 77
Virgilio, Giovanni del, 236

Wagner, Richard, 80, 82, 84, 86n2, 87n4
Walcott, Derek, 117, 121–22, 123
Wallace-Hadrill, Andrew, 17n13
Waller, Edmund, 23
Warner, Marina, 87n6, 190, 218n3
Watson, Thomas, 131
Weil, Elizabeth, 211n12
Weisenberger, Steven, 105
Weisstein, Ulrich, 107n1
Wells, H. G., 95, 100n3
Wells, Stanley, 193
Wheeler, A. L., 74, 75, 76, 90
White, P., 227
Whitney, Isabella, 93–94
Wilford, John Noble, 151
Wilkinson, L. P., 16n10, 50, 73
Williams, Gareth, 51–52, 73, 76, 125 (nn 2, 5)
Williams, Gordon, 169n2
Wilson, N. G., 27
Wind, Edgar, 53, 245, 246
Wiseman, T. P., 248n6
Wishart, David, 12
Wittstock, Uwe, 250
Wöhrle, Georg, 250
Woodard, R. D., 44
Woods, John E., 250
Woolf, Virginia, 204, 207–09, 211n11
Woudhuysen, H. R., 203n1
Wroth, Mary, 197
Wycliffe, John, 144

Xenophanes, 16n3
Xerxes, 152

Yeats, William Butler, 84
Yglise, Saint, 20

Zimmerman, Mary, 43, 134, 139–41, 158, 218n2, 221
Ziolkowski, Theodore, 45, 55, 87n6, 118, 124n1
Zyroff, Ellen S., 68, 70

Modern Language Association of America
Approaches to Teaching World Literature

Achebe's Things Fall Apart. Ed. Bernth Lindfors. 1991.
Arthurian Tradition. Ed. Maureen Fries and Jeanie Watson. 1992.
Atwood's The Handmaid's Tale *and Other Works*. Ed. Sharon R. Wilson, Thomas B. Friedman, and Shannon Hengen. 1996.
Austen's Emma. Ed. Marcia McClintock Folsom. 2004.
Austen's Pride and Prejudice. Ed. Marcia McClintock Folsom. 1993.
Balzac's Old Goriot. Ed. Michal Peled Ginsburg. 2000.
Baudelaire's Flowers of Evil. Ed. Laurence M. Porter. 2000.
Beckett's Waiting for Godot. Ed. June Schlueter and Enoch Brater. 1991.
Beowulf. Ed. Jess B. Bessinger, Jr., and Robert F. Yeager. 1984.
Blake's Songs of Innocence and of Experience. Ed. Robert F. Gleckner and Mark L. Greenberg. 1989.
Boccaccio's Decameron. Ed. James H. McGregor. 2000.
British Women Poets of the Romantic Period. Ed. Stephen C. Behrendt and Harriet Kramer Linkin. 1997.
Charlotte Brontë's Jane Eyre. Ed. Diane Long Hoeveler and Beth Lau. 1993.
Emily Brontë's Wuthering Heights. Ed. Sue Lonoff and Terri A. Hasseler. 2006.
Byron's Poetry. Ed. Frederick W. Shilstone. 1991.
Camus's The Plague. Ed. Steven G. Kellman. 1985.
Writings of Bartolomé de Las Casas. Ed. Santa Arias and Eyda M. Merediz. 2008.
Cather's My Ántonia. Ed. Susan J. Rosowski. 1989.
Cervantes' Don Quixote. Ed. Richard Bjornson. 1984.
Chaucer's Canterbury Tales. Ed. Joseph Gibaldi. 1980.
Chaucer's Troilus and Criseyde *and the Shorter Poems*. Ed. Tison Pugh and Angela Jane Weisl. 2006.
Chopin's The Awakening. Ed. Bernard Koloski. 1988.
Coleridge's Poetry and Prose. Ed. Richard E. Matlak. 1991.
Collodi's Pinocchio *and Its Adaptations*. Ed. Michael Sherberg. 2006.
Conrad's "Heart of Darkness" and "The Secret Sharer." Ed. Hunt Hawkins and Brian W. Shaffer. 2002.
Dante's Divine Comedy. Ed. Carole Slade. 1982.
Defoe's Robinson Crusoe. Ed. Maximillian E. Novak and Carl Fisher. 2005.
DeLillo's White Noise. Ed. Tim Engles and John N. Duvall. 2006.
Dickens's Bleak House. Ed. John O. Jordan and Gordon Bigelow. 2009.
Dickens's David Copperfield. Ed. Richard J. Dunn. 1984.
Dickinson's Poetry. Ed. Robin Riley Fast and Christine Mack Gordon. 1989.
Narrative of the Life of Frederick Douglass. Ed. James C. Hall. 1999.
Duras's Ourika. Ed. Mary Ellen Birkett and Christopher Rivers. 2009.
Early Modern Spanish Drama. Ed. Laura R. Bass and Margaret R. Greer. 2006

Eliot's Middlemarch. Ed. Kathleen Blake. 1990.
Eliot's Poetry and Plays. Ed. Jewel Spears Brooker. 1988.
Shorter Elizabethan Poetry. Ed. Patrick Cheney and Anne Lake Prescott. 2000.
Ellison's Invisible Man. Ed. Susan Resneck Parr and Pancho Savery. 1989.
English Renaissance Drama. Ed. Karen Bamford and Alexander Leggatt. 2002.
Works of Louise Erdrich. Ed. Gregg Sarris, Connie A. Jacobs, and James R. Giles. 2004.
Dramas of Euripides. Ed. Robin Mitchell-Boyask. 2002.
Faulkner's The Sound and the Fury. Ed. Stephen Hahn and Arthur F. Kinney. 1996.
Fitzgerald's The Great Gatsby. Ed. Jackson R. Bryer and Nancy P. VanArsdale. 2009.
Flaubert's Madame Bovary. Ed. Laurence M. Porter and Eugene F. Gray. 1995.
García Márquez's One Hundred Years of Solitude. Ed. María Elena de Valdés and Mario J. Valdés. 1990.
Gilman's "The Yellow Wall-Paper" and Herland. Ed. Denise D. Knight and Cynthia J. Davis. 2003.
Goethe's Faust. Ed. Douglas J. McMillan. 1987.
Gothic Fiction: The British and American Traditions. Ed. Diane Long Hoeveler and Tamar Heller. 2003.
Grass's The Tin Drum. Ed. Monika Shafi. 2008.
Hebrew Bible as Literature in Translation. Ed. Barry N. Olshen and Yael S. Feldman. 1989.
Homer's Iliad *and* Odyssey. Ed. Kostas Myrsiades. 1987.
Hurston's Their Eyes Were Watching God *and Other Works*. Ed. John Lowe. 2009.
Ibsen's A Doll House. Ed. Yvonne Shafer. 1985.
Henry James's Daisy Miller *and* The Turn of the Screw. Ed. Kimberly C. Reed and Peter G. Beidler. 2005.
Works of Samuel Johnson. Ed. David R. Anderson and Gwin J. Kolb. 1993.
Joyce's Ulysses. Ed. Kathleen McCormick and Erwin R. Steinberg. 1993.
Works of Sor Juana Inés de la Cruz. Ed. Emilie L. Bergmann and Stacey Schlau. 2007.
Kafka's Short Fiction. Ed. Richard T. Gray. 1995.
Keats's Poetry. Ed. Walter H. Evert and Jack W. Rhodes. 1991.
Kingston's The Woman Warrior. Ed. Shirley Geok-lin Lim. 1991.
Lafayette's The Princess of Clèves. Ed. Faith E. Beasley and Katharine Ann Jensen. 1998.
Works of D. H. Lawrence. Ed. M. Elizabeth Sargent and Garry Watson. 2001.
Lazarillo de Tormes *and the Picaresque Tradition*. Ed. Anne J. Cruz. 2009.
Lessing's The Golden Notebook. Ed. Carey Kaplan and Ellen Cronan Rose. 1989.
Mann's Death in Venice *and Other Short Fiction*. Ed. Jeffrey B. Berlin. 1992.
Marguerite de Navarre's Heptameron. Ed. Colette H. Winn. 2007.
Medieval English Drama. Ed. Richard K. Emmerson. 1990.
Melville's Moby-Dick. Ed. Martin Bickman. 1985.
Metaphysical Poets. Ed. Sidney Gottlieb. 1990.
Miller's Death of a Salesman. Ed. Matthew C. Roudané. 1995.

Milton's Paradise Lost. Ed. Galbraith M. Crump. 1986.
Milton's Shorter Poetry and Prose. Ed. Peter C. Herman. 2007.
Molière's Tartuffe *and Other Plays*. Ed. James F. Gaines and
    Michael S. Koppisch. 1995.
Momaday's The Way to Rainy Mountain. Ed. Kenneth M. Roemer. 1988.
Montaigne's Essays. Ed. Patrick Henry. 1994.
Novels of Toni Morrison. Ed. Nellie Y. McKay and Kathryn Earle. 1997.
Murasaki Shikibu's The Tale of Genji. Ed. Edward Kamens. 1993.
Nabokov's Lolita. Ed. Zoran Kuzmanovich and Galya Diment. 2008.
Works of Ovid and the Ovidian Tradition. Ed. Barbara Weiden Boyd and Cora
    Fox. 2010.
Poe's Prose and Poetry. Ed. Jeffrey Andrew Weinstock and Tony Magistrale. 2008.
Pope's Poetry. Ed. Wallace Jackson and R. Paul Yoder. 1993.
Proust's Fiction and Criticism. Ed. Elyane Dezon-Jones and
    Inge Crosman Wimmers. 2003.
Puig's Kiss of the Spider Woman. Ed. Daniel Balderston and Francine Masiello. 2007.
Pynchon's The Crying of Lot 49 *and Other Works*. Ed. Thomas H. Schaub. 2008.
Novels of Samuel Richardson. Ed. Lisa Zunshine and Jocelyn Harris. 2006.
Rousseau's Confessions *and* Reveries of the Solitary Walker. Ed. John C. O'Neal
    and Ourida Mostefai. 2003.
Scott's Waverley Novels. Ed. Evan Gottlieb and Ian Duncan. 2009.
Shakespeare's Hamlet. Ed. Bernice W. Kliman. 2001.
Shakespeare's King Lear. Ed. Robert H. Ray. 1986.
Shakespeare's Othello. Ed. Peter Erickson and Maurice Hunt. 2005.
Shakespeare's Romeo and Juliet. Ed. Maurice Hunt. 2000.
Shakespeare's The Tempest *and Other Late Romances*. Ed. Maurice Hunt. 1992.
Shelley's Frankenstein. Ed. Stephen C. Behrendt. 1990.
Shelley's Poetry. Ed. Spencer Hall. 1990.
Sir Gawain and the Green Knight. Ed. Miriam Youngerman Miller and
    Jane Chance. 1986.
Song of Roland. Ed. William W. Kibler and Leslie Zarker Morgan. 2006.
Spenser's Faerie Queene. Ed. David Lee Miller and Alexander Dunlop. 1994.
Stendhal's The Red and the Black. Ed. Dean de la Motte and Stirling Haig. 1999.
Sterne's Tristram Shandy. Ed. Melvyn New. 1989.
Stowe's Uncle Tom's Cabin. Ed. Elizabeth Ammons and Susan Belasco. 2000.
Swift's Gulliver's Travels. Ed. Edward J. Rielly. 1988.
Teresa of Ávila and the Spanish Mystics. Ed. Alison Weber. 2009.
Thoreau's Walden *and Other Works*. Ed. Richard J. Schneider. 1996.
Tolstoy's Anna Karenina. Ed. Liza Knapp and Amy Mandelker. 2003.
Vergil's Aeneid. Ed. William S. Anderson and Lorina N. Quartarone. 2002.
Voltaire's Candide. Ed. Renée Waldinger. 1987.
Whitman's Leaves of Grass. Ed. Donald D. Kummings. 1990.
Wiesel's Night. Ed. Alan Rosen. 2007.

Works of Oscar Wilde. Ed. Philip E. Smith II. 2008.
Woolf's Mrs. Dalloway. Ed. Eileen Barrett and Ruth O. Saxton. 2009.
Woolf's To the Lighthouse. Ed. Beth Rigel Daugherty and Mary Beth Pringle. 2001.
Wordsworth's Poetry. Ed. Spencer Hall, with Jonathan Ramsey. 1986.
Wright's Native Son. Ed. James A. Miller. 1997.